Race after Hitler

Race after Hitler

BLACK OCCUPATION CHILDREN
IN POSTWAR GERMANY
AND AMERICA

Heide Fehrenbach

PRINCETON UNIVERSITY PRESS

PRINCETON AND OXFORD

Copyright © 2005 by Princeton University Press
Published by Princeton University Press, 41 William Street,
Princeton, New Jersey 08540
In the United Kingdom: Princeton University Press, 3 Market Place,
Woodstock, Oxfordshire OX20 1SY

Library of Congress Cataloging-in-Publication Data
Fehrenbach, Heide.
Race after Hitler : Black occupation children in postwar Germany
and America / Heide Fehrenbach.
p.   cm.
Includes bibliographical references and index.
ISBN-13: 978-0-691-11906-9 (cl : alk. paper)
ISBN-10: 0-691-11906-6 (cl : alk. paper)
1. Racially mixed children—Germany—History—20th century.
2. Racially mixed children—Services for—Germany—
History—20th century. 3. African American soldiers—
Germany—History—20th century. I. Title.
HQ777.9.F44   2005
943′.004059073031—dc22   2004043162

British Library Cataloging-in-Publication Data is available

This book has been composed in Palatino

Printed on acid-free paper. ∞

pup.princeton.edu

Printed in the United States of America

1   3   5   7   9   10   8   6   4   2

For David and Dabi

CONTENTS

ILLUSTRATIONS

ACKNOWLEDGMENTS

THIS BOOK WOULD not have been written without the generous financial support of the American Council of Learned Societies, the German Academic Exchange Service, and the National Endowment for the Humanities. I am also indebted to the universities with which I've had the good fortune to be affiliated—Colgate, Emory, and most recently Northern Illinois—for providing research funding and release from teaching. A postdoctoral fellowship from the Rutgers Center for Historical Analysis in 1994–95 provided critical gestation time for this project to take shape. My thanks to John Chambers, the director of that year's seminar, as well as fellow participants for creating a stimulating venue for intellectual exchange.

I would like to thank the archivists who have assisted me in the course of my research. Particularly helpful were Dave Klaassen of the Social Welfare History Archives at the University of Minnesota; Peter Latta at the Filmmuseum Berlin/Stiftung Deutsche Kinemathek; Dr. Gerhard Hetzer at the Staatsarchiv Augsburg; Herr Jochen at the Stadtarchiv Nürnberg; Dr. Saupe at the Bayerisches Hauptstaatsarchiv; Rüdiger Koschnitzski at the Deutsches Institut für Filmkunde in Frankfurt/Main; Paul Reichl at Taurus Film; Dr. Verlande at the Bundesarchiv in Koblenz; Herr Theurer at Bamberger Stadtarchiv; Herr Freund at the Bundesarchiv-Filmarchiv in Berlin; Frau Krieg at the Staatsarchiv Freiburg; Dr. Hochstuhl at the Hauptstaatsarchiv Stuttgart; and Dr. Talazko and the friendly staff of the Archiv des Diakonisches Werk der Evangelischen Kirche in Deutschland, e.V. Thanks also to Dr. Christoph Münz of the Deutscher Koordinierungsrat der Gesellschaft für Christlich-Jüdische Zusammenarbeit for help with illustrations.

The NYC German Women's History Group provided critical feedback back in 1995 on a proposal for this project; my thanks for their early encouragement and support. I've been pleasantly surprised, when delivering bits and pieces of my research in lectures over the past years, how unanticipated questions and comments helped stimulate new insights or clarify vague ideas. For such interventions I thank colleagues and audience members at Cornell, Emory, Ohio State, Rutgers, Trinity College in Dublin, University of Buffalo, University of Illinois-Chicago, University of Washington-Seattle, and the German Historical Institute in Washington, D.C. I'd also like to express my appreciation to Brigitta van Rheinberg, my editor at Princeton University Press, for her initial enthusiasm and continuing support, and to Thomas Borstelmann and an anonymous reader for useful suggestions. Thanks also to editorial assistant Alison Kalett and copyeditor Cindy Crumrine, and to my graduate student, Helen Bailitz, for her comments on the manuscript and for ongoing discussions regarding our mutual research interests.

At Emory University, the founding members of the Race and History reading group—Leslie Harris, Mary Odem, Jeff Lesser, and Eric Goldstein—provided lively and convivial intellectual companionship as well as the opportunity for a thoroughly enjoyable reunion in Atlanta to present my research. My time at Emory and knowledge of Central European history were enriched by friendship and frequent lunches with Jamie Melton and Dirk Schumann, who is now at the German Historical Institute and provided thought-provoking feedback on several chapters. I miss all of you guys. My thanks to Volker Berghahn and Omer Bartov for writing on behalf of my research over the years, and to Christine Worobec for her friendship and support here at NIU. Uta Poiger has been an important sounding board and source of moral support for the past decade. It was she who first urged me to expand a chapter I had planned to write on black occupation children into this book. Finally, I cannot adequately express my debt of gratitude to Bob Moeller, who quickly, carefully, and repeatedly read parts (and ultimately all) of this book manuscript when I felt I needed input or a reality check. His unwavering goodwill, generous spirit, and astute comments have sustained me over the long life of this project and improved this book in too many ways to acknowledge.

Serendipity is always a part of the research process. One of the real delights of this project has been my unexpected acquaintance with Lisa Hein Dixon, which has grown into a valued friendship and has deepened my understanding of the history about which I have written. My thanks to her daughter, Shirley Peeples, for introducing us, and to Lisa for her openness and generosity in sharing her experiences with me. Henriette Cain, a virtual neighbor here in northern Illinois, entered my life out of the blue one day. It has been a pleasure getting to know her and I very much appreciate the perspective she too has provided me and my work.

Finally, I'd like to express my deep appreciation to my parents, Herbert and Gladys Fehrenbach, for a lifetime of emotional and other support, and to my siblings, Lori, Robin, Herb, and Krista, their families and significant others, for recuperative visits on the East Coast. Special thanks to Herb and Keith for pet care and furniture storage during research trips and for holiday accommodations and birthday parties for many years running.

I dedicate this book to my brilliant and loving husband, David Buller, and his spitting image, our son Dabi. We've bounced around a lot over the past few years, but one thing has never changed: you provide the life I want to come home to.

Race after Hitler

DEMOCRATIZING THE RACIAL STATE: TOWARD A TRANSNATIONAL HISTORY

[R]acism dreams of eternal contaminations, transmitted . . . through an endless sequence of loathsome copulations. . .

—Benedict Anderson

If Germans endowed themselves with a "racial" identity and then excluded others from it, Americans tended to racialize others and consider themselves simply human—citizens of the "Universal Yankee Nation" and beneficiaries of what was promised to "all men" by the Declaration of Independence.

—George M. Fredrickson[1]

IN 1937, the Nazi regime ordered the sterilization of all black German children fathered by foreign occupation troops of color stationed in Germany after World War I. A few years later, as German troops marched across Europe in World War II, at least one sterilized teenage girl narrowly escaped being pressed into prostitution for the Wehrmacht on the Eastern front. The history of Black Germans during the Third Reich is still being written, and their individual and collective fates remain unclear.[2] What is uncontroverted is that during those terrible years, state power served a racist fantasy intent on engineering a purebred Aryan *Volk*, resulting in the mutilation or murder of millions deemed racially alien to it.

After World War II, Germany again was occupied by foreign troops, and a new cohort of German children of color—the so-called *Mischlinge* or mixed-bloods—was born. Citing rumors that the previous generation of black German children had all wound up "in bordellos or circuses," died of climate-related illness, or "fallen victim" to the Nazi regime's racial policies, one Protestant social worker in early 1950s western Germany mused about what should be done with the current cohort. There were, she wrote, "three incompatible views" on the subject. The first suggested the children should remain in Germany, to be raised by families or in orphanages and socialized with other (white) children so they could learn to cope with "life's struggles" from an early age. A second view held that children who "showed physical signs of their father's racial inheritance" should be adopted to America. And a third view argued that the children should be segregated into group homes in Germany, where they should be carefully educated with an eye to their future emigration.[3]

Postwar German social policy toward the children ultimately combined a bit of all three views. Nonetheless, the segregationist approach did not dominate. And as early as 1952, the National Association for the Advancement of Colored People (NAACP) and the African American monthly *Ebony* made a point of publicly praising West Germany for its enlightened treatment of the children when compared to racial practices in contemporary American society and schools.[4]

In spite of the positive African American press extended West German officials a few years after the defeat of the National Socialist state, the primary goal of this book is not a congratulatory one. Rather than merely chronicle the apparent successes of the postwar democratization of West Germany, I seek to explore it as a social and cultural *process*. As the attention of the NAACP and *Ebony* suggests, the task of democratizing Germany after 1945 involved not only the transition from fascist to postfascist social ideologies and policies. It also involved the active oversight of Allied authority and troops on the ground. As Cold War hostilities rapidly replaced wartime ones, American influence in the western zones of Germany gradually became predominant. When democracy arrived in western Germany after 1945, the United States was its midwife.

This book focuses on a formative, yet understudied, moment in the racial reconstruction of postfascist Germany: transnational responses to black "occupation children" born to German women and Allied soldiers after World War II. Four years of military occupation between 1945 and 1949 produced some 94,000 occupation children, but public attention quickly focused on a small but visible subset, the so-called *Mischlinge* distinguished from the others by their colored paternity.[5] Although they comprised a small minority of postwar German births (some 3,000 in 1950 and nearly 5,000 by middecade), biracial occupation children took on a disproportionately great symbolic significance on both sides of the Atlantic. Their existence challenged historical definitions of ethnic German-ness and sparked heated debates about the social effects of occupation, as well as the character and consequences of democratization.

In the U.S. zone of Germany, where a substantial number of the children resided, official American response—which mandated the children's legal and social equality—served to highlight not only the lofty principles of American democracy, but also its hypocrisies and failings. Germans were quick to perceive, and to protest, that they were being reeducated by a nation with a Jim Crow army and a host of antimiscegenation laws at home. What is more, the NAACP and the African American press trained a critical eye on how the American government and military would reconcile its inspiring international rhetoric of democratic equality in Germany and elsewhere with the ongoing realities of racial discrimination within its own ranks.

German and American responses to black occupation children after 1945 were therefore conditioned by an ironic yet momentous bit of historical synchronicity. The American occupation and democratization of Germany coincided with a postwar push by African Americans and white liberals at home to democratize American society and its institutions.[6] As a result, the study of transnational responses to the children constitutes a rich field for the investigation of postwar reformulations of race, citizenship, and nationhood on both sides of the Atlantic.

Recent studies by historians of the United States have investigated the links between American foreign policy interests abroad and the emerging Cold War mandate to attend to the issue of civil rights abuses at home in order to avoid providing grist for the Soviet Union's propaganda mill during the superpowers' struggle for international influence in a budding bipolar world.[7] American "race relations" became an issue of particular concern in the aftermath of World War II. American wartime propaganda had, after all, pointed to venomous Nazi racism as an indication of the enemy's evil inhumanity.[8] The Allied liberation of the death camps and Nuremberg Trials publicized the horrendous dimensions of racialized murder in Nazi-dominated Europe. And shortly thereafter, the United Nations issued the 1947 Universal Declaration of Human Rights, a global denunciation of racial classification, discrimination, and inequality in favor of the "inalienable rights of all members of the human family."[9] Given the altered geopolitical climate and heightened sensitivity to racial abuses, America's own racial practices represented a potentially serious political liability for the United States, at a time when it was engaged in a historically unprecedented worldwide expansion of its political, military, economic, and cultural presence. As a result, American federal policymakers recognized the need to "control the narrative by which the domestic struggle for reform unfolded in the media." The liberals among them worried aloud that American racism threatened "the national interest" by undermining the United States' message and moral standing abroad.[10]

While informed by such scholarship, my study aims to supplement this bird's-eye view of the interdependence of American foreign policy and domestic civil rights initiatives with a worm's-eye view that explores the social interactions and racial conflicts appearing on the ground in Germany as initially segregated American occupation troops pursued their mission to democratize that defeated country. This focus contributes a fresh perspective on the history of the desegregation of the U.S.

military, which has been almost exclusively examined in relation to *war-time* conditions (during hostilities in World War II, Korea, Vietnam) while the important impetus and experiences of military occupations has been inexplicably ignored.[11] However, a more primary point is to suggest that the American image abroad was not beholden merely to press coverage, whether negative or positive. Rather, in areas of American military presence it was also informed by the *social practices of race* that Germans (and others) observed among U.S. occupation troops or between U.S. soldiers and native populations.[12]

In studying the American occupation, historians have tended to treat democratization as a one-way process, a forcible transformation of West German society. While there is much truth in this, I am interested in looking at the occupation as a period of interaction and mutual transformation—and one with enduring implications for the postwar and post–Cold War eras. This study of the transnational response to black occupation children focuses on this crucial historical moment in order to probe its *constituent* effects on post-1945 social and legal deliberations on—and cultural expressions of—the fit between race, ethnicity, and national belonging. Moreover, it is designed to historically situate and illuminate contemporary debates about citizenship and multiculturalism in (re)unified Germany.

The postwar logic of race that emerged in Germany was beholden to an internationally enforced injunction that Germans differentiate their polity and policies from the Nazi predecessor. It reflected both a self-conscious democratizing impulse and, for the Federal Republic, a new Western orientation. What is more, it promised a fresh start through abrupt disavowal of state-sponsored racism.

A brief anecdote from my own experience in researching this book suggests how heavily white Germans may be invested in the postwar narrative of a radical rupture when it concerns notions of race. Several years ago, in the early stages of this project, I wrote to select archives inquiring whether they had material on social policy toward postwar *Mischlingskinder*. Within a few weeks, I received a curt reply from a western German archivist, admonishing me that the term *"Mischlingskind"* belonged to the racist vocabulary of the Third Reich and had been extinguished along with it. Like the Nazi Regime, he suggested, it did not survive defeat. Surprised by his sermon but undeterred, I visited that and other municipal, state, and federal archives in the Federal Republic of Germany, locating along the way a depressingly broad array of official, scholarly, school, and social welfare reports and memos devoted to *"Mischlingskinder"* and *"Negermischlinge."* This wealth of material only made the archivist's inaccurate historical lesson more unsettling. How could he claim the postwar extinction of racialist classificatory schemes when the

A map of occupied Germany, 1945–1949. The American zone of
occupation was comprised of Bavaria, Hesse, Württemberg-Baden, and Bremen.
In 1949, the states of East and West Germany were founded: the Soviet zone became
the German Democratic Republic; the western zones merged into the Federal Republic of Germany, which achieved full sovereignty in 1955. *Source*: O. J. Frederiksen,
The American Military Occupation of Germany (Historical Division, Headquarters,
U.S. Army, Europe, 1953), 15.

very archival holdings he administered contradicted this assertion? Did he really believe in a "Stunde Null" when it came to racial ideology?

Over the course of my research, I have come to realize just how much historical evidence and social experience had to be ignored to claim the emergence of a race-blind German polity and bureaucracy after 1945. I have also come to understand how generalized this perception is. Indeed, one need only examine the trends of postwar historiography to see how little attention has been devoted to the historical linkages between race and nation after 1945, compared to the intense scrutiny it has received for the pre-1945 period.[13] To some degree, of course, historical inquiry on Germany has been dominated by the need to probe the relationship between National Socialism and the longer German nation. A significant focus of historians has been the particular ways that the German *Volk*, German citizenship, and German identity were reformulated in accordance with specific racial prescriptions and eugenic principles, and how this ultimately led countless thousands of Germans to assist in the sterilization, ghettoization, enslavement, and murder of millions of fellow Germans and Europeans due to their Jewish, Slavic, "Gypsy," or "Negro" descent.

In view of the intense scrutiny that the racist policies of the Third Reich have received from historians over the past thirty years or so, it is striking that more attention has not been devoted to the postwar *devolution* of the Nazi racial state, particularly given the more recent boom in the study of the postwar Germanys. Historical studies of the postwar period in both German states tend not to be conceptualized around the general category of "race." Rather, they explore state policies toward, or the social experiences of, specific groups such as Jews or Displaced Persons (DPs, an often implicitly racialized category), migrant ("guest") workers, asylum seekers, and so on. This tendency, I would argue, is largely unconnected with the current critical practice of dismissing the scientific basis—if not the historical salience—of "race" as a fictional, if intensely ideological, construct. Instead it is a more direct result of the way that historical inquiry has shaped itself in relation to the language of difference contained in its sources. For the Nazi period, this language of difference was expressed in the language of "*Rasse*" (race), "*Blut*" (blood), and "*Erbe*" (biological inheritance). And over the past few decades, historians increasingly have organized their research around the exploration of such categories. In the postwar period, while reference to these concepts was not completely absent, especially in the first decade or so after the war, the public invocation of "*Rasse*" became taboo over the course of the 1950s. This resulted in a gradual shift away from public discussions of "*Rasse*" in favor of "*Anderssein*" (difference) by about the mid-1950s in the Federal Republic. In the Democratic Republic, in contrast, socialist ideology declared *"Rasse"* an extinct category of social classification and ordered it excised from official rhetoric. Each Germany declared the concept inconsistent with their founding documents (the West German Basic Law) or doctrines (East German socialism).

Nonetheless, "race" was instrumentalized for political purposes by both postwar German states, East and West. As each Germany's officials eagerly sought to establish their ideological distance from the Nazi predecessor, as well as their estranged Cold War twin across the border, they articulated new national cultural identities by drawing on eugenic imagery and even, as historian Uta Poiger has shown, by alternatively denouncing or embracing Germans' cultural consumption of black American music.[14] However, the social politics of race were not something the West German state could easily marshal to public effect to establish moral superiority over its socialist sibling. The new Bonn republic could and did point to its rejection of "race" as a legal classification and basis for discrimination in order to differentiate itself from the Berlin dictatorship. But the dictatorship countered was that of the recent past, not the socialist present. After all, by 1949 both states barred discrimination on the basis of race in their constitutions. Moreover, the socialist German Democratic Republic went further than the West German Federal Republic in expunging racial terminology from its official utterances (even if racial considerations continued to influence East German social policy more silently). The social language of race had distinctly different trajectories in East and West Germany. Where possible, I highlight aspects of those differences, along with their social policy consequences, when examining official responses to perceived miscegenation in the immediate years following military defeat. In this book, however, I have chosen to focus on developments in the Federal Republic, which was home to the majority of black "occupation children" and has persisted as the post–Cold War successor state.

After the defeat of National Socialism, the social landscape and national imaginary of both Germanys remained highly racialized, if in ways distinct from the wartime and interwar years. What Barbara Fields has said of the American reconstruction of the late-nineteenth century also holds for reconstructing Germany of the mid-twentieth: "It is easy enough to demonstrate a substantial continuity in 'racial attitudes.' But doing so does not demonstrate a continuity of racial ideology. . . . [A]lthough there was no appreciable decline or mitigation of *racialist* thinking, there was a decisive shift in its character."[15] And, I would add, in its function.

Racialist thinking did not disappear from postwar Germany, but gradually the use of the term *"Rasse"*—and its association with Jewishness—did, particularly in German official and academic circles. Nonetheless, in the cultural and social-scientific articulations of "race" after 1945, the recent German history of antisemitism and the Shoah remained a significant, if sometimes unstated, subtext.

The term "*Mischling*," for example, persisted well into the 1960s in official, scholarly, media, and public usage in West Germany. But its content changed markedly. It was no longer used to refer to the progeny of so-called mixed unions between Jews and non-Jewish Germans. Rather, after 1945, it was used to connote the offspring of white German women and typically foreign men of color. Thus "*Mischlinge*" remained a racialized category of social analysis and social policy after 1945, as before. But its definition of *which races* had mixed, as well as the social significance of such mixing, was fundamentally altered.

As a result of sustained official and scholarly attention to the so-called *Mischlingskinder*, "color" and "blackness" became significant referents for postwar German definitions of race in the first decade after the war. Moreover, for various reasons, this focus on blackness echoed the simplified black-white binary that emerged over the course of the 1920s and 1930s in the United States and came to characterize American definitions of race in the postwar period.[16]

This book seeks to chart the postwar devolution of the Nazi racial state in two ways: first, by tracing the shifting taxonomies and social policies of race and nation across the 1945 "divide" within Germany; and, second, by investigating the impact of international developments and impulses—via military defeat and occupation, Cold War, and the U.S. civil rights movement—on postwar reformulations of racial policy and practice within German society and the U.S. military. One goal, then, is to uncover the process by which German understandings of race came to resemble those informing postwar American social science and liberalism.

MILITARY OCCUPATION, INTERRACIAL SEX, AND POSTWAR IDEOLOGIES OF RACE

For the majority of Germans who were not among the minority groups persecuted by the Nazi state and its accomplices, 1945 initiated a new era that was marked by the trauma of defeat, the shock of contact with enemy troops, and rapid regime change—first to the occupation governments of the American, British, French, and Soviet zones, and then after 1949, to the Cold War states of East and West Germany. In addition to the political revolution accompanying Allied victory, military defeat served to destroy and delegitimate the particular national-communal ideal of a superior Aryan *Volksgemeinschaft* that was officially advocated and murderously enacted not only in Nazi Germany, but throughout

Nazi-dominated Europe. With the demise of the Nazi Regime, Germans entered a phase in their national history that was characterized by the challenges of material want, political division, national redefinition, and social reconstruction. Postwar Germans faced the task of recasting the social and ideological parameters of their national identity. The first decades after World War II were dominated by debates regarding communal self-definition as contemporaries were compelled by circumstances to grapple with the question of what it would it mean to be German after Hitler and the Holocaust.[17]

This process was complicated and conditioned by the unique international matrix within which it occurred. Clearly, certain political and legal aspects of this national reconstruction and redefinition were compelled by the victorious powers. However, in addition to alien official directives, Germans, in shaping the postwar parameters of their national identity, proved intent on responding to what they perceived as the negative social and moral consequences of military occupation. Nineteen forty-five had been experienced by many Germans as a national humiliation. With the influx of foreign troops, outbreak of rape, and the advent of heterosexual fraternization, it came to be understood as a sexual humiliation as well.

Much of the moral and social dislocation following defeat was attributed to perceived abnormal relations between German men and women, and in particular to the active displacement of native masculinity by foreign troops and the German women who pursued sexual relationships with them. Beginning in the early days of the occupation and persisting for a good decade, public attention in western Germany was drawn irresistibly to relations between native German women and foreign occupiers as *symptomatic* of the postwar problems confronting Germany. What was at issue for many contemporaries was the very integrity of the German nation as it had been defined prior to 1945, along with its significant correlates of German honor, German manhood, and the German family.[18]

Postwar attempts to address issues of national self-definition necessarily involved confronting issues of race since defeated Germany was occupied by the multiethnic armies of hostile nations. What is more, these former racial subordinates now occupied a position of political superiority due to their membership in the Allied forces. Clearly, then, the very nature of the occupation challenged Germans to learn to function within a context that was radically postfascist in terms of social composition and political authority, if not yet in terms of ideological disposition or social policy.

As historians have noted, postwar Germans may have avoided—or even resisted—a thorough reckoning with their murderous past beyond the feeble native denazification efforts of the 1940s, remunerative agreements signed with Israel in the early 1950s, and sparse number of trials against war criminals that decade and the next that, following Allied tribunals, cast race-based murder in the more generic language of "war crimes" or "crimes against humanity."[19] However, in response to the occupation and the interracial relationships and children that resulted, Germans felt themselves confronted with the need to assert or recast the fit between race and notions of national belonging. In a very real sense, then, military occupation stimulated and shaped the contours of postwar racial ideology in Germany. And this was because the most *explicit* discussions of race after the war occurred in response to interracial sex and reproduction between German women and Allied soldiers of color. Postwar West German notions of race were intimately connected with notions of proper *female* social and sexual comportment—as lovers, as wives, as mothers.

Over the course of military occupation, the specific interracial relations most discussed in public venues became those between white German women and black American troops. Although Germans after 1945 continued to operate within the context of a highly differentiated racial paradigm (developed over the course of the prior eighty or so years, which extended well beyond a simple reliance upon skin color to include a hierarchal racial valuation of various populations within Europe), postwar German officials, scientists, and social workers increasingly focused on distinctions between blackness and whiteness. In part, this may have resulted from Germans' unwillingness to speak openly about Jews in racialized terms, although antisemitic utterances and actions certainly were not uncommon or unrecorded.[20] However, as the Nazi era receded into the past, West German officials (if not the German public at large) gradually learned to adjust their language and self-censor their *public* statements on race, particularly—if not always successfully—as these concerned Jews.

German racism prior to 1945 was not limited to antisemitism, though its history often (and understandably) has been written that way due to the Nazi era's obsessive murderous policies targeting European Jews. Nevertheless, German racism was broader in scope. While antisemitism was an important, even central, ingredient of German racism, it was not the sole one. As Victor Klemperer noted in his poignant reflections in *The Language of the Third Reich*, the hatred of the Jews was "embedded" in the larger category of race.[21] Nazi fantasies of engineering a purebred Aryan *Volk* dictated that desirable Germans be delineated—socially and sexually segregated—from a host of foreign inferior races. Since Germany had been a colonial power prior to its defeat in the First World War, and since the German Rhineland had been occupied by French North African troops in the early 1920s, "racial mixing" between Blacks and whites was both a social fact *and* perceived as linked to the loss of national status. Thus antiblack racism was a constituent part of a larger German racism that included but was not exhausted by antisemitism. An examination of social and scientific rationale that culminated in sterilization of "mixed-bloods" during the Third Reich (taken up in chapter three) illustrates this point.[22]

• • •

This book is not a social history of Black Germans, although it aims to contribute to that emerging historical literature.[23] Rather, it examines the shifting racial assumptions, language, and social policy that framed the lives, and often determined the fates, of black German children after 1945. The evolution of racial understanding and policies in West Germany occurred in constant dialogue with Americans in the United States, be they in the Washington offices of the NAACP or State Department, the New York offices of the National Council for Christians and Jews or the International Social Service, or the Chicago offices of *Ebony* and the *Chicago Defender*. The children were variously understood as Germans or Americans, "occupation children" or "illegitimate children," "mixed-bloods" or "half-Negro." And the precise ways they were categorized helped to determine the social prognosis or social policy initiatives suggested for their future. What is more, since the children came to be perceived—by Germans and Americans alike—as the offspring of white German women and American (rather than other Allied) soldiers of color, they were also thought to embody and potentially upset the specific *national* racial ideologies of white domination those countries historically embraced. Therefore discussions regarding the children could be cast in the language of antiblack racism or enlightened postwar liberalism; could play upon anti-American or anti-Nazi (rather than anti-German) sentiment; and could serve or subvert the agenda of racial equality and civil rights.

In addition to the history of racial integration, this project speaks to the history of cultural transfers—especially those involving the sociology of racial knowledge and the social practices of race. The chapters are intended, moreover, to elucidate the range of official, public, and scholarly response that accompanied interracial heterosexual socialization, sexual relations, and reproduction between occupying troops and German women in western Germany and the United States. Chapter 1, "Contact Zones," focuses on the U.S. zone of occupied Germany to study the interaction of two distinct national-historical idioms of race. It considers how American race relations in the U.S. military (where practices of racial segregation persisted) and social contact between American occupiers and

German civilians affected racial ideology and policy in Germany and, to a lesser degree, the U.S. military. Of special interest are the experiences of African American soldiers in Germany, the occupation's effect on military policy toward those soldiers, and the impact of both on German public opinion and behavior. Chapter 2, "Flaccid Fatherland," discusses the gendered and racial dimensions of defeat. This chapter interprets the military occupation of Germany as unleashing a crisis of German masculinity; describes German experiences of, and responses to, rapes by Allied troops, including those considered racially foreign; and explores social policy—especially regarding female sexuality, abortion, and reproduction—developed in response to interracial rapes and sexual relations between Allied soldiers and German women.

Chapter 3, " 'Mischlingskinder' and the Postwar Taxonomy of Race," takes up the issue of black occupation children born to German women and fathered by Allied soldiers of color to investigate the range of ways Germans constructed and investigated the children as a significant social "problem" in the 1950s. This chapter charts shifts in the social language and social policies of race in the decade following the end of the war and is particularly attentive to the transnational influences of American "prejudice studies" and "intergroup relations" models on West Germany. These influences, I argue, help to differentiate West German responses from those of East German officials to their much smaller population of biracial children. Chapter 4, "Reconstruction in Black and White," focuses on the popular 1952 West German feature film, *Toxi*, and the short career of its Afro-German child star, Elfriede Fiegert, who was six years old at the time of filming. This chapter examines the strategies by which the film popularized and disseminated a liberal discourse of race around the problem of the black occupation child in order to win social acceptance for the children as they entered West German schools. It also charts the rapid demise of this cultural strategy of racial tolerance by considering subsequent films in which Fiegert appeared, as well as the truncated trajectory of her career.

Chapter 5, "Whose Children, Theirs or Ours?" traces the evolution of social policy toward Afro-German children and transnational debates about their national belonging from the early 1950s into the 1960s. Specific attention is paid to debates regarding the children's upbringing and education, the desirability of the children's adoption abroad to the "land of their fathers," and the children's long-term prospects for social integration in West Germany. The chapter explores the transition from fascist to postfascist adoption practices in Germany as well as the significant role played by international NGOs like the International Social Service in arranging intercountry adoptions of black German children to the United States. It also considers the efforts of African American individuals and organizations (such as the black press and the NAACP) to publicize the plight of the children; denounce U.S. military policies that adversely prejudiced applications of black GIs seeking to marry their German girlfriends; and facilitate adoptions of Black German children by African American families. In tracing the two-way travels of African American troops and Afro-German children between Europe and the United States, I hope to contribute to detailing another dimension of the Black Diaspora and Black Atlantic.

Chapter 6, "Legacies" examines the integration of Afro-German teenagers into the West German workforce in the 1960s and casts a critical eye on the accompanying official rhetoric proclaiming the triumph of the principles of racial liberalism and racial equality in the postwar German state. The chapter concludes by suggesting that early postwar attention to racism was ultimately displaced by attention to xenophobia—the hatred of *foreigners*—in response to increasing numbers of immigrant workers from Italy, Spain, Turkey, and the former Yugoslavia who labored, and later settled with their families, in the Federal Republic. This shift away from intensive postwar engagement with issues of race and racism to debates about immigration and xenophobia was of great consequence to German understandings of national and cultural belonging, for it rendered invisible the longer historical experience of *native* racial diversity *within* the German nation.

An important goal in writing this book was to demonstrate that the reformulation of race after 1945 was not merely a national enterprise, but an international one. Since I am a historian of Germany, I have focused on German-American relations and transatlantic interactions concerning racial ideologies, practices, and belonging after World War II. However, it is worth noting that when it came to racial reconstruction, this was but one node in a much larger international web of social interaction and signification. In the context of early postwar Germany, for example, white German women had social and sexual relations with other perceived racial aliens—such as French colonial troops from North Africa and Indochina or "Asiatic" Soviet soldiers—and I have analyzed German responses against this broader social interaction and racial imaginary. Yet historians could cast a wider conceptual net and investigate the process of racial democratization in the postwar and Cold War periods as a more expansive international and transnational phenomenon. After all, democratizing American troops occupied Japan as well. Could we conceive of writing a comparative history of military occupations and racial reformulation? Or a comparative history of postwar racial liberalisms?[24]

Perhaps. But the contributions of this book are more modest. In chronicling contemporaries' responses to interracial relations, sex, and repro-

duction in occupied and semisovereign West Germany, it explores an extended moment when the issue of race and its peculiarly postwar
meanings were explicitly addressed and performed by and for West Germans. This was accomplished by shifting the location of race from Jewishness to blackness in order to distance it from the Holocaust and Germans' crimes against humanity which, after all, were still on trial in these
postwar decades. The postwar focus on *"Mischlingskinder"* and blackness
rendered the racial issue one of juvenile stewardship and German control. And although it permitted racist response, it also facilitated the
emergence and articulation of a brand of racial liberalism that both drew
upon American social science and was offered as proof of West Germany's successful racial reeducation and rehabilitation after Hitler.

Finally, the postwar focus on blackness also allowed white West Germans, like their white American contemporaries, to draw the line at
white women's involvement in interracial sex and reproduction. In fact,
postwar German notions of race were formulated through sustained reference to German women's social roles and sexual behavior. Even in its
most liberal version, the revamped German racial ideology that emerged
was, like its American counterpart, intimately bound up with prescriptions for normative white German femininity. In a reciprocal fashion,
gender norms after 1945 were informed by social ideologies and experiences of *race* in ways that most historians of Germany have not yet recognized.[25] The postwar language of race, nation, and proper women's behavior was a shared one and, as before 1945, their meanings were
mutually constitutive.

• • •

NOTE ON LANGUAGE

In this book, I use the word *"Mischlingskinder"* when referring to the specific term and attendant perceptions Germans brought to their discussions of the children. In the United States, Afro-German children were
most typically called "half-Negro children" or, more colloquially, "brown
babies." One of the purposes of this study is to investigate the specific
social and cultural meanings attached to perceived "mixing" between allegedly distinct races. I do not subscribe to such understandings of racial
difference. Scientists have shown that race has no foundation in biology,
and what little application it has to the study of genetics derives solely
from its use in indicating *closed* intrareproducing populations, which are
by definition contingent.[26] There is no ideal racial category of "white,"
"Black," "Asian," "Jew," nor do I mean, by employing such terms, to indicate otherwise. Rather, when I use phrases like "black German chil-

dren" or "white Germans" or "biracial teenagers," they refer not to some distinct biological category of people, but connote social ascriptions or— in the case of "Afro-German" or "Black German" —self-ascriptions and therefore sociopolitical identities that have grown from the continued social salience, rather than some fictional "scientific fact," of race and racial difference.[27] It is precisely the historical and cultural contingency of this phenomenon, along with the process by which such social ascriptions and self-identities get formulated, reformulated, and invested with meaning, that this book seeks to explore.

An American GI from New Jersey relaxes with newfound friends
in occupied Berlin. The photo appeared in the October 1946 issue of *Ebony*.
Courtesy of The Newberry Library, Chicago.

Chapter One

CONTACT ZONES: AMERICAN MILITARY OCCUPATION AND THE POLITICS OF RACE

> I like this goddamn country, you know that? That's right. . . .
> You know what the hell I learned? That a nigger ain't no dif-
> ferent from nobody else. I had to come over here to learn
> that. . . . They don't teach that stuff back in the land of the
> free.
>
> Maybe I'll write a book about all this. . . . I'll write a book and
> tell how the Germans listen attentively to speeches on democ-
> racy and then look around at the segregated camps and race
> riots over white women and listen to the slurs on Negro sol-
> diers on the streets, and then how Germans in the coffee
> houses along the Hauptstrasse . . . gather and laugh at the
> Americans who preach a sermon on what they, themselves,
> do not yet know.
>
> —William Gardner Smith, *Last of the Conquerors*, 1948[1]

THE MILITARY occupation of Germany by American troops elicited two striking responses that were organized around irony and issues of race. One came from Germans, who noted with incredulity and derision that they were being democratized by a nation with a Jim Crow army and a host of antimiscegenation laws at home. The second came from African American GIs who, in their interactions with Germans, were stunned by the apparent absence of racism in the formerly fascist land and, compar-ing their reception with treatment by white Americans, experienced their stay there as unexpectedly liberatory. Both responses criticized the glar-ing gap between democratic American principles and practices; both ex-posed as false the universalist language employed by the United States government to celebrate and propagate its political system and social values at home and abroad. Yet both also suggested the centrality of in-tercultural observation and exchange for contemporaries' experience and understanding of postwar processes of democratization.[2]

From their inception, the occupation zones in Germany were zones of social and cultural contact between occupier and occupied. Rapidly, they emerged as informal sites of racial reeducation and reconstruction as well. When the victorious allies subdued Germany in May 1945, their most urgent agenda centered upon the need to demilitarize, denazify, and democratize their defeated foe. Dismantling attitudes of racial superiority among Germans was understood by the Western allies as an implicit part of this process. But aside from the first year of occupation— when American officials in particular insisted on mandatory screenings of atrocity films like *Todesmühlen* (*Mills of Death*), with its graphic scenes of liberated death camps, denunciation of notions of Aryan supremacy, and blunt accusations of collective German guilt—"race" barely figured in formal reeducation programs, nor did it play a central role in allied policies for German reconstruction.[3] Racial reeducation in early postwar Germany resulted primarily *not* from the official programs of occupation authorities, but rather more spontaneously through the experience of social interactions between Germans and Americans or through German observations of social relations among the multiethnic American occupation forces.[4] In the public behavior of U.S. troops on the street and in the pub, the current complexion of American race relations was on display for postwar Germans to see.[5]

It was in the specific historical circumstances of the occupation that two distinct national-historical idioms of race—the American and German—confronted and instructed each other. Under these circumstances, Germans reformulated their notions of race after National Socialism, and African American GIs experienced and appraised the comparative state of race relations between democratic America and its fascist foe. It is in this context, then, that racial reeducation as an informal *interactive* process must be investigated and understood. Encounters between white Germans and African American GIs after 1945, moreover, were not merely transitory phenomena; rather, they had a constituent effect on postwar racial understanding in both countries that outlived the period of occupation.

• • •

German-American interactions were embedded in a larger field of power relations dominated by the United States and structured by official American policies and practices. As is well known, the United States conquered and occupied National Socialist Germany with an army in which troop units, training, work assignments, housing, recreational and other facilities, and even religious worship, were segregated by race.[6] And although President Harry Truman formally began the process of desegregating the U.S. military in 1948, when he issued an executive order proclaiming "equality of treatment and opportunity for all persons in the armed forces," a corresponding commitment to the principle of racial integration was not at that time a value held by most American commanders in general, nor by those responsible for Germany in particular. As a result, the actual integration of American military forces stationed both within and outside of the United States dragged on well into the 1950s.[7]

Ultimately Cold War considerations, and especially the United States' entry into the Korean conflict in 1950, helped dictate the timing of desegregation of the U.S. military, which emerged as a pragmatic response to the pressing exigencies of mobilizing manpower and fighting the Korean War. Commitment to the social value of integration had little to do with it. Predictably, then, its application was uneven. Where wartime exigencies did not exist, leadership response was lethargic or temporizing. According to historian Bernard Nalty, "the need for efficiency imposed by the Korean War did not make itself felt in Europe . . . where enthusiastic reports from Korea [regarding the performance of integrated troops] went unread or encountered disbelief."[8] In Germany, the mandate to integrate U.S. army bases was ignored until the spring of 1952 and then took over two years—into August 1954—to complete.[9]

Nearly a decade after defeating and occupying Nazi Germany, and some five years after overseeing the foundation of a democratic West German state, the United States finally dismantled its almost century-long tradition of racial segregation in its armed forces.[10] The slow pace of postwar integration of the U.S. military—and the even slower pace of postwar integration of American society—meant that for the entire period of military occupation (1945–49), and throughout most of the High Commission in Germany (1949–55), postfascist German society was democratized by a country whose institutions, social relations, and dominant cultural values were organized around the category of race and a commitment to white supremacy.

Fighting the War, Winning the Peace: "The Problem of Negro Troops"

Like Germany, American society too was undergoing an uneasy period of challenges and adjustments to entrenched racial ideology after 1945. Unlike Germany, however, the postwar years in the United States represented a continuation and intensification of social transformations that began in earnest during World War II. The important point for our purposes is that at the same time it was fighting Nazi Germany, the U.S. government was under considerable public pressure by a growing number of African American activists and organizations to democratize the United States and dismantle its discriminatory policies and practices toward its own citizens of color. Democratic America of the 1930s and 1940s can not be said to have enjoyed a stable or consensual understanding of the significance of race.[11] Rather, the social ideology and organization of race was hotly disputed and, with mobilization for war, gave rise to a new sort of advocacy politics that was attentive to both national and international developments and ultimately succeeded in affecting the political decision-making process in Washington, D.C.[12]

Prior to the bombing of Pearl Harbor, African American newspapers tended to express an isolationist view, characterized by a 1940 essay in the NAACP's mouthpiece, *The Crisis*, which proclaimed that while they were: "sorry for brutality, blood, and death among the peoples of Europe . . . the hysterical cries of the preachers of democracy in Europe leave us cold. We want democracy in Alabama and Arkansas, in Mississippi and Michigan, in the District of Columbia and *the Senate of the United States*."

Or as C.L.R. James pithily put it, "the democracy I want to fight for, Hitler is not depriving me of."[13]

After the attack on Pearl Harbor in December 1941, however, the battle broadened to two fronts for most African American leaders. Instead of characterizing war as an either/or proposition, black leaders and newspapers fused domestic and international quests for democracy into a campaign for "double victory." To modify columnist George Schuyler's 1940 dictum in the *Pittsburgh Courier*, their motto became "our war is against Hitler in Europe *and* against the Hitlers in America." From early 1942, African American leaders and the press overwhelmingly supported black participation in the war effort while continuing to lobby against racial discrimination and injustice at home.[14]

The United States' entry into war—and especially its official justification of fighting Nazi Germany and Imperial Japan in order to free the world for democracy—created a useful context for African Americans to press their case for social equality and civil rights. Black leaders well recognized the wrenching irony of the situation and did their best to use it to its greatest political effect. As the *Pittsburgh Courier* noted, "What an opportunity the crisis has been . . . to persuade, embarrass, compel and shame our government and nation . . . into a more enlightened attitude toward a tenth of its people!"[15]

One of the most prominent organizations to lobby on behalf of "Negro" interests was the National Association for the Advancement of Colored People, which, during the wartime and postwar years, became an outspoken advocate of African American soldiers' rights. NAACP leaders scrutinized the relevant policies of U.S. officials in the War Department and White House, and later in the American Military Government in Germany, and publicized their reactions and recommendations in the African American press. Complaints centered around racial inequities in soldiers' recruitment, training, assignments (most black troops were relegated to service, housekeeping, supply, or transport duties), promotion, housing, entertainment, and other facilities. In addition to frequent episodes of violence directed at black servicemen by white American citizens and soldiers in the United States and overseas, African American leaders and the black press documented and publicized widespread discriminatory practices exercised by the Selective Service, white military officers, white communities surrounding the predominantly southern U.S. military bases, and by the Red Cross, which segregated by race not only the soldiers' social functions it hosted, but also the blood plasma it collected.[16]

African Americans bristled at the poor treatment accorded black troops. Soldiers wrote letters to loved ones and the black press that chronicled the wide range of indignities they were subjected to, which resulted in a profound sense of demoralization and disgust. Soldiers from the northern United States were shocked by official expectation that they adjust to the overtly racist Jim Crow practices of the southern states and proved unwilling to adopt the self-effacing posture demanded of them by white southerners. Black inductees clearly expected that as American soldiers in uniform, they should receive the respect extended their white compatriots. When this did not occur—when, for example, African Americans in uniform were refused service in local restaurants, were ordered to the back of the bus when traveling off base, were subjected to racist epithets, physically assaulted, or saw their black officers mistreated or passed over for promotion, to name but a handful of common occurrences—they became disillusioned or embittered.[17]

Throughout the decade of the 1940s, and extending well into the 1950s, African American soldiers' experience was dictated by the U.S. military's insistence on the primacy of race and the "fact" of their Negro blood. According to official military policy, African American soldiers— unlike their white counterparts—were not treated as individuals with specific abilities, aptitudes, or educational accomplishments. Rather, their military selection and assignment were made according to their group identity as "Negro" with all of the racist valuations that accompanied that social classification. As a result, skilled African American soldiers rapidly became insulted and dejected by assignments to labor and service units that derived solely from their race and failed to recognize or utilize their abilities.[18] As one soldier remarked: "Civilian life is one thing, but to be drafted and fight to save the world for democracy only to find that you have entered the most undemocratic and racist organization in the whole country is quite another thing. This . . . turned me off completely."[19]

One of the greatest insults to African American soldiers—and one repeatedly commented upon in the black press—was the comparatively better treatment, even camaraderie, extended to German POWs by white American soldiers and civilians in the presence of black American troops.[20] Since numerous complaints were recorded on this issue, a few examples will have to suffice. Sergeant Edward Donald of the 761st Tank Battalion remembered that African American soldiers were housed in the segregated "swampland" of Camp Claiborne, Louisiana, while German POWs were accommodated in a more desirable area of the camp, "had access to facilities denied black American soldiers . . . and were given passes to town when black soldiers were confined" to base. "This was one of the most repugnant things I can recall of the many things that happened to Negro servicemen," he concluded.[21] Captain Charles Thomas of Detroit remembered having hunger pangs on his return trip to his camp in Texas and looking for a place to eat:

> The station restaurant was doing a rush business with white civilians and German prisoners of war. There sat the so-called enemy comfortably seated, laughing, talking, making friends, with the waitresses at their beck and call. If I had tried to enter that dining room the ever-present MPs would have busted my skull, a citizen-soldier of the United States. My morale, if I had any left, dipped well below zero. Nothing infuriated me as much as seeing those German prisoners of war receiving the warm hospitality of Texas.[22]

Black soldiers weren't the only ones infuriated. Singer Lena Horne was scheduled to give two concerts at Camp Robinson in Alabama, the first for white officers, the second for black GIs. However, the second concert was also attended by German POWS, who were given the best seats up front, while black American soldiers were relegated to the back. Realizing the outrage, Horne responded, "Screw this!" stormed off the stage and refused to perform. Following that incident, she consented to sing only for African American troops.[23]

As the comparative official and informal treatment of German POWs and African American soldiers in the United States makes clear, the "problem of Negro soldiers," from the perspective of African Americans, had its origins in the prejudicial practices and policies of white America. The first point made by the preceding testimony was that African Americans—whether in uniform or out—were not accorded the rights or recognition of their American citizenship. Rather, they were treated as subordinates—as inferior or "not-quite" Americans—by white compatriots and military leaders, as evidenced by the preferential treatment extended white prisoners of war. While the American rhetoric of war pivoted on the appeal to a national "we," African Americans learned time and again from their wartime experience that this was empty rhetoric. The second point derives from the first. This was that race—and especially a shared whiteness—trumped nationality when it came to social privilege and prerogative. As a result, even though German soldiers were, and remained, the military enemy throughout World War II, once they were pacified as POWs, they were treated as social equals in a way that African American soldiers never were. And to a large extent these sociocultural presumptions and practices of whiteness survived the war to shape postwar reconstruction in occupied Germany.[24]

The blatant abuses and indignities perpetrated on African American men in uniform mobilized black leaders, citizens, and newspapers. In addition to headlining domestic expressions of racial inequality and violence, African American newspapers sent correspondents overseas to cover the condition and contributions of "Negro troops" abroad. Walter White of the NAACP toured U.S. installations in Britain, France, Northern Africa, and the Mediterranean to interview African American troops about their treatment and morale.[25] In response, U.S. officials in the White House and War Department grudgingly learned to consult representatives of the NAACP, Urban League, and other black organizations for their opinions before making or announcing major policy decisions, if only to try to deflect criticism and negative publicity.[26]

From the official perspective of Washington, the "problem of Negro troops" was first and foremost a political one: How to appear responsive to black leaders and their constituencies, in order to effectively mobilize them as workers and soldiers for the war effort, without having to concede to their demands for wholesale racial equality. Just before the presidential election in 1940, for example, FDR appointed a black aide to the director of the Selective Service and a black civilian aide to the secretary of War to illustrate his responsiveness to African American concerns. Once the United States entered the war and the Army's racial policy came under increasing fire by black leaders and the black press, the War Department established an "Advisory Committee on Negro Troop Policies" which failed to coordinate effectively with the War Department's civilian aide. In sum, official and institutional attention to the "Negro problem" stemmed more from official assessments of political expediency than any wholehearted interest to right discriminatory policies and practices. Throughout World War II, the U.S. president and his military officers single-mindedly prioritized fighting and winning the war and actively resisted calls to revamp the military's policy of racial segregation, which they dismissed as a dangerous "social experiment" that would sow conflict among the troops and result in markedly weakened troop morale, performance, and cohesion.[27]

The War Department considered the need to induct black soldiers as presenting irksome organizational challenges and problems of performance and morale. The military leadership tended to view black troops as a drag on military efficiency and effectiveness and, in group terms, as not combat worthy. Noting the small numbers of African Americans assigned to combat units, critics accused the military of considering black soldiers "too stupid to fight."[28] Since War Department officials paid little attention to the demoralizing *effects* of racial stereotyping, institutionalized racism, and segregation in the military, they blamed black soldiers for being disloyal, unpatriotic, and overly "race conscious."[29]

As military intelligence registered the large readership newspapers like the *Afro-American, Pittsburgh Courier,* and *Chicago Defender* enjoyed among African American soldiers, the War Department became concerned that news coverage of racial discrimination was fostering "agitation" and disaffection among them. During the war, circulation numbers for the African American press increased 40 percent and membership in the NAACP multiplied tenfold. Detecting a similar pattern among its black troops, the War Department issued a secret order banning "Negro newspapers" on military bases. Ultimately, the ban was lifted in 1943, the year pent-up frustration regarding racial discrimination burst forth in a wave of riots that swept American cities, workplaces, and military bases.[30]

Widespread social unrest caught the attention of the White House and War Department, which recognized the need to respond to the political pressure of disgruntled African American opinion. This they did in selective areas: by instituting black officer training programs, by mounting a publicity campaign to recognize African American contributions to the war effort (most notably in the 1944 motion picture, *The Negro Soldier*), by issuing Army recommendations to its white officers on "the command of Negro troops," by increasing the numbers of black troops shipped overseas, by assigning some black soldiers combat duties, and by integrating troops on the battlefront in isolated emergency situations. Nonetheless, for the duration of the war, the American political and military leadership staunchly resisted a more general policy of racial desegregation. Despite this fact, African American organizations, through their unrelenting attention to racial inequities in the U.S. military and workforce, played an important and productive role in unsettling entrenched racist ideologies and practices, fostering African Americans' expectations, and setting a broad social reform agenda for the postwar period.[31]

Once war in Europe began to wind down, the War Department and European Command questioned the merits of having black troops participate as occupation forces, particularly in Germany. General McNarney, commander of the U.S. Army in Europe, went "on record with a recommendation to recall all black troops from Europe, citing the absence of Negroes from the U.S. Occupation Army in the Rhineland after World War I." Off record, he judged "the Negro . . . a failure as a soldier," adding that "it will be 100 years before he . . . will be on a parity with white Americans." His successor, Lucius D. Clay, commander of the European Theater and American military governor in Germany, thought African American soldiers should be "used primarily as parade troops."[32] There was a general concern about how receptive Germans would be, steeped as they were in Nazi-style racism, to the occupation goals of a multiracial army.

But this was not the only, or even overriding, concern.[33] Following the end of hostilities, the army was expected to shrink from approximately 8 million troops to 1.8 million, but the percentage of black troops was projected to increase from about 10 to 15 percent due to new and reenlistments. The anticipated increase in the percentage of black troops concerned the U.S. State Department, which had earlier made "informal arrangements" not to post black U.S. troops to countries like Iceland, Panama, and China that refused to host them, even within a segregated army. As a result of these agreements, black troops would have to be concentrated elsewhere, and both the War Department and European Command had reservations regarding their placement in Germany for reasons of both political prestige and effectiveness.[34]

With the end of war in Europe in May 1945, the demobilization of combat troops proceeded apace, although at a much slower rate for black soldiers than for white. Within the year, the number of U.S. troops in the Europe was reduced from just over 3 million to 342,000; by mid-1947, it stabilized at around 135,000, until the mid-1950s, when the numbers again nearly doubled. The proportion of African American troops hovered around 10 percent.[35] During this time, wartime troops were replaced by younger, inadequately trained troops of uneven aptitude, skill, and commitment. In 1946, the European Command began to register a marked decline in performance and discipline and a rise in rates of venereal disease as well as serious criminal incidents against property and civilians among its troops in Germany. Statistics showed, moreover, that black troops were disproportionately more involved in disciplinary infractions and criminal activity.[36] In response, the NAACP—inundated by letters from black GIs complaining of discriminatory treatment in matters of military discipline and struck by the stark overrepresentation of Blacks in military arrests and punishment, including courts-martial and executions—launched an investigation and publicly questioned officials about the racist assumptions and practices underlying military justice. The American military leadership, however, continued to make policy decisions on the basis of these statistics, treating them as objective and value-neutral.[37]

Due to negative publicity regarding the behavior of occupation troops in the white mainstream press, a Senate Special Investigation Committee undertook a study on the conduct of "Negro soldiers" in Germany as part of a larger inquiry into the operations of military government in Europe. Chief counsel George Meader produced the 1946 report, subsequently described as a "curious amalgam of sensational hearsay, obvious racism, and unimpeachable fact, " in which he recommended that black troops overseas be returned to the United States.[38] Meader's biased report provoked outraged response by black newspapers like the *Pittsburgh Courier*, which noted that Meader hadn't even bothered interviewing black soldiers on his four-week tour of Germany, but relied exclusively on information provided by white officers.[39] Over the course of late 1946, the secretary of War's civilian aide, Marcus Ray, also studied the situation of black troops in Europe and ultimately concluded that "substandard troops" of *both* races were the cause of increased indiscipline, crime, and venereal disease rates overseas.[40]

The War Department and the European Command concurred with Ray about the poor quality of troops, but remained concerned about an anticipated "glut" of enlistment by black soldiers with poor education, skills, and motivation. As a result, they took steps to address these concerns within the larger context of efforts to upgrade the overall quality of the postwar army. The Army discharged any soldier who scored in the lowest category of the general classification test (many of whom were black, due to widespread economic hardship and limited access to quality education among African Americans), and the War Department set the lowest acceptable test score for African Americans a full thirty points higher than for whites. In addition, they exercised a racially differentiated approach to first enlistments by accepting only those African Americans possessing required skills, and instituted remedial military training and basic academic programs (at Käfertal, Grafenwoehr, and Kitzingen) for African American soldiers in Germany. Through these methods, they raised the performance level of black troops abroad while at the same time studiously limiting their numbers.[41] As historian Bernard Nalty summarized, in the first years after the war, "Little change took place in the treatment blacks received. . . . The retraining program for blacks in Europe, instead of broadening opportunities for graduates, served mainly to increase effectiveness of existing segregated units, many of them service organizations. . . . Segregation remained the first consideration, . . . the gap in power and privilege between black soldiers and whites [persisted]."[42]

Throughout the decade following V-E Day, African American organizations and newspapers continued unabated their wartime strategy of lobbying for desegregation of the military and equal rights for black soldiers. After 1945 they often turned their eyes to conditions in Germany to focus more sharply their political and ethical points.[43] In June 1946, for example, in response to official attempts to suspend—or at least drasti-

MAP 5

MILITARY DISTRICTS & MILITARY POSTS

US ZONE-GERMANY

1 AUGUST 1947

SECOND MILITARY DISTRICT
LAND HESSE &
LAND WÜRTTEM-
BERG-BADEN

LEGEND:

———— *MILITARY DISTRICT BOUNDARIES*
‑ ‑ ‑ ‑ ‑ *MILITARY POST BOUNDARIES*
● *MILITARY POST HEADQUARTERS*

WETZLAR

FULDA

WIES‑
BADEN   FRANKFURT

FIRST MILITARY DISTRICT
LAND BAVARIA

DARM‑
STADT   WÜRZBURG   BAMBERG

HEIDELBERG   NÜRNBERG   GRAFENWÖHR

REGENSBURG

STUTTGART

AUGSBURG

MUNICH

TÖLZ

GAR‑
MISCH

Military districts and posts in the U.S. occupation zone. By early 1947, all
black American troops assigned to Germany were trained at Kitzingen, just
south of Würzburg. Afterward, they served near all the major military posts.
Source: O. J. Frederiksen, *The American Military Occupation of Germany*
(Historical Division, Headquarters, U.S. Army, Europe, 1953), 37.

cally reduce—overseas service by African American troops, the United Negro and Allied Veterans of America (UNAVA) announced that "the ghost of Hitler . . . [is] very much alive" in American-occupied Germany. But this time around it was haunting American military bases rather than German public spaces. The next month, the Negro Newspaper Publishers Association submitted a report to the secretary of War cataloguing instances of abuse that they collected on their tour of U.S. bases in Europe. Among the grievances were those of soldiers stationed in Nidda, Germany, who alleged that their white commanding officer refused them the right to attend Sunday religious services, "drew his gun when reprimanding them," and referred to them as "niggers" when speaking to German civilians.[44] That same summer of 1946, the War Department received a letter from a black U.S. soldier stationed in Auerbach, Germany, complaining that his regiment was quartered in barracks that recently housed German prisoners of war. Surrounded by barbed wire fences, the barracks had been neither cleaned nor upgraded after the German POWs were vacated. The black troops entered a filthy, garbage-filled, louse-ridden compound with overflowing, noxious latrines, and no electricity or bathing facilities. The letter writer was rightly outraged that African American troops were assigned to live literally amidst German shit, while their white officers took up residence in homes located in a village two miles from base.[45]

While conditions for African American troops in Auerbach may have been extreme, they were indicative of an ongoing attitude among white military officers who saw nothing wrong in segregated substandard facilities for African American troops. Due to soldiers' complaints and political pressure from black leaders and newspapers, the quality of housing, leisure and sports facilities, and work assignments would gradually be improved for black American troops. But well into the 1950s African Americans in Germany continued to be drastically underrepresented in Military Government headquarters, in the officer ranks, in medical and professional services, among chaplains and the military police, and in assignment to combat duties. As a reporter for the Baltimore *Afro American* noted in mid-1948, after chronicling some of these inequities in an article on "racial bars" in occupied Germany, "The Germans know these things, and it doesn't help promote the so-called democratic way of life being introduced" to them.[46]

OCCUPATION, AMERICAN STYLE

While Germans' reception of American troops in the spring of 1945 was certainly marked by the bitterness of defeat, it was also influenced by Germans' assessment of the practical alternatives. As is evident from postwar testimony, Germans felt it far preferable to be occupied by the

Americans or British than by the Soviets or (later) the French. Like the British, the Americans were generally considered disciplined and well-mannered, but with none of the famous British reserve. Alone among the Allied troops, American GIs, both black and white, were described as friendly and informal, inordinately tall, broad-shouldered, and healthy, with unimaginably good teeth. From the first, their casual demeanor and physical appearance made an indelible impression.[47]

Germans were also struck by American soldiers' affluence, generosity, and access to consumer goods, which far exceeded not only the miserable material circumstances of early postwar Germans, but also the more meager resources of the other Allied soldiers as well. The stereotype of the gum-chewing, chocolate-bar-dispensing GI originated both in the actual social practices of U.S. occupation troops and in German perception of these behaviors as somehow uniquely American. GIs were the informal source of that unofficial currency of the booming black market in occupied Germany, American cigarettes, as well as other diverse gifts to Germans such as supplemental food, nylon stockings, and rock and roll. A bit later in the occupation, GIs rolled through German towns in big American sedans, occasionally offering ogling German children or, more frequently, young German women a ride. The spectacle of American soldiers' cultural modernity and avid consumerism evoked strong responses in Germany, both positive and negative. But it served to differentiate them from the British and especially the Soviets and French, who were denounced by Germans for their particularly punitive provisioning policies during the first years of occupation. American GIs, in comparison, are remembered for an openhanded largesse, which reinforced in most Germans the image of the United States as a land of material—if not necessarily cultural or moral—abundance.[48]

In the months following the defeat of Nazi Germany, occupiers and occupied alike were struck by the high incidence of fraternization between American troops and German civilians. As historian Elizabeth Heineman has pointed out, "in the western zones, fraternization became one of the most-discussed aspects of the occupation," and a focus on fraternization has shaped the historical understanding of postwar reconstruction in West Germany. In contrast, Germans' experience of Soviet occupation, and their retrospective historical assessments of it, have been dominated by references to Soviet authoritarianism, coercion, brutality and, at the earliest stages of contact, rape. Such perceptions and distinctions were, of course, forged and refined in response to a quickly evolving political and ideological context in which wartime gave way to postwar, out of which the Cold War would rapidly emerge.[49]

Nonetheless, it is significant that Germans' personal and historical narratives of life in the American and Soviet zones are structured around *different dynamics of social interaction* between occupier and occupied. The

Soviet approach preached socialist equality via policies that increasingly isolated Soviet troops from Germans, in part due to official fears of reciprocal negative political and ideological influences if social interaction were allowed.[50] The American approach—after a failed attempt to prohibit fraternization between its troops and a presumed Nazi-infected German public in the first few months of occupation—permitted its soldiers to live among Germans in private housing and to socialize with them off base. Moreover, they encouraged organized contact through official American sponsorship of cultural and sporting events, holiday parades, parties for children, and the like.[51]

In stark contrast to early interactions between Soviets and Germans—which were marred by terrifying incidents of Soviet vengeance that included mass rapes in the spring and early summer of 1945—social contact between Germans and Americans was perceived as elective, rather than coercive. This was not due to an absence of violent crimes, including rape, perpetrated by American troops against Germans. These did occur, but not on a mass scale and widespread basis over a relatively short amount of time, as was the case with Soviet troops.[52] Moreover, while some Soviet soldiers cultivated consensual relations with Germans, and particularly German women, after 1945, such opportunities were officially discouraged by late 1947. At that time, Soviet soldiers and officers were prohibited from cohabiting with Germans in private arrangements and were rehoused. In order to create segregated billets for its troops, Soviet officials evicted Germans and confiscated their housing and gardens, forcibly transforming whole city streets and rural villages into Soviet military districts. With housing scarce, the results for affected Germans were devastating.[53]

In the American occupation zone, an opposite trend was evident, as GIs increasingly took advantage of the possibility to rent private housing from German landlords, sometimes using the opportunity to cohabitate with German girlfriends or to import their own wives and children from the United States in a wave of family reunions. Housing and servicing American GIs became a highly lucrative business, which provided Germans both an additional reason to welcome them to the neighborhood and an unprecedented level of contact with American soldiers, their families, and their distinctive way of life. By late 1946, family reunion was well underway for American officers and soldiers in Germany and, within the year, American families and soldiers were integrated into surrounding German residential areas.[54] Unlike the Soviets who opted, for ideological reasons, to rule at a social distance, the more informal interactive American approach appeared based on a presumption of social (if not political) equality between Americans and the nonsovereign Germans, and could work to the economic benefit of the latter.

If Germans pragmatically preferred Americans over other Allied soldiers, American GIs in Europe overwhelmingly returned the compliment. When asked to assess European countries and peoples among whom they served, American GIs disregarded the battle lines of World War II and expressed a strong preference for Germany and the German people over Allied countries and their inhabitants. In a Red Cross register signed by soldiers returning to the United States, for example, about four out of five named Germany as their "favorite foreign country." During the first year of the occupation, a poll taken by the U.S. Army found that nearly 60 percent of enlisted men serving in Europe who spent at least one month in Germany reported their opinion of that country as "favorable" (compared to 32 percent of enlisted men who had not had a German tour of duty). By early 1946, GIs' partiality toward Germans attracted the attention of sociologists and the popular press. Under the ominous caption, "Disaster lies ahead for a nation which cannot tell its enemies from its friends," the *Reader's Digest* featured an article titled simply "Why So Many GIs like Germans the Best."[55]

The reasons for these preferences appear to be many, and surely included the enforced political subservience of the Germans and the corresponding heightened political authority of the American occupiers, though GIs rarely referred to this in their responses. U.S. soldiers commonly praised the Germans for their cleanliness, friendliness, compliant attitudes, relatively good health, and habituation to a "higher material standard of living"—attributes that stuck them as admirable and somehow "familiar" when compared with the French and even the British. For a considerable number of GIs, moreover, this familiarity derived from heredity and heritage, and from the first days of military occupation, many disregarded the fraternization ban to contact and visit relatives still residing in Germany. Whatever the complex of motivations—which doubtless ran the gamut from political to material, genealogical to sexual—American occupiers and German civilians sought each other out. Normalized postwar relations between Americans and Germans derived in large measure from such practices of social proximity and intimacy.[56]

"DEMOCRACY'S NEGROES" IN "NAZILAND": GERMANY MEETS JIM CROW

It should not be forgotten that such practices of social proximity and intimacy were undergirded by the highly asymmetrical power relations existing between American occupiers and their German subjects, on the one hand, and among members of the American occupying force, on the other. The racial hierarchy of the American military—along with its explicit policies and social practices towards minority members—affected and helped to rescript the hierarchical relationship between victor and vanquished. Race fractured the social binary of American-German relations under the occupation into a more complicated and less predictable social triad. And since it was structured around the contested category of race, the dynamics of this triad wreaked havoc with notions of loyalty, belonging, and difference based upon national identification. Any assessment of the military occupation of Germany, then, is incomplete without a consideration of the impact and consequences of the social dynamics of race.[57]

On their march into Germany in the spring of 1945, African American soldiers reported experiencing unpleasant receptions by German civilians. Several recalled being spat upon or glared at by hostile German women, acts that may well have been directed at all conquerors, regardless of race. Others remembered that Germans were told they had "tails and other such garbage," the sort of racist propaganda that also circulated in Italy and even England during the war and originated in both Axis sources as well as rumors spread among native populations by white racists in the U.S. forces.[58]

Germans, for their part, greeted the sight of African American troops with a mixture of trepidation and disgust. In an interview with an American sociologist a few years after defeat, a member of the Christian Democratic Party in Hesse scolded: "We were deeply hurt when you Americans sent Negroes to Germany in soldiers' uniforms. How can America do this to us, a white people? We are not used to Negroes here; you in America are because you have mongrels of all kinds; but here in Germany we are a pure white race. To see a Negro shocks us, as we would be shocked to see a poisonous snake while walking through the woods."[59]

Germans' negative reactions were shaped by long-held antiblack stereotype, as well as more recent wartime propaganda disseminated by the Nazi Regime. Women and girls were particularly affected by rumors that stereotyped black soldiers as primitive savages and rapists. As American forces entered their communities, Germans found it "scary" since they "did not know what the Blacks would do to" them.[60] One woman, who was a child at the time, recalled "For the first time in my life I now saw Blacks. They were 'cannibals,' we were told by the older children whose word meant something to us. Nothing, however, happened. The unit passed by us completely peacefully."[61]

While fear of black soldiers persisted among some Germans, others reported "experiencing or witnessing pleasant contacts" with African American GIs. By September 1946 in Mannheim, nearly one in six Germans polled by the American military government (OMGUS) claimed to have a relationship (of some sort) with black soldiers.[62] Six years later, one-quarter of West Germans polled said they would be "willing to invite a Negro soldier" into their home, while a larger number, some 30 percent, said they would not.[63] Although the percentage of hospitable Germans was not high, one cannot help but wonder what sort of comparative numbers this question would have yielded in the United States at the time, and whether OMGUS pollsters ever gave serious thought to this issue when analyzing survey results.[64] While it is difficult to get a clear picture of the extent of interracial U.S.-German socializing that developed in the American zone and, later, in West Germany, available data suggest that it was confined to a minority of Germans—albeit a highly significant one, both in statistical and symbolic terms.

Antiblack racism has a long historical legacy in Germany and frequently was fused with anti-Americanism and antisemitism during the first half of the twentieth century—something that will be discussed at greater length in subsequent chapters. Nonetheless, the problems that confronted officials in occupied Germany did not derive for the most part from Germans' wholesale unwillingness to mingle with American troops. Quite the opposite, in fact. Shortly after Germany's unconditional surrender, American officials reported an unanticipated "epidemic" of fraternization between African American troops and the native population.

Prior to 1948, during the worst of the hunger years in occupied Germany, fraternization between black GIs and Germans extended beyond the heterosexual romantic relationships that would increasingly become the obsessive complaint of white Americans and Germans alike to the larger German community. In contrast to the superior attitude and "conquering hero" posture evinced by some of their white counterparts, black GIs appeared less likely to treat Germans as subordinates. Germans tended to consider them more affable, modest, courteous, and compassionate than white American soldiers and officers. Black GIs were known at the time, and have been remembered since, as especially kindhearted and generous toward children, but also as responsive to the stark misery of other Germans after the war as well. "In a village near Ulm, during the their six-month tour, nearly every German household had its own 'house-negro' [Hausneger]" to supply it with scarce food or goods, recalled one German woman in offensive, if characteristic, fashion. In other localities, German women reportedly "refuse[d] to take in the laundry of white soldiers if black soldiers were stationed in the area," presumably because the latter compensated the women more liberally. In Kitzingen, the site of a training center for African American GIs, where two thousand Blacks mingled off hours in a small town of 17,000, inhabitants uniformly described the soldiers as "very friendly" and prone "to share cigarettes, wine, or beer." Friction occurred only when such generosity was declined, since this tended to be interpreted by black GIs as a racially motivated insult.[65] Clearly, then, contact with black soldiers could offer significant material advantages to Germans.[66] But it also caused headaches for American officials, who complained in an OMGUS memo on Bavaria in 1946 that "the core of the problem did *not* consist in educating racially prejudiced Germans to refrain from the display of a hostile or disrespectful attitude towards the negro soldier, but rather in supervising the springtime of fraternization" that allegedly resulted in the siphoning of military rations and clothing into German homes.[67]

Perhaps the greatest surprise of intercultural contact in occupied Germany was reserved for African American soldiers, who—after the initial shock of contact, which for some included the revolting, firsthand observation of the horrors of Dachau and Buchenwald—reported surprisingly cordial relationships with Germans.[68] They commented upon the striking *absence* of racism in postwar German society: the relative friendliness of the German population and their ability to move about without undue restriction and to socialize with anyone they pleased regardless of race. Although they had "heard about Hitler's autobiography, 'Mein Kampf,' with its unflattering reference to Negroes as 'Semi-Apes,' . . . had heard of Germans' prejudices, and . . . were prepared to hate them," as Bill Smith of the *Pittsburgh Courier* noted, African American soldiers experienced their stay in this formerly fascist country as both eye-opening and emancipating. Germany's reputation as a desirable place to be stationed spread among African American troops, and it remained a sought-after assignment throughout the American civil rights era.[69]

Germans' positive public reception of black GIs and perceived lack of racial discrimination toward the soldiers was headlined in the black press in the first years of the occupation and even resonated in the mainstream American press in publications like *Newsweek*. As a 1946 report in *Ebony* magazine put it: "Strangely enough, here where once Aryanism ruled supreme, Negroes are finding more friendship, more respect and more equality than they would back home either in Dixie or on Broadway. . . . Race hate has faded with better acquaintance and interracialism in Berlin flourishes. Many of the Negro GIs in the German capital are from the South and find that democracy has more meaning on Wilhelmstrasse than on Beale Street in Memphis."[70] Of course much of this German response can be attributed to African American soldiers' stature as representatives of a victorious occupying power. "Here in Naziland," noted the *Pittsburgh Courier*, black GIs began "to feel equal or even superior to everyone around him. And they liked for a change to feel superior."[71] African American soldiers in Germany were struck by the novelty of being treated courteously as "Yanks," or representatives of the United States and its military. In Germany, unlike in the United States and its military, their uniform and national affiliation dictated German response

and superseded their racial classification as "Negro" in spite of the privately held racial attitudes of individual Germans. African Americans
immediately registered and responded to this outward show of respect,
precisely because it was an unprecedented social experience for them.[72]

In his 1948 novel, *Last of the Conquerors*, William Gardner Smith (the
same Bill Smith who wrote for the *Pittsburgh Courier*) drew on his own
tour of duty as occupation soldier in postwar Germany to produce a critical commentary on the social and emotional effects of antiblack racism
and racial segregation in American society and its military. Described as
the "first twentieth-century novel by an Afro-American writer to deal
with the sensitive matter" of black soldiers' experience in a Jim Crow
army, *Last of the Conquerors* is set in occupied Germany and narrated from
the perspective of its protagonist, Hayes Dawkins, whose duties, assignment, and social contacts in the novel closely echo those of Smith, who
was inducted into the army in December 1945 and served as clerk-typist
with the 661st TC Truck Company in Berlin from June 1946 through January 1947.[73] *Last of the Conquerors* chronicles Dawkins's introduction to
Germany and his easy integration into the army and a wider social life
in Berlin, the site of his initial posting. It explores his friendships with
other black soldiers and their interactions with white officers, both be-
nign and, with a transfer out of Berlin to the "nigger hell" of Bremburg,
increasingly brutalizing. Throughout, however, the social critique of
American race relations is juxtaposed against the interwoven story of
Dawkins's ready social acceptance by the Germans he meets, both male
and female. This includes, first and foremost, a developing love affair
with Ilse—a beautiful yet respectable German secretary who works for
the U.S. chaplain on the base in Berlin and initiates their romance by asking him out on their first date—as well as his warm relations with her
family and friends, first in Berlin and later near Bremburg, where the
devoted Ilse follows him, unbidden, at risk to her personal safety.

Smith makes clear in the novel that time abroad in a different national
context—even and especially in postfascist Germany—provided African
American soldiers with a new, and quite unforgettable, perspective. A
quarter of the way into the novel, Dawkins and friends throw a going-
away party for Murdock, whose tour of duty is up. After an evening of
drinks, Murdock breaks down in front of Dawkins:

> I can't leave this place. I can't. . . .
>
> You don't understand. . . . You ain't been away from all that s—— as long
> as I have. You ain't yet got the feel of being free. I like this goddamn country,
> you know that? That's right. I like the hell out of it. . . . [N]ow I know what
> it is to walk into any place, *any* place, without worrying about whether they
> serve colored. You ain't been here long enough to feel that like I do. You

know what the hell I learned? That a nigger ain't no different from nobody else. I had to come over here to learn that. . . . They don't teach that stuff back in the land of the free.[74]

Contact with Europeans provided black soldiers with expanded cultural knowledge and a comparative vantage point from which to assess American racial practices. As one soldier put it: "It was the biggest thing that ever happened, and it touched everybody's life who was around at that time." Some men expressed their intention to stay in Germany after their tours of duty ended. In early 1947, William Gardner Smith advertised such sentiments in a front page article for the *Pittsburgh Courier* titled "Few GIs Eager to Return to States." In the article, which likely served as inspiration for his novel and the character, Murdoch, he quotes a soldier as saying: "I don't want to go home again, ever. . . . How can I leave these people who have treated me so swell . . . like a man, not like some damn animal?"[75] Others appeared to have toyed with the idea of fleeing to the Soviet zone of Germany, hopeful that socialist promises of equality rendered race and racism irrelevant there. By the early 1950s, African American newspapers reported "scores of American ex-servicemen . . . now listed as 'missing' or 'AWOL' or 'deserters' . . . [who] constitute a kind of 'invisible army' wandering illegally over the face of Europe, on both sides of the 'iron curtain.' "[76]

Overseas experience had a transformative political effect on many black American GIs, rendering them "less willing to accept discriminatory treatment." In contrast to would-be expatriates, however, other black GIs found that intercultural contact reaffirmed their national identity and made them "feel more American." Consequently, some returned to the United States determined to support the fight for black civil rights.[77]

In *Last of the Conquerors*, another of Smith's characters, a former reporter for the *Pittsburgh Courier*, dubbed the "Professor" by fellow GIs for his serious manner and facility with words, contemplates the effects of his stay in occupied Germany and offers the following analysis:

> You know what? I don't think I'll ever be happy at home again. . . .
>
> I was born there, and my parents were born there. I'll go back, because it's the only place I know. But you know, before I came here I just ignored the things that went on there. I mean, I knew what was going on, I wrote about it in fact, and I hated it, but I was used to it. It had been with me all my life. Now it's different. I've gotten away from that stuff and I'll never be able to take it calmly again. I'll endure it, I guess. I might even become sort of used to it again. But not the way I was before. I'll never take it the way I used to. . . . Because I'll always remember the irony of my going away to Germany to find democracy. That's bad.[78]

African American soldiers' positive response to Germany shouldn't be taken to indicate that Germany had been transformed overnight into a racial paradise; it hadn't. Rather, the soldiers were indicating a heightened sense of personal safety, freedom of movement, and freedom of association. As members of a well-paid U.S. military, they enjoyed an elevated economic status and sociopolitical power vis-à-vis ordinary Germans. Yet these benefits had their downside as well, and from the earliest years of occupation through the 1950s, African American soldiers attracted the resentment of white competitors—both American and German—for white German women precisely *because* they had the opportunity and the means to attract and court them.[79]

In American-occupied Germany, interracial dating, sexual relations, and reproduction became a flash point for white male resentment and official regulation that transcended national lines. Both countries had histories in which interracial sex, marriage, and reproduction between Blacks and whites were legally proscribed. Germany's attempt to discourage and disadvantage black-white marriages and reproduction developed out of its experience with colonies in the final quarter of the nineteenth century, and accelerated in the years leading up to the First World War. It was not until the so-called Nuremberg Laws of 1935 under the Nazi Regime, however, that interracial sexual relations and reproduction between white Germans and "jews, blacks, gypsies and their bastards" were explicitly prohibited and subject to punishment and persecution by the state.[80]

In the United States, social and legal proscriptions against interracial sex and reproduction had a longer history and reached back well into the nineteenth century, only to be reinvigorated with a vengeance with the end of slavery and the social controls that institution afforded propertied whites. In the aftermath of the American Civil War, the Ku Klux Klan organized as a kind of terror organization led by prominent local white businessmen, politicians, professionals, and other property owners devoted to the preservation of white supremacy and privilege. A cornerstone of white supremacy became the policing of white women's sexual purity and propriety—ensuring, that is, that white women socialized and reproduced "within their race." Any infraction—real or imagined—was punished quickly and lethally, with vigilante action targeting the alleged black male "perpetrator" and only rarely his white female companion. By the turn of the twentieth century, lynching became an endemic cultural practice throughout the United States that persisted into the post-1945 period. In its unique American form, it developed into a surprisingly popular spectator sport that drew crowds of white onlookers—male and female, children and adults—and spawned a gruesome commercialized souvenir market of postcards and other memorabilia.[81]

Black soldiers' assessments of their experience abroad are relative and therefore always at least implicitly critical of the comparatively more dangerous ways that racism was mobilized and expressed in the United States than in occupied Germany. Given the tremendous importance that white Americans placed on policing their women's "virtue" and, by extension, their white bloodlines, and given the terrifying illicit violence that putatively "respectable" white American citizens historically proved themselves willing to marshal and condone in order to punish—or merely prevent—interracial sex, reproduction, and or even just heterosexual socializing, it is no wonder that African American soldiers in Germany were most struck by their unprecedented ability to date white women there. This becomes evident in *Last of the Conquerors*, when Hayes Dawkins, on his first date with Ilse, finds himself sunbathing next to her on the beach at Wannsee, a lake on the outskirts of Berlin: "I had lain on the beach many times, but never before with a white girl. A white girl. Here, away from the thought of differences for awhile, it was odd how quickly I forgot it. It had lost importance. . . . No one stared as we lay on the beach together, our skins contrasting but our hearts beating identically and both with noses in the center of our faces. Odd, it seemed to me, that here, in the land of hate, I should find this one all-important phase of democracy. And suddenly I felt bitter."[82]

As Smith indicates in this passage, this is not an issue of black men finding white women somehow more desirable than black, or—as racists would have it—of black men cravenly craving carnal knowledge of white women. Rather, Dawkins experiences a moment when "race" as a marker of difference and social place is nearly forgotten and he is given the freedom—as an unmarked individual—to choose a partner from among other, similarly unmarked individuals. With "hearts beating identically and both with noses in the center of our faces," the only race restriction is their shared humanity. Toward the end of the novel, Dawkin's fantasizes, lying in bed next to Ilse, in "a dream without sleeping." But his fantasy—with its focus on domesticity, sociability, middle-class sensibility and respectability—is poignant for its mundane quotidian detail and the stark contrast it presents to his ghettoized life in Philadelphia:

A house in Wannsee in Berlin. With ivy on the walls and a flower garden with lawn chairs. A small house, but a house that is clean, to which many friends come to talk, and play cards, and drink beer, or maybe schnapps. With books along the walls and scrubbed paint and windows that open out and a bathtub that is always well washed and always being used. A porch, and nighttime sitting on the porch looking at the water of Wannsee, hearing the wind through the trees, smelling the scent of the grass and trees and water and flowers. With quiet in the night and rising early in the morning and the wife who puts the blankets and sheets and pillows in the window at eight o'clock to air out. Paintings on the wall and lis-

tening to operas and symphonies over the radio or in the theater. Head held high and smiling people. To dances that are not in tiny halls and dancing not the jitterbug all the time, but the waltz and the tango and the rhumba and the samba and the polka. Singing "I'm in Love with Vienna."

Wie geht's, Herr *Dawkins*?
Danke, sehr gut. Und Dir?
Auch gut, danke.
Und deine Frau?
Auch gut. Es geht uns sehr gut.

Shall we go to the coffee house? Why yes, I would like that. The coffee house warm and cozy on a winter's night with many people at the tables smiling red-faced and merry. The Fraulein: *May I serve you, sir? Yes. What do you have? Well, we have wonderful Kartoffel Salad, gnädiger Herr. Would you like that, Ilse? Yes. I think it would be nice. All right, we'll take it. And anything else, sir? Well, the coffee of course. Thank you, sir. And in the coffee house everyone looking up at me in admiration, admiration, admiration . . . not disdain . . . because my skin is brown and healthy-looking and as a man's skin should be. With the barber saying,* Herr Dawkins, *you have wonderful hair. And the laugh inside.*[83]

Time spent in Germany was instructive to many black GIs because it provided them with the ability—via a different cultural frame—to think beyond their social experience as black men in the United States. It gave them a sense of the historical and cultural contingency of American racial practices. It extended the possibility of escaping prejudicial legal and social prohibitions based upon entrenched notions of race.[84] (For although the novel concludes with Dawkins returning to the United States, novelist William Gardner Smith ultimately chose to become an expatriate, settling in Paris.)[85] It could also fuel aspirations for social reform since it brought the realization that racial segregation, antimiscegenation laws, and lynchings were not universal practices common to all white societies, but socially and culturally mutable, differing from nation to nation. While such cultural comparisons might generate despair regarding the condition of American society, they could also fuel hope by suggesting that racism was not the *essential* condition of all whites.

Learning from America: Democracy Imposed, Whiteness Unchallenged

It was precisely a realization of the potential emancipatory effect of such experience abroad on black soldiers' social perceptions and behavior that accounted for the zealous rage and condemnation of some of their white compatriots. In a series of intelligence debriefings of U.S. troops returning from overseas in 1945, for example, numerous white officers and

GIs denounced interracial dating by black GIs abroad as a significant *cause* of racial violence in the military. Beginning with the entry of U.S. troops into England and Europe during the war, white GIs publicly harassed white women in the company of black GIs and hurled insults, fists, and in one case even a sledgehammer, at the latter.[86] Antiblack slurs and violence within the American ranks abroad caused one angry soldier, interviewed in the European Theater of Operations (ETO) by the NAACP's Walter White, to ask, "What are we fighting for over here? Are we sent . . . to fight the Nazis—or our white soldiers?"[87]

In a mid-1945 interview regarding "Colored Soldiers in the ETO," a white Lieutenant Ducharme asserted that "the problem of social equality" and particularly the willingness of "large numbers of women" to socialize with black American troops "created a feeling of resentment on the part of white soldiers." Tellingly, the lieutenant complained that their dating of white women encouraged a "new found assurance" by black troops "that frequently resulted in over-stepping the limits of propriety."[88]

White male resentment was not limited to troops abroad. In 1946, Dwight D. Eisenhower received a letter from Alvin M. Owsley, an "indignant former national commander of the American Legion" who was irate after seeing a photo of a black GI fraternizing with a white German woman: "My dear General, I do not know . . . where these negroes come from, but it is certain that if they expect to be returned to the [U.S.] South, they very likely are on the way to be hanged or burned alive at public lynchings by the white men of the South. . . . There is only one way to stop the white men of the South from burning and hanging blackmen [*sic*] who lay their hands on our white women and that is . . . [for] . . . the blackmen [*sic*] to associate with black women and leave *our* white women alone."[89] As an American sociologist, writing about the racial friction in the U.S. Army abroad, astutely summarized:

> There can be no doubt that the new situation required considerable adjustment . . . and was more difficult for white officers and men than for the Negro. . . . As can be readily imagined, the issue revolved largely around women and the fact that they made little or no distinction between colored and white and, in some cases, even preferred the Negro male to the white. The whites expressed the fear that the Negro would never be satisfied to go back to his old status and would continue to expect white women to submit to his sexual desires. The Negro expressed similar sentiments. . . . Negro troops were under the impression that white women in America were perfectly willing to accept them as sexual partners and that only the American male stood in their way.[90]

The battle, then, was one involving American "manhood." Although expressed through the language of sexual competition for white women, the stakes—it should be clear—were perceived as much more profound and far-reaching by Blacks and whites alike. This was not just a contest over access to white female bodies, but over access to political and social equality. For the history of antimiscegenation laws in the United States reveals that such laws were (merely) the emotionally charged touchstone for a more comprehensive *program* of legal and extralegal initiatives to bolster white supremacy via white patriarchy, on the one hand, and to effect the permanent political, social, and economic subordination of African Americans, on the other. "Manhood"—in all of its dimensions—had been crafted as the exclusive domain of white men in the United States, and therefore was a fundamentally racialized term. So when African American men claimed the privileges of sexual manhood through elective relations with white women, they were perceived by white men—and also perceived themselves—to be attacking the entire edifice of white (male) superiority.

White American hostility toward interracial relations between African American troops and German women persisted throughout the first twenty-five years or so after 1945, but was especially heated through the 1950s. White American servicemen vehemently, and sometimes violently, opposed interracial fraternization and, like Alvin Owsley above, sought to defend an imagined transnational community of inviolable whiteness—"*our white*" German women—from the attentions of their black compatriots. In shifting the emphasis from national to racial belonging when it came to interracial heterosexual relations, white American soldiers redrew the battle lines between "us" and "them."[91]

But because U.S. troops were in postwar Germany to assist in the official American program of denazification, political democratization, and social and ideological reconstruction, and because in this period Germany was literally rendered a borderland for Cold War skirmishes between hostile socialist and capitalist systems, good public relations and the ability to project a positive image was of paramount political importance in securing American interests internationally. As a result, public displays of American antiblack racism at home and abroad became increasingly worrisome to American officials both because of the disillusionment it could sow among occupied populations, but also because of the negative publicity it could provide Cold War enemies regarding American values—or rather American hypocrisy in the *social transubstantiation* of those values.[92]

During the years of occupation through the 1950s, American officials devoted resources to intelligence gathering among Germans and attempted to ascertain, for example, Germans' attitudes toward the goals of the American occupation and the behavior of its troops, and the level of anti-Americanism and, to some extent, also antisemitic sentiment "on

A private club for black GIs in Berlin in which, according to *Ebony*,
"only ice cream and Coca-cola were served." German women were welcome;
German men were not. Courtesy of The Newberry Library, Chicago.

the streets" in western Germany. Moreover, U.S. occupation and military
officials were acutely aware of German reactions to the public displays
of interracial friction in the U.S. Army. The most common incidents were
white-on-black verbal and physical assaults—including, for a time, white
soldiers' practice of driving their vehicles onto sidewalks in the attempt
to run down black GIs in the company of German women—or raucous
barroom brawls in or near German establishments. White soldiers were
also alleged to have detonated two bombs on a base in Bremen in order
to dissuade black soldiers from dating German women. Occasionally,
brawls got out of hand and fatalities occurred. In one case, white American southerners of the 29th Division amused themselves in a pub by fir-
ing their guns at the feet of two black GIs to "make them dance." Incensed friends of the victims, upon hearing of the incident, rushed to the
scene and returned fire. At a dance at an enlisted men's club in Asberg,
Bavaria, when white GIs threw beer bottles at black GIs dancing with
white German women, angry black soldiers turned .30 caliber carbines
on the culprits. One white soldier died and as a result, "three Negro soldiers were sentenced by court martial to hang on the gallows."[93]

As historian Maria Höhn has pointed out, by the 1950s the American
civil rights struggle was transferred to Germany, resulting in bloody
street fights and riots between white and black American troops in western German towns like Baumholder, Kaiserslautern, and Butzbach. The

integration of the U.S. military did not end racial segregation: it merely moved it off base. Under pressure from white GIs, German bar-owners near U.S. bases excluded black soldiers from their establishments, forcing the soldiers to carve out their own social space in less desirable areas of town and frequently in bars owned by Eastern European Jews. As a result, Jim Crow practices were transferred to German garrison towns, with whites cleaving to whites and Blacks relegated to areas of racial otherness. Such informal practices, moreover, became subsequently formalized by the endorsement of white officers and enforcement of white Military Police (MPs) on patrol, who would chase away any black would-be interlopers with the threat of violence or incarceration.[94]

As telling were cases in which black GIs alleged racial discrimination on the part of German landlords or shopkeepers who refused to rent to or serve them or their families, and who presumably could justify their actions with appeal to racially discriminatory American practices in Germany. In these instances, the U.S. military declined to intervene, either by labeling these actions "anti-American" rather than racially motivated, or by maintaining that "community mores with respect to race vary" and were "beyond the direct purview of the DOD [Department of Defense]." However, the real concern was that if they did intervene in German cases, they would have to respond to black allegations of discrimination in garrison towns in the United States as well. In refusing to act, they upheld the principles of racial segregation and antiblack racism in postwar America and Germany.[95]

However the most heated racial animosities centered on black-white dating. While U.S. officials—and the African American press—noted that sexual competition between white and black troops over German women exacerbated hostilities, and that black GIs' fraternization with white women drew particularly condemnatory opinion or action by white U.S. soldiers, little was done over the years of the occupation and High Commission to defuse white soldiers' hostile responses. Disturbances and fights between white and black GIs remained frequent and ferocious and were assiduously reported in the German press.[96] In response, American military courts doled out the severest sentences to retaliatory action by black GIs, who had been targeted for racial violence and even murder by whites and, pushed well past their boiling point by an unresponsive command, had determined to meet violence with violence.[97] More lenient sentences tended to be meted out to their white antagonists.[98]

The U.S. military in Germany initiated policies of social control that managed the problems of racism and racist violence rather than confronted them. A major, stationed at Roth Army Air Base, wrote to the *Chicago Defender* in late 1946 to report that when a black enlisted man "is caught with a German girl, he is given up to six months in the so-called guard-house. The girl is beaten and locked up in German prison."[99] Local commanders would monitor the off-duty activities of black GIs, and MPs would cooperate with German authorities to regulate the behavior of white German women seen in the company of black troops.

During the occupation, American military police routinely hauled women dating or socializing with black GIs into custody for venereal disease (VD) checks. Motivation for such action ranged from officially endorsed racist white assumptions that only the lowest forms of white femininity—namely, prostitutes or the pathologically promiscuous—would associate with black men to concerted attempts to pressure women to renounce interracial fraternization.[100] Black GIs stationed throughout Europe complained that such prejudicial assumptions and actions negatively affected the views of local populations toward them and caused respectable women, out of fear for their reputations, to disassociate themselves increasingly from black soldiers.[101]

In *Last of the Conquerors*, Ilse is picked up for a VD check one night while returning with Dawkins from a visit to her aunt and uncle. When she is finally released, she is reluctant to give him the details of her incarceration. At his insistence, she describes her interrogation by an American lieutenant: "[T]he lieutenant spoke to me very softly like a child. He said I must know that the colored man was not like everybody else, and that an American white woman would never go out with one. He said that the colored man was dirty and very poor and had much sickness. He said everything soft and sounded very kind. He said I could go, only I must promise not to go with the colored soldier any more." This Ilse refuses to do, responding that she loves her soldier and will stay with him. She is locked up with other women in similar circumstances and, over the course of her stay in jail, is propositioned by white MPs, who promise to release her if she has sex with them. When she declines, they call her a "nigger-lover" and tell her she will never again experience the love of a white man. Ten days later, she is handed over to the German police, "friends" of the MPs, who "said the same thing . . . that we should not go out with colored soldiers. They were very angry when we did not say we would no longer see you. . . . After a time they let us go. They said if they did see us again with a colored soldier they would put us in prison. Many of the girls are now afraid and will not again go with a colored soldier."[102] The novel suggests the ideological affinity and practical cooperation between the American military police and the German civilian police on the issue of race and racial mixing—something borne out by reports of American military government authorities and the German police during the period.[103]

And this, ultimately, became a central problem of the occupation since interracial fraternization between black GIs and white German women was treated as an unbearable provocation by numerous white American soldiers and officers, and by white German men more generally. Moreover, white men of American and German nationality employed a common epithet: "nigger lover" or "*Negerliebchen*," newly popularized in the German language, to slander German women who associated with black troops. Although white Americans and Germans drew on distinct national-historical idioms of race, both agreed upon the necessity—for peculiarly postwar reasons—to "defend" white manhood and to police white women.

This is not to argue that postwar Germans learned antiblack racism from American occupiers. After all, Germans already had a long tradition of such bigotry that predated and was intensified by both Germany's short stint as a colonial power prior to 1918 and shorter stint as National Socialist power between 1933 and 1945. Rather, at the level of the street, Germans were absorbing the *postwar* lesson—inadvertently taught by their new American masters—that democratic forms and values were consistent with racialist, and even racist, ideology and social organization. Informal contacts between occupier and occupied—along with the discriminatory policies of the U.S. military toward its minorities and the tense relations among occupation soldiers of differing ethnicities—affected the ways Germans perceived and received American political and social values after 1945. German understandings of the *content* of "democratization" were conditioned by the implicitly racialized *context* within which this was delivered. As a result, military occupation reinforced white supremacy as a shared value of mainstream American and German cultures.[104]

Chapter Two

FLACCID FATHERLAND: RAPE, SEX, AND THE REPRODUCTIVE CONSEQUENCES OF DEFEAT

Exhausted, after many long weeks,
We German soldiers crawled along streets,
With aching feet and a question in mind:
When we reach our homeland what will we find?
Already prepared for the very worst,
What we found was even more cursed.
German women, in a most shameless way,
Are whoring with strangers, it's clear as day . . .
With an insolent smile still on your face,
German women, don't you feel the disgrace?
You've defiled us all—you know it's true—
And German woman's honor with what you do!
To beat German soldiers it took them six years,
But in five short minutes, German women were theirs!
We have neither cigarettes nor butter
Yet the foreigner has both coffee and sugar.
And if he comes by, offering chocolate
His skin color won't matter—you'll jump at it!
In closing, we wish you much pleasure and fun,
And that the Russians will come for you soon.
From this time forward, you've now been instructed,
By no man again will you be respected!

—Street poster in Munich, 1945[1]

It now, for all intents and purposes, has become legally possible to do everything with the German girl except marry her.

—*Newsweek*, 1947[2]

MILITARY DEFEAT often initiates a painful process of social disruption and ideological revaluation. In 1945 Germany, to judge from contemporary accounts, one of the most shocking aspects of defeat and occupation for

German men was their immediate loss of social and sexual prerogative, made manifest in the challenge by foreign troops to their *exclusive* claim to bodies of white German women.

This claim was one invested with legal authority by the National Socialist state. During the Third Reich, a litany of laws were promulgated that restricted the social and sexual choices of "Aryan" German women (those deemed racially and eugenically "valuable," whose prescribed duty was to reproduce and rear a racially superior German *Volk*) to Aryan male partners.[3] Relations between Aryan German women and "racially foreign" men, whether Jewish, Polish or Soviet—to name only the most prominent and reviled groups among the millions of forced laborers and POWs quartered in the Greater German Reich during World War II—were strictly prohibited and severely sanctioned. Tellingly, however, Nazi-era laws were not similarly restrictive for German men. Rather, since masculine vitality and military prowess were assumed to be "highly dependent upon sexual gratification," the German military leadership provided brothels for their men and often turned a blind eye to incidents of rape by German soldiers—particularly on the Eastern front against Jewish and Slavic women considered for racial reasons to be essentially devoid of value or honor.[4] During its twelve-year rule, National Socialism forged a culture predicated on a "thorough racialization of sex" in which the bodies of Aryan women were stringently policed, while the bodies of non-Aryan women were expressly—and often violently or murderously—exploited.[5] In both cases, female sexuality was instrumentalized for national purposes by a regime hell bent on building a powerful, racially pure state to dominate the European continent.[6]

Significantly, then, by opening access—albeit sometimes forcibly—to German women's bodies and permitting them expanded choice in sexual partners, military defeat in 1945 represented a radical rupture with the Nazi Regime's prescriptions and legislation regarding normative German sexual and reproductive behavior. However, the ideological impact of defeat and occupation on popular perception, public discourse, and social policy regarding these issues, particularly with respect to race, is not well understood.[7] How did German contemporaries experience and describe the fundamentally altered power and sexual relations in and after 1945? What language did they use; what meanings did they draw? Did military defeat and its aftermath nullify the Nazi era's obsessive racialization of sex and regulation of women's bodies? Or did race and female sexuality remain central categories of analysis and concern in postfascist German society?

This chapter and the one that follows represent a preliminary attempt to sketch some of the ways that issues of race, female sexuality, and reproduction were addressed in public discourse, national mythology, and social policy as Germans were compelled by victorious foreign troops to transition from a national socialist to a democratic context. In particular, these chapters focus on exploring the fraught process of ideological transformation after 1945 through attention to Germans' uneven efforts to grapple with and reformulate racial and sexual ideologies in the immediate aftermath of the Nazi regime's failed attempt to engineer an Aryan nation. The intention is to probe the *devolution* of the Nazi racial state as a social and cultural process.[8]

FOREIGN TROOPS, FEMALE BODIES, AND THE CRISIS OF GERMAN MASCULINITY

The crisis years of the early occupation have often been referred to as the "hour of women" due to the inordinate amount of productive and reproductive work assumed by women in the wake of defeat and the absence or low public profile of German men, who were either killed or missing in the war, held in prisoner-of-war camps, physically or mentally disabled, emotionally exhausted, or unemployed due to ill health or their former political loyalties.[9] In the early postwar years, women commanded a strong public presence for demographic, social, and symbolic reasons. According to the first postwar census of 1946, the ratio of German men to women was 100:126; numbers in urban areas, and particularly the former capital city of Berlin, were even more skewed. Adding to contemporary alarm was the official estimate that among the reproductively active "marriageable" age groups, there was a mere 1,000 men for 2,242 women. Even after adjusting the numbers to include German POWs expected to return from captivity, census officials projected that "one-third of all women of child-bearing age" would have no prospect of finding a mate.[10] This imbalance between the sexes triggered anxiety and pessimistic prognostications for the future. In public and private parlance, German defeat became widely identified with demasculinization, as countless contemporary stories thematizing missing husbands, fatherless households, and humiliated husbands unable to work, earn, or function—whether professionally, socially, or sexually—suggest.[11]

Despite the prevalence of such accounts, this characterization was not quite accurate. Public life in postwar Germany retained a masculine profile, as the ubiquitous uniformed men of the occupation forces attested. All Germans, male and female alike, were subject to the masculine military governments of the victorious Allies. And that was precisely the problem. The issue was not the putative wholesale demasculinization or even feminization of daily life, but the absence of adequate *German* male authority and a corresponding increase in displays of female autonomy. This lack of German male authority was sorely felt both in the overtly political public sphere and, in an era of severe housing shortages, the less-than-private domestic sphere, where there could be, at least initially, no ready reversion to normative social and sexual relations between the sexes. In the wake of defeat and occupation, German men lost their status as protectors, providers, and even (or so it seemed for a short time) as procreators: the three "P"s that had traditionally defined and justified their masculinity.[12]

The influx of occupation forces in 1945 effected not only a displacement of native masculinity in political, social, and sexual terms. It also ended a decade of prescribed Aryan exclusivity in social and sexual relations for German women. After all, what came home to the Germans after 1945 was not just their former state enemies, but their declared *racial* enemies as well: Blacks, Jews, Slavs, and other so-called "Asiatics" who served as non-German nationals in allied armies or were liberated as slave laborers, POWs, or concentration camp inmates and represented groups the Nazi Regime had declared inferior (*minderwertig*) and marked for segregation, sterilization, and murder. The result for German women was that the restrictive, state-mandated Aryanized sex of the Third Reich gave way to a broader range of choice in social relations and sexual partners.

However, not all sexual contact between the "liberators and liberated" was elective, as the high incidence of rape in the spring and summer of 1945 indicates.[13] German men's powerlessness vis-à-vis Allied soldiers troops was revealed immediately and traumatically in violent sexual assaults on German women by invading troops. In diary entries and subsequent oral histories describing their rapes by Allied soldiers, German women repeatedly mentioned the submissive or cowardly behavior of German men and their notable unwillingness or inability to come to the women's aid, in some cases due to overriding concerns for their own safety. In the spring of 1945, a Berlin woman registered the disruption to conventional gender norms when she observed that it was only after Soviet troops withdrew from that part of the city that German men finally began "acting in a practically masculine way—or in a way that used to be called 'masculine.'" "Now," she added, "we're going to be on the lookout for a better word, one that can still be used even in bad conditions."[14]

Although women acknowledged the physical and emotional pain of their rapes, they often tallied it as but one form of hardship in a long list of others—bombing, hunger, lack of housing, the stress of caring for children in wartime conditions, and gut-wrenching fear—that they suffered at the time. Nonetheless, the women did distinguish between rape and other wartime experiences in one way: in their common reluctance to tell husbands or other male relatives about the attack. In those cases in which they did, women remarked that "it changed everything" between husband and wife, or that after one conversation, it was never mentioned again. One woman remembered her attempt to tell her husband, a recently returned POW whom she described as "a broken man . . . an honest-to-goodness lethargic" about her rape, but he walked out before she finished the story, never to return. Divulging the details or even the fact of a rape could result in emotional alienation, separation or divorce or, in the most extreme cases, the murder of women by husbands or fathers seeking to neutralize dishonor to his name, person, or family by slaughtering the victim's defiled body. As these examples make clear, husbands (and some fathers) tended to interpret rape as a grave personal affront and the mark of a woman's shame. Commonly, then, women were left to deal with their trauma privately and in isolation from others—even those with whom they had been most intimate. Out of sheer necessity, women typically responded by pushing the experience to the margins of their memory and by minimizing or deleting it from the narratives of their lives.[15]

Unlike women's response to their own rapes, Germans as a whole did not remain silent on the matter. If many German husbands "experienced" their wives' rapes as a serious personal indignity about which they refused to speak, other Germans publicly excoriated the rape of German women as a national and sexual humiliation. As a result, rape—and especially German women's rape by Soviet soldiers—became central to postwar West German national identity and by the 1950s was readily transformed into one of the founding mythologies of the West German state. As the Cold War emerged, so too did a stylized West German narrative of mass female rape by "Asiatic" Red Soldiers that served to recast the German nation—in the form of its self-professed "legitimate" West German successor—as an innocent victim of a barbaric Bolshevism.

In public policy debates of the 1950s regarding the reconstitution of the postwar family and gender roles, the political rhetoric of all major West German parties conflated "anticommunist with anti-Asian sentiments." "The East," as historian Robert Moeller has observed, "became a highly elastic designation, extending from the border separating the two Germanys to the Sea of Japan" and was deployed as imprecise shorthand for the enemy territory of "Soviet and Chinese communism." Similarly, the words "Asiatic" and "Mongol" persisted during the early decades of the Cold War as powerful slurs to evoke the presumed racial inferiority and cultural backwardness of Soviet society when compared to West Germany and the Christian Occident more generally. Such derogatory characterizations became part of the mainstream political culture of the early Federal Republic, and were given credence through Chancellor

Konrad Adenauer's impassioned calls to his fellow West Germans to fight for all "that seems of value in life" against the incursions of the Soviet Union, that "monstrous power of Asia."[16] Emotional denunciations of "Asiatics" and "Mongols" continued to play a role in respectable anticommunist politicking after the war and helped foster a specifically West German political and cultural identity. *This* part of the German racial imaginary—or, rather, racial demonology—that predated 1945 was not interrupted, but reestablished and reinforced due to Cold War preoccupations of the 1950s. [17]

Anticommunism both fueled and was fueled by stories of sexualized Soviet brutality, as German "women's violated bodies took on an enormous emotional and symbolic value" in postwar West German society and historiography.[18] This focus helped to finesse the issue of broader German responsibility for the crimes of National Socialism by relativizing the German state's atrocities in relation to those of the Stalinist Soviet Union's. Mass rape and slaughter by Soviet soldiers were offered as explanation for why the Wehrmacht continued to battle so tenaciously against the Red Army in the last weeks of the war. According to this logic, German soldiers on the Eastern front were *not* convinced Nazi ideologues fighting *for* Hitler, but rather desperate husbands, fathers, brothers, and sons attempting to protect their women and families—and indeed the "Christian West"—from the cruel vengeance of a savage foe.[19]

There was, of course, a large enough kernel of truth in this interpretation to make it plausible to postwar Germans. Soviet troops *did* engage in large-scale rape and murder as they invaded the expanded German Reich and its capital city, and vengeance appears to have been an important motivating factor for their behavior. Retrospective testimony from German women, moreover, show that they too anticipated violence against them by Soviet troops. While much of this expectation was fueled by Nazi propaganda intent on encouraging active German resistance to invaders in the final stages of the war, it was also based upon their knowledge or informed suspicions regarding the murderous wartime behavior of their own German troops against combatants and civilians on the Eastern Front that preceded, and likely informed, Soviet attacks. Yet little attention was paid to this larger historical context, and public discussion of the topic remained conspicuously silent in the first several decades after the war.[20]

References to Bolshevik barbarism were predictably absent from the official rhetoric of the East German Democratic Republic, whose patron state was, after all, the Soviet Union. While the eastern German population was most affected by the experience of the mass rapes by Soviet sol-

diers, and while it is clear that resulting resentments fueled intense popular anti-Soviet attitudes among East Germans, this occurred at the level
of the street and in early election results that disadvantaged the Soviet-
sponsored Communist Party (later the Socialist Unity Party of Germany
[SED]). By early 1949, after the issue of rape was tentatively raised by
the public at a massively attended discussion on the topic "About the
Russians and About Us" held at the Soviet-German Friendship Society
in Berlin, East German officials realized that rape was a political hot po-
tato that could only harm SED interests, and shut down the possibility
of airing the issue in public. Months before the official foundation of the
East German state in October 1949, rape by Soviet troops was rendered
a taboo topic there and would remain that way for the next forty years.[21]

For West Germans, the Bolshevik enemy—and its racialized incarna-
tion, the Asiatic or Mongol soldier—remained stable across the 1945 divide. As a German woman who was raped in 1945 recalled in an interview some fifty years later: "I was most scared of the Mongols at that
time. [Nazi] propaganda had influenced us completely. . . . At the time I
thought that all Russians were wild beasts, brutal, instinctual, without
any self-control.[22]

This image persisted unchallenged in West Germany and was enshrined in official discourse and putatively objective historical scholarship of the postwar period. In a massive oral history project undertaken
with federal sponsorship in the early 1950s and published over the
course of the decade by the federal Ministry for Expellees (Bundesministerium für Vertriebene) as "The Expulsion of the German Population
from the Regions East of the Oder-Neisse,"[23] historians interpreted the
mass rapes by Soviet troops in the spring of 1945 as "grounded in conduct and a mentality that is foreign and repugnant to European conceptions. . . . The fact that Soviet soldiers of Asiatic descent behaved with
such savagery and lack of restraint confirms that certain inclinations of
the Asiatic mentality contributed fundamentally to the those outrages."[24]

Consisting of over "4,300 densely printed pages" and 11,000 "reports
of experience," the volumes were deposited in the new West German
federal archives and became an important foundational source for official national history and popular conceptions of the war, as Robert
Moeller has persuasively argued. In them, unlike subsequent published
histories however, "women's voices are legion" and stories of horrific
rapes of German females "ranging in age from nine to ninety" appear
throughout. Most central for this discussion is that West German official
and scholarly culture, as well as popular memory and testimony, cast
the Soviet troops as national *and* ethnic aliens. Rapes were recorded and
remembered in racial terms.[25]

Racialized Rape as National Mythology
in Western Germany

Although racially inflected tales of rape by the Soviet Red Army played a dominant role in the postwar mythology of the West German state, if not its East German sibling, this retrospective focus has been tellingly myopic and overdetermined by Cold War considerations.[26] If one surveys the social experience and mythology of rape outside of Berlin and eastern reaches of the former Reich—the areas that have dominated historical discussions thus far—a somewhat more complex picture emerges.[27] In southern Germany, the zones of French and U.S. occupation, terrifying stories circulated about the violence done to German women by black troops, both French colonial and, to a lesser extent, African American.

German reception of black troops after World War II was informed by earlier German responses to the previous French occupation of the Rhineland after the First World War by colonial troops from Algeria, Morocco, Tunisia, Madagascar, Senegal, and Indochina. In 1918, as in 1945, occupation followed military defeat. The German nation and German masculinity were perceived as severely weakened, and sexual relations and reproduction acquired heightened social and symbolic significance. The presence of nonwhite troops sparked a furor in Germany (and beyond) and was denounced as an intentional French strategy to destroy Germany's racial purity, cultural patrimony, and national pride. Drawing on current racial stereotypes common throughout Europe and the United States at the time, German pamphleteers and the press portrayed the soldiers as a herd of sexually rapacious, syphilitic black beasts, intent on the rape, torture, or murder of German women, girls, and boys. Despite evidence that allegations of widespread rape were utterly fallacious and that relations between white German women and French colonial troops were mutually elective rather than unilaterally coercive, perceptions regarding the violent nature of the occupation endured and figured prominently in the fashioning of indignant national narratives of Germany's victimization, which was dramatically enhanced by the feminization and juvenilization of the German innocents. In 1920, the German Constitutional Assembly nearly unanimously denounced "the abusive employment" of black troops as a "horrible peril for German women and children." Shortly thereafter, the German Federation of Protestant Churches called upon "Christendom all over the world [to] raise your voice against the atrocity of these ravages." The same year the Bavarian mint released a commemorative medal adorned with a naked woman bound to a helmeted phallus, accompanied by the inscription, "The Black Shame" (*Der schwarze Schmach)*.[28] Thus gendered and sexual stereotypes of national humiliation via foreign black masculinity were at the ready for rapid re-mobilization after 1945.

Due to Western-oriented Cold War politics and an international alliance system that ultimately tied the Federal Republic to NATO, tales of rape by American and French troops became something of a footnote to West German narratives of victimization as the postwar years receded. However, if one looks at commemorative practice at the regional level, and particularly at the local vernacular of *Heimat* histories that flourished in the 1950s, violence by black French and U.S. troops figured promi-nently and was featured in the national press.[29] Through the 1950s and significantly longer in certain localities, black-on-white violence played an important role in establishing the "national community of suffering" Germans were so keen to document and proclaim for themselves follow-ing defeat and the ensuing exposé of the Nazi death camps.[30]

In his book *Ten Years Ago, 16–17 April 1945: How Freudenstadt Came to Be Destroyed*, for example, Hans Rommel depicts defeat as a second visi-tation, likened to that after World War I, of marauding and murdering French Moroccan troops. He ends his town history with a list of Germans slain over the course of several days in April 1945 and includes brief de-scriptions of German women abducted and killed by the troops, as well as German men done in trying to protect them.[31] Rudolf Albart, in his description of the "last and first days" in Bamberg—those, that is, lead-ing up to and following defeat and occupation by American troops—tells the story of a rape that allegedly took place the day the Americans en-tered the town: "That evening the engineer's wife, Betty K., was dis-turbed by a loud banging on the door while sitting in her kitchen. As she opened the door with her one-and-a-half year old in her arms, two tree-tall negro soldiers stood before her and immediately pushed past into her apartment. . . . According to her account, they jumped on her and raped her three times. During the crime, her father was forcibly re-strained and finally *gunned down*. He died instantly. Only after complet-ing their gruesome deed did the negroes depart the scene of their out-rage, leaving behind a dead man and a degraded woman." What is paradigmatic about this account is the representation of rape by soldiers of color as a victimization of both the German woman, who is depicted as maternal rather than sexual, and the German man (or more precisely, the German father), an insubstantial image of ineffectuality. This double victimization narratively linked female racial and sexual defilement with the displacement and, ultimately, the demise of native masculinity and patriarchy.[32]

Two points should be made at this juncture. First, the female victims featured in postwar tales of rape by Soviet and black troops were coded

German in terms of nationality and ascribed ethnic identity. So, for example, although Soviet soldiers did not always distinguish between privileged Aryan women and persecuted ethnic minorities in perpetrating rapes as they moved westward into Germany, West German chroniclers most certainly did when it came to *representing* mass rape by Soviet troops. As a result, although Jewish women and other Displaced Persons were subject to "rape and sexual assault at the hand of their liberators," *this* form of racialized violence did not enter the annals of postwar German history. It remained both undocumented and uncommemorated by West German historians, media, and the state. Thus the victims depicted as deserving public sympathy and recognition were only some of those affected by actual rapes. The female victim of West German historical and commemorative discourse was therefore delineated in ways that were beholden to, and helped perpetuate, notions of cultural and ethnic homogeneity rather than diversity. White, non-Jewish, and German, she implicitly embodied the Aryan ethnoracial ideal.[33]

The second point is that sustained attention to racialized rape occurred in spite of the fact that attacks were perpetrated by *white* Allied soldiers as well as white German men, as crime reports show. For a short time in mid-1945, German men prowled the streets asking German women whether *they* could "offer them a little abuse."[34] There is little statistical evidence to indicate that rapes by nonwhite soldiers were numerically higher than those perpetrated by whites—unless, that is, *all* rapes by Soviet soldiers are considered rapes by racial others, regardless of the actual ethnic background of the individual.[35] Thus the focus on the racial dimensions of rape derived less from *prevalence* than from *perception*. In Stuttgart, for example, statistics show that the police classified perpetrators according to nationality and race or a confused conflation of both. So, for instance, police tabulated rapes by "white Frenchmen," "white Americans," and "colored *(farbige)* Americans," but also by otherwise undifferentiated "Russians" (who nonetheless came from diverse parts of the Soviet Union) and "French colonial troops" (who could be Moroccan, Algerian, Tunisian, or Indochinese).[36] Thus, three racialized categories emerged: "colored Americans," "French colonials," and "Russians." Significantly, it is only the first group—Americans—that was explicitly distinguished by race, if only in terms of the simplistic racial binary of white/colored. The other two groups—French colonials and Russians— were already racial designations as indicated by their very imprecision.

Such categories both derived from and, conversely, helped to construct the victims' descriptions of attackers.[37] Since individual raping soldiers often went unapprehended, identification of perpetrators for administrative purposes depended upon a woman's ability to "recognize" physical and cultural markers such as phenotype, demeanor, uniform worn, or language spoken. This privileged visual and aural cues; in order to register, "race" had to be something visible or audible. So while many women could likely identify national uniforms, distinctive European languages, and "colored" complexions—and therefore the putative marks of "Slavs," "Mongols," "Moroccans," or "Negroes,"—they would have been hard-pressed to detect among enemy troops that supreme racial Other of the Nazi period, namely Jews, by such methods. As a result, "Jewishness" disappeared almost immediately from popular and official discussions of German women's rape, abortion, sexuality and reproduction in the spring of 1945. And discussions of race in matters of sexuality and reproductive policy contracted to a focus on the "Asiatic" Russian and the Black.

Thus categories convey important information about the ways victims "read" and reported their attacker's racial and national attributes, and how race was processed and recorded by police bureaucrats. They also provide clues about how race as a social category was already being subtly deployed and redefined in the days surrounding defeat.

As will become clear in the discussion of abortion that follows, in describing their rapes, women had a significant personal investment in presenting certain information and images to police and medical authorities. The reporting of rape betrayed a shared cultural knowledge of race, and women learned to use description as culturally coded shorthand to win sympathy and desired medical intervention. As social process and in social policy, military defeat both represented, and was represented as, the replacement of Aryanized sex by racialized sex. But after 1945, unlike during the decade before, this racialized sex did not involve Jews.

Abortion as Racial Eugenics during the Early Occupation

In a period of debilitated German patriarchy and pride, native officials responded to instances of rape by Allied soldiers with emergency social policy provisions. Beginning in the spring of 1945, German state officials sought to nullify the reproductive consequences of conquest by relaxing, temporarily, Paragraph 218, which outlawed abortion. Under National Socialism, a state-sponsored policy of "coercive pronatalism" emerged in which access to abortion was severely restricted for Aryan women, who were prohibited from terminating pregnancies (under threat of the death penalty) unless they had severe medical problems or unless pregnancy had resulted from sexual relations with "racial aliens." Pronatalist policies directed at Aryan Germans were counterbalanced by policies of coercive antinatalism targeting eugenically undesirable residents. In these cases, women deemed non-Aryan, asocial, or mentally or physically disabled were routinely subjected to abortions and mandatory subsequent sterilization. By the late war years, Reich officials "began organizing abortions of 'unworthy' fetuses on a massive scale."[38]

In the first months of 1945, in the face of Soviet invasion and impending defeat, this was extended to include the unwanted pregnancies of Aryan Germans. This unprecedented liberalization of Aryan women's access to abortion under National Socialism was limited, however, to instances of rape and was dictated by ongoing concerns regarding racial pollution of the German *Volk*. In liberalizing abortion policy, German officials were specifically targeting miscegenist rape by enemy soldiers. In early March 1945, the Reich Interior Ministry issued a decree with detailed instructions to doctors, health offices, and hospitals on expediting abortions of "Slav and Mongol fetuses."[39] Sometime during the spring the Bavarian Landesregierung followed suit, issuing a secret memo that expressly encouraged abortions in rape cases involving "colored" troops. Evidence from Augsburg indicates, moreover, that state and municipal authorities continued to refer to those orders in authorizing abortions during the months following defeat.[40] So while compulsory abortions and sterilizations ceased in May 1945 due to the nullification of Nazi laws, *elective* abortions of fetuses continued apace from the first months of 1945 and over the course of the year "became a mass phenomenon."[41]

Although not all abortions occurred in response to rape by perceived racial aliens, the majority were, and it is clear that a commitment to racial eugenics continued to inform the practice of abortion after defeat.[42] In large measure, this was due to the fact that German authorities at the local and state level were left to deal with women's health and medical issues without firm instructions from the Allied powers. Given the Allies need to establish order, disarm and imprison Nazi officials, secure or reestablish communications, utilities, and the food supply, control communicable diseases and so forth, they paid little attention to local initiatives regarding abortion. Although the Allied Control Council abrogated Nazi penal law, it took until late November 1945 to formally rescind the 1933 Law for the Prevention of Hereditarily Diseased Offspring and capital punishment for miscegenation. Moreover, the Allies failed to reach firm conclusions regarding what to do about the abortion law, even after their first discussion of it in late 1946.[43]

As a result, through 1946 the legal status of abortion was murky throughout Germany, which allowed state and local medical and health officials a good deal of latitude in their interpretation and implementation of this public policy.[44] In fact, there are indications that state officials in Bavaria met the suspension of national law regarding abortion with covert decrees of their own. In a memo to district officials and doctors in early June 1945, the mayor of Sonthofen announced that

Cases are multiplying in which German women are being successfully raped by Moroccans (or other colored men).

According to German law until now, the termination of pregnancy was permitted only for eugenic reasons. Because these indications were related to race, it appears that this legal criteria is out of date. The possibility of abortion does not now exist. . . .

Yesterday, the head of the state health office, Dr. Bertram, informed me that a secret decree was issued by the Bavarian state government [*Landesregierung*] according to which the termination of a pregnancy is possible in cases of rape by colored troops [*farbige Truppen*]. Once noted, this secret order was returned to the district magistrate by the state health office. This paper was destroyed by fire. . . .[45]

In the wake of defeat and for the year after, local health officials—with reference to (suspended) Nazi-era law or ad hoc decrees—continued the late wartime practice of granting abortions to German women who provided a sworn affidavit detailing "forceful" rape by enemy soldiers.

Applications for abortion followed a particular pattern: women's statements described the "stage setting" of the rape—focusing on where the attack took place, how they came to be in the place it occurred or, if at home, how or why the assailant gained admission. If considered nonwhite, the assailant was immediately identified in terms of racial difference, with women employing the culturally loaded shorthand of "Russen," "Marrokaner" or "Neger." The victim would then describe her attacker's use of overpowering force—through focus on his considerable size, weight, and strength, or the presence of a weapon—as well as her own often numbing fear, concern for the welfare of her children if present, and her frantic but failed attempts at physical resistance. In some cases, affidavits were over a page in length and rich in voyeuristic detail. In others, they were short and perfunctory, absent a blow-by-blow description of the attack.[46]

In narrating the story of their rapes, however, all women appeared attentive to how they constructed themselves as victim. They typically identified themselves with home and family and emphasized their wifely or maternal roles and loyalties: they were, their testimony implicitly asserted, good and proper German women. Such a narrative strategy was prudent. For in addition to the alleged rape victim's affidavit, officials solicited supporting statements from witnesses or acquaintances who were clearly asked to describe not only the incident, if they had firsthand knowledge of it, but also the victim's reputation and standing in the community. In one case for which there were no witnesses, the local mayor attested to the woman's good reputation. All of this material was to be reviewed by a committee of three doctors (preferably gynecologists) including, if possible, the chief medical officer of the local health office (*Gesundheitsamt*). Together—and often with the help of German police—they would decide whether the alleged rape had actually occurred and whether the application for abortion would be approved.[47]

Throughout 1945, German officials in the southern states of Bavaria, Baden, and Württemberg continued to ponder the legal status of abortion and the criteria for its authorization. On three separate occasions in June, August, and again in November, the Bavarian Ministry of the Interior issued memos to local authorities establishing mandatory criteria for authorizing abortions in instances of rape. According to these instructions, abortions were permitted only if accompanied by severe medical problems certified by a doctor.[48]

In insisting on the presence of serious medical indications, Bavarian officials modified their informal stance from the spring of 1945 and began to declare that abortion could not be authorized on purely eugenic grounds in cases of rape. However, while formally abandoning eugenic principle as grounds for abortion, they informally allowed eugenic practice to continue by pioneering a more expansive interpretation of what constituted medical necessity. According to the Bavarian Interior Ministry, in addition to physical maladies, "a serious danger to health can also especially be present if the rape and its consequences could result in severe emotional or psychological impairment, in particular when it is feared such injury could accompany or follow the giving of birth."[49] Bavarian officials were not alone in their interpretation. By January 1946, the State Justice Department in Tübingen adopted similar provisions in a secret memo circulated to state attorneys and courts throughout Württemberg-Baden.[50] The practical result of these quasi-legal determinations was that, at least in cases of rape, "miscegenation" continued to be recognized as grounds for the termination of pregnancy over the course of 1945 and early 1946.

In their applications for abortion, women emphasized the detrimental impact of interracial rape and pregnancy on their own mental health and family's welfare. They also alluded to the power that racist norms exercised both through external social pressures and internalized values. While the trauma of rape should not be minimized, women focused more on the issue of racial repugnance in their testimony: "I am experiencing terrible emotional suffering as a mother and wife from this incident," wrote one thirty-six-year-old woman claiming rape by a Moroccan. A thirty-one-year old single mother noted, "It affects me mentally when I think I shall bring a Moroccan child into this world." "Under no circumstances can I accept this pregnancy because I refuse to carry and raise the child of a black man," declared a twenty year old, "and above all because I am hoping that my fiancé will return, especially since he is ill, limps, has frostbitten legs and suffers from sciatica, so he shouldn't remain in enemy hands."[51] "No, I cannot bring a black man's child into the world," insisted another woman. "I already feel like I've been disparaged as morally inferior by this. And how would it be afterwards, if I were to bring a half-black child into the world? I would feel completely rejected as a German mother."[52]

German officials usually found such arguments persuasive, provided they had no serious qualms about the woman's veracity or virtue. In the case of the thirty-six-year-old mother mentioned above, the district magistrate noted that "one has to be careful because the incident took place in a forest inhabited only by the Moroccan and because even though she could have contracted venereal disease, she didn't tell her husband." Nonetheless he found "the details of her story and the reasons for her silence"—namely, an ailing and excitable husband—convincing. "If she was really raped by a Moroccan, which in any case can't be disproved, then the emotional injuries must also exist," he concluded and authorized the abortion.

Strikingly, women who alleged rape by white soldiers appear to have faced a more skeptical official response. A thirty-three-year-old widowed mother of three children, for example, alleged rape by a white French soldier—"kein Marokkaner," she noted—while in the laundry room of a Frauenhaus. Finding it useless to scream or report the rape to French authorities, she now sought an abortion. The official in question doubted whether it was a genuine rape and speculated that "she could have received help if she screamed. Perhaps he would have desisted." But the most telling difference between the case of black-on-white rape and white-on-white rape was his assessment on medical grounds: "it is questionable whether there would be physical or emotional problems if she bore the child," he wrote. The abortion for this, and for other cases of alleged rape by white French and American occupation soldiers, was denied.[53]

Thus in both women's representation of the circumstances and consequences of rape and in medical officials' authorizations of abortions, notions of "Rassenschande," or race pollution, persisted. Shared cultural assumptions condemning miscegenation informed the language and social policy of abortion in the early years of occupation.

Nonetheless, Allied victory did mandate some subtle changes in justification within the first year of occupation. For the most part, arguments to abort fetuses of white German mothers were based not upon racist arguments regarding the inherent inferiority of resulting offspring, but rather upon the expected negative effect bearing and raising a Mischlings-

kind, or "mixed-race" child, would have on white German women. In shifting the diagnostic focus from offspring to mother, German officials and abortion applicants anticipated a crucial postwar development in the rhetoric and rationale of social policy: namely, the transition from emphasis on the biology of race to the psychology of racial difference.

Restricting Abortion and Women's Sexual Autonomy

Beginning in early 1946, there was a swift tightening around the issue of the women's "innocence" as access to abortion came to be increasingly restricted, especially in the western zones.[54] If either her reputation or the details of her story appeared suspect, abortions were denied. Medical review boards, local and state officials, and Christian clergymen rapidly began to voice concern that women were relying on officially sanctioned abortion to rid themselves of the unwanted consequences of casual consensual sex with occupying soldiers. They feared that the availability of abortion was encouraging wily German women to surrender to their promiscuous proclivities and afterward misuse abortion as a form of state-sponsored birth control. These fears were expressed with force and frequency in Bavaria, where in 1947 the leadership of the Evangelical Church issued a position paper arguing against abortion, even in the case of rape, in part because it could not be proved with certainty that the sexual relations were not consensual. On this point, the Evangelical Church reiterated the position of the Bavarian Interior Ministry from late 1945, which had declared that "actual or alleged rape *by itself* does not justify terminating pregnancy" and warned doctors that performing an abortion on this criterion alone exposed them to the risk of punishment.[55] Within the first year of occupation, then, concerns about policing women's behavior competed with concerns to address national and racial defilement.[56]

Typically, however, women's motives were suspected, and their requests for abortion rejected, when the putative perpetrator's race was white. In cases involving soldiers of color, applications continued to be approved on the basis of applicants' uncontested claims that bringing the pregnancy to term would result in unbearable psychological or emotional suffering for the woman and, not incidentally, for her husband or fiancé, who could not be expected to bear with equanimity such a grievous sexual and social affront. In the first days of occupation, racial stereotypes of sexually predatory black males tipped the balance in favor of women's applications. Within months of defeat, however, the image of the pathologically promiscuous and materialist *"Negerliebchen,"* or "nigger-lover," were propagated and popularized.[57]

"*Negerliebchen*" and Black Occupation Children

If one trope that conditioned national narratives of victimization and early postwar social policy centered on white German women violated by national and racial aliens, a second trope focused on the willing sexual fraternizer. This distinction between victim and fraternizer was clearest at the level of discourse and representation. At the level of social interaction, the picture was more diffuse. Evidence from the street suggests that public reception of rape victims was not always sympathetic. Women's allegations of rape, even those occurring during "mass rapes" within communities, could attract suspicion and derision. Such was the case for a woman from a small village in the southwestern state of Baden, who explained, while petitioning for an abortion, that she did not report her rape by a "Moroccan soldier" to the police because when she went to do so, she witnessed the other female victims gathering to make their complaints being rudely mocked by onlookers.[58] Like German religious and state leaders, ordinary Germans too evidenced a good deal of skepticism regarding undomesticated female sexuality.

By early 1946, as the incidence of rape and legal abortions declined, the first "occupation children" were born. As a result, public attention and social policy increasingly shifted from a focus on coercive sex to *consensual* sex between masculine occupiers and native women in the western zones. Evidence from southern Germany suggests that in addition to elective liaisons with American occupiers, German women also chose French occupation soldiers—including those from Algeria, Morocco, Tunisia, and French Indochina—as lovers, bore their children, and in some cases married them and emigrated.[59] The social history of relationships and reproduction between the full range of multinational, multiethnic Allied troops and German women still needs to be written. Nonetheless, despite this broader range of social interaction and experience, when it came to discussing and addressing consensual heterosexual sex, American soldiers attracted the lion's share of Germans' attention and aggression.

Over the course of mid-1945 through 1946, the American zone of occupation experienced a small but significant flurry of "antifraternization" actions by German men, and especially returning German soldiers, against American soldiers and their German girlfriends. Although the incident rate was low—no more than about 5 per 100,000 and perhaps fewer—the targets and symbolism of the attacks were highly significant. Most telling was the castration of U.S. soldiers by German assailants. This was a rare practice, claiming but three victims, but was a clear physical and symbolic challenge to the sexual, and perhaps also political, prerogatives of American masculinity.[60] More commonly, offending German women were targeted. In the first case to go to trial, a twenty-year-old former German soldier in Heidelberg attacked a young German woman seen in the company of a GI and attempted to shear her head with nail scissors. Into 1946, women fraternizing with American GIs—regardless of skin color—were harassed and subjected to hair-cutting or beatings by their angry countrymen, the same type of popular punishments directed at German women accused of "*Rassenschande*" under the Nazis.[61] But the postwar situation also encouraged the invention of neologisms, with offending women denounced as "*Schokoladensau*" (chocolate pigs), "*Schokoladenhure*" (chocolate whores), *Amizonen* (a word play on "American zone" and "Amazon"), "*Amihuren*" (Ami-whores) or "*Negerliebchen*" (nigger-lovers), a slur that may have been borrowed from white GIs.

Physical and verbal assaults against female fraternizers were accompanied by public castigation. Anonymously authored posters appeared on German streets over the course of 1946, addressing the women and a broader German public: "For six years the German soldier offered brave resistance. The German woman cannot resist one bar of chocolate. Did none of your relatives die at the front or through air attack?"[62] This sentiment was echoed in a circular letter by the Protestant High Consistory in Stuttgart, which censured German women and girls who "degrade themselves through licentious behavior. . . . They forget the thousands of graves that surround them. . . . They forget their husbands, brothers, sons, boyfriends, who are still imprisoned or missing. They forget the many thousands of war-wounded. They forget the entire plight and affliction of the Fatherland. Their conduct is an affront to the returning men and a vexation for the entire public."[63] German women's fraternization with occupation soldiers was widely characterized as dishonoring the memory and martial sacrifices of German men, and desacrilizing—and in some cases, literally denigrating—the German fatherland. Women who engaged in sexual relations with occupation troops of color became particular targets of public condemnation.[64] An American intelligence report from January 1946, for example, noted that in a cluster of small towns west of Würzburg, six girls were hospitalized after being sheared and beaten for associating with black GIs, and a girl was jailed by the local police because they suspected her of "bearing the child of a Negro soldier." As the report summarized: "Conversations among civilians in this area indicate that anti-Negroism has replaced anti-Semitism as an expression of German race superiority."[65]

Sex between German women and black American troops provoked censure and an unusual measure of consensus among German and American officials. During the years of military occupation, U.S. intelligence memos and German police reports focused on such interracial relationships, generated an image of African American GIs and German "whores" in criminal alliance to undermine law and order. As discussed in the previous chapter, the American forces in Germany were organized in accordance with a binary understanding of race that segregated black from white. This social practice affected official assessments of interracial fraternization among both victor and vanquished alike.[66]

Understandably, given the goals of their mission in Germany, American officials preferred publicly to downplay the current complexion of race relations in the United States and the U.S. military. Nonetheless, in internal administrative operations, they consistently scrutinized the behavior of black troops and invoked race as a category of analysis when it came to studying the incidence of disease (especially VD), reproduction, and marriage, along with misconduct of various sorts. In one notable example, army intelligence accused a "colored" platoon of the 596th Laundry Company of taking over a Bavarian village and terrorizing local German officials into providing accommodations for "various and sundry imported prostitutes." When the case was investigated, it was decided to remove the company to a less "isolated" area "where adequate American law and order exists"—in other words, where black troops would be subject to the closer supervision of their white compatriots. In other cases in Bavaria, OMGUS reports alleged black market activities, "alarming VD rates," and the siphoning of U.S. military rations and clothing into German homes. Here and elsewhere, American investigators noted the readiness with which African American troops intervened to protect their "mistresses" from VD raids or arrest or, if the women had already been taken into custody, mounted jail breaks to secure their release by threat of force.[67] The point here is not that black American troops were free from indiscipline and disease; that was not the case.[68] The point, rather, is that American officials exhibited an explicit interest in a soldier's race, and then only if he were black, when reporting behavior they feared would undermine either the status or the political aims of the U.S. Military Government in Germany. As a result, American officials tended to *record* and *assess* African American masculinity nearly exclusively in terms of negative undisciplined, sexual, or unsoldierly qualities.[69]

Needless to say, the example of official American treatment of their black troops did not serve as a positive example for reeducating Germans in liberal racial attitudes.[70] Like their American counterparts, German officials frowned on interracial sexual fraternization. Over the course of 1945 and 1946 in Nuremberg, for example, German police staked out "Neger-clubs" like the "Tally-Ho," rounding up any and all women in the vicinity under suspicion of prostitution. In November 1945, police raids netted up to 120 women a day. Most were described as between the ages of seventeen and thirty, and while some women were identified as refugees or itinerants, the majority were natives of Nuremberg "who were caught in the bars or barracks of the black occupiers." The female suspects were held in jails or later remanded to workhouses, which continued to operate in Bavaria after 1945 until American officials belatedly took notice and ordered them closed in the final year of military occupation.[71]

When it came to relations between black GIs and German women, what emerged from reports by native local authorities were not tales of German female victimization similar to the "Black Horror" stories that circulated after the First World War following the French occupation of the Rhineland by Algerian, Moroccan, Tunisian, and Senegalese troops, or tales of mass rape by Soviet troops in the East during the spring of 1945. Rather, officials after 1945 spun narratives of national disorder that linked racialized American masculinity with unrestrained native female sexuality, criminality, and materialism. Strikingly, while much German oral lore still circulating to this day about the American occupation lauds the friendliness, compassion, and generosity of black American troops compared to their white counterparts, it was precisely this perception— and particularly the popular association of African American soldiers with black marketeering and ample gift-giving—that was employed first to characterize, then condemn, the women they socialized with.

The black GI came to represent a kind of hyperversion of American materialism and sexuality whose potency—and appeal, it was feared— was enhanced by racial difference.[72] In a survey conducted in the early 1950s, German social workers queried German women to determine why they became involved with black troops. (Tellingly, this question was not posed to women who fraternized with white troops). On the basis of interviews with 552 women, social workers concluded that for 56 percent "material benefits were decisive": "For the women themselves, it was naturally a great inducement to satisfy their hunger with American canned foods and, in addition, obtain tasty treats, cigarettes, silk stockings and money from their colored boyfriends." However, such incentives were not the only motivation, as social workers found. Of the remaining 44 percent of women polled, 27 percent responded that they had chosen African American lovers on the basis of affection or love, and 17 percent said they were motivated by sexual curiosity, carnal desire, or "simply the wish not to be outdone by their friends who already had Negro boyfriends."[73]

Relations between black GIs and white German women were condemned not because they were perceived as coercive—as in the case of "Moroccan" or Soviet troops—but because women willfully embraced them for material advantage, sexual pleasure, and romance (although such emotional "compensations" were rarely recognized by contemporaries).[74] Because black American men, unlike their German counterparts, apparently had so much to offer destitute German women, and the women offered companionship and often more in return, the latter were denounced as selfish and transgressing sirens.[75]

Such negative characterizations of women with black boyfriends cannot be attributed to a more general condemnation of out-of-wedlock sex. As historian Dagmar Herzog has recently shown, Germans in the late 1940s considered "non-marital heterosexual activity . . . not only prevalent but reasonable." In a survey from 1949, 60 percent of Germans judged sex between consenting unmarried adults "not immoral." In another survey from the same year, over 70 percent of respondents approved of premarital sex and 52 percent declared it "desirable" for women in particular. When queried about their own personal experience, just under 90 percent of German men and 70 percent of German women confessed having had premarital sex.[76] What was significant for contemporaries, then, was not the sex itself but the woman's choice of partner.

Moral assumptions about the women who engaged in interracial fraternization lived on after the occupation to condition the ways that the "problem" of biracial occupation children was formulated in the Federal Republic of Germany. From their first births in late 1945 through the 1950s, every German commentator, even the most conscientiously liberal among them, insisted that the child should not be made to suffer for the "sins" of the mother. The high number of births in Bavaria rankled state officials there, who sought in vain to negotiate with the American military government regarding the citizenship status of the children. Ultimately, all occupation children—including those of color —were grudgingly extended German citizenship, but only after Allied Military Government officials made it clear that they would neither entertain paternity suits nor readily grant citizenship to their troops' illegitimate offspring abroad. Despite this resolution, between 1946 and 1948, state officials attempted to deny public support to the mothers of biracial children in Bavaria, where the greatest percentage resided.[77] In a period marked by a fierce nonpartisan commitment to German sexual and social normalization and the reversal of wartime dislocations of gender and familial relations, the mothers of biracial children were held up to public scrutiny as an unacceptable antinorm, in large measure because their behavior was thought to undermine both the principle of (white) German paternity and native postwar efforts to reconstitute viable postwar German masculine and national identities.[78]

The women's deviance from the norm, moreover, was linked to their presumed class and social status. Most were assumed, incorrectly, to be prostitutes or from the "lowest levels of society" and therefore, by defi-

A "Sunday stroll" on the streets of Berlin. The photo
appeared in the October 1946 issue of *Ebony* magazine.
Courtesy of The Newberry Library, Chicago.

nition, outside the boundaries of respectable German femininity. This despite the fact that a contemporary study showed that of 600 mothers of
biracial children surveyed, 134 were upper class and 180 were middle
class. In 80 percent of cases, pregnancy resulted not from a presumptive
one-night-stand, but from a relationship that lasted several months to
several years.[79] And although almost half of these women expressed their
intention to marry their black beaus, German and official American commentators were united in their inability to imagine that interracial relationships grew out of genuine mutual love and desire.[80] As a result, the

reigning interpretations of women's motivations were moral or mental deficiency, and they were characterized as mentally impaired, asocial, or as prostitutes.[81]

Notably, then, by the end of the occupation in 1949, women's real or putative victimization played an ever-diminishing role in the formation of social policy regarding black occupation children and their mothers. With the gradual return of German husbands from the war and from POW camps, in fact, there was a marked increase in divorce and paternity suits, particularly if a new child had appeared during a husband's long absence. In many such cases, the husband contested paternity and petitioned to be absolved of his legal and financial responsibilities; under German law, all children lacking a male guardian became wards of the local or state youth office and hence eligible for public support.[82]

German state officials and social workers gradually retreated from their hostile attitude toward women's fraternization with white soldiers, particularly by 1948 when marriage was permitted between American occupation soldiers and German women in the U.S. zone and currency reform promised an end to the "hunger prostitution" thought to motivate much of the sexual promiscuity of the immediate postwar period. Relations between black soldiers and white Germans women, however, continued to be considered transgressive of racial and national boundaries and subject to general condemnation, in part, ironically, *because* interracial marriages remained rare. Emigration would likely have satisfied such critics, but official American policy made this all but impossible.[83]

U.S. military policy had enforced an outright ban on marriage between its occupation troops and German women through the end of 1946. Even after lifting the ban, the American military government continued to discourage such marriages by elaborating a set of complex procedures whose implementation was particularly prejudicial to black applicants.[84] GIs seeking to marry their German girlfriends required the permission of their (typically white) commanding officers. The prospective bride was screened by an American chaplain and the unit commander, as well as denazification and counterintelligence officials, and subjected to a battery of medical and psychological exams by which time "she is not only lily-white, she is practically bleached" noted *Newsweek*.[85] Certainly the requirements were cumbersome to white GIs and drew much complaint from them. But for black applicants, the screening process frequently made rejection of the marriage application a foregone conclusion by allowing the personal biases of individual commanders, chaplains, and medics against black soldiers or their white fiancées to intervene in the process and dictate the outcome.

Statistics are hard to come by. However, a 1949 survey funded by an American doctoral student showed that of 500 African American soldiers queried, 280 wanted to marry their German girlfriends and had filed the required forms. Of these "110 were pending, 57 had had no response, 91 had been disapproved, and only 22 had been approved." By the early 1950s, a study undertaken by German social workers painted an even grimmer picture. Although 20 percent of 552 interracial couples surveyed (or 96 couples) applied to marry, only one actually received permission and went through with it.[86]

The result of American policy, from the German perspective, was an unfortunate paucity of transnational interracial marriages. This foreclosed the possibility of emigration for female fraternizers and rendered the offspring of such relationships overwhelmingly "illegitimate," thus ensuring that biracial occupation children and their offending mothers would remain German citizens on German soil.[87]

"FATHER STATE": OCCUPATION CHILDREN AND THE REASSERTION OF GERMAN SOVEREIGNTY

Occupation children—black and white—became the subject of sustained West German official inquiry only with the end of military occupation.[88] This timing is telling. Through 1949 American military government officials expressly forbade German state youth and welfare offices in their zone from surveying the numbers of occupation children, regardless of race, for a number of compelling reasons. These included a fear of embarrassing negative publicity regarding the moral behavior of American troops abroad as well as a determination to avoid the appearance of giving implied official sanction to German paternity and child support suits when sexual relations resulted in out-of-wedlock births.

In fact, from 1945 until the Federal Republic achieved full sovereignty a decade later, it was legally impossible for German women to file paternity or child support suits against the American fathers of their children. On the one hand, American occupation soldiers were prohibited from appearing before German civil courts by occupation statute. On the other, German women were blocked from filing such suits in American courts by state laws that required either that the child be born in the United States or that the maternal complainant and her child reside on U.S. soil. As a result, German mothers of occupation children were trapped in a legal bind. Shortly after the foundation of their fledgling postwar state, West German politicians and the press began to denounce American policies of paternal and financial irresponsibility and seek avenues of redress.[89]

In 1950, the popular German weekly, *Revue*, ran a caustic feature article on occupation children under the caption: "Citizens of Tomorrow Seek their Fathers of Yesteryear." Leading with the zinger, "the Americans don't need an occupation army in Germany any longer, they just need to send uniforms for the children they've sired," the article soon settled on its central point: "Who pays for child support? Until now Father State has been the true Papa."[90]

In fact, the West German state had retained paternal power over all illegitimate children and their unwed mothers upon its founding in 1949. For the next two decades, single mothers had no legal standing before German courts in issues regarding their out-of-wedlock children. Rather, the interests of the children and their mothers were represented by a male guardian appointed by the public youth office. Thus the perceived threat to male authority in the postwar period derived from a focus on the circumstances of *individual* German men and their uncertain status in the households, hearts, and boudoirs of German women. When it came to reconstituted *state* power and civil law in West Germany, patriarchy persisted unscathed.[91]

Nonetheless, the two appeared fused in the thinking of many contemporaries. Although West German law rendered all out-of-wedlock children potential recipients of state support, by the turn of the 1950s, West German politicians and the press focused on a very select sample: illegitimate children of Allied paternity. In 1951, representatives of the Social Democratic Party (SPD) petitioned the West German Parliament (Bundestag) to take up the issue of occupation children and their financial burden to the public purse. Declaring the situation "unbearable," a representative of the conservative Protestant German Party (Deutsches Partei) jumped on the bandwagon and demanded that the recently constituted German Foreign Office (Auswärtiges Amt) inform the Bundestag about any dealings it had on the matter. This initiative engaged national feeling and ultimately garnered diverse political support that included Social Democrats, Christian Democrats (CDU/CSU), the liberal Free Democrats (FDP), and the German Party (Deutsches Party). Political scrutiny and the resulting press coverage caused the federal Ministry of the Interior to survey state and local youth offices regarding both the number of occupation children born in West Germany for the year 1951–52 and the cases in which paternity was acknowledged. Of the nearly 15,000 children counted for that twelve month period, less than 8 percent (or 1,267) had fathers who voluntarily declared paternity.[92]

One of the most striking characteristics of both the *Revue* article and the subsequent political dealings regarding occupation children in 1950s West Germany was the central role accorded American policy and paternity. This was due not to any obvious peculiarities of the official American position regarding paternity and child support suits. In fact, West German officials in the federal and state Ministries of the Interior carefully studied the relevant national laws of *all* Allied countries governing possible paternity and child support suits by German women on behalf of their illegitimate children and found prospects equally dismal for Britain, France, and the Soviet Union.[93]

Nonetheless, press and political attention focused on the Americans for two apparent reasons: first because official statistics indicated a higher prevalence of American paternity among West German occupation children.[94] Once this statistical prevalence was established, the German press jumped in to do the math—in American dollars. The relative wealth of the United States vis-à-vis other Allied countries suggested to Germans that it might bear a larger financial obligation when it came to costs. As an early 1952 newspaper article titled "Who Pays for Occupation Children?" summarized: "According to estimates, the number of occupation children in Germany may reach 280,000. If we calculate $10 per child per month in child support, which is equivalent to German contributions, then the obligation would amount to $2,800,000 a month and $33,600,000 a year. This sum would be a far better material and psychological investment than the many other allocations America so liberally makes."[95] The West German public appears to have concurred with such sentiment. In an opinion poll taken by the U.S. Information Agency, 71 percent of West Germans responded that when "soldier fathers" fail to pay child support, their governments should.[96]

Another reason for highlighting American responsibility, however, was that it allowed critics in the Bundestag and social welfare institutions, such as the German Association for Public and Private Welfare (Deutscher Verein für öffentliche und private Fürsorge), to claim that the long-term care of occupation children was not a specifically "German problem," but a larger "European" one. After all, they pointed out, American troops stationed throughout England and the continent since the war years cavalierly fathered and abandoned untold thousands of illegitimate children without concern for their welfare or future. By January 1952, members of the parliamentary Committee for Legal Matters and Constitutional Law (Ausschuss für Rechtswesen und Verfassungsrecht) took up the issue and declared it "less a legal problem than a political and humanitarian one." By unanimous vote the committee suggested the West German Bundestag appeal to the United Nations to reinstate the "human rights" of illegitimate occupation children currently denied protection under West German law due to stipulations in the Occupation Statute.[97] Explicitly, such analysis questioned the social implications of both American military power and it democratizing mission abroad.[98]

Throughout the decade, these German children were tallied along with other costs of military defeat and foreign occupation, and the resolution of their social and cultural status was linked to the reassertion of (West)

German sovereignty.[99] When, by 1954, relief still was not forthcoming as a result of earlier efforts, the West German federal Interior Ministry ordered another more thorough nationwide survey of all occupation children. While the explicit purpose of this census was proclaimed as *economic*—to determine how many offspring of Allied soldiers were supported by German public funds—other concerns were also at work.

The tabulations were desired by the Foreign Office (Auswärtiges Amt) for negotiations concerned with terminating the Occupation Statute and providing for a military defense contribution to NATO by West German troops. A larger point, then, was to abolish all remnants of subordinate status and, more specifically, to claim the Federal Republic's right to establish jurisdiction in the area of civil law over all inhabitants within West German borders—but most particularly over the masculine military forces of the former enemies-turned-allies. While this was clearly an overt political move to reclaim parity on the level of international relations, it was also an attempt to regain domestic control in the national arena. As such, it highlighted the perceived need—expressed by diverse federal, state and local officials, party-political interests, and social workers—to reign in the formerly underregulated social and sexual behavior of foreign troops on West German territory, subject them to German law and custom, and in the process reestablish the corresponding prerogatives and privileges of native German men in domestic public and private life.[100]

Ultimately, the strategy proved only a partial success. The 1955 agreement governing the rights and duties of foreign troops in Germany did establish that the soldiers were subject to German law and the power of German authorities, a clear departure from the provisions of the Occupation Statute. Beginning 6 May 1955 (but not for births preceding that date), foreign soldiers in the Federal Republic could be summoned before West German civil courts for paternity suits and ordered to pay child support. Hailing "the altered humanitarian and legal status of the children and their mothers," the *Stuttgarter Nachrichten* (Stuttgart news) credited the "re-won sovereignty of the Federal Republic."[101]

As West German judges and youth officials soon found, however, getting soldiers to appear in court and collecting their money was a completely different matter. During the second half of the decade, in fact, West German officials in the federal and state Ministries of Justice continued to track and lament the notable lack of paternal responsibility among resident U.S. troops. This, they argued, was the direct and deliberate result of an American military culture that actively intervened to protect its soldiers from the long-term consequences of casual sex with German women. In 1956, for example, the Bavarian ministry of Justice polled its district and municipal courts regarding the disposition of cases involving

American servicemen. Consistently, reports were returned chronicling intentional bureaucratic foot-dragging at U.S. Headquarters in Heidelberg and rapid transfers back to the United States for men summoned before German civil courts. In his detailed memo to the federal Ministry of Justice, the Bavarian minister of Justice summarized that "the difficulties arise because American headquarters claims not to be able to locate the defendant even though the complainant has provided an exact address. Virtually all the court cases are terminated prematurely because the soldier is returned to the United States," rendering him legally untouchable.[102]

State-sponsored initiatives addressing the illegitimate children of Allied soldiers thus conjoined issues of German *political* and *patriarchal* rehabilitation. Moreover, such West German efforts at postwar rehabilitation were informed by ongoing reference to—and dialogue with—the United States. In its dealings with American officials regarding occupation children, the Federal Republic rhetorically assumed the mantle of "Father State," claiming its actions were based upon a desire to protect the welfare and rights of innocents and heal the breach left by Americans who individually and collectively chose to abdicate that responsibility. By grounding moral comparisons in the international present, West Germans deflected attention from a murderous Nazi past that had actively targeted innocents of "alien blood."

The following chapters focus on responses to biracial occupation children in order to explore the ways "race" was understood and investigated in the decade following Nazi Germany's defeat. Over the course of the 1950s *"farbige Besatzungskinder"* became a favorite topic of anthropologists, psychologists, sociologists, social workers and educators, as well as media reports and feature films. The studies and images they generated conditioned not only the children's social treatment, but also postwar notions of the fit between racial and national identities in the Federal Republic.

Chapter Three

"MISCHLINGSKINDER"
AND THE POSTWAR TAXONOMY
OF RACE

The Kaiser Wilhelm Institute for Applied Anthropology will undertake a study of the children resulting from relations between German women and colored men. The following questions will be considered: 1) what are the morphological consequences of race mixing? Do specific constitutional and developmental problems occur? 2) How does the mental and intellectual development of mixed-blood children unfold over time?

—Hermann Muckermann, 1951

We all live with the painful knowledge of the deadly divide that separated the principle of decency from the practices of barbarism at that time. . . . The existence of 3,100 colored children in this traditionally white land is a problem, even if not one small hair on these dark-skinned, curly-headed children is harmed.

—Hermann Ebeling, Society for Christian-Jewish Cooperation, 1952[1]

FOLLOWING the end of military occupation in 1949, West German officials tallied some 94,000 occupation children fathered by Allied troops residing within the boundaries of the newly established Federal Republic. Although biracial children constituted only a small fraction of occupation children and a tiny minority of postwar German births overall—just under 2 percent of out-of-wedlock births in 1947, for a total of fewer than 3,000 children in 1950—contemporary media reports inflated their numbers exponentially. Estimates ranged from a low of 10,000 to the egregiously exaggerated 950,000 put forth in all seriousness by a Pater Leppich and disseminated in German newspapers.[2] While the actual demographic presence of black occupation children in West Germany was minuscule, the hyperbolic response to the children indicates the disproportionate symbolic significance accorded them. This chapter seeks to survey the range of ways West Germans articulated and investigated that significance.

Concerns about biracial occupation children—variously dubbed by Germans *farbige Besatzungskinder* (colored occupation children), *Mischlingskinder* (mixed-blood children), or *Negermischlingskinder*—engaged public opinion, sparked scientific study, shaped social policy, and imprinted cultural representation. Although the children commanded a good deal of official, academic, and media attention between 1949 and 1963, this attention was informed by disparate politics and ideological commitments. Simply stated, German response to the children was far from monolithic. Rather, for the decade following 1950, biracial occupation children became a nexus around which social, cultural, and scientific debates about the meaning of race—and its implications for postwar German society—whirled.

Scholarly, media, and social welfare discussions regarding the children not only invoked, but also reconstituted, German understandings of race by revising racial classifications, often with reference to contemporary American race relations and social science. Collectively, these initiatives produced a new, and peculiarly postwar, taxonomy of race in the West German Federal Republic.

German commentators on *farbige Besatzungskinder* were acutely aware of both the postfascist context in which they operated and the compulsory moral mandate to excise Nazi-style racism from postwar social ideology and policy. Nonetheless, continuities in racial assumptions and analysis persisted across 1945. Scientific studies of the children during the 1950s, and the articulation of social policy regarding them, document the highly self-conscious yet deeply ambivalent ways in which German authorities and academics sought to revamp racial understanding and practice in Germany. As such, they encapsulate key elements of the ideological transition from National Socialist to democratic approaches to race in Germany. Unavoidably, they also betray the limits of democratic principles when applied to issues of race.

One important factor accounting for the significance of black occupation children after 1945 is that this was a juvenile population of German citizens subject to the control and in some cases under the legal guardianship (*Vormundschaft*) of West German authorities. In this way, they differed from the much larger population of Jews in West German territory who numbered some quarter million by late 1945. Although the postwar birthrate among Jews in Germany was exceedingly high, well outstripping the overall German birthrate, West German officials paid scant attention to it. This was because the majority of Jews were Displaced Persons, often of Eastern European origin, and therefore subject to Allied—and particularly American—supervision and care (assisted by UNRRA, the United Nations Relief and Rehabilitation Administration). Moreover, Jewish DPs considered themselves, and were considered by American

and German officials to be, a *transitory* population in Germany, temporarily biding their time while they sought permanent homes in more
hospitable lands.[3] In the case of the offspring of occupation soldiers
and German women, in contrast, Allied officials made it clear that care
of the children was not their concern. Their legal status, moreover, was
unambiguous: as the illegitimate offspring of German women, they inherited their mothers' citizenship according to the 1913 German Nationality Law.

As a result, German official and academic response to the children differed *in kind* from their response to other resident minorities after 1945.
As a population of minors with German citizenship, biracial occupation
children were indisputably a German responsibility. Because of their foreign paternity and racial difference, however, they were constructed as
a serious social problem in the Federal Republic of the 1950s. Subject to
censuses in 1950, 1951, and 1954, they were also singled out during these
years for a series of anthropological studies of the sort that would be
unimaginable if conducted after 1945 on Jews, Slavs, or so-called Gypsies—groups that had been targeted for sterilization or extermination on
the basis of race under the Nazi regime.[4]

This chapter examines the emergence and evolution of the social problem of biracial occupation children in the Federal Republic in order to
elucidate the precise ways West Germans reformulated the language and
categories of race after 1945. Of specific concern will be the process by
which West German officials, academics, and journalists, among others,
struggled to articulate a suitable terminology and coherent social policy
toward the children that was consistent both with Allied mandates for
democratization and the postwar need to rethink the racial dimensions
of German identity.

Counting "Coloreds"

While state officials and politicians in West Germany lobbied nationally
and internationally on behalf of the general problem of "occupation children" in the early 1950s, they concurrently created a distinct social problem around "colored occupation children" (*farbige Besatzungskinder*) by
singling them out for special tabulation and treatment. In 1950, after the
Protestant social welfare organization Inner Mission gathered and disseminated anecdotal evidence alleging miserable social circumstances
and the maternal abandonment of *farbige Besatzungskinder*, West German
officials in the federal and state Interior Ministries joined forces to count
them—a full eight months before they found it necessary to conduct a
similar survey of all occupation children. Underlying this tabulation was
the somewhat contradictory assumption that while *farbige Besatzungs-*

kinder were part of the larger problem of occupation children due to their foreign paternity and claims on public funds, they nonetheless presented a unique social challenge to German officials. A primary justification for the survey, indicated in draft memos but omitted from official correspondence, was to establish an empirical basis upon which the West German government could "initiate negotiations so that Negro mixed-blood children [*Negermischlingskinder*] be raised—when possible—in the homelands of their fathers."[5] In the case of occupation children of color, the relevant issues were not merely those of costs and care, but also racial difference and national belonging.

The most striking feature of these censuses was their use of racial categories, which effectively revised an earlier German lexicon of race, reaching back to the nineteenth century, that drew fine distinctions and valuations among European "races," paying particular attention to Slavs and Jews.[6] Although Blacks were certainly not absent from Germans' historical hierarchy of race, they did not dominate it either, in part because German colonialism in Africa (and Asia) came late and was short-lived compared to that of other European powers.[7] German official and scientific preoccupation with racial difference among Europeans derived from both geography and the political exigencies of belated nationhood. Founded in 1871, and therefore a latecomer to the imperialist scene, Germany's territorial aspirations and security concerns resided primarily within Europe rather than without. By the turn of the twentieth century, German military and political elites set their sights on Eastern Europe as the primary target for their expansionist ambitions. However, those same Eastern European regions provoked anxieties among German nationalists because they bordered German territory and were the source of minorities—Jews, Poles, and other Slavs—whose ethnic and cultural attributes were judged foreign and inferior to that of the Germans. Although resident minorities within German borders may have held state citizenship, they were nonetheless perceived, and at times persecuted, as un-German and even anti-German. Their presence challenged notions of nation based upon German bloodlines and ethnocultural belonging that achieved legal expression during the Wilhelmine period. German citizenship derived from the principle of jus sanguinis rather than jus soli: German descent rather than birth on German territory. By the eve of World War I and during the years that followed, Jews and Slavs—as well as Blacks—were perceived as alien to *Deutschtum* (Germandom) and, more tellingly, to the *Volkskörper*, the very "body of the nation."[8]

By 1945, however, a number of factors including the genocidal Nazi death camps and subsequent emigration of surviving Jews; westward expulsions of ethnic Germans from the eastern reaches of the former Reich; and an increasingly impermeable Iron Curtain dividing West Germans from Slavs (as much as capitalists from communists) imposed a form of ethnic "unmixing" on Cold War Central Europe.[9] For West Germans, although "the East" continued to present a political and ideological threat, by the early 1950s its perceived threat to West Germans' racial integrity was vastly diminished.[10] Following geopolitical developments, their point of reference shifted radically west to the United States.

After 1950, in fact, West German federal and state Interior Ministry officials explicitly constructed the postwar problem of race around skin color and, even more narrowly, blackness. This they accomplished by focusing exclusively on *Negermischlingskinder* when surveying state and municipal youth offices (*Jugendämter*) regarding the number and living arrangements of the children. Since the survey was limited to southern West German states of Baden, Bavaria, Hesse, Rheinland-Pfalz, Württemberg-Baden, Württemberg-Hohenzollern—territories constituting the former zones of French and American occupation—German officials' attention to color/blackness, as opposed to a presumed normative whiteness, suggests their simplified appraisal of the racial composition of, and racial distinctions within, those occupying armies. What is more, this telescoped focus on color/blackness set a precedent for subsequent surveys of occupation children. As a result, the attribution of other racialized identities previously, obsessively, and at times lethally targeted by the German state—be they Jewish, Slavic, or "Mongoloid/Asiatic"—were displaced, and ultimately erased, by a preoccupation with blackness in bureaucratic record keeping as well as official and public discourse.[11]

One might be tempted to argue that the revised racial categories of the early 1950s merely reflected the demographic "facts" of a West German population truncated from the East, and therefore from areas of Soviet troop presence, by the international politics of the Cold War. To some extent, this is true. By the mid-1950s, the official census of occupation children born since 1945 showed that 55 percent were fathered by American troops, 15 percent by French, 13 percent by British, and only 5 percent by Soviet (with the majority of the remaining 12 percent declared of unidentifiable nationality). However, in 1951, West German officials in youth offices, social welfare organizations, and state and federal Interior Ministries noted with some surprise that although there had been an expected decline in the birthrate of occupation children following currency reform in 1948 and the end of the worst "hunger years" in western Germany, beginning as early as 1949 cities like Wiesbaden and Munich in the vicinity of American garrisons were reporting noticeable increases in the birthrate of out-of-wedlock occupation children. The results of the 1955 census confirmed this trend, with the Federal Office of Statistics reporting a sustained rise in the national birthrate of occupation children since 1952, and a corresponding jump in the rate of American paternity—

including that of "colored troops." By 1953, U.S. soldiers fathered nearly 75 percent of all occupation children; within the year, this rate had increased to 80 percent "and was still climbing." As a result, the problem of occupation children and the attendant problem of race were increasingly perceived as American ones.[12]

This was also the case in Berlin—that divided city whose western sectors were declared a democratic outpost in an inhospitable socialist east by the emerging American-led Atlantic alliance. Although Berlin had been the site of mass rapes by Soviet troops, the children of such encounters and of subsequent consensual unions between Soviet soldiers and German women were effectively deracialized by both German states in the early 1950s. In East Germany, this happened somewhat differently and earlier than in the West. There the children of Soviet soldiers, colloquially called *"Russenkinder"* (Russian children), initially commanded special consideration as a problem due to the presumed violent circumstances of their conception. In the first year after defeat, East German officials freely employed the term as they struggled to formulate policy in response to demands by German mothers for financial assistance or, in many cases, placement of unwanted children in institutional homes.[13]

But because of the political sensitivity attached to *"Russenkinder"* as children of rape, East German authorities only reluctantly engaged the issue since it undermined official representations of Soviets as "benevolent liberators." Instead, they articulated policy in fits and starts at the prompting of local administrators attempting to grapple with the financial and institutional burdens of the children's care. Unlike their counterparts in the West, East German officials proved unwilling to pursue the issue of paternal child support with their occupiers, and in any case the Soviet Military Government (like the other Allies) permitted only voluntary declarations of paternity by its troops. As a result, mothers were subjected to considerable official pressure to develop a "maternal affinity" for their child and provide for its upbringing. By early 1946, as local communities struggled to respond to the upsurge in births of *Russenkinder*, East German officials firmly excised the term from their correspondence, replacing it with the euphemism "fatherless children." This linguistic shift reflected a new legal position. From mid-1946 on, *"Russenkinder"* were no longer treated as a distinct category of children but were designated as of unidentifiable paternity. And although East German officials had earlier requested that localities submit monthly statistics on "fatherless children" conceived by Soviet soldiers, by mid-1947 such reports were terminated along with official attention to *Russenkinder* as a special social problem. From that point on, their legal treatment was to be identical to that extended illegitimate children of *German* fathers.

From the official bureaucratic perspective, *Russenkinder*—those popularly perceived products of racialized rape—ceased to exist.[14]

In West Germany, the surveys of occupation children in the first half of the 1950s similarly whitewashed the offspring of some fathers formerly categorized as racial enemies. This was accomplished by the strategy of segregating only the "coloreds" among occupation children for separate tabulation. The detailed federal census of all occupation children, taken in 1954–55 as West Germany was achieving full sovereignty, requested that states classify resident occupation children according to their biological father's origins. Among the categories established for the children's paternity were the predictable "USA," "France," "Great Britain," and "Soviet Union." However, a fifth column recorded "children of colored parentage [*farbige Abstammung*]" without reference to the father's national affiliation, thereby uncoupling racial from national difference. As a result, the statistical categories deraced Soviet paternity and rendered Jewishness invisible, implicitly coding the occupation children of formerly racialized Soviet and Jewish soldiers "white." What remained were distinctions of nationality on the one hand and blackness on the other.[15]

In reducing a subset of occupation children to the category of undifferentiated "color," official statistics erased precise national attributions of their paternity from public record and representation. At the same time, since federal and state censuses established the statistical dominance of American paternity among all occupation children, the colored among them were rapidly "renationalized" as children of black American soldiers in media coverage and, increasingly, among state officials, social scientists, and social welfare workers dealing with youth issues. An important consequence of this genealogical imprecision was that as "race" in West Germany became equated with blackness rather than Jewishness, blackness was increasingly equated with African American origins. In just over a half-decade after the defeat of National Socialism and the Allied liberation of the death camps, the problem of race was embodied in the *Mischlingskind* and linked to America.[16] A putatively "new" and peculiarly postwar problem of race had been born.

Anthropological Investigations of Race: "Mixed-Bloods" in Historical Perspective

During the first half of the 1950s, two young German anthropologists, Walter Kirchner and Rudolf Sieg, independently undertook studies on black *Mischlingskinder* ranging in age from one to six. Assisted, respectively, by Berlin's youth and health offices and by Christian social welfare organizations in West Germany proper, Kirchner and Sieg minutely recorded the children's skin color, lip thickness, and hair texture; the breadth of their noses, shoulders, chests and pelvises; the length of their arms, legs, and torsos; the shape of their dental bites and circumference of their heads and chests, documenting their physical traits in a series of photographs that Kirchner (but not Sieg) appended to his study. In addition, both authors analyzed the children's medical and psychological records, as well as their social, familial, and moral milieu, and subjected the children to a series of intellectual and psychological examinations. The point of this exercise, according to Kirchner, was to establish the extent to which *Mischlingskinder* deviated from the white norm and whether such "deviations in development were localized in specific characteristic mental or emotional regions" or in particular circumstances of social milieu. Sieg too sought to identify and account for the children's "anomalies."[17]

In probing the somatic, psychological, and behavioral effects of "racial mixing," both anthropologists took as their starting point the problems and methodologies developed by racial scientists and eugenicists between the 1910s and 1930s. Citing the work of such German luminaries as Eugen Fischer, Wolfgang Abel, Hermann Muckermann, and Otmar Freiherr von Verschuer (as well as Americans Charles Davenport and Melville Herskovits), they uncritically and unapologetically built upon the principles and practices of interwar anthropologists.[18] But while the cumulative efforts of earlier German anthropologists resulted in the compulsory sterilization of an estimated six hundred black German children under Hitler, the postwar work of Kirchner and Sieg was necessarily directed at other social policy applications since the foundational law of the West German state prohibited discriminatory treatment on the basis of race.

Beholden to an earlier German literature on racial hygiene that informed, and in some cases justified, Nazi racial violence, Kirchner's and Sieg's interpretations nonetheless departed from that literature in small but self-conscious ways. As products of younger anthropologists who had not yet established their professional credentials during the Third Reich yet were trained by those who had, their studies stand as transitional texts between Weimar- and Nazi-era anthropological paradigms and their postwar successors. As such, they represent the work of men who felt the pressure to abandon the worst abuses of Nazi-era racial science and, responding to an altered postwar legal structure, attempted to feel their way to a less morally reprehensible alternative.[19]

German scholarly impulses after 1945 to segregate out and study black occupation children must be read against a longer history of German preoccupation with black-white miscegenation that emerged in response to German colonialism and culminated under Hitler. In order to register the subtle differences between the postwar studies of Kirchner and Sieg and those of their predecessors, we must return briefly to the first decade of the twentieth century. It was during this time that heated debates regarding the legal status of "race-mixing" and *Mischlingskinder* in the German colonies of Southwest Africa, East Africa, and Samoa raised the question of the legal and cultural relationship between "blackness" and "Germanness." While the legal resolution to the issue was ambiguous and geographically bound—with German colonial administrators in Southwest Africa, for example, insisting on withdrawing political rights and German citizenship from the offspring of African women and German men, while jurists in mainland Germany favored the patriarchal right of white German fathers to pass citizenship onto their sons, regardless of race—the cultural resolution was more clear-cut. That is to say, the very *fact* of the debates—and especially the tendency to classify heterogeneous heterosexual relations between colonizer and colonized under the unified rubric of "race mixing"—established a strong cultural presumption of race-based nationhood, which considered blackness antithetical to a color-free German *Volk*.[20]

The perceived problems of "racial mixing" rapidly spilled out of this legal frame to become the subject of scientific investigation in Germany. In 1913, on the eve of World War I, Freiburg-based anthropologist Eugen Fischer achieved international reputation and pioneered a new subdiscipline that merged the study of anthropology with biology with the publication of his book, *The Rehobother Bastards and the Bastardization Problem among Humans* (Die Rehobother Bastarde und das Bastardisierungsproblem beim Menschen). Noting anthropologists' lack of knowledge concerning the effects of racial-crossing (*Rassenkreuzung*), Fischer drew upon Mendel's laws of biological inheritance to document the physical and emotional consequences of interracial reproduction between German or Dutch colonists and native Nama (or in European parlance, "Hottentot") women. Focusing on hair texture and color, eye and skin color, along with other measurable body parts and behavioral traits, he examined the offspring of such unions with the goal of discerning the rules of human inheritance in order to establish a scientific basis upon which to conduct "practical eugenics and racial hygiene." Although he conceived of races as true types, Fischer found that "racial crossing" did not give rise to new races but resulted in racial mixture, in which racial qualities of both parents were differentially dispersed, in accordance with Mendel's laws, among affected individuals and populations. In arguing that interracial "bastards" received traits of both parents, Fischer posited the plasticity of reproduction in racial terms. Racial-crossing, rather than spawning an "either-or," combined racial traits in one body. Projected into the future, it was expected to have a long-term impact on the genetic inheritance—the character and capabilities—of national populations. As Fischer concluded: "an improvement in our race is not possible through such crossing; a degeneration—in the best case by means of the inheritance of disharmonious traits—will surely prevail."[21] As historian Fatima El-Tayeb has observed, already by 1914, Germans' "confrontation with the 'black race' (defined in terms of its absolute difference and inferiority) and with 'mixed-bloods' (classified as 'unnatural' and 'race-destroying') . . . as *potential members of one's own community* led to a sharpening of racial thinking. . . . Given the 'objective' foundations laid by 'respectable' scientists like Eugen Fischer, the concepts of 'Volk' and 'Race' were rendered synonymous and became part of general consciousness."[22]

A second formative episode in the historical relationship between blackness and German notions of national belonging followed Germany's defeat in World War I, when the French occupied the German Rhineland with colonial African troops. Fabricating stories of mass sexual violence by "colored" troops against German women and youth, government officials, politicians (in all parties but the radical left), clergymen, and journalists denounced the so-called Black Horror (*Schwarzer Schmach*) in a propaganda campaign of national and international dimensions, fanning the flames of antiblack sentiment at home and abroad. In an effort to counter what they considered to be an overly punitive peace treaty, German officials attempted, and in large measure succeeded, in currying international sympathy and support by portraying the occupation by North African troops as part of a French vendetta intent on the forcible destruction of German national and racial integrity. (A few years later in his political autobiography, *Mein Kampf*, Hitler embroidered upon this charge, rendering it a world-class conspiracy by an unholy trinity of the French, Jews, and Blacks.)

Early on, German authorities were aware that unions between German women and nonwhite French soldiers had produced "illegitimate" interracial offspring—the so-called Rhineland Bastards—who took their mothers' German citizenship. Although officials quietly condemned the births on eugenic grounds as contributing to, or symptomatic of, the degeneration of the German Volk, they did not publicize the children's existence. They feared undermining their own propaganda by advertising the existence of consensual sexual relations between German women and nonwhite troops.[23]

Between 1923 and 1927, there were scattered attempts to count the children and contemplate ways to defuse their eugenic threat to the German nation. During these four years, state officials in the Palatinate, Prussia, Hesse, Bavaria, Baden, and Oldenburg succeeded in identifying 385 children—about half of the total 600 children estimated by historians. Realizing that appearance alone was not a fail-proof method of detection, they were forced to rely on voluntary declarations of the children's paternity by mothers who proved less than forthcoming, given the antiblack racism driving the survey. By mid-1927 the Palatinate Commissar, together with the Privy Councilor of the Bavarian Interior Ministry, urged Reich officials to "protect the purity of German race" by neutralizing the threat of the Rhineland bastards via emigration or sterilization. Although these appeals received a serious hearing in Berlin, officials ultimately declined to challenge the children's citizenship and reproductive rights, declaring intervention politically inadvisable. To be legal, emigration or sterilization would have to be voluntary and would require receiving the unlikely permission of the children's mothers. To render either compulsory would necessitate new legislation. However, whether voluntary or compulsory, such action would likely provoke unwanted negative publicity at the domestic and international levels. For these reasons, official pursuit of solutions to the "bastard problem," as it was called, was abandoned for the duration of the Weimar Republic.[24]

Within three months of Hitler's ascent to power, however, the problem of the "Rhineland bastards" was placed back on the agenda. In April 1933 Prussian Interior Minister Hermann Göring ordered a detailed survey of the children (the oldest of whom were approaching puberty) in his jurisdiction and engaged Wolfgang Abel of the Kaiser Wilhelm Institute for Anthropology, Genetics, and Eugenics in Berlin to perform anthropological examinations on them. Drawing on Eugen Fischer's methods, Abel examined twenty-seven "Moroccan bastards" between the ages of five and eleven, judging their health to be poor. He noted a higher than average incidence of tuberculosis among the children, which he attributed to their Moroccan paternity, and declared that many exhibited symptoms of "early psychosis" such as nighttime screaming, nail biting, fluttering eyelids, and speech impediments. In examining the children's school records, he concluded their performance was below average (in contrast to six "Annamese bastards," who were deemed easier to educate). In sum, Abel described the "Moroccan mixed-bloods" as "uneducable, disobedient, slovenly, excitable, and hot-tempered, with a predilection for the life of the streets"—in effect credentialing them as racially inferior asocials.[25]

The following year, in April 1934, the Reich Minister of the Interior followed up on Abel's study and ordered the states of Baden, Bavaria, Hesse, Oldenburg, and Prussia to conduct a thorough accounting of all "bastards" in their territories so that officials in Berlin could gauge the size of the problem and "decide on measures to counteract the pressing threat of these racially alien [fremdrassige] bastards mixing with pure German blood." Police and youth officials in these states were to report the child's name, address, birthdate and place, and racial background of the father (categories provided were "Neger, Marokkaner, Anamite"). The responses returned from Baden show that the children's mothers would sometimes dispute the paternity of the child in an attempt to keep the child off the official rolls. One woman from the outskirts of Heidelberg, for example, claimed her child's father was French or Spanish. Since her mayor contradicted her and said he was Moroccan, the child was counted. In Konstanz, one mother claimed her son was not "from a Neger" but fathered by a German from Thüringen: "What is more, when questioned by the police, she explained that during her pregnancy in Karlsruhe, she once witnessed two Negroes boxing. This sight so shocked her that her son apparently took on the appearance of a Negro." This report went on to state that her response did not fit with the "facts" since her son, on the basis of his physical attributes, was most certainly the product of Negro paternity. This judgment was seconded by the doctor examining the boy.[26]

Although Baden submitted the requested information in July 1934, within the year the state received word from the Reich minister of the Interior that it was "not thorough enough." The Reich Interior Ministry now ordered that each child be examined and evaluated "according to biological-inheritance criteria" by the medical staff of the local health office. Unlike Abel in his 1933 examinations of children, local health office doctors from southern Baden overwhelmingly returned positive reports of the children's physical and mental health in the summer of 1935. In twelve out of fifteen cases reported for southern Baden, the doctors judged that the children showed no indications of hereditary illness and that therefore the children were not candidates for sterilization. Out of three negative reports, two concerned a "pure-blooded Negro" boy and a girl of Moroccan paternity who were alleged to be mentally impaired. In the former case, the doctor noted that the boy had already been sterilized; the doctor in the latter case recommended the girl's sterilization. In the third case, a Dr. Roeder from Ludwigshafen, appeared as repulsed by the family as by their child, who had "the pronounced racial phenotype of a Negro": "My attempt to advise and instruct the mother [regarding the desirability for her son's sterilization] was a complete failure," he wrote in disgust. "And the child's foster parents appear to me to be stricken with a pathological monkey-love [*Affenliebe*] for the child."[27]

Apart from such displays of rabid antiblack racism, two tendencies stand out from these reports. The first is that in the examinations, the children's family situation—and especially their mothers' moral, mental, and physical "health"—were often taken into account when assessing the child. However, the outcome of such calculations was not always predictable. For example, a health office doctor in Offenburg noted that sixteen-year-old Edwin had "frizzy, matted, and very black hair," brown

eyes, and "skin that was almost as darkly pigmented as one sees in Negroes." Nonetheless, he judged Erwin's physical and mental development as good and praised his performance in school. The doctor also
examined Erwin's white mother. Like her son, she had black, curly hair
and brown eyes. Unlike her son, she was judged a half-wit. The doctor
ordered her sterilization, but concluded that "for Erwin, sterilization is
not appropriate."[28]

A second point is that in mid-1935, most local health office doctors in
Baden did not consider racial difference alone as a sufficient indication
for social or medical intervention. In examining their subjects and making evaluations for sterilization, they looked for negative physical or
mental indications attributable to degenerate heredity. If those indications were absent, the doctors judged the child healthy in both medical
and national-racial terms. Thus, for example, although one fifteen-year-
old boy near Konstanz was described as "a decidedly Negroid type," the
doctor nonetheless found "no inferiority or hereditary deficiencies." In
their summary to the Reich Interior Ministry, moreover, Baden officials
noted that for some of the children of Moroccan and Algerian paternity,
doctors detected "no non-Aryan ancestry." Clearly, in mid-1935, the Nazi
version of racial ideology was not being applied—or at least applied consistently—by medical practitioners in the provinces.[29]

Although it took Reich officials four years from Hitler's ascension to
power in 1933, the children were ultimately sterilized. The reasons for
the delay are attributable not to a failure of will among Nazi officials, but
to ongoing legal constraints as well as foreign policy concerns expressed
by the German Foreign Office. Although the Nazi regime enacted a 1934
law that provided for sterilization of individuals suffering from "hereditary disease," there was no legal basis to support sterilization on racial
grounds alone. Reich Interior minister Wilhelm Frick believed that "Moroccan bastards" could nonetheless be sterilized under the existing law
due to their "mental inferiority." But as we have seen, doctors in Baden
did not always agree with his assumption, and this argument did not
prevail at the time.

In addition, international considerations played a role. As the Nazi regime began to draw negative response to their racially exclusionary laws
from African, Asian, and Latin American countries, the German Foreign
Office urged caution in promulgating new measures, fearful of the effect
on Germany's foreign and commercial interests. The Foreign Office suggested that racial legislation be narrowed to target Jews alone since, they
argued, this was a purely "internal affair" unlikely to trigger international response (an assumption that proved tragically correct). For his
part, Frick urged the Foreign Office to enlighten the world that the re-

gime's racial laws were an "act of self-defense" by the German Volk against an "incursion of alien Jewish blood."[30]

In early 1935, by which time the Nazi Party had more firmly consolidated its power in Germany, Frick assembled anthropologists and medical experts to brainstorm a solution to the "Rhineland bastard problem." Their first suggestion was sterilization. Their second (when Foreign Office concerns still precluded the former) was to pay the children to emigrate to Africa to be raised by missionaries—a solution soon rejected as "unrealistic and too expensive." The final resolution to the problem, coming in 1937, was to sterilize the children by applying the same legal criteria used in cases of eugenic abortion: to do it "illegally"—and secretly—at the order of the Führer and with the help of loyal Nazi doctors. Before being sterilized, the children were required to be examined and racially classified by trained anthropologists in order to certify paternity since the sterilization order applied only to "Rhineland bastards" and not to all children of color resident in Germany at the time (again due to fear of international repercussions).[31]

Eugen Fischer and Wolfgang Abel, among others, conducted racial examinations, "condemning 385 children between the ages of seven and seventeen to sterilization." While the majority of children targeted were of North African paternity, one was the teenage daughter of a black American soldier who had been stationed along the Rhine after the First World War.[32]

Having helped solve the eugenic problem of the "Rhineland bastards," Fischer, Abel, and their colleagues at the Kaiser Wilhelm Institute for Anthropology, Genetics, and Eugenics turned to the scrutiny of Jews. They provided scientific expertise and legitimacy for the Third Reich's increasingly radical program of eugenic engineering targeting human beings deemed "unworthy of life" due to physical or mental infirmity, asocial behavior, or racial difference. Fischer and Abel assisted in the classification of "full, half- and quarter-Jews" for these purposes, contributing to the bureaucratic process of racial selection that facilitated the segregation and subsequent shipment of German and other European Jews to the death camps once war and eastward territorial expansion were underway.[33]

Due to the Nazi regime's increasing ideological fixation on solving the "Jewish problem" (expressed publicly in the branding of those of "Jewish blood" with the yellow Star of David), the term *Mischling* became popularly applied to the offspring of unions between Jewish and non-Jewish Germans during the Third Reich.[34] This narrowing of contemporary linguistic usage, in conjunction with the sheer magnitude of Nazi crimes against Jews, has tended to obscure the issue of state-sponsored violence against Black Germans. As a result, historians have typically treated the story of *"Mischlinge"* during the Third Reich as an exclusively Jewish one. But as the fate of the Rhineland "mixed bloods" makes clear, this ignores a significant dimension of Nazi racial ideology and social policy and conceals an important prehistory of post-1945 racial reconstruction.

CONSTRUCTING THE POSTWAR *MISCHLINGSKIND*

After 1945, the story of German *Mischlingskinder* is marked by significant continuities as well as ruptures. One of the most striking continuities—along with its reliance on the methodologies of Fischer and Abel—was institutional. The first postwar anthropological study of *Mischlingskinder* by Walter Kirchner emerged out of the newly reconstituted Kaiser Wilhelm Institute for Applied Anthropology (KWI) under the directorship of Hermann Muckermann. Kirchner was a doctoral student at the Free University in West Berlin working under Muckermann, a former Jesuit priest and well-known eugenicist during the interwar period, who had served as director of eugenics at the KWI from its beginnings in 1927 through 1933. After the war, Muckermann was intent on resurrecting the Institute, which he accomplished with American permission.[35] An influential advocate and "the greatest popularizer" of eugenic thinking during the Weimar Republic due to his tireless program of popular pamphleteering and lecturing, Muckermann was ejected from the KWI in mid-1933, some six months after the Nazis took power, due to "ideological differences." Unlike his new masters, he supported voluntary, rather than compulsory, sterilizations for those deemed unfit to reproduce. Despite his ouster by the Nazis, his professional record was hardly free of that era's brand of racism. In an attempt to retain his job, he declared that he shared with the Nazi leadership "the common goal of surmounting the degeneration of ancestral biological inheritance and encouraging the preservation and propagation of our nation's hereditarily healthy families."[36] Although Muckermann denounced antisemitism, he considered Jews a distinct race and in his writings invoked typical anti-Jewish stereotypes of the day, including references to Jews' extraordinary "hypersexuality, influence, and subversive potential." Similarly, he absorbed and reproduced extant antiblack stereotypes noting, for example, the susceptibility of the "Negro race" to sensory impressions, as well as their limited cognitive and intellectual powers and lack of cultural achievement. Defending his work in 1936, Muckermann emphasized that he, like his Nazi critics, never doubted "that mental and emotional characteristics derive from race and that the Nordic race in particular well deserves its high valuation."[37] So although Muckermann could claim to have been professionally victimized by the Nazis since

1933, a claim that bestowed substantial moral authority after 1945, his commitment to eugenics and racial hygiene dovetailed with aspects of Nazi racial ideology.[38]

Kirchner's postwar work clearly continued his adviser's proclivity to think within a racist eugenicist paradigm in its attention to the effects of racial mixing. But what *is* peculiarly postwar is his choice of subject: the black *Mischlingskind*. This was not a logical choice in demographic terms. The vast majority of black occupation children resided in the southern states of mainland West Germany; Kirchner's study was based in Berlin, where fewer than 2 percent of the children (about eighty in total) were located.[39] A focus on Jewish- or *Russenkinder* would have yielded a larger sample. But there is no indication that Kirchner ever considered such a study, and that is precisely the point. It was politically impossible to contemplate studying Jewish or Russian *Mischlingskinder* after the death camps, Nazi defeat, and the onset of the Cold War. The postwar political situation helped shape the postfascist study of race and the delineation of racial categories in Germany. And this makes the linguistic survival of the term *Mischling* particularly surprising and its ongoing anthropological study all the more significant.

What was symptomatic about Kirchner's study—as well as Sieg's and virtually all studies of black German children in the 1950s—was their nearly exclusive emphasis on children of African American paternity. Kirchner, for example, examined the medical records and social welfare and school reports of fifty "Negro mixed-blood children" in Berlin ranging in age from one to twenty, but focused his analysis on a subgroup of twenty-three children, ages one through five, of predominantly "American Negro" paternity. Similarly, Sieg had access to children of Algerian, Moroccan, and American paternity, but deliberately excluded from his study all but the latter.

This focus was key to both authors' arguments. In establishing the theoretical basis of his study, Kirchner dismissed the notion that one could render a "general judgment about racial mixed bloods." Rather, he argued that in addition to considerations of race, anthropologists must attend to the "role of individual traits" and the specific social factors leading to "race mixing."[40] Focusing on "American Negro" paternity and post-1945 circumstances of conception allowed both Kirchner and Sieg to render a relatively rosy picture of the postwar *Mischlingskind's* physical, mental, and emotional health when compared to the supposedly more negative impact of Moroccan paternity and interracial relations on the "Rhineland *Mischlinge*" after the First World War. Admitting he lacked information about the health and intelligence of American soldiers, Kirchner nonetheless "assumed that the U.S. army had certain standards." In accounting for the absence of serious disease among postwar

Mischlingskinder, both Kirchner and Sieg credited the relative health and wealth of black American GIs. Unlike North African soldiers after 1918, who "presumably represented a thoroughly unfavorable selection" in eugenic and material terms, African Americans were assumed to have few serious maladies yet ample resources with which to provide for their offspring.[41] These national biases had racial overtones. Invoking Herkovit's 1928 analysis of the racial constitution of the "American Negro," both Kirchner and Sieg emphasize that unlike Africans, few black GIs were "pure Negroes" but rather racial mixtures of Negro, Mongoloid, and particularly European inheritance.[42]

This, apparently, made all of the difference for the children. Neither Kirchner nor Sieg found significant deviations in the health, intelligence, or emotional disposition of postwar *"Mischlingkinder"* when compared to their white counterparts. However, they did note certain developmental, physical, and behavioral characteristics which they attributed to the children's "Negroid biological inheritance" [*negrides Erbteil*]. These traits were diverse and in most cases echoed the stereotypes handed down by previous generations of racial scientists. Aside from early rapid growth in infancy and young childhood, Kirchner and Sieg noted a disposition for respiratory disease (due to maladjustment to the European climate); abnormalities of dental bite; long legs; lively temperaments; a marked joy in movement, including dance; and well-developed speaking abilities, with particular talents for rhythmic speech, rhyme, and imitation. Although the children were described as open to social contact, they were also declared willful, impatient, and uncooperative at times, given to strong (although not necessarily ungovernable) impulses.[43] So although Kirchner initially asserted the importance of weighing the role of individual traits in examining the children, his conclusions centered around identifying instances of racially based inheritance.

A final significant feature of these early postwar studies was their ambivalent treatment of the children's German mothers. Sieg reproduced the negative assessments of the immediate postwar years regarding German women who consorted with black occupation soldiers by claiming that 50 percent came from an "asocial milieu" and that most were likely prostitutes. Since Sieg focused solely on children placed in institutional care [*Heimkinder*], his sample was inherently skewed. However, this did not stop him from generalizing. Judging the absent mothers harshly, he assigned them responsibility for any signs of poor nutrition or disease among the children. Moreover, he was one of the first in a series of commentators to cast *Mischlingskinder* as *Heimkinder*, thus affecting public opinion about the children and the nature of their putative problems.[44]

Kirchner's sample examined children in diverse living arrangements, and as a result his analysis of the mothers was somewhat more differentiated and positive. While suggesting that most of the children's mothers hailed from the "simple social classes," he also noted that most children were well cared for within their mother's meager means and saw evidence of "a genuine and deep emotional bond between mother and child."[45] Overall, he judged maternal influence on their children as generally beneficial, which, he argued, was decidedly *not* the case when one considered the example of the earlier "Rhineland bastards" who suffered disproportionately from psychopathologies. Following Abel and others, Kirchner blamed their poor mental health on the miserable genetic stock of their "asocial" mothers. Since the German population rejected contact with occupation troops after 1918, he reasoned, those who engaged in sexual contact were a "particularly negative" type of woman. However, he reassured readers, "in the case of the Berliner Mischlinge" after 1945 "no such factor presented itself, and therefore no especially adverse social selection has occurred." Or as Sieg put it, at the conclusion of his study: "No detrimental consequences of bastardization were perceptible among *our* Mischlingskinder."[46]

Ultimately, then, these young postwar anthropologists articulated a less negative assessment of "race mixing" and "mixed-blood children" by reading the contemporary episode in relation to earlier historical experience and through the lens of racist racial science. Their upbeat prognostications, moreover, rested on evaluating the distinct national and gender dimensions of each case. "Our" *Mischlingskinder* present fewer problems than those of the past because they were fathered by healthy, wealthy "American Negroes," rather than diseased and uncultivated Africans; because they were born to caring lower-class mothers, rather than asocial lunatics.

But perhaps the most significant departure of the postwar studies from their precursors was in their focus on the social environment, and particularly its potentially mitigating effect on residual areas of intransigent racial inheritance. Here Kirchner had more to say than Sieg. Kirchner, it will be recalled, identified some troublesome areas of "Negro inheritance" among the children, such as their tendency to be hotheaded, impulsive, willful, and disobedient. Yet these presumed inherited racial qualities were not immutable: they could be tempered by the proper positive influences of attentive mothers, childhood friendships, and a well-disposed public. Arguing that the "psychical" legacy of their racial inheritance need not be an insurmountable burden, Kirchner concluded by urging that "everything possible be done" to improve the living conditions of the children.[47] If Kirchner (like Sieg) aped his predecessors in his conviction that racial distinctions existed in the biology and psychology of his subjects, he departed from them in articulating the possibility of social solutions to this purported "problem of race."

"Fighting Ignorance": Transatlantic Impulses in Racial Reeducation

While German anthropologists continued to seek expressions of race in the bodies and behavior of their subjects, others turned to an examination of racism in postwar society. By the early 1950s, a rather inchoate movement emerged among diverse state and municipal officials, educators, social workers, and journalists to reeducate the German public away from racist response by focusing on black German children in their midst. To the extent that these efforts found an institutional home, they were centered in local West German chapters of the Society for Christian-Jewish Cooperation (Gesellschaft für Chistlich-Jüdische Zusammenarbeit [SCJC]). Founded in 1948 with the assistance of the American Military Government's Office of Religious Affairs, the Society's mission was to "analyze and eliminate existing prejudices, . . . strengthen the social order, [and] promote justice, understanding and cooperation between Protestants, Catholics, and Jews." SCJC members considered their work compatible with the American reeducation program during the occupation and devoted particular attention to youth, education, teacher training, and curriculum reform in West German schools.[48]

Modeled on the National Council of Christians and Jews (NCCJ), which had been founded in the interwar United States to fight antisemitism and the racist violence of the Ku Klux Klan, the Society for Christian-Jewish Cooperation resulted from the transatlantic transfer of this American organizational form. Following the destruction of World War II and the murderous racism of National Socialism, the interfaith initiative was exported to Europe, and International Councils of Christians and Jews were established between 1946 and 1947 in England, France, and Switzerland. In late 1947, Everett Clinchy, president of the American NCCJ, toured Germany, working closely with American occupation officials to cultivate support among prominent German Christian and Jewish leaders, both lay and religious, for the interfaith initiative. By mid-1948, having received official U.S. approval and material assistance, Minnesota minister Carl Zietlow became the American NCCJ's man-in-the-field in Germany, recruiting Germans in government, education, and the media to begin branches of the organization in Munich, Wiesbaden, Frankfurt, Stuttgart, Berlin, and other cities. The goal was to use these local chapters to lead the fight against racial discrimination and antisemitism and foster tolerance and interconfessional understanding in postwar Germany. Over the course of the next two years, the American patrons of the Society for Christian-Jewish Cooperation prodded their German counterparts to broaden their aims, encouraging them to counter all forms of prejudice and to cultivate a broad sense of humanism and brotherhood among all people of the world. By 1950, American NCCJ president Everett Clinchy created a new international organization called World Brotherhood with headquarters in New York City and sought to centralize the nationally based initiatives under American leadership. This organizational and ideological refashioning appears to have been developed as a strategic way to transmit American values and enhance U.S. influence abroad in response to the new challenges posed by decolonization and Cold War. While some of the German branches of the SCJC affiliated themselves with World Brotherhood, others, including the Society's West German Coordinating Council (Koordinierungsrat) resisted surrendering their autonomy.[49]

Despite the varied response by the German branches after 1950, there were a couple of noteworthy consequences of the Society's founding. First, it transferred to the Federal Republic the American model of "intergroup relations" that first emerged in the 1930s United States and sought to counter racial bias and violence by building a viable educational and activist network across confessional, ethnic, and racial lines. Second, it introduced into West Germany the reigning American social-scientific tool for investigating racism, namely prejudice studies, which had important consequences for how race was discussed and understood in the postwar German context.[50]

The prejudice studies approach is evident in the Society for Christian-Jewish Cooperation's early engagement with the topic of the *Mischlingskind*. Beginning in 1952, the year that black occupation children were first entering German schools, the Society played a prominent role in bringing the postwar race problem to the attention of German state officials, educators, social workers, and the press by organizing conferences in Wiesbaden, Nuremberg, and Frankfurt titled "The Fate of Colored Mixed-Blood Children in Germany," and by sponsoring the publication of Alfons Simon's booklet *Maxi, unser Negerbub* (Maxi, our Negro lad). This booklet, which told the fictionalized story of a teacher's journey toward understanding the causes, manifestations, and costs of prejudice through his efforts to integrate a black German boy into his white classroom, was widely disseminated and became recommended reading for all teachers throughout West Germany.[51] Such SCJC initiatives were crucial in shaping social and school policy regarding the children and in establishing the ways the children would be presented to the public at large as they made their way from the privacy of home to the classroom. What is more, they pioneered the principles upon which a liberal discourse of race would be constructed in West Germany.[52]

In August 1952, 170 participants gathered at the Amerika Haus in Wiesbaden for a two-day forum intended to facilitate the exchange of information about the children, fight public misconceptions, and formulate "concrete educational and social welfare guidelines" to aid their successful integration into West German society. In attendance were state and municipal authorities, education and youth officials, teachers, clergy, journalists, social welfare workers (including the head of the German Association for Public and Private Welfare) representing the cities of Wiesbaden, Frankfurt/Main, Giessen, Kassel, Marburg/Lahn, Nuremberg, Offenbach, and Wetzlar, among others. Two Americans, Dr. J. Oscar Lee, from the National Council of Churches, and a Catholic priest from Ohio rounded out the guest list.

World Brotherhood members Claire Guthmann and Hermann Eberling opened the Wiesbaden proceedings by defining the postwar race problem in relation to *farbige Mischlingskinder* and establishing the urgency of its address. On the one hand, Guthmann suggested that Germans' engagement with the *"Wohl und Wehe"*—welfare and woes—of the children was part of the global struggle to ensure the peaceful coexistence of "human beings of different races and beliefs."[53] On the other hand, Hermann Ebeling, who was based in Frankfurt and emerged as a central advocate for the children in Germany, centered on the peculiarly national and moral dimensions of the task confronting Germans:

> The question has been posed: Why treat something like a problem when it isn't one? It would be wonderful if this were not a problem. It would be a sign of our overall humanitarian, moral, and religious maturity. But the experiences of the not-too-distant past cannot justify such a response. We all live with the painful knowledge of the deadly divide [*Grabeskluft*] that separated the principle of decency from the practices of barbarism at that time. . . . It is both terrible and notable that our consideration of the minority problem . . . stands in the shadow of this tragedy. The existence of 3,100 colored children in this traditionally white land is a problem, even if not one small hair on these dark-skinned, curly-headed little children is harmed.[54]

Ebeling explicitly framed the postwar challenges of race and racial tolerance in relation to recent German history and constructed it as an issue of social responsibility—indeed, social maturity. His was not a lone voice in the postwar wilderness. A survey of the literature on biracial children in professional journals for youth and social workers indicates that the children's presence in the Federal Republic was viewed as a stimulus to a belated but necessary "training in tolerance" among its predominantly white population.[55]

The first task of the SCJC, then, was to reformulate the nature of the problem that confronted West German society. Through 1952, most public commentary focused on the financial costs of the "foreign-looking" children, who were viewed as resulting from the sinful, selfish, or greedy actions of their mothers or, to a much lesser extent, from the mother's rape. Such commentary tended to portray the children as outsiders to German society and advocate their "return" to the land of their fathers. A primary goal of the Society for Christian and Jewish Cooperation was to domesticate postwar biracial children by recasting them as a *German* problem—rather than an American import—that required sustained German compassion and attention.

In order to facilitate that aim, German participants of the 1952 Wiesbaden conference focused on language—what the children should most properly be called—and resolved to reject the terms "*Mulatten-*," "*Neger-*," or "*farbige Besatzungskinder*," which they felt emphasized their foreign paternity, in favor of "*farbige Mischlingskinder*." While this may have served to nativize the children in terms of nationality, it also reproduced preexisting notions of the children's essentialized racial difference from their white counterparts. Strikingly, it was a self-consciously liberalizing organization like the World Brotherhood/SCJC that explicitly authorized the continued use of "*Mischling*" in official and public venues. Ebeling's historical references notwithstanding, conference attendees appear to have endorsed this resolution without examining the racial assumptions upon which it was based or the history of racial persecution it connoted. While the term remained a common colloquialism in private and public parlance after 1945, its official adoption by the SCJC indicates a critical blind spot in West Germans' articulation of a liberal analysis of race.

It must be added, however, that this was not an exclusively German failing. While the resolution was regrettable in hindsight, it nonetheless conformed to widespread American legal and social practices of racing individuals on the basis of *any* black heredity, according to the so-called one-drop rule. In his comments to the conference, Oscar Lee of the National Council of Churches similarly dehistoricized the German experience of race by asserting that the children's difference in skin color presented Germans with unprecedented challenges since "in the past, Germany has had relatively little experience with the problem of race relations." Lee's utterance appears to betray a surprising ignorance about Nazi Germany's well-known persecution of racial minorities, particularly Jews. However, it may merely betray his unquestioned internalization, as an African American, of an American paradigm of race dominated by the black-white binary.[56]

Viewed in concert, the Wiesbaden conference, the official and semiofficial censuses, and the anthropological studies of *Mischlingskinder* produced a shift in definitions of race in early 1950s West Germany. Through these initiatives, race became inscribed as *Neger/farbige* in accordance with a black-white binary familiar to Americans. (In fact, the leading German dictionary of 1952 defined *farbige* as "Nicht-Weisser [nonwhite], in Amerika Neger or Mulatte.)"[57] As a result, Negro/colored *rather than*

Jewish heredity was labeled, understood, and investigated in racial terms. This is not to argue that antisemitism disappeared from West German life or that Jews and other "white" European minorities were not still perceived as distinct and different races by postwar West Germans. There is ample evidence that they were.[58] Rather, it is to argue that West German social policy and academic scholarship of the 1950s did not *authorize* defining those differences as *racial*. In this sense, postwar West German definitions of race paralleled those of the postwar United States. For in the United States over the course of the 1930s and 1940s, social scientists softened the differences among whites of European origin (including, in particular, Jews) to a cultural one and conceived of these groups in terms of "ethnicity." Race, as a concept, continued to be employed, but was reduced to the radically simplified terms of the black-white binary—or at its most articulated, the black-white-yellow triad—thus redrawing the lines of meaningful difference according to stereotypical phenotype.[59] There was, then, at least in the 1950s, a *confluence* of the broad forms of racial taxonomy in both West Germany and the United States.

From Biology to Psychology, from Jews to Blacks: Race à la America

This confluence of racial taxonomy between West Germany and its Cold War patron does not imply a wholesale "Americanization" of German racial ideologies and race relations after 1945. Rather, it resulted from the efforts of West Germans like those discussed above who worked quite consciously to Americanize the postwar German *problem* of race. In large measure this was because some would-be reformers looked to American social science to provide guidance on democratic approaches to race.

Alfons Simon's pedagogical booklet, *Maxi, unser Negerbub*, is a representative example of these efforts. A close reading of the text yields important clues about the particular ways West German advocates of racial liberalism sought to educate their compatriots on racial issues and wean them away from entrenched racial biases and practices. *Maxi* is structured as a brief Bildungsroman in which a middle-aged male teacher must confront his unexamined prejudices in order to do justice to the biracial child scheduled to join his class. He decides to visit Maxi's foster home before the school year begins. Our first acquaintance with the child takes place in the context of a respectable, orderly household dominated by Maxi's "cheerful" foster mother, who is lauded for having become a "real mother" to the boy due to her "healthy maternal instinct" and her deep concerns regarding the potential future "dangers" he faces.[60] The boy's home and family life are normalized, uncoupled from associations with prostitution, moral delinquency, national betrayal. We are encouraged to focus on the child, who is rendered German in the text—the embarrassingly possessive and patronizing "our" Maxi of the title—through a series of progressive domestications (a respectable mother, a tidy home, a weighted observation that he speaks the local dialect) which seek to reinterpret, rather than erase, racial difference.

The author is intent to showcase Maxi's positive personal qualities: he is good natured, generous, and displays a natural grace when he moves. The objective was clearly to make the boy likable and unthreatening, to evoke sympathy in the reader. Unfortunately, this was accomplished in inadvertently racist ways and with appeal to the usual litany of commonplace racial stereotype. It was not uncommon, for example, for black German children to be likened to house pets (with their "sweet, black, poodle hair-dos") or dubbed "chocolate princes" or "Moor-heads" (after the German confection); much was made of their physical agility, robust sportiness, musical talents, and rhythm.[61] In efforts to establish the children's "innocence" and untainted moral state, liberal commentators would remark that while they might be black on the outside, on the inside—where it counts—the children had a "white heart."[62]

Emphasis was placed on the here and now, and particularly the question of how to ensure the "normal development" of the children in order to make them socially "useful *Mitmenschen*," or "fellow" human beings, as they matured. In 1952, Alfons Simon reassured his readers that his subjects were "all still just children; we don't need to think too far into the future. What will happen to them later? Who are they going to marry? What sort of employment will they find among us? We should respond to such considerations that we are not yet able to answer these questions, especially in such uncertain times as ours when we can't see further than tomorrow. None of us knows what the following years will bring."[63] Thus Simon skirted the sensitive issue of a new cycle of interracial reproduction and appealed instead to thoughts of the common good and a future of frictionless *"Zusammenleben,"* or coexistence, for the sake of the reconstructing nation. "All prejudices," wrote Simon in the preface, "threaten the healthy development of the individual and society." If altruism was insufficient motivation, Simon suggested the personal benefits to be gained: "things will go better for your child," he counseled recently denazified German parents, "if he learns to live peacefully with others in this new democracy."[64]

In a departure from German tradition, but consistent with contemporary American practices, Simon psychologized the problem of racial prejudice. This meant that racism began to be understood as a virulent psychological malady that, when acted upon, had serious effects—both for the emotional health of its target and for society's well-being as a

whole.[65] If the psychological approach to racism was an American import, it was one of the few popular ones in the 1950s, precisely because
of its value in denationalizing the postwar German problem of race. In
other words, this explanation construed racism as a function, and disorder, of *human* rather than German psychology. Prejudice was universal-
ized as an ahistorical malady that plagues all people at all times, thereby
exorcising the specter of racially motivated murder during the Third
Reich as a specifically German social pathology. As the fictional teacher
of *Maxi* researches the problem of racisms, he finds to his relief: "a scientific explanation: how prejudice has always existed in the world, how it
typically arises, how it functions, what one can do about it. He likes the
fact that the many examples that make the book so readable are drawn
from outside of Germany. That others can also make mistakes can only
reassure us."[66]

When historical examples were offered, they were situated in the land
of Jim Crow. This symptomatic shift from the German to the American
experience is evident at the outset in the pamphlet *Maxi*, as the fictional
teacher reflects on race. His first association is with Jews, but rapidly his
thoughts settle on the "Negerfrage," "the Negro problem, " and the
American South as he recalls reading newspaper reports of yet another
"Negro lynching."[67] Thus the United States became inscribed as the leading site of racial problems, and racism was reformulated as a problem
common to modern Western democracies.[68]

One striking feature of this and similar texts of the period—including
the highly popular 1952 West German film *Toxi*, discussed in the following chapter—is that the journey toward racial enlightenment was consistently undertaken by a middle-aged middling-class male.[69] Initially reluctant to engage in a process of critical self-examination on the issue of
race and racial bigotry, our budding hero's professional commitment to
teaching gradually compels him to confront his unquestioned prejudice.
Significantly, his racial reeducation is not imposed by Allied policy but
is autodidactic. Once stimulated by awareness of a proximate social
problem, it springs from his curiosity about the nature of prejudice
and an inner conviction to rid himself of any inadvertent or unconscious
racialist response. It is, then, both self-imposed and self-prepossessed,
accomplished by means of a self-directed program of study, thoughtful
reflection, and critical analysis. Racial enlightenment and racial liberalism are represented not as consequences of military defeat and foreign
mandate—a forcible transplant from distant democratic shores—, but
as the homegrown accomplishment of a rational, moral, and sovereign
German (man).[70]

Upon learning that an interracial child will enter his classroom, for example, Herr Schmidt, the teacher in *Maxi*, reflects that "he had always

tried hard to be a good person and a good teacher, but he never had anything to do with these sorts of things. Mixed-blood children—the Negro problem—the race problem—never in his life did he have the occasion to engage with these in a serious way. The race problem—yes; but that had to do with the Jews." He proceeds to assert the sympathy he felt for "persecuted Jews from 1938 on" and that he considered their mass murder a horrible crime "when he learned of it after 1945." Although he admits to having felt some annoyance at the sight of Jewish blackmarketeers at the train station after the war, since he had no Jewish acquaintances he never felt compelled to engage personally with the problem of race until now.[71]

Herr Schmidt functions in the text as a German everyman: a decent nonpolitical person who denies overt complicity with the racial policies of the Third Reich and who, as a result, feels no need to assess his inner feelings and assumptions about race until it emerges as a rather unwelcome issue of professional responsibility. The character's ordinary qualities in an extraordinary age are intended to encourage identification among the readers and to reassure them that their good-faith involvement with the sensitive issue of race required no form of retrospective judgment: neither condemnation nor theories of "collective guilt" would be applied to them. Rather, the text exonerates German everymen for the crimes of the Third Reich and reassures them of their innate, if unexpressed, moral goodness. In attributing the race problem to inadequate introspection and social action, the story holds out the promise of atonement for the Jewish genocide if Everyman Schmidt can manage to make amends in the treatment of his postwar charge. Thus broadening the focus to the more general "race problem" permitted the displacement of Jewishness by blackness; past crimes by current concerns; and the issue of culpability by the practice of caregiving.

The rehabilitation of Germans via the German man was not, however, merely the stuff of fiction. At the 1952 World Brotherhood conference in Wiesbaden, Erich Lißner, editor of the prominent West German newspaper, *Frankfurter Rundschau*, was fêted as a "hero of humanity" for becoming adoptive father to Donatus, a black German child. In his remarks at the conference, Lißner's anecdotes chronicling Doni's integration into his white family emphasized less the personal relationship between adoptive father and son than the social implications and social utility of interracial fathering after National Socialism. Describing Doni's adoption as a "refutation" of past racial hatred, Lißner articulated the lofty principles underlying the decision: "We simply need to summon the courage to view these brown children as having equal rights as the white and to raise them accordingly. They will, one day, assume jobs and work among and with us. However, we cannot accept that someone will once again

This photo appeared facing the title page of *Maxi, Our Negro Lad*. Note the foregrounding of the black child and the staging of the photo, which suggests a cheerfully integrated classroom and signals the boy's German-ness through his traditional Bavarian dress. If the photo provoked, rather than persuaded, the viewer, the pamphlet at least reached its target audience. A very similar picture of Erich Lißner's adopted son Doni, sporting lederhosen and a white schoolmate at his side, appeared in *Ebony* in 1953. Courtesy of the Deutscher Koordinierungsrat der Gesellschaft für Christlich-Jüdische Zusammenarbeit. *Photo*: General Research Division, Schomburg Center for Research in Black Culture, New York Public Library, Astor, Lenox and Tilden Foundations.

come along and solve such a 'problem' through deportations, gas chambers, and other similar 'humane' means. It is a disgrace that time and again it is suggested that these children must be expelled to countries with mixed populations. Are we really completely incapable of living with others without prejudice?"[72]

At the conclusion of their 1952 conference in Wiesbaden, World Brotherhood/SCJC participants produced an ambitious list of resolutions to improve the condition and public reception of the children. To aid the "detoxification" [*Entgiftung*] of opinion regarding the children, conference participants advocated an extensive program of public and professional education, grounded in the methods of intergroup relations and based on up-to-date psychological theory and pedagogical practice. Specific suggestions included: the development of juvenile literature featuring the biographies of prominent Negroes of high achievement; professional training and workshops in racial sensitivity for youth workers and schoolteachers; school-sponsored parents' evenings to fight existing prejudices and win cooperation for racial tolerance; the co-operation of state culture ministers in racial education programs; the creation of a central information office for issues concerning *Mischlingskinder*, as well as a central fund to collect private German and American donations to aid the children. Conference participants also called for a nationwide information campaign by churches and religious organizations, adult education classes, newspapers, radio, and film to educate the public about the children and away from racist response. Toward the end of the list of resolutions came the stern reminder that the children enjoyed equality under the law and that care should be taken to avoid singling them out for special attention, lest they become "conscious of their difference." "It is inhumane and psychologically damaging," declared the resolution, "to treat the children as if they were specimens in a side-show [*Schaustücke*]."[73]

Liberalism's Lessons

In the early 1950s, West German Interior Ministry officials followed the recommendations of the Society for Christian-Jewish Cooperation/World Brotherhood and integrated schools. But truth be told, the small number of the black children entering West German schools would not have lent itself to racial segregation unless German officials were willing to mandate their residential schooling away from home—something that appears not to have been seriously contemplated. Nonetheless, officials continued to solicit and review data on the children, with the clear intention of monitoring anomalies in psychological, behavioral, moral, or social development.

In 1954–55, the federal Ministry of the Interior ordered states to collect detailed reports by local school and youth officials on noteworthy characteristics of school-aged *Mischlingskinder*. States were to document educators' impressions of the children's intellectual, moral, and religious development; whether the children exhibited special talents or dispositions

that distinguished them from white children; their academic performance at school, including any educational deficits that existed; and
whether problems of upbringing or socialization were present that could
hamper "integration into our social and civil order."[74]

Although white ethnic German refugee children from eastern Europe
entered West German schools in far greater numbers than black German
children, the federal Interior Ministry opted to have school and youth
officials investigate the character, abilities, and integration prospects of
only the latter—this despite the fact that white expellees and refugees
from the eastern reaches of the former Reich "accounted for more than
90%" of population growth in the Federal Republic in 1950s, and constituted nearly one-quarter of the West Germany's total population by the
end of the decade.[75] Clearly, then, the overriding concern was not to facilitate social integration. Rather, such selective study shows that official
anxieties regarding the social and somatic consequences of "race mixing"
persisted well into the postwar period.[76]

Reports submitted to the federal Ministry of the Interior ran the
gamut. A few teachers and school officials returned negative assessments
couched in bald racist stereotype or physical-anthropological descriptions of facial and physical features in the tradition of Fischer, Abel,
Kirchner, and Sieg. Most, however, submitted mixed reports that cited
average or weak academic performance while praising the children's
lively personalities or (no surprise here) physical prowess. A third group
of reports resolutely maintained that the children were no different from
white classmates and refused to countenance the racial problem implied
in the questionnaire. These, however, were in the minority.[77]

The school reports provide a glimpse into the social and emotional effects on the children of their prescribed racial difference. Testimony from
Berlin was particularly poignant. A report noted that one boy began to
display behavioral problems at school after working as an actor in the
production of a children's film *Ten Little Niggers* (*Zehn kleiner Negerlein*),
based on a well-known German children's rhyme.[78] Similarly, a five-year-
old girl refused to participate in the singing of "Zehn kleiner Negerlein" in her Berlin kindergarten. The enlightened author of the report
suggested that the problem was attributable not to any deficiency in the
children, "but rather that their [social] adjustment was made more difficult by the environment."

The same report chronicled children's deeply felt sense of damaged
self-worth and social isolation resulting from repeated exposure to hostile situations or unwanted negative attention:

> Seven-year-old Maureen lives in the household of her employed mother,
> who is very fond of her. . . . She is an average student, but has the ability

This special one-hundredth installment of the popular comic strip *Herbert* appeared in the 1952 Easter issue of the Munich-based magazine *Revue* and was timed to coincide with the entry of black children to German schools. In the cartoon, Herbert and his mother fetch a newly adopted little sister, who immediately becomes the object of curiosity among neighborhood children. In the bottom frame, Herbert stands at the open door and proclaims: "He's allowed to take a look. He gave us an Easter egg for it." The adopted sister, rendered as black stereotype, remained a fixture in the comic strip and a frequent butt of jokes. A later installment of the comic depicts the sudden appearance of her face scaring an attacking dog into retreat.

to achieve more. The mother has engaged a tutor for her. During the first lesson, in order to break the ice, the tutor suggested to Maureen that she pretend to be the teacher and that she would pretend to be Maureen, where-upon the child said to the tutor: "Maureen, you are ugly! You are a Misch-ling! I can't stand you." The child is also mistrustful. . . . Maureen recently, and for no apparent reason, hit a boy [at school]. When the teacher ques-tioned her about this, she explained: "But he whispered 'Negerkind' to me."

Nine-year-old Anita was raised in a children's home, [in which] she is neither rejected by the other children in her group nor assumes a special position due to her racial difference. Unfortunately, she is strongly con-scious of her race. In the home and in the classroom she shows no signs of suffering from it. However, outside of the home it has been observed that she self-consciously looks away when she encounters strangers. She has been heard to say, "I'm horrified by summer because I get so brown and everybody laughs at me." Her face often has a tormented look. . . .

[Seven-year-old] Leonhard was placed under the beneficial influence of a foster mother and foster father during his mother's employment and expe-rienced an upbringing in a complete family since the foster parents had their own adoptive daughter. Initially, when Leonhard was a small child, he was sometimes called "Neger" by neighborhood children due to his dif-ferent appearance. This could cause him to become excessively angry. He always answered with the same words: "I am not a nigger, I'm a German!"[79]

Having absorbed the pejorative meanings attributed to darker skin, Leonhard made his choice. The open question, of course, was whether the emerging racial liberalism in the Federal Republic, in conjunction with public education programs, would forge a postwar German culture in which blackness and German-ness could be perceived as something other than mutually exclusive, even antithetical, categories.[80]

•   •   •

The school reports returned on *Mischlingskinder*, while hardly homoge-neous, suggest that by middecade many West German school officials, teachers, and youth workers had begun to absorb and employ the basic language and lessons of the racial liberalism sponsored by the Society for Christian-Jewish Cooperation/World Brotherhood. One indication of this was a tendency, when identifying problems, to include a consider-ation of nurture as well as nature in assessing the children.

Postwar anthropologists, educators, and youth workers expanded a predominantly biological understanding of race to include attention to social factors. Initially more supplement than conceptual shift, the postwar emphasis on "the social" in identifying and investigating racial difference was fundamentally gendered and came at the expense of the children's mothers. In a self-conscious effort to renounce racial hierarchies, West German educators and youth workers, in their reports, tended to attribute any apparent moral, intellectual, or behavioral lapses detected in the children to their maternal source, rather than to black biological inheritance. Thus, German mothers of black children perceived as troubled, disruptive, or of below-average abilities would be faulted for their neglectful or overly indulgent mothering; running a dirty or disorderly household; being dimwitted, disreputable, or of weak moral character; or for having serial monogamous relationships with black American soldiers. In rejecting biological explanations of race and shifting the focus to social environment, psychology, and family relations, liberalizing West Germans followed the trends established by postwar American social science and tended to blame the mother.[81]

On the one hand, this gendered analysis continued—and continued to legitimate—interwar assessments of women who engaged in interracial sexual relations as immoral or asocial. And although, after 1945, such women would not be subjected to sterilization or worse, they could be tossed in reconstituted workhouses for wayward women in states like Bavaria and Hesse.[82] It may be true, as historian Gisela Bock has argued, that German women were "liberated from state antinatalism" in 1945 (or shortly thereafter, if one considers the state-supported abortions extended women alleging rape by foreign soldiers after defeat). But misogynist criticisms of women's social and sexual independence, and patriarchal attempts at women's social and sexual regulation, persisted both in society at large and in reconstituted social science and social policy after the war.[83]

However, the fact that West German social scientists learned from their American colleagues in revamping their understanding of race in the 1950s was significant, for American-style liberalism, like its German protégé, relied heavily on a gendered analysis. The psychosocial approach favored by American liberal thinkers from the 1930s through the 1960s invested women, *as mothers*, with the power to raise well-adjusted citizens. Social pathologies (including racism, crime, or inadequacies in economic, or other, performance) were understood to stem from problems of socialization and family dynamics, and therefore from maternal failure. What is more, such failures were perceived to present serious negative national consequences. As historian Ruth Feldstein has argued, American "representations of women as mothers developed in conjunction with debates about who was a healthy citizen and what was a healthy democracy."[84] A similar argument can be made for the postwar Federal Republic.

Gender conservatism, moreover, was a shared characteristic of the 1950s in the United States and West Germany and, as Feldstein has noted, its "symbolic significance was considerable." "It is perhaps *because* traditional gender roles did not capture the varied experiences and attitudes of Americans that gender conservatism assumed significance as an ideological norm, and stood in for a collective dream of social harmony."[85] For West Germans, part of the "collective dream of social harmony" after 1945 involved reconstituting a viable German state and society while fulfilling the Allied mandate to denazify and democratize. As in the United States, racial liberalism and gender conservatism worked together to produce a new postwar understanding of nation.[86]

In invoking Feldstein's arguments for the German context, I do not mean to suggest that the national experiences and discourses of race and gender were identical in the postwar United States and Germany, or that political or cultural contexts out of which racial liberalism emerged in each country were more similar than not. I am merely suggesting that there was an important dialogue between postwar American and West German liberalism that appears to have resulted in a transfer of cultural logic. This is not to say that the practice and rhetoric of "blaming the mother" was not evident in Germany prior to 1945. It certainly was, as this and previous chapters have shown. However, the attention devoted to women as mothers in postwar German social science cannot be understood as a simple continuation of pre-1945 eugenic and racialist commitments. Rather, I am suggesting that it represents both departures from and reformulations of earlier explanations. Biological racism was rejected, even if its assumptions were not thoroughly excised in *either* postwar nation's liberal thought. Gradually, as American social science was digested and deployed in West Germany, the focus on women expanded from an obsessive interest in the biology of interracial reproduction to include the sociopsychology of mothering. In this way, West German studies of race were both Americanized *and* retained a "gender conservative" logic.

Chapter Four

RECONSTRUCTION IN BLACK AND WHITE: THE *TOXI* FILMS

> If, from their earliest days of youth, these children are sub-
> jected to prejudice and viewed as foreigners and aliens, how
> can they later fit into a nation (even one in which they were
> born) which has never provided them a home [*Heimat*]?
>
> —Claire Guthmann, World Brotherhood, 1952

> I would like so much to go home
> To see my homeland [*Heimat*] once again
> I can't find my way on my own
> Who will love me and take me along?
>
> —Toxi's theme song[1]

SOMETIME in 1951, five-year-old Elfriede Fiegert traveled with her mother to Munich from their Bavarian village of Markt Schwaben to au-dition for a film. Elfie had no acting experience, but her foster mother had read in the newspaper that talent scouts were seeking "mulatto chil-dren" for a new production and was determined to have her daughter considered for a part. In Munich, the film's well-known director, Robert A. Stemmle, had already auditioned four hundred children for the title character and was despairing about having not yet found "the one"— until, that is, the fateful day a "small brown thing" in a hand-stitched dirndl and alpine hat burst into his office. "My name is Elfie," said the girl in the most proper German. "No, you are *Toxi*," responded Stemmle and immediately cast her in the role of her life.[2] The following year, Ger-man moviegoers flocked to the fictional story of an abandoned black oc-cupation child, making *Toxi* a box-office hit and Elfie Fiegert a star.[3]

The story of Elfie's discovery is, of course, the stuff of movie publicity. Nonetheless, Stemmle's pronouncement to Elfie proved portentous. The marketing campaign for the film consistently submerged the identity of the historical Elfie in her fictional counterpart and played up the parallels between Elfie's and her character's biographies. Elfie's father, like Toxi's, was an African American soldier. While he initially supported the child, he was soon ordered back to the United States and disappeared from her life. Her birth mother, again like Toxi's, was similarly out of the picture, having placed the child in a home. Press reports insisted on treating Elfie's early days in an orphanage as representative of the experience of "almost all" black German children: "parentless, homeless." However, readers were reassured, Elfie was exceptional in having found a happy ending. She was adopted by the Fiegerts, former cinema owners and German refugees from Silesia, whose own two-year-old daughter died after their arduous flight west from Soviet troops. Elfie's biography—at least as packaged for public consumption—neatly interpreted the traumatic past through the lens of the Cold War, casting Soviets as eternal enemy and Americans as allies. Moreover, by merging the fates of two groups produced by the war—ethnic German expellees from the east and black occupation children—the film's publicity appeared to advocate, and celebrate, the principle of social integration in fledgling West Germany.[4]

Toxi was notable on a number of counts. It was the first feature-length film to explore the subject of black occupation children in postwar Germany. Released to coincide with the start of the school year for the oldest of the postwar *Mischlingskinder*, the film had the explicit purpose of cultivating, in addition to profit, "social understanding" for the children as they made the difficult transition from the privacy of home to public school.[5] What is more, it was one of the few postwar films—and to my knowledge the only one in the early 1950s—to explicitly thematize the *"Rassenproblem"* in Germany and call it by its name.[6] The sentimental story, tearjerker finale, and neat resolution of the postwar problem of race made it a runaway commercial success, which resulted in overnight celebrity and a brief acting career for Elfriede Fiegert, who would reprise the role of a black occupation child in the 1955 West German film *Der dunkle Stern* (The dark star).

Toxi yields insight into some precise ways that "race" was visualized and narrated in German film culture after 1945. Because it was a smash hit among West German moviegoers, the film played a crucial role in establishing a liberal discourse of race in postwar Germany and popularizing it for the public at large. While the film obliquely acknowledged a national legacy of lethal antisemitism, it oriented the viewer toward the German future by articulating the revised taxonomy of race, discussed in the previous chapter, that was beholden to the more recent social relations accompanying the American occupation of Germany and based upon a black-white binary more familiar to American experience. This chapter examines *Toxi*'s narrative strategies and cinematic "sequels" in some detail to explore the centrality of race to both the reconstitution of

Actress Elfriede Fiegert signing autographs in a publicity appearance for
the 1955 film, *Der Dunkle Stern* (The dark star). Courtesy of Filmmuseum Berlin-Stiftung Deutsche Kinemathek.

postwar gender norms and German mythologies of national belonging.
Attention to actress Elfie Fiegert's brief career offers context and counter-
point to the fictional films, and permits insight into the cultural contours
and personal costs of racial ideology in Adenauer's Germany.

Toxi's Liberal Vision

Toxi opens in the evening with a street shot of a handsome single-family
home. The main action is the return from work of Dr. Theodor Jenrich at
the end of the day. Entering the home, he finds the household in the
throes of hectic preparations for a birthday celebration for Grandma
Rose, Theodor's mother-in-law. It quickly unfolds that Theodor, his wife,

and two young daughters share the house with Theodor's parents-in-law, Grandfather and Grandmother Rose and their grown daughter, Herta. This German home, it seems, has two patriarchs, and much of the domestic drama of the film centers on the battle between their diverging views on race and social responsibility.

This battle is first unleashed and articulated when Toxi, a black German child, arrives unexpectedly on the doorstep of the white German family. Toxi's African American father is absent, having returned to the United States, and her mother is inexplicably dead, which leaves only an ailing maternal grandmother who is unable to care for the child and deposits her at the door of the middle-class home. Like the pedagogical pamphlet, *Maxi*, this film severed the fate of the child from the "fall" of the mother, shifting the focus away from the latter's sexual and racial transgressions. Toxi is unburdened from the taint of past national traumas, both military and moral. References to defeat and occupation are elided since the sexually transgressive mother has mercifully disappeared. As a result, the racial problem was construed less as persistent than presentist and purged of reference to the double pasts of National Socialism and the later loss of national sovereignty. Viewers were encouraged to focus on the plight of the child, rather than the circumstances of conception.

Toxi's arrival disrupts Grandma Rose's birthday party, causing consternation and establishing the central conflict in a dramatic drawing-room scene that will be played out in the film. When Theodor and Grandpa discover a suitcase left outside the house with Toxi's belongings, the assembled party concludes that they are confronted with a case of child abandonment and call the police. In the meantime, Herta and her beau, Robert, tend to Toxi and feed her leftover dinner after which the child is questioned by the police. As the police officer prepares to depart without Toxi, Theodor unsuccessfully demands he take the child with him. Theodor's protest initiates an exchange that exposes the adult characters' racial attitudes and sketches the topography of the possible dramatic solutions to the problem of race that the film invokes.

As Toxi is led off to bed by Grandma Rose, Theodor expresses his disapproval of Toxi's overnight stay.

> *Grandpa Rose*: You'd rather we put her out on the street, suitcase and all?
> *Theodor*: If you want the child to stay in the house tonight, fine, it's your house. . . . But I forbid her to be with my children in the morning.

Herta's fiancé, Robert, objects to Theodor's attitude, but Theodor is adamant and counters that the child could have a communicable disease. When a guest who is a doctor leaves the room to examine the Toxi,

Theodor continues, "But even if the child is healthy, I don't want her with our children." As Robert criticizes Theodor's focus on skin color, and Grandpa Rose agrees, Theodor gets to the heart of the matter:

Theodor: I can't speak to you about this problem. This *Negerkind* . . .

Robert: . . . is also just a person.

Theodor: Right, but nevertheless there are differences

Robert: I don't see any differences, perhaps because I'm not a philistine [*Spiessbürger*].

Grandpa: Don't make such a big deal of this. I don't see any problem either. One child more in the family is only a problem if there is no food. Otherwise there is no problem.

Theodor: I mean the race problem.

(*Silence, exchange of meaningful looks. Closeup shots of Theodor and Grandpa together in one frame, Herta and Robert in another, then back to Theodor and Grandpa.*)

Grandpa responds: "Of course, that still exists. But I think we've learned to see with different eyes." (*Theodor's wife tries to interject, but is cut off.*)

Theodore: You know that our opinions differ on certain points.

Grandpa: Yes, I know and I don't take offense at you for it. But you must break the habit of approaching all people and things with prejudice.

Herta: You have your opinion and we have ours, as every person does. But you have to recognize that the child can't be blamed; such a child is innocent.

Male guest: In any case, the child will leave the house tomorrow

Guest's wife: No, tomorrow is Sunday!

Male guest: Ok, then the day after.

Guest's wife: I know what Herr Doktor Jenrich means. It's a child of shame.

Male guest: Anna! Please be quiet.

(*Closeup of Theodor and Grandpa.*)

Theodor: You spoke of prejudice. I find it a matter of sensibility [*Gefühls-sachen*].

Grandpa: Sensibility!? A small black child comes to us, helpless. Who knows what has been done to the child. And your first emotion is "racial difference"! Now listen . . .

Robert: Herr Doktor, I've only just met you today, but . . .

Herta: Please be quiet!

Robert: If I'm not permitted to speak I'd rather leave. (*Leaves, slamming the door*).

Grandpa: It appears he wasn't properly raised.

Robert returns: I'm sorry, the door slipped. (*Leaves again, this time the front door slams off camera. Herta starts to exit room*).

Grandpa: Please stay here, Herta. Don't run after him.

Herta: But I may be allowed to go upstairs. Excuse me. (*Camera follows Herta into front hall, where Doctor emerges, pronouncing Toxi healthy. Guests depart.*)

As this scene illustrates, and the film bears out, the family's response to Toxi and her black skin fractures along generational lines. She is treated sympathetically by the family's young adults, Herta and her fiancé Robert. While Herta's and Robert's formative years technically wouldn't have postdated the Third Reich (they appear to be in their early twenties in the film), they—along with Theodor's younger daughters, who later befriend Toxi—are meant to represent the new postwar generation, graced by late birth and therefore unmarred by the racist ideology of the Nazi past. Grandpa Rose, in contrast, is clearly of a generation whose coming of age predated the Third Reich. This grace of early birth, the film seems to suggest, inoculated him against the disease of racism that ravaged his son-in-law's generation, freeing him to see in Toxi "only a child" and not a problem. Thus in this scene, the film defines the postwar *Rassenproblem* as Theodor's inability to dispense with racial classifications and hierarchies when encountering individuals or social situations. Grandpa, in effect, articulates the problem by suggesting that, rather than "learn to see with new eyes," Theodor continues in the habit of confronting the world through the prejudices he carries with him like so much outdated baggage. It is precisely this act of locating the problem of race in the skewed perspective of the *white* beholder, rather than the body, culture, or intellect of the black individual, that constitutes the liberal kernel of this film's own ideology of race.

Nonetheless, there are some notable amendments to this liberalizing discourse of race in the film. As noted above, the film identifies the residue of racist perspective and practice as adhering most stubbornly to the middle-aged ranks that came of political age under Hitler. While the film avoids explicitly demonizing Theodor as a Nazi holdover—opting instead for a softer, less controversial approach to characterization to avoid alienating its postwar German viewers—the generational topography produced by the film anchors racist ideology firmly and exclusively in the Nazi past (rather than a longer German history) and in the belief system of its adult generation (rather than Germans in general). The problem is thereby minimized and made manageable: broad-minded Germans need only help reeducate the tainted cohort of the Nazi years.

If *Toxi* is unambiguously liberal in the way it articulates the problem of race early in the film, this dramatic scene of articulation also represents the culmination of the film's liberal perspective. In fact, the liberal perspective is unsettled—and the dialogue on race terminated—as the scene breaks down due to Robert's impassioned exit, quickly followed by Herta and the rest of the group. This scene and its disruption point to the perceived dangers of race in postwar Germany, for it indicates Germans' inability to confront the issue of racial prejudice—even within that most intimate social grouping, the family—without the threat of social dissolution. This becomes clear as we move from a consideration of the problem posed to solutions proposed by the film, for it is here that we run smack into the limits of postwar racial liberalism in 1950s West Germany.

Before considering the full range of the film's solutions for *Toxi*, I would like to consider what at first seems the likely solution, but is quickly betrayed as a fleeting utopian moment in the film.[7] Toxi has been taken to stay in an orphanage (*Kinderheim*) following the weekend she made her appearance at the Rose/Jenrich home. To fulfill his promise to her, Grandpa Rose arrives at the *Kinderheim* for a visit, where he sees a clean, orderly home for mostly black (and a sprinkling of white) German children. As Toxi greets Grandpa and leads him into the room, the children begin to sing in unison: "I would like so much to go home / To see my homeland once again / I can't find my way on my own / Who will love me and take me along?" This song of homelessness—which characterized the representative fate of Afro-German children as unloved *Heim-kinder*—is reprised throughout the movie at critical points and comes to serve as Toxi's theme song.

As Grandpa Rose's visit comes to an end, Toxi is permitted to accompany him to the outside gate. Grandpa, clearly moved by the sight of the roomful of unwanted children and by concern for Toxi, uncomfortably comments on the time and begins to say goodbye to her. But then he says, "Wait, I'll bring you back," takes Toxi's hand, and proceeds to walk her back in the direction of the *Kinderheim*. This begins the filmic moment (lasting less than 30 seconds) of promise and possibility. The camera pulls in for a close-up of Grandpa's face as they walk, which observes Toxi with affection and enjoyment; a reverse shot shows her smiling back at him, innocent and undemanding. Again, reverse shot to Grandpa, and back to Toxi. It is during these brief fleeting seconds that Toxi and Grandpa interact as individuals outside of a racialized perspective, as individuals who share a human connection, a compatibility that renders race irrelevant. Within a few minutes, we realize that he had decided not to "bring her back" to the children's home, but to his family's home. Racial integration—even in that most intimate sphere of the family—appears imminent.

However, this moment is over just after it begins, and the scene concludes with the camera settling on a less fortunate black German girl, nose pressed against the window glass, apparently observing the happy scene from inside the *Kinderheim*. This concluding shot reminds us of the

After Grandpa Rose rescues Toxi from the children's home,
the camera settles on a girl left behind, visually coding black German
children as abandoned and unwanted. Courtesy of Filmmuseum
Berlin-Stiftung Deutsche Kinemathek.

children left behind, establishing the abandoned anonymous child as
norm and Toxi, as the object of Grandpa's attention, as a rare exception.
Not incidentally, this shot of the tragic abandoned child also begins to
transform the race problem within the film. It is no longer a narrow issue
of white racism but has been broadened to include the social alienation
and loneliness experienced by forsaken, institutionalized children. One
might suppose that attention to the plight of black German children
might have a salubrious social effect, but there is little evidence that that
was the case. Rather, it diffused (one is tempted to write *de*fused) the
issue of white responsibility, since the camera lens shifts focus from the
social fact of white racism to that of the putatively unwanted black children yearning in vain for love, family, and home in the Federal Republic.[8]
Later in the action, moreover, the film closes off the possibility of
Grandpa becoming the solution for Toxi and children like her. The utopian moment of mutual enjoyment gets subverted, as we shall see.

The second solution proposed by the film is—predictably enough, following the generational analysis of the film—adoption by the young couple, Robert and Herta. In reaction to Theodor's continued insistence that
Toxi leave his home, Robert and Herta decide to marry quickly and raise

the child. This decision follows an earlier scene in which Herta and Toxi visit Robert at his studio and Robert photographs the child after handing her a chocolate bar to nibble. When Herta asks what he's doing, Robert, who is in advertising, answers simply "poster." The scene in which Robert and Herta agree to care for Toxi opens with a shot of the advertising poster he has made featuring a coal-black caricature of a girl with white saucer-shaped eyes and protruding lips. Robert clearly required no photo of Toxi to draw this image which, rather than betray a likeness of the child, draws liberally on familiar tropes of racist black stereotype. He marvels at his work, declaring that the company "will have to reorganize production around it." In fact, shots of the poster and his response to it serve to frame the short scene in which the couple decide to adopt the child. After appearing to admire the poster, Herta leaves rather abruptly following Robert's prideful display. As the camera follows them to the door, the poster of Toxi moves out of the frame and the backdrop to the action is dominated by another advertising poster of a snowy-white sheep inscribed with the word "Dura-wool" (*Durawolle*). The camera work is subtle, but in establishing Robert's representational equivalence of black child and white sheep, can be taken as critical commentary on his readiness to exploit the child and exaggerate her "difference" for commercial gain. The poster, in effect, allows us to see Toxi through Robert's professional eye, which reduces the child to racist caricature.

As Herta moves toward the door to leave, and the scene concludes, the couple's embrace is filmed through a divider in the room that resembles a wire fence. Both the "Dura-wool" poster and the fencing visually suggest the inability of even this younger generation to break out of the constraints of enduring cultural bias since Robert—at some less than conscious level—appears as conditioned by the same careerist ambitions as Theodor and is willing to resort to racial stereotype to realize them. This scene, in fact, is the first and last in which Robert and Herta are proposed as surrogate parents to Toxi. The film abandons the theme of their marriage and adoption altogether although they continue to appear as a couple. Thus solution number two is quietly killed as an option.

The third possible solution the film proposes revolves around Theodor's character. Throughout much of the film, Theodor protests Toxi's presence as an economic burden and epidemiological hazard, prohibiting his young daughters from playing with her. That command is quickly subverted by the curious girls, but he continues to devote his energies to having Toxi removed from the family home when he's not busy pursuing business investments. The dramatic culmination comes when Grandpa suffers a heart attack after a heated showdown with Theodor, which allows Theodor the opportunity to act. Early the next morning, while the household sleeps, Theodor awakens Toxi and

Robert proudly displays his advertising poster of Toxi to Herta.
Courtesy of Filmmuseum Berlin-Stiftung Deutsche Kinemathek.

readies her for a drive to the orphanage. On the way, however, his car
breaks down. While the car is repaired, the two become better acquainted
over breakfast. In a comedy of errors, Toxi gets lost. Theodor gets
worried, searches frantically for the child, and in the process gains a
healthy dose of paternal and social responsibility. Following a telephone
lead, Theodor and the police rescue the hapless Toxi just before she is
spirited away in a gypsy caravan by a disreputable family of street performers who have realized her economic value as curiosity to their panhandling. The rescue scene concludes with a medium close-up of a re-
lieved Theodor warmly hugging a grateful Toxi, as an instrumental
reprise of Toxi's theme song swells on the soundtrack. Thus Theodor's
conversion story and Toxi's search for home appear to reach a happy,
shared conclusion.

Blood is Thicker than Good Intentions: The Failure of Integration

In the film's narrative, the German father is successfully weaned from
his recidivist racial prejudices of yesteryear and Toxi finds herself in the
embrace of white father and family. However, the filmmakers do not
leave it at that. One of the most striking things about the film is that it

Theodor and Toxi en route to the orphanage. In a last-minute change of plans, Theodor and Toxi stop for breakfast. When they get separated, Theodor gains a sense of paternal responsibility for the child. Courtesy of Filmmuseum Berlin-Stiftung Deutsche Kinemathek.

refuses to end on the high celebratory note of this first, transformative ending. Rather, the first ending turns out to be a false one, and the drama continues. Toxi is returned to the family home and readily included in the family's preparations for the Christmas holidays. The long final scene that concludes the film begins with the apparent effacement of race as Theodor's white birth child plays one King of the Magi in blackface in the family Christmas drama, while Toxi performs in whiteface. Yet rather than undermine the significance of race and the salience of the color line, the painted faces initiate a scene that reasserts both (a point reinforced by the fact that the filmmakers felt the need to darken Elfie's light brown skin with makeup during the filming of the movie so it would not "appear too light"), vigorously reestablishing racial boundaries and race-based definitions of German identity.[9]

In the second—and final—happy ending, Toxi's African American father arrives unexpectedly at the family's door that Christmas eve to collect his child and take her "home" to the United States. This over-determined sentimental finale was foreshadowed in the Christmas drama, in which Toxi, while performing as a King of the Magi, abruptly steps out of character to reprise her theme song. The camera moves in

The children's Christmas procession at the Rose-Jenrich
home. Toxi plays in whiteface on the right, while her white
foster sister appears in blackface on the left. Courtesy of
Filmmuseum Berlin-Stiftung Deutsche Kinemathek.

for a tight close-up of Toxi, establishing a psychological moment that betrays her ongoing yearning for a home and sense of belonging that she
has not yet found. Within minutes that search is over, and the film concludes with Toxi's introduction to her African American father. The last
sequence of shots, in which the camera pulls in for increasingly tighter
close-ups of the reunion and filial embrace, visually disengages the pair
from the German domestic scene and releases a carefully choreographed
crescendo of emotion that anticipates—and justifies—Toxi's imminent
emigration. As a result, the German family, and German identity, is

healed first through inclusion of the racialized other, then restored to whiteness by her *elective* exit.

Promotional literature for the film speculated that its tug on the audience's heartstrings would result in a sizable increase in adoptions for black German children, who were otherwise markedly shunned by most prospective adoptive parents in West Germany.[10] Such adoptions did not, in fact, increase. Rather, the film had the opposite effect: of facilely encouraging among its German viewers fantasies of *repatriation* as a solution to the problem of what to do with the living "legacies of the occupation." Well into the 1950s, in fact, a notable number of youth and social workers, educators, and state and federal officials continued to argue for the need to provide black German children good educations and solid job training so they would have the option, upon attaining majority, of emigrating to the "land of their fathers."[11]

Toxi's finale reveals that the film all along had been advocating the principle of tolerance over integration. Moreover, the film appears to imply that racial integration would have destructive social and psychological consequences for white family and black child alike. This is dramatized toward the end of the movie in a confrontation between Theodor and Grandpa, two scenes before Theodor loses Toxi on the drive to the *Kinderheim*. In the scene, Theodor again demands that Toxi be removed from the house, but this time threatens that if she is not, he and his family will leave instead. The threat triggers a violent reaction from Grandpa, who condemns Theodor's "heartless principles" and declares that he never wants to see his son-in-law and daughter again. With this, Grandpa appears to have a heart attack and collapses. While Grandma rushes to his aid, Theodor mutters to his wife that Grandpa's "love for this exotic [*fremdartigen*] child is not normal." After Grandpa is seen by the doctor and his condition stabilizes, Grandma Rose, who has been sympathetic to Toxi all along, tells Grandpa that he "cannot allow his grandchildren to leave the house on Toxi's account." Strikingly, neither Grandpa nor the film argue with this. Delivered by Grandma with calm demeanor, her counsel is treated as common sense and indisputable assertion. It is precisely this "common sense" response that begins to defuse the ideological rift between Grandpa and Theodor and shift the terms of the conflict. For Grandma's response implicitly questions whether Grandpa has the right to assert equivalence between Toxi and his own white grandchildren; whether Grandpa is right to stubbornly elevate Toxi and the principle of racial integration over their own progeny and loyalty to bloodline. Confronted in this manner, and assured by the doctor that Toxi will thrive in the healthy, stable environment of the *Kinderheim*, Grandpa immediately relents and agrees to have Toxi returned there. But do it quickly, he orders: "I can't look her in the face."

Toxi's American father, who appears unexpectedly on Christmas eve, is greeted by family members. Grandpa Rose is in foreground at left; Toxi's ailing grandmother (wearing eyeglasses) and Grandma Rose are beside him. Theodor and his wife occupy the background. Toward the end of the scene, it is Theodor who physically hands Toxi over to her biological father. Courtesy of Filmmuseum Berlin-Stiftung Deutsche Kinemathek.

Thus commitment to intact family trumps commitment to intact principle. And so Theodor wins the battle (if only to be converted from his most overtly racist ways a bit later in the film), and the scene ends without seriously challenging the reasonableness or racial assumptions of Theodor's demand.

In fact, the film establishes a symmetry that works to reinforce and ultimately reify the black-white binary, since it insists that the pull of race is as strong among black as among white characters. Despite Toxi's being welcomed into the family at the end, we hear a reprise of her theme song "Ich möchte so gern nach Hause geh'n / Die Heimat möchte ich wiederseh'n" at the very moment her father enters the family home. This refrain is intended to serve as a window into her emotional and psychological state, to signal a condition of incompleteness. Heredity and belonging is envisioned as inherently racialized—after all, Toxi's devoted maternal grandmother is never entertained as a possible solution for Toxi's placement, even after the old woman recovers—and racial segregation is depicted as unconscious *natural* mandate.[12]

Toxi's Plight

"I guess that's the dream most of us black children had," commented a Black German woman I know after she viewed the film.

Thus far, my discussion has focused on the way the film's treatment of the *Rassenproblem* helped construct a normative national identity predicated on whiteness in postwar West Germany. Yet my friend's comment indicates that certain aspects of the film resonated with her experiences and fantasies growing up in the Federal Republic of the 1950s.[13] Initially I was surprised by her response, perhaps because my analysis of the film focused so single-mindedly on deciphering the racial ideology it articulated for the white German audiences it addressed. My friend, however, viewed the film in terms of its "accuracy"—judging it by how well it conformed to, or diverged from, her personal experiences and social treatment. In fact, the film cultivates an aura of sociological accuracy in examining the plight of the black German child, in order to make its case for both racial tolerance but also, ultimately, for segregation through expatriation. And it does this precisely in the ways it chronicles and dramatizes Toxi's fate—and by extension, that of every black German child of the era—as one of abandonment, social isolation and marginalization, and cultural stereotyping.[14]

Toxi is deposited on the doorstep of the Rose/Jenrich home by her grandmother early in the film. Aside from a couple of shots of child and grandmother outside the home, which convey little about Toxi or her emotional state (except to establish the characters' liminal qualities in terms of race and class), the film introduces meager biographical details of the child only during interrogations by the white police officer and family members. Within the film, neither the child nor her plight exist apart from them. Any psychological or emotional depth she has as a character is revealed in interaction with white family members or white society. The film accords her little independent subjectivity.

Rather, the character Toxi functions as a kind of cipher onto which white Germans project their racial attitudes and fears. The social analysis of the film, in fact, is driven by white concerns regarding the implications of racial difference for German society. Displaced from their white source to Toxi's fate, potential perils are dramatized as targeting the well-being of the black child rather than white society. So, for example, while Toxi is depicted as receiving the compassion and concern of most family members in the Rose/Jenrich household, barring Theodor and perhaps his wife (who is interrupted as she tries to speak her mind on the issue), Toxi's brief forays into public at the beginning of the film show the opposite: hostile glances, contempt from the friends of Jenrich daughters, treatment as a curiosity. The film suggests that while black German children may be able to find the necessary *"Nestwärme"* in the private sphere of home, their experience in public is fraught with dangers. But even here, the film's depiction of home is ambivalent and ultimately problematic for Toxi—for the child is bounced between an ailing white grandmother who cannot care for her, a home inhabited by a surrogate white family rift by conflict over her, and an institutional home peopled by abandoned children like herself. None, then, are presented as optimal solutions or as places where Toxi unambiguously *belongs*.[15]

Although *Toxi* is fundamentally a domestic drama, with most of the film's action occurring within the confines of the family home, there is one noteworthy scene in which Toxi wanders the city alone after being separated from Theodor. Intercut with shots of Theodor's frantic search, this sequence provides hints about the dangers confronting Toxi, which are not, for the most part, immediate but incipient. In her public wanderings, Toxi scarcely attracts racist remarks—except when a man in a clearly disreputable part of town dubs her a "little black beast"—but she hardly attracts social interaction either. We see her nose pressed against store windows: the first shot shows her hungering for food. In a second shot, a night scene, she inspects the showcase of a lingerie store, with an interior camera position looking out through the window at her. Toxi is shown peering in, occupying barely a quarter of the frame to the far left, while two pairs of white opaque mannequin legs displaying women's stockings dominate the rest of the frame and tower over Toxi. Her placement at the edge of the frame, with the window acting as a barrier cutting her off from the symbols of white female sexuality, is telling. It depicts her as an observer—suggesting her outsider status—along with the unattainability of German norms of femininity, desirability, and reproduction, which are coded as exclusively white. That shot fades to a tilted-angle shot of Toxi on some stairs, indicating her dislocation. We hear the sounds of a toy piano, and she's drawn to its player, a boy panhandling. A gathering crowd of white adults assume Toxi is part of the show and readily hand her loose change. When the boy senses the police, he folds up his piano and runs with Toxi back to his caravan home and unsavory parents. As they register Toxi's commercial value as curiosity—their son has brought home more money than usual, which he attributes to Toxi's presence—they resolve, without consulting the girl, to take her with them when they depart later that night, thus initiating the rescue scene with Theodor and the police.

In sum, this extended scene indicates that the filmmakers could imagine only a future of social isolation, commercial exploitation, and economic marginality for Toxi and children like her. In the lingerie window shot, the film obliquely raises the question of what would happen when

Toxi on her own in the city as night falls. The camera position
of this studio shot differs from the footage that appeared in the film,
which emphasized her outsider status and enhanced the whiteness of the
hosiery on the mannequin legs. Courtesy of Filmmuseum Berlin-Stiftung
Deutsche Kinemathek.

Toxi reaches sexual maturity. The panhandling scene and attempted ab-
duction, along with Robert's earlier advertising poster of Toxi's stereotyped caricature, suggest that she would always be treated as an exotic
object of curiosity, that exploitation was inevitable. It also, however, signals her anticipated social and economic status in West Germany if left
to her own devices: not the lofty ranks of the respectable bourgeoisie that
Theodor and family inhabited, but the more lowly ranks of "gypsy"
street performers or ailing indigent grandmothers.

This cultural conceit, which preached racial tolerance but insisted on
maintaining racial difference and gauging relative worth, was pervasive
in the liberalizing discourse of 1950s West Germany and appears to
account for the alignment of *Toxi*'s fictional ending and my friend's
desire to be united with her unknown father. As it was not culturally
permissible for her to be classified according to her white maternity, her
social experience taught her not to self-identify that way. Rather, she
fantasized about embracing her black paternity in order to escape the
subordinate social status assigned her as racialized other. The desire may

Toxi greets and embraces her biological father. During the scene, Toxi self-consciously wipes at the white face-makeup on her cheek, commenting "This comes off." Courtesy of Filmmuseum Berlin-Stiftung Deutsche Kinemathek.

have been motivated in part by genealogical pull, but it was certainly also a self-preserving strategy to foster a personal sense of dignity and worth by shaking off a destructive, socially ascribed identity of immutable difference.

Toxi's Trajectories

Although *Toxi* is a highly ambivalent text that forsakes the principle of racial integration in favor of racial tolerance—and ultimately exhibits more concern about rehabilitating the German patriarchal family through the maintenance of racial boundaries—it nonetheless represented a banner moment in the cultural expression of postwar racial liberalism in West German popular cinema of the 1950s. Plainly stated, it was downhill from here. This becomes evident when one examines the next film Elfie Fiegert appeared in, *Der dunkle Stern* (The dark star), released in 1955.[16]

Der dunkle Stern has been dubbed inaccurately a "sequel" to *Toxi* in the film's promotional materials and press reviews from the 1950s (and by an archivist at the federal film archive in Berlin when I was doing research there a while back). The film, however, is not a sequel in any meaningful sense of the word. Although its script, like *Toxi*'s, was authored by Maria Osten-Sacken, and both films featured Elfriede Fiegert in the role of a black occupation child, there was no carryover of storyline or characters. Any continuity between the films has to do with the ways the second film selectively amplified some of the themes of the first within its new fictional constellation. And this selective amplification resulted in a retreat from the expressly liberal commitments of its predecessor. A reading of *Der dunkle Stern* reveals a noticeable narrowing of the definition of tolerance; a marked unwillingness even to entertain the possibility of racial integration, if only for most of the duration of the film as *Toxi* had; and an overwhelming obsession—from the film's very beginning—both to locate a suitable place for the black German child outside the white German nation and to reconcile the child intellectually and emotionally to the wisdom, and indeed compassion, of this choice.[17]

The film opens in an "idyllic village" in the mountains of Upper Bavaria. Moni, the black German child played by Elfie Fiegert, lives in a small cottage with her foster mother, Frau Lechner, loves rural life, skis to school in winter, and is well-regarded by the villagers, none of whom remind her of the "the blemish of her heredity [*Makel der Herkunft*]."[18] One day in school, Moni's teacher, Fräulein Rieger, asks the children what they want to be when they grow up. Few of the children have well-formed answers, but Moni replies with passion, "I'd like to have a farm [*Hof*]! I'd like to be a peasant-farmer [*Bäuerin*]!" The children quickly taunt her, "A black peasant! . . . Even the chickens would laugh! There's no such thing!"[19]

Moni's aspirations, and not the other children's mockery of them, stimulate Fräulein Rieger to take action on Moni's behalf. Convinced that Moni's dreams cannot be realized, Fräulein Rieger consults the village veterinarian, who puts her in touch with an agent for the circus where he once worked. In short order, the Italian circus artist Casseno shows up at the village to collect Moni, who will live and work with him and his family. Frau Lechner agrees to the plan since she has been notified that she will lose her rental cottage soon and cannot continue to care for the child. Moni, meanwhile, is told that the arrangement is temporary and embarks on the adventure, but quickly develops a case of homesickness for the Bavarian mountains. Once at the circus, she is readily befriended by the circus performers. She helps a traumatized young woman, who has witnessed her mother's fatal fall from the ropes, get over her fear of the trapeze. She becomes surrogate sibling and caretaker to a blind orphaned boy-clown, and after a stint serving as human target for Casseno's knife-throwing, ultimately discovers her own stereotypical "natural talent" as clown and trapeze artist, as well as her popularity with audiences. By the end of the film, as the circus director announces that they'll be embarking on an international tour through South America and after a brief reunion with Fräulein Rieger, Moni finally surrenders her dream of returning to her mountain village and accepts the circus as her new *Heimat*.

The film's treatment of racial difference is so outrageous by our contemporary standards that it begs the question of how this was justified and rendered acceptable within the context of the film's fictional space. The answer, I would argue, resides in the way that the film's narrative was organized around the cultural logic and postwar mythology of *Heimat*.

Der dunkle Stern opens by invoking the visual conventions of *Heimat* and *Heimatfilme*, with shots of the natural majesty of the Bavarian Alps and nostalgic scenes of rural village life. Postwar *Heimatfilme*, the most prolific and popular film genre in 1950s West Germany, sought to locate an "authentic" Germany—unmarred by passing political regimes—in the values and practices of hearth, village, and church. At the same time, however, they also recognized recent traumas unleashed by the war and frequently peddled new norms of moral German masculinity and femininity to postwar German audiences. In short, *Heimatfilme* appealed to their audiences because, unlike Hollywood imports, their orientation was fundamentally *national*: they addressed their audience first and foremost as Germans. *Heimatfilme* released through the mid-1950s tended to acknowledge and engage critical issues of the day, such as the benefits and boundaries of national belonging, the desire for national rehabilitation, and the need to adjust to new postwar realities.[20] However, this was done in ways that emphasized the reassuring stability and longevity of the German *Heimat*, which was accorded a nurturing maternal essence and an existence independent of the more volatile, transitory, and politicized German *Vaterland*.[21]

Heimat, then, was ideologically encoded as something fixed and eternal, Christian and white. Its evocation of natural beauty, community, and security could stimulate longing in the child, Moni, but by definition it was not something that could readily assimilate *her*. This is made apparent in the school essay Moni writes on the topic "What I Want to Be When I Grow Up," which Fräulein Rieger reads aloud to her veterinarian friend, and in the exchange between the two that follows:

> "I want to be a farmer. Just like I said today at school when everyone laughed. But that's the most wonderful thing there is in the world. It's lovely to walk through the grain fields when the stalks are high. It's lovely to lead the cows to pasture. They have large and small bells hanging around their necks that jingle and ring all together—it's wonderful, just like in

church. It's lovely to be in the fields early in the morning when the sun rises, and to spend the whole day working together with the farmhands [*Knechten*] and milkmaids [*Mägden*]. But my favorite time is the harvest festival when everyone is happy and dances and sings. I would like to marry a hardworking farmer, have a farm, and many children."

"And she'll get him!" responds the vet, impressed by the author's conviction and unaware that the author is Moni.

"She will not get him," counters Fräulein Rieger. "Or do you really think that some farm boy will lead Moni to the altar?"

The veterinarian considers a moment, "Yes, well, what with our tiny village here! As long as she's a child it's still all right. But as soon as she turns seventeen or eighteen, she'll be run out of town like a unwanted dog!"[22]

The scene conforms, at least initially, to the conventions of *Heimatfilme* in Moni's veneration of the natural beauties of the rural landscape and the cyclical yet steadfast quality of agrarian life which, even in their most mundane details (bells on cow's necks), are infused with Christian imagery (or aurality) and likened to church bells. Moni has demonstrated through her essay both her love of *Heimat* and her intimate cultural familiarity with its iconography. Yet this mastery is rapidly revealed to be transgressive. She may fervently *desire* it—along with marriage and children within the *Heimat*—but her love must remain unrequited since *Heimat* by definition is constant, unchanging, and therefore unable to accommodate "difference."

This is made manifest in an earlier scene, when Moni tells her foster mother of the schoolchildren's taunts. "Black peasant!" her mother questions. "Where did they get that?" As Moni explains how she responded to the teacher's question at school, her mother effectively dismisses the child's aspirations as inappropriate, admonishing: "Well it really would have been best if you hadn't said that." Thus the film, through its responsible adults, consistently declares Moni's heartfelt desire an impossible and, more significantly, a *forbidden* one (that achieved legal expression in the first year of Hitler's rule).[23] The dramatic action of *Der dunkle Stern* pivots and is predicated upon an unquestioned affirmation of the exclusionary ideology—and racial immutability—of *Heimat*, that dominant cultural category of 1950s West Germany.[24]

What makes the exclusionary ideology of *Der dunkler Stern* all the more striking was that it was an anomaly among *Heimatfilme*. In fact, some of the most popular examples of *Heimatfilme* from the early 1950s were notable for advocating social integration. The box-office hit *Grün ist die Heide* (Green is the heath, 1951), for example, dramatized the successful social integration of ethnic German expellees from the eastern reaches of the former Reich into the West German rump state.[25] While avoiding

Moni, in jungle costume, with circus-owner Casseno in *Der Dunkle Stern*. Courtesy of Filmmuseum Berlin-Stiftung Deutsche Kinemathek.

reference to National Socialism and its expansionist policies of military conquest and mass murder, the film preached a moral message: it instructed newcomers to respect the laws, traditions, and conventions of their new homeland, on the one hand, and urged sympathy and social acceptance among West German viewers for their ethnic brethren from the East on the other. In *Grün ist die Heide* the logic of integration took the form of romance, and by the end of the film viewers eagerly anticipated the marriage of an upstanding West German forester to the charming daughter of a dispossessed Pomeranian landowner. Two formerly distinct German branches have been merged into one family tree.[26]

A related point is that the trope of *Heimat*, precisely because it was invested with the function of encapsulating an authentic German community, *enabled* filmmakers and other cultural producers to envision and enforce a fundamentally racialized definition of the German nation without having it appear to be an overtly political or even racist move. *Heimat*, after all, resided in locality, home, family, emotions; as such, it was understood to stand apart from politics. It was rooted not only in the soil, but in the very viscera of Germans. This sense of intimate connection is what gave it its strength and staying power as a cultural concept. This is also what accounts for the fact that most Germans "knew" that their *Heimat* was traditionally, historically, irrevocably white.[27]

Placing the issue of racial difference within the context of *Heimat*, then, nullified integration as a possibility precisely because of the hundred-year history of the concept. The film *Toxi* could entertain the issue of integration, if temporarily, because the drama played out in the urbanized context of modern postwar family life in which the need for national reconstruction and moral rehabilitation was at least recognized. *Der dunkle Stern*, by opening in the Upper Bavarian *Heimat*, set as its stage the supposedly timeless German community, that bedrock of German identity that could tolerate no reform without jeopardizing its imagined nature. As a result, the question of integrating Moni could not be raised, for racial integration would alter its immutable "essence." *Heimat*, then, continued to be a fundamentally racialized concept.[28] In spite of the fact that it was presented as an innocuous cultural building block of German (and not incidentally also gender) identity after 1945, *Heimat* played an important role in *reconstituting* racially exclusive notions of national belonging after National Socialism.

At the end of the film *Der dunkle Stern*, Moni is exiled to the circus, that "colorful world" of diverse ethnicities where she "must—no! wants to—find a new *Heimat*," and is booked to depart for a year-long tour of the great cities of South America: from Rio to Buenos Aires to Montevideo.[29] Coincidentally or not, perhaps, Elfie Fiegert next landed on the screen in *Das Haus in Montevideo* (1963). By now a young woman of seventeen, Fiegert played a bit part as the exotic attendant in a hyper-sexualized fantasy villa owned by lead character Herr Professor Dr. Nägele's recently deceased sister. Having left Germany years before under a cloud of shame due to an out-of-wedlock pregnancy, Nägele's sister subsequently made a fortune, which the white German patriarch has now come to claim on behalf of his teenage daughter. The film treats the sexual impropriety with a light touch, engages in double entendre, and finally teaches the Herr Professor to be less judgmental and morally rigid. As such, the film evinces a more general transition in mores occurring in popular commercial feature films by the early 1960s.

For the purposes of this argument, however, the important points are three: first, that the onset of puberty demoted Elfriede Fiegert from leading roles to bit speaking parts. Second, it altered the roles into which she was typecast from black occupation child to exoticized, sexualized beauty. And third, it changed the location of her character from Germany to abroad, a transition that was already underway in *Der dunkle Stern*. She no longer played the exotic German girl, but rather the exotic foreign one. And most importantly, perhaps, no explanation or apologies were deemed necessary for this ascription. The retreat from the liberal discourse of race, at least as it concerned the intersection of blackness and German-ness, was complete.

Despite this evolving disassociation of Elfie Fiegert's characters from Germany, Fiegert continued to be referred to as "Toxi" or even "Toxi Fiegert."[30] In part, of course, this was a marketing ploy that attempted to capitalize on her early success and popularity in her original role as a black occupation child. Even so, it is telling. For prior to the film's release and box office success, the historical Elfie Fiegert had already been literally reinscribed as her fictional counterpart: while the names of all other actors are provided in the film credits and publicity materials, "Toxi" is listed as played by "Toxi." As a result of the repeated identification of actress with character in a stream of personal appearances, interviews, and press releases, the story of Toxi became the story of all West German *farbige Mischlingskinder* and the name "Toxi" entered the German language as a generic term for black German children. And the term stuck. The print media, over the course of the following decades, would continue to invoke "Toxi" as shorthand when titling articles discussing Black Germans and their social condition.[31]

Elfriede Fiegert, too, began using the stage name and by the early 1960s, as she continued to have trouble getting parts, expressed her intention to have her name legally changed to "Toxi." This insistent identification with character can be attributed to her attempt to build a professional career by reminding the industry of both her early professional success and the critical recognition she received in the role. Yet she also seems to have experienced a certain wistfulness about playing Toxi: positive attention from public and press, media events fêting her as a budding and adorable star and, one would suppose, the professional career these seemed to portend.[32]

By the time she reached her teens, Elfriede, like her characters, became trapped by a socially ascribed identity of immutable difference. Industry interest in her had dried up, the promise of her early career had dwindled into a couple of bit parts, and her father was firmly encouraging her to reorient her career aspirations downward—to the office job she held at an insurance firm in Munich. Asserting that "dark types are harder to sell than blonds," her agent too tried to reconcile the teenager to the decline in demand.[33] By the early 1960s, Elfie Fiegert—along with sustained public attention to the "fate of the postwar *farbige Mischlingskind*"—had been rudely pushed from the limelight.

In periodic interviews over the course of the 1960s, Elfriede insisted that she had experienced little racial prejudice and discrimination in her life, something she attributed to her upbringing, attitude, and persistence in meeting hostility with friendliness. As a seventeen year old intent on pursuing a film career, she noted hopefully, "If one achieves the artistic success of someone like Josephine Baker or Dorothy Dandridge, then skin color no longer plays a role." Nonetheless, it appears she herself wasn't convinced of this, for when asked about her future plans, she expressed the desire to emigrate to South America where she believed "people of all colors coexist without distinctions." Within a year, however, eighteen-year-old Elfie Fiegert married a thirty-five-year-old Nigerian engineer studying in Munich and announced that she would return with him to his homeland. The press reported the marriage under the headline, "Film Child Toxi goes to Africa." The union did not last, and within a few years Elfriede, who returned to Germany and continued to cobble together small parts, acknowledged the tendency of German filmmakers to repeatedly buttonhole her in feature films or documentaries concerned with the social problem of *Mischlinge*. "One is always a type," she sighed in 1968 at the age of twenty-two.[34]

Chapter Five

WHOSE CHILDREN, THEIRS OR OURS?
INTERCOUNTRY ADOPTIONS
AND DEBATES ABOUT BELONGING

Have you ever been in a [German] beer saloon on a pay day and seen the mothers with their little brown children gathering to watch how much money the servicemen are spending there? [H]ow the little dark girls' hair is cut so short that they look like little boys, because their hair needs a special treatment? . . . I have innumerable letters from mothers who get no support for their children and whose hearts are breaking because their children are insulted at school as "niggers" and who ask for a solution to their problems from me. Would your agency provide money to apply special treatment for the little girls' hair? Would you be able to guarantee their future equal to that of a white child when they grow up? . . . [If so] I would immediately inform my newspaper and the colored Americans would . . . be fully satisfied and no longer worried about the dark children in Germany.

—Mabel A. Grammer, *Afro-American* correspondent, 1953

Well-meaning friends suggested to us during the worst [economic] times in 1947, that we should separate from Doni for the sake of our own children. One day, they sent a colored professor from the United States to us. He wished to adopt Doni . . . "The child will live well in the United States, much better than here with you," he declared. "Just give him to us!" I refused the professor as politely as I could. . . . Doni's brothers were thoroughly incensed, which shows how much they loved him from the beginning. "Where does he get the idea . . ." they wanted to know. "Doni is no rabbit which one may give away. . . . Nobody can take him from us!" . . . Their concern showed how much children can love each other even if they are not "blood relations." . . . [It] is not a "catastrophe" for a colored child to be in a white family, as people warned us seven years ago. . . . Doni, our son, has perhaps already taught some people that every human being, no matter to which nation he belongs, no matter to which religion he belongs, no matter what kind of nose he has or what color skin, is first of all our brother.

—Erich Lißner, "We Adopted a Brown Baby," *Ebony*, 1953[1]

IN LATE 1947, widowed schoolteacher Ethel Butler was reading her Chicago newspaper when she came across a photograph of ten small children living together in an orphanage in southern Germany. The children, little more than toddlers, were seated in a row along a wall, arranged by size from smallest to largest. Nearly all looked squarely at the camera; none was smiling. Overwhelmed with compassion for the "half-Negro waifs," Mrs. Butler resolved to provide at least some of the children with a loving home in the United States. Over the course of the next three years, the persistent Mrs. Butler overcame substantial bureaucratic indifference and red tape to travel to Germany and locate two children, a three-year-old girl and five-year-old boy, whom she planned to raise as a family in Chicago.[2]

Ethel Butler was merely one of countless hundreds of black Americans who sought to adopt black German children beginning in the late 1940s. Although exact numbers are hard to come by due to the decentralized nature of such arrangements,[3] by 1968 experts estimated that in the two decades since the war as many as seven thousand black German children had been adopted by American citizens.[4] Virtually all of the prospective parents were black, with the notable well-publicized exception of author Pearl Buck, who adopted a black German daughter along with other biracial children of American paternity from Japan and India during the 1950s. Unlike Pearl Buck, who sought to demonstrate the irrelevance of skin color in forming affective relationships, Ethel Butler and other prospective African American parents tended to be motivated by notions of racial identity and responsibility. Although they, like most adoptive parents, were doubtless driven by desire for a child, they also wanted these *particular* children cared for and regretted that the children's black fathers were unable or unwilling to take on the task.[5] What is more, they feared for the children's future in what had recently been a rabidly racist Germany. As one commentator provocatively put it in a personal note to Walter White of the NAACP in 1950, after reading a newspaper report on Germans' alleged efforts to establish a "central colony" for several thousand "brown babies": "Is Germany to be allowed to substitute her concentration camps and persecution of the Jews for *children* who happen to be brown in color? . . . Heaven help us!"[6]

In this instance, as in the case of Ethel Butler, press coverage played an important role in stimulating awareness and action among African Americans on behalf of black German children abroad. From the late 1940s through the mid-1950s, in fact, stories about "brown babies" fathered abroad by black American occupation troops appeared with regularity in the American press.[7] Newspapers such as the *Pittsburgh Courier* and the Baltimore *Afro-American* published appeals to their predominantly black readership, urging them to send special CARE packages to black German children residing in German children's homes or with their unwed mothers. The *Pittsburgh Courier* went so far as to publish the names and addresses of two hundred German mothers of black children. Readers were encouraged to contact the women directly and pledge long-distance material and moral support over the long term.[8]

In addition to responding to the news, people like Ethel Butler *became* news. By early 1951, her quest to adopt German children was fêted in popular glossy magazines on both sides of the Atlantic and, the following year, in the promotional literature for the film *Toxi*.[9] The mainstream West German weekly, *Stern*, ran an offensively titled feature, "*Mammies für die Negerlein*" (Mammies for the little Negroes), which praised Ethel Butler's heroic "fight against the white bureaucracy in America" and chronicled her "frosty reception from U.S. officials" upon her arrival in Germany to locate children for adoption. Lauding Butler's "resolute" efforts on behalf of the orphans in the face of negative official American response, the article reminded readers that this "means something in a country where racial segregation is exercised with unrelenting rigor." By early 1952, *Revue*, a Munich-based magazine that covered Butler's trip, reported receiving inquiries from "hundreds of Negro families" regarding black German children available for adoption. As a result, one of their staff reporters sought, and received, assistance from state and city youth officials in North Rhine-Westphalia, Bavaria, and Munich, to identify appropriate *Mischlingskinder* and match them with African American families for adoption to the United States. *Revue* planned to cover the "*Adoptionsaktion*" and issue follow-up reports on the children once they arrived in America.[10]

In the United States, the African American monthly *Ebony* also featured Butler's trip to Germany and, adopting a similar editorial line to *Stern*, characterized it as a mission of "mercy" frustrated by restrictive U.S. immigration laws and an indifferent American bureaucracy. This was contrasted to Butler's warm welcome among Germans "who did everything they could to help" her. *Ebony* reported the widespread positive publicity Mrs. Butler received from the German press, as well as the generous assistance and hospitality extended her by a white West German journalist and his wife. The article concluded on a critical note, with a final paragraph devoted to the hostility that greeted Butler upon her American homecoming. Following publicity of her efforts in a Chicago newspaper, the schoolteacher reported receiving "an anonymous letter berating her for 'trying to bring more Negroes into the U.S.'" It was signed, *Ebony* noted ironically, "A True Patriot."[11]

As this press coverage illustrates, the "fate" of black German children was as much a political issue as a social one. For an extended moment in the 1950s, some prominent black Americans and white Germans dis-

Mrs. Ethel Butler of Chicago finds a daughter to adopt in a
Bavarian orphanage. *Ebony* featured Butler's story in January
1951, claiming that "at first sight," the child ran directly into
her future mother's arms. Courtesy of the
Newberry Library, Chicago.

covered in the children a common cause and found they could further
their distinct agendas by engaging in transnational dialogue and cooperation. An important basis of this temporary identity of interests was the
strategic utility of exposing and publicizing the injustices of American
racial practices and policies at home and abroad.[12] By these means, African Americans variously sought to improve the lives of children, end racial injustice, and initiate an era of civil and social equality for black
Americans. White Germans, on the other hand, had a different mixture
of motives. While some sought primarily to rid Germany of unwanted
"colored" children by cultivating interest among African Americans, others sought to assist the children and thereby shake off the stigma of Nazi-
era racism. All, however, sensed the utility of transnational interaction

for the desired reform or rehabilitation of their respective postwar nations, American and German alike.

This chapter reconstructs the emerging discourses and policies informing intercountry adoptions of black German children in order to sketch a social history of this postwar phenomenon, explore the racial and national ideologies underpinning adoption practices, and consider the range of destinations and destinies pursued for the children.

•   •   •

From the early 1950s, statistics consistently showed that a minority of black German children—just over 10 percent—lived in institutions rather than with families. Nonetheless, German commentators in federal and state ministries, youth offices, and the press persistently presented international adoption as the preferred solution to a more generalized social problem of postwar *Mischlingskinder*. As in *Toxi* and *Maxi*, the children were portrayed as unloved and abandoned victims of their mothers' immoral proclivities and their father's national and racial otherness. West Germans, from across the political spectrum, emphasized the myriad forms of discrimination that the children attracted—as a result of their illegitimacy, foreign paternity, and racial characteristics—or referenced these as the multiple ways in which they did not belong.

This characterization permitted counterstrategies to the self-proclaimed goal of racial integration advocated by the Society for Christian-Jewish Cooperation/World Brotherhood. Since the occupation, German officials at the local, state, and federal levels were mandated—first by the Western Allies and then by the West German Basic Law—to support the principle of integration. As a result, their consistent if somewhat mechanical response to questions regarding the status of *Mischlingskinder* was to assert that the new constitution prohibited discrimination on the basis of race, and that the children would be treated in ways equal to their white counterparts. Nonetheless, this official public line reflected neither the range of opinion nor the variety of solutions proposed by municipal, state, and federal officials, social workers, educators, and interested others for the disposition of the children.

Similar to some African Americans at the time, West German authorities tended to perceive black German children as an American problem demanding "Negro solutions." But whereas the children's racial and national paternity stirred feelings of kinship in concerned black Americans, those same attributes connoted problematic difference for most West Germans.

As a result, following the 1949 foundation of the West German state, federal and state Interior Ministry officials, as well as numerous youth workers, openly advocated the "Toxi" solution—the children's emigration from this "traditionally white land" to a historically multiracial one. The early destination of choice was, unremarkably, the United States, where West German officials hoped the children would be adopted by "their own kind"—that is, within the embrace of African American families and communities.

THE GERMAN LEGAL LANDSCAPE AFTER 1945

In part, this reflected the realities of German adoption practices. As German social workers and youth officials repeatedly pointed out, prospective parents in Germany—much more than their American counterparts—rejected out-of-hand children of perceived negative biological inheritance. For a good decade and a half after the war, in fact, German professionals marveled at Americans' apparent belief in the mitigating effect of positive environmental influences on a child's development and their corresponding faith in the possibility of moral or mental improvement. German prejudices regarding the children's eugenic and moral background, in contrast, rendered them virtually unadoptable in their own country.[13]

Such prejudices were both prevalent and persistent, dating back to at least the early decades of the century. However, during the Third Reich, they had been invested with legal authority when, over the course of 1938 and 1939, adoption law was racialized and all adoption applications were subject to the review and approval of "higher administrative authorities": "If, from the viewpoint of the adopter's family, or *in accordance with public interest*, there are important reasons [which militate] against the establishment of a family tie between the contracting parties," adoption applications were to be denied. But state intervention didn't stop there. The law gave the authorities broad powers to review legal adoptions that had already been concluded and to nullify them without the consent of adoptive parent or child.[14]

Thus Nazi-era amendments to the law shifted authority over adoptions from local and sectarian to state hands, in the process denying Christian organizations any role in a process they had previously dominated. After 1945, and indeed throughout the military occupation, the legal basis for adoption (as for abortion) remained murky and took a good half decade to be clarified. In spite of the elevated influence of Christian social work after the war, it was not until 1951 that the Federal Republic formally reinvested Christian organizations with the legal right to conduct adoptions (although, in practice, they reasserted that right before that date).[15]

This delay was attributable to the lack of legal directive by Allied and especially American authorities, since the bulk of intercountry adoptions originated in the U.S. zone. As late as 1948, an official of the Protestant Inner Mission, Dr. Becker, penned a report attempting to sort out the legal status of adoptions in Germany and, in particular, whether a 1939 law on adoption was still in effect. On the one hand, he noted, Military Government Law No. 1, "proclaimed immediately after Germany was occupied, abrogated all laws and decrees that were Nazi in character or content." However, he added, the military government never issued a catalogue of laws they considered to be "typically Nazi," so the matter required interpretation. Nonetheless, "official [1939] commentary on the law indicates that racial and national [völkischen] criteria for adoption took precedence and that the state, in its totalitarian strivings, wanted to dominate this area of human life as well. . . . [The intention was] to guarantee the consideration of heredity and racial-biological factors and to impede adoptions in which the prospective guardian could not warrant that the child would be raised in the spirit of the National Socialist Weltanschauung." "In view of the motives and the wording of the law," Becker argued, "there cannot be the smallest doubt" that it was nullified in accordance with Military Government Law No. 1.[16]

Although Becker's reasoning was sound, his conclusion proved incorrect. In June 1948, in fact, the Central Committee for the Protestant Inner Mission received a memo from the Religious Affairs Branch of the U.S. Military Government announcing that the 1939 law remained in effect. After reviewing the law and deleting a reference to the Reich Adoption Office, the legal branch of the American Military Government ruled that it could *not* be regarded "a Nazi law." In support of this decision, American officials invoked the commentary of the Reich minister of Justice from 1939 which, they claimed, established that the primary purpose of the law was to foster the professionalization and more effective regulation of German adoption practices. American legal logic thus held that since "these motives cannot be said to be typically National Socialist, the Law is therefore . . . politically and ideologically neutral."[17]

How do we make sense of this decision's stunning silence on Nazi racial politics? The most charitable answer would be that the American ruling was likely attributable to the laws' wording, which euphemistically invoked "public interest" rather than racial criteria more explicitly. However, German commentators like Becker—as well as British and Soviet authorities, who rescinded the Nazi amendments in their zone and returned adoption law to its pre-1933 form—recognized a clear racial and eugenic intention. The Americans were fully aware of this. Moreover, American authorities *did* create a legal mechanism to deal with one consequence of Nazi-era adoption law: They issued an American Military

Government law in November 1947, which permitted adoptive parents or children to petition for the reinstatement of adoptions that were terminated, against their will, by German authorities between 1933 through 1945. However, this law was temporary and targeted at that one provision; the balance of adoption legislation of the Nazi period was allowed to stand.[18] The answer to the question of American inaction on this issue lies in part, I would suggest, in the rigorously racialized adoption practices of the United States, in which whites cleaved to whites, Jews to Jews, and Blacks to Blacks. Racial restrictions in forming German families attracted little American attention because the assumptions underlying such policy were not viewed as necessarily Nazi or even undemocratic.[19] Moreover, the sense of retrospective surprise generated by this decision—and particularly the jarringly divergent assessments of the law by the German Protestant official, on the one hand, and the American Military Government, on the other—points to a gap in our historical understanding of the *process* of democratization during the occupation. It suggests that more research is needed to reconstruct the legal transition in social policy from fascist to democratic state.

However, before we too quickly valorize the German Christian leadership as more racially progressive than their American occupiers, a few words about their motives are in order. In raising the question of the legal status of the 1939 adoption law, the Protestant Inner Mission was primarily concerned to reestablish the right of Christian organizations (like its own) to reenter the adoption business. Protestant officials were not fundamentally, or even tangentially, interested in deracializing adoption practices. Rather, they wanted to denazify them. To them, this meant decentralizing authority over adoptions in order to remove state monopoly over the constitution of families and the socialization of children. The Christian churches and their social organizations were eager to resume adoption activities in order to influence the character of families and parent-child relationships that were established after the war. But their self-stated goal was to dispense with the 1939 law in order to "foreground confessional considerations" in the adoption process. So while "race" proved handy in denouncing the Nazi-era law, it disappeared as a referent in the Protestant Inner Mission's projections for postwar adoption practices. The German families that dominated their thinking on this issue were normative and the children white.[20]

Although harsh economic conditions into the 1950s initially discouraged adoptions of any kind in the Federal Republic, West German adoption policy continued to be influenced by unspoken racial and national considerations. By 1950, for example, a number of West German states passed legislation, which ultimately culminated in a federal law, provisionally lifting the restriction that only childless couples could adopt.

Citing the "special circumstances of the war" and its serious human consequences, these laws temporarily extended the right of adoption to couples with living children, provided such adoption would not negatively
impact the welfare of the birth children.[21] Although the laws contained
no explicit racial language, commentary at the state level as well as heart-
rending national press coverage of blond-haired, blue-eyed orphans suggest that such laws were framed with the large numbers of unclaimed or
orphaned ethnic German children in mind.[22] This category of child was
considered separately from the "occupation child" of foreign paternity,
as such social policy solutions illustrate. For as West German state and
federal officials worked to mitigate adoption law to integrate unrelated
white German children into West German families, they simultaneously
eagerly sought ways to release German taxpayers from the maintenance
costs of German "occupation children" of foreign paternity.[23]

THE ADOPTION SOLUTION: PERCEPTIONS AND PROVISIONS

As a result of this constellation of factors, the West German popular press
enthusiastically reported initiatives, such as Ethel Butler's, to facilitate
adoptions of German *Mischlingskinder* to the United States. Articles like
"Mammies für die Negerlein," accompanied by photos of an ever-smil-
ing black schoolmarm (who, against stereotype, held an advanced university degree unreported by *Stern* magazine), reflected a generalized
conviction, shared by many West German officials and youth workers
through the mid-1950s, in the superior capacity of African American
women to better nurture, love, and understand the biracial German child
than its own white biological mother.

What is striking, if not surprising, in this regard is the consistency with
which postwar Germans—similar to their American counterparts—insisted on defining the children as a product of their black father's, rather
than white mother's, racial ancestry. This established both the children's
essentialized difference from white children as well as the social need for
German contemporaries to seek solutions to this "problem of race." As
colored children in a putatively lily-white nation, they were never
viewed as unproblematically German. Rather, they were tagged with a
group identity that allowed West Germans of various political and ideological stripes to posit in them an affinity for things African, or more typically African American, on the basis of foreign paternal ancestry. So, for
example, representatives from the Protestant Inner Mission could suggest to the Hessian *Landtag* in 1947 that the children be educated in spe-
cially segregated German schools and afterward shipped to Africa to
serve as Christian missionaries.[24] And by the early 1950s, West German

newspapers could advertise black American "mammies" as the most natural and compassionate caretakers for the children despite the fact that the two shared neither common language nor culture; and the prosperous American North could be imagined as their most propitious destination due to overly optimistic assessments of possibilities for easy integration there.[25]

Initially, then, West German federal, state, and youth officials were heartened by Ethel Butler's adoption inquiries in the late 1940s and expressed hope that other black Americans would follow her lead. However, like Butler herself, German authorities rapidly realized that what appeared an auspicious solution was turning into a bureaucratic mire due to restrictive American immigration policies. Although the 1948 Displaced Persons Law permitted entry of war orphans, among others, from Germany, Austria, and Italy into the United States, occupation children were not initially eligible under its provisions. However, by 1950, concerns regarding the narrow manner in which "orphan" was defined were addressed, and the law was amended to include children (age sixteen or under in June 1948) rendered parentless by "contingencies other than death or disappearance of both parents." In addition, a new category of special nonquota visas was created for "orphaned children under 10 who were not eligible displaced orphans."[26]

In February 1951, several months after the amended legislation went into effect, West German federal Interior Ministry officials met with Lois McVey, a representative of the U.S. Displaced Persons Commission, to discuss the eligibility of occupation children for immigration into the United States under the revised provisions. In particular, German officials appeared eager to present the case for intercountry adoptions of *Mischlingskinder* to America and informed McVey that their ministry was in the process of conducting a survey of "*Negerkinder*" to determine the number available for placement. In response, McVey noted noncommittally that the Commission agreed "that the part-Negro child is a social problem since there is no Negro group [in Germany] for him to assimilate into" and that she and her colleagues had made inquiries to their office stateside to ask whether "they could encourage the adoption of some of these children." However, she simultaneously requested Ministry officials to provide any figures they might have on the number of *Volksdeutsche*—white ethnic German—children available for adoption to the United States, thus indicating where she sensed American demand would prove strongest and least controversial.[27]

In May 1951, federal Interior Ministry officials pressed the issue further during a second visit by Lois McVey. West German officials suggested to McVey that their Ministry and the U.S. High Commission for

Germany (HICOG) each appoint representatives responsible for organizing the "deportation of Mischlingskinder to the homeland of their fathers." In developing this proposal, Ministry representatives had sought advice from a putatively knowledgeable and trustworthy German American, a certain Pater Alkuin Heibl, recommended to ministry officials by the head of the German Catholic Social Welfare Association (Katholische Fürsorgeverein). Queried on his response to the emigration plan, Heibl extended his enthusiastic encouragement, maintaining that "as soon as they grew up" "the . . . *Negermischlingskinder* would prove to be a problem for Germany. The fertility of the Negro is such that it would affect the color of a nation's blood [*Blutfärbung eines Volkes*] in a short time. The conflicted nature of these children leads them astray and causes them to become a threat to a land. . . . Half-blood Negroes, insofar as they do not become reconciled to their fate . . . can very easily become asocial." Heibl's pseudobiological interpretation, which echoed that of prewar German eugenicists, appears to have been received by ministry representatives as instructive, rather than off-putting.[28]

Reinforced by Heibl's racist counsel, Interior Ministry officials' emigration proposal was not limited to children whose mothers had relinquished their custodial rights, but was more ambitious in scope. In fact, they extended their desirable target group to include "children whose mothers were *willing* to relinquish them," but presumably had not already done so, as well as children who were institutionalized or "lived in unfavorable family circumstances." What is more, Ministry officials made it clear that while it would be preferable to place the children with their (presumed) American fathers or fathers' relatives, in some cases they would need to be transferred to foster care or children's homes in the United States. Such a plan not only betrayed ministry officials' bias that the paternity of *Mischlingskinder* was exclusively African American. It also revealed them as quite prepared to recruit German children for emigration, even those currently living in family arrangements, and ship them to a foreign American environment for institutional placement.[29]

McVey proved intent on discouraging such a plan, maintaining that as a member of the Displaced Persons Commission, she did not have the authority to entertain the suggestion of appointing a HICOG representative for this matter. More to the point, however, she informed Ministry officials that half-Negro children "would still suffer considerably due to the antipathy towards colored people" in the United States and "suggested that the attempt be made to make arrangements for the children in Central or South America, where the issues of race hold less significance." Neither West German nor U.S. officials, it seems, were eager to claim responsibility for the children and the social problem they were perceived to embody.[30]

American Deliberations: The Committee to Consider the Immigration of German Orphans of Negro Blood

Lois McVey's response to West German Interior Ministry officials appears to have been informed by discussions that took place in New York City in late January 1951, when the U.S. Displaced Persons Commission convened a committee of representatives from interested religious, social welfare, and African American organizations "to consider the possibilities and resources for the immigration of a group of German orphans of Negro blood."[31] The DP Commission representative, Evelyn Rauch, presented the committee with background on the children, noting that the Commission had learned from HICOG that some five hundred children "of Negro blood" and American paternity were available in Germany for adoption. Since they constituted a "social problem that the [West German] government would like to have help with," the committee was charged with discussing the possibility of their "resettlement" to the United States.[32]

The ensuing discussion revealed that, unlike their white German counterparts, these children thus far had received few formal expressions of interest from prospective American parents and that those who did present themselves were black families unable to afford transportation costs for the children to the United States. As a result, one of the issues considered was a financial one: whether the Displaced Persons Commission would be able to help fund the travel costs of "German children of Negro blood" to the United States. While this issue was not resolved, committee members expressed interest in assisting the German government and its agencies, and declared their intention "to find what it could do to be most helpful" in the matter. Like their German equivalents, white American social welfare officials tended to define the issue in black and white terms and agreed that the children, because of their color, presented Germans with a legitimate social problem.

When the committee chairman turned to the "representatives of the American Negro community" at the meeting to seek their advice, responses were somewhat more varied. Black committee members expressed a number of concerns regarding both the adoption of black German children to the United States and the committee's approach to the issue. A fundamental criticism came from Channing H. Tobias of the Phelps Stokes Fund, who objected to the Committee's fixation on issues of race. These were "disadvantaged children," he argued, who "should not be classified [according to] their mixed blood. . . . [W]hatever is done, it should not be assumed that the only adjustment can be an American Negro adjustment, and that only American Negro homes will be available to them. . . . [T]rue democracy and double standards of citizenship do not go together."[33] Others at the meeting voiced their agreement that the children should be approached as a "human problem" without special consideration of race or skin color.

Not all, however, found Tobias's objections realistic. Mrs. Gordon of the Child Welfare League, who had experience in adoption matters, felt strongly that in seeking a solution within the United States, "the difference in this group of children should not be evaded." "It cannot be denied that adverse feeling toward Negro children exists" in Germany and the United States, she noted, and that "not much is being done to overcome it." Cognizance must be taken of the children's social environment and social reception, she suggested. If the children were to be brought to the United States, she maintained that "they should be placed if possible with families whom they resembled in appearance," in conformity with American adoption practices a the time. But if the children were refused entry, she queried, what were the alternatives? "What could be done if the United States does not take them?" In response Roland Elliot, committee chairman and director of the Church World Service, proposed that the children could either remain in Germany or be sent to "some South American country," adding that expressions of interest had been received from Venezuela. Elliot's suggestion drew immediate criticism from the representative of the Brooklyn Catholic Interracial Council, who objected that this was no solution, but rather an "evasion of the problem."[34]

Ultimately, the deliberations yielded no consensus. Rather, the committee reiterated its interest in helping with the "problem of these children" and seeking a solution "on a humane basis, shared by the Negro community and other communities represented." "Whatever is done should be done on an interracial basis," it resolved, and emphasized the need for financial assistance. A subcommittee was formed to solicit opinion, disseminate information regarding the children, and otherwise consider what more could be done. Here the archival trail runs cold. It appears that the committee and subcommittee achieved little in the way of tangible results. Yet the issue lingered to be taken up by individual organizations and the black press.[35]

THE NAACP RESPONSE

Following this committee meeting in January 1951, the National Association for the Advancement of Colored People continued to track the fate of black German children for several years. In early 1952, the NAACP contacted the German Embassy in Washington, D.C., to solicit further information about their social condition in the Federal Republic. The embassy, in turn, passed the request on to the German Foreign Office and federal Interior Ministry officials in Bonn, who agreed it would be useful to share the census information on "colored occupation children" with the NAACP in the hope that they would act as advocates for the children in America.[36] In addition, the NAACP received missives from West Germans involved in the care of black German children, who appealed to the NAACP for financial support or assistance in facilitating the children's emigration to the U.S.[37]

While NAACP officials provided no material support in such instances, they nonetheless clearly considered the issue of the children's welfare connected to the larger political agenda of their organization's mission.[38] Serving as lobbyists for biracial German children's interests permitted African American activists to voice trenchant observations regarding comparative race relations in the postwar United States and West Germany while playing to a national and international audience of officials and publics.

In a press release distributed to the Associated Press in September 1952, for example, Walter White of the NAACP argued that the plight of postwar black occupation children was created by discriminatory official U.S. policies toward their African American fathers, which "varied materially from the pattern of white soldiers." "Where other factors were favorable, white soldiers were not only permitted but encouraged to marry the mothers of their children. In the case of Negro soldiers, every possible obstacle and particularly outright refusal of commanding officers to grant the necessary permission was placed in the path of would-be couples. . . . For this reason, as well as the color of the offspring, there has been much more discussion of these partly colored children than of the far greater number of illegitimate children whose fathers are white."[39] White's point echoed the position taken by the NAACP representative at the committee meeting on the immigration for children of Negro blood the previous year, who argued that black occupation children were "a political problem . . . created by the [U.S.] Government's refusal to allow soldiers to marry. . . . [T]he Government has some responsibility . . . for these children. . . . The Negro community would like to know what responsibility would be taken by the Government, and if any effort has been made . . . to bring them to this country."[40] *Ebony* magazine picked up the issue and expanded criticism to highlight the corrosive international effects of American racism abroad, charging that: "More than one German child has been taught to shout 'nigger bastard' [at black German children] by American soldiers who neglect to tell them the meaning of the words."[41]

Negative perceptions regarding the current state of American race relations caused some representatives of African American organizations, from the early 1950s, to express doubts about the wisdom of encouraging the children's adoption to the United States. Lester Granger from the Urban League explicitly posed the "question as to whether German children rejected in their own country because of their color would be any better off in this country. . . . There [are] colored children in this country, in Georgia for example, who probably were much worse off than the colored children in Germany."[42] Writing several months after black German children entered German schools in 1952, Walter White cast the comparison in even starker terms:

> What is . . . immensely significant in view of the racist doctrines of the Nazis is what is now being done in Germany to assimilate these children. . . . It was most interesting, in light of the impending argument in the U.S. Supreme Court dealing with segregation in education, that the German teachers who had lived under Hitler voted unanimously that the only right, just, and sensible way to handle the situation is on a basis of full integration and without any kind of segregation based on race. The Bavarian Minister of Education has issued a law to all school superintendents, . . . principals, and teachers that Negro children must be fully integrated into the schools, and any practice of segregation based upon race are contrary to policy and will be dealt with accordingly. Somewhat similar steps are beginning to be taken in Japan.

In a release to the Associated Press, White lauded West German efforts and singled out the pamphlet *"Maxi, Our Negro Lad"* as particularly praiseworthy due to its presentation of "physically beautiful" black German children and its "straightforward and non-sentimental" discussion of the "human problems" connected with the children.[43] White had been informed of SCJC-World Brotherhood efforts on behalf of biracial children by J. Oscar Lee of the National Council of Churches, who, it will be recalled, visited Germany in 1952 to attend SCJC conferences on *Mischlingskinder* in Nuremberg and Frankfurt. Lee kept White apprised of West German plans to integrate the children into German schools and educate teachers and youth workers on issues of race. White, in turn, used this information to good effect in his press release, concluding with the trenchant observation that "It is significant that these two nations which have recently undergone violent indoctrination in racism appear to have recovered from the virus of racial supremacy to a greater extent than some sections of the United States."[44]

Thus the NAACP's analysis and international engagement on behalf of black occupation children was grounded in a social critique of racist American culture and practices. By focusing on the comparative national responses to the children and their fathers, moreover, this prominent African American organization, the black American media, exposed the Achilles heel of the American race relations and advertised their own just cause of racial equality and black civil rights—along with the pressing need for America's *own* postwar democratization. And what is more, they did this in a way that inadvertently highlighted the West German state's impressive moral progress when compared to that of the United States.

The NAACP ultimately extended little practical assistance to the children or their caretakers on either side of the Atlantic. As Roy Wilkins had noted in response to a request for financial help, the NAACP was not, after all, a social welfare agency. What the organization did do was to articulate and publicize a critique of the racial inequities underlying both official American military policy and ongoing social practices within the United States proper. It would be left to prospective African American parents, however, to test whether and how those inequities would affect their attempts to adopt "half-Negro" children from abroad.

INTERCOUNTRY ADOPTION IN PRACTICE:
AFRICAN AMERICAN INITIATIVES

If African American leaders painted a rosy picture of race relations in post-fascist Germany it was either because they were situated in the United States and focused primarily on achieving civil liberties and social equality for black Americans at home, or, like J. Oscar Lee, had gone abroad and formulated their opinions in response to personal interaction with progressive elements—in his case, budding racial liberals—while in the Federal Republic. African Americans on the ground in West Germany saw things quite a bit differently. Their attention was drawn to black German children living in miserable conditions due to the poor economic situation of their mothers or the loveless and harsh realities of institutional life in the case of those children whose mothers couldn't or wouldn't care for them.

One woman who was appalled by conditions under which some of the children lived, and determined to do something about it, was Mabel Grammer, a sometime correspondent for the Baltimore newspaper *Afro-America* and the wife of U.S. warrant officer Oscar Grammer who was stationed with the 62nd antiaircraft artillery regiment in Mannheim. Shortly after arriving in Germany in 1951, Grammer visited a German orphanage near her husband's base. As she recalled in a 1953 interview with the *Chicago Daily News*, upon entering the children's home she found herself surrounded by children of color, "all pleading 'I want a Mummy.' It nearly broke my heart and of course we decided to adopt a child ourselves. And we just kept on. . . . Being in Europe has made me appreciate the privilege of being an American more than ever and I made up my mind that as many of these children as possible should have that privilege. These children aren't going to have silks and satins but they will have good decent American homes and parents"[45] Grammer's encounter initiated a long-term engagement on behalf of biracial German children. Over the course of the next decade, she and her husband would adopt eleven German children and receive the praise of German authorities for providing them an "unusually warm" and caring home environment.[46]

In addition, in 1951 Mabel Grammer began an enterprise in West Germany to match black German children to African American parents for adoption to the United States. To publicize the plight of the children and the availability of her services to compatriots back home, Grammer enlisted the help of the *Afro-American* newspaper in Baltimore, which ran regular articles and announcements.[47]

Grammer worked through local West German youth welfare offices and orphanages, both public and religious, making it impossible to get an accurate count of the number of intercountry adoptions she arranged. Evidence suggests that German youth officials at the local level were pleased with the quality of placements arranged through Grammer and with the corresponding increase in requests for children they received from the adoptive parents' African American acquaintances and neighbors.[48] Press reports in Germany credited Grammer with placing some 326 children with black American families residing in the United States and abroad during her first two years of operation alone. Other agencies—such as the International Social Service, which emerged during the 1950s as a coordinating agency for international adoptions and had offices in New York, Frankfurt, and Munich (among other cities worldwide)—judged the number of Grammer-facilitated adoptions totaled closer to seven hundred during those two years. This is likely an overestimation, based upon the fact that the International Social Service (ISS) eyed Grammer's activities and competence in intercountry adoption with suspicion, in large measure because she operated independently of their organization and without recourse to their expertise. Since she was active in promoting American adoptions of biracial German children into the early 1960s, she doubtless arranged well over a thousand adoptions all told. Moreover, she inspired a decade's worth of ISS memos exchanged between New York, Frankfurt, and Munich on the topic of "what to do about Mrs. Grammer."[49]

From Mabel Grammer's perspective, she was simply a "colored American woman . . . trying to help these little illegitimate children and give them a chance for their future." To justify her work, she invoked the sad circumstances of numerous children whose lives she hoped to improve through adoption into loving American homes. There was Paul, who as a baby "had been left in an orphan home" and "spent seven years [there] without the love of a mother who was full of anxiety having been raped by a colored soldier in World War II." Grammer helped place him with an African American family in California. Another boy, Hans, had been living with his mother, but when she fell ill with tuberculosis and was hospitalized, the boy began hanging around bars frequented by American soldiers in order to beg money. Concerned for her son's future and determined to protect his health, the ailing mother asked Grammer to "find a new home for her child." He was placed with an educated and propertied African American family in the Washington, D.C., area, along with an unrelated black German girl whose mother had tearfully appealed to Grammer for help since "she could not feed the child and could not find employment just because she had a colored child." Another girl, Hanna, had been living with her mother in "deplorable conditions" in a city shelter. "Her mother was expecting a baby and the German man refused to marry her as long as the colored child was with her." Grammer intervened and sent Hanna to live with a "teacher's family" in Maryland. In a similar case, four-year-old Dieter was given for adoption by his mother, an unmarried domestic living in East Berlin, whose white fiancé refused to become stepfather to a child of black paternity and demanded she choose between him and her son. Dieter was placed with an African American couple from New York—a retired civil servant in his early forties and his teacher wife, who had previously tried to adopt an American child, but were rejected despite their good physical and financial health because the husband's age slightly exceeded the forty-year limit.[50]

Grammer represented her efforts on behalf of "colored children in Germany" as motivated not only by compassion, but also by a pragmatic desire to counter the adoption practices of official American agencies and nongovernment organizations, dominated by "so many narrow minds and so much red tape." If an American couple attempted to locate and adopt a German child through the Refugee Relief Act, they were required to subject themselves to the scrutiny and approval of an authorized child welfare agency in the United States. This process could drag on over a year and more, often without reaching a successful conclusion. What is more, many U.S. states did not allow for the adoption of "alien" children in their courts, even if the petitioner was the child's biological father or grandparent. There was, however, one legal loophole for prospective adoptive American parents of non-U.S. nationals: if they were living or traveling abroad when they adopted, they could petition for adoption in foreign courts and return with the child to the United States. In addition, by the mid-1950s, the U.S. military set up local American military adoption boards in West Germany, to which servicemen could appeal to establish their suitability as parents and receive permission to adopt through the German courts.[51]

Mabel Grammer cultivated her contacts with local German orphanages and youth welfare offices to identify children available for adoption and initiate the legal adoption process for her American clients. Her role was mostly one of facilitator, although in some cases she assumed power of attorney to represent those who could not be present for court proceedings, since West Germany was one of the few European countries that permitted adoption by proxy. Grammer saw herself as performing an important service to the children and their mothers, as well as to prospective African American parents who, she suggested, offered their hearts and homes to children in need only to be disrespected and derided by high-handed (typically white) social workers and social service professionals in the United States. American ISS officials, who were otherwise critical of Grammer's activities, admitted that child placement agencies in the United States "have lofty standards . . . and rarely approve of the preferred Negro homes." This, they argued, was because prospective black parents often hailed from rural southern states like Alabama or Virginia, "where economic standards are not high" and an overabundance of unplaced "local dependent Negro children" already existed—an analysis contradicted by the geographic and financial profile of Grammer's documented placements.[52]

Grammer, in turn, registered her indignation and sense of injustice regarding the situation in a letter to the New York office of the ISS. Responding to perceived allegations that "Colored People of America are not able to take care of these children" and that "there are already enough of us there as it is," she countered: "I resent this statement very much. America is our Country as well as anyone else's. . . . I for one will fight for my country and will also fight anyone trying to deprive me or any other American colored citizen [of] the right to find happiness in helping one or more of these little children. I can understand the attitude of such a big organization as yours if I was sending children in wholesale lots to America. . . . But [this focus on] such few [children adopted by] such outstanding citizens who could pass any test . . . is beyond me. Why should so much stress be put on helping a few colored German-American children when literally thousands of other nationalities are coming to 'my country'?"[53]

THE INTERNATIONAL SOCIAL SERVICE AGAINST PROXY ADOPTIONS

Mabel Grammer's impassioned defense of her right—and by extension that of all upright African Americans—to adopt "colored children" from abroad was provoked by a series of inquiries into her adoption placements by International Social Service personnel in New York and West Germany beginning in 1953. A few of Grammer's adoption cases came to the attention of the American ISS when German youth authorities requested reports on the children in order to formally release their German legal male guardian (appointed at birth for every illegitimate German child) from that duty. In a handful of other cases, ISS advice was solicited by child welfare agencies in the localities in which the children were placed, due to changes in the health or marital status of the adoptive parents or suspected maladjustment of the children. The ISS, which previously had no involvement with Grammer or her cases, soon began a file on them and a protracted correspondence with ISS offices in West Germany about her adoption activities.

On the face of it, ISS officials identified the "problem of Mrs. Grammer" with the more general "problem of proxy adoptions," and characterized both as "casually tossing children across the Atlantic" without the careful preparation and high standards of "modern" professional child-placing practices. Proper adoption methods, they asserted, should encompass "a very careful study of the home, including everything the parents have to offer in the way of economic security, wholesome influences, physical care," emotional responsiveness, and understanding.

> The measure is taken of the community, schools, church, neighbors. . . .
> Then there begins the study of various available children, their health, mental equipment, and above all their need for understanding and their capacity to respond. After all of this is assembled, there is a thoughtful "matching" of the child to the home, with a time to get acquainted. Even after the child is chosen and settled, there is still a trial period of a year or so, during which the skilled advice of understanding counselors is available for working out problems of adjustment. And only if, at the end of this period, there is every indication that the plan will work, does the child-placing agency give its blessing before the Adoption Court and the legal proceedings go through.[54]

The fact that Grammer's placements, whether by proxy or not, short-circuited that process provoked the concern of ISS officials, who charged that inadequate preparation and unprofessional practices created unhappy situations requiring crisis management on the part of youth welfare workers.

Although Grammer was cited as a negative example in numerous ISS memos, reports, and publications on adoption practices, it is difficult not to conclude that she was unfairly scapegoated. She was not, after all, in the same league as the man who reportedly arrived in the United States on a plane from Germany "accompanied by eight babies in gaily covered boxes" adopted by proxy in German courts, and later offered "to their new parents like prize packages."[55] Grammer, at least, claimed to gather and utilize background information on prospective parents and children in arranging placements. But such comparative judgments don't get to the heart of the issue.

As ISS officials themselves admitted, intercountry adoption was a completely different animal than its domestic equivalent. The president of the American ISS, in a speech on the topic, complained that in "intercountry adoptions there is no adequate machinery for the protection of the child or the home or the community."[56] International law regulating intercountry adoptions did not exist, in part because the practice only blossomed as a notable phenomenon during the mass population dislocations of World War II and its aftermath. As a result, the International Social Service, whose branches had been founded in the interwar years to deal with refugee problems of the First World War, rapidly emerged as an international liaison for such adoptions because of their infrastructure of offices located in Europe, North and South America, North Africa, and Japan.[57] Thus this particular NGO played a critical role in sorting out legal adoption requirements of both sending and receiving countries, and facilitating the exchange of information and documents between them; arranging for "matching" of parents and children; communicating with local public or sectarian social services overseeing specific adoptions; and lending professional support in crisis situations requiring consultation with people or agencies in two or more countries. By the 1950s, intercountry adoptions between Europe or Asia and the United States, for the most part involving the out-of-wedlock offspring of American servicemen abroad, dominated the ISS workload in the New York office.[58]

The ISS representatives in New York regretted people like Grammer, who, they claimed, however well intentioned, operated in an uninformed and potentially damaging manner for all involved. As a result, they communicated frequently with their counterparts in West Germany, and especially with Dr. Ursula Mende, head of the ISS office in Frankfurt (who in 1955 would make a study visit to the United States under ISS-NY auspices). The New York office urged her to educate public and private youth workers in West Germany regarding the "proper" methods of child placement, such as the need for written histories of the children, family background checks, and home visits prior to and following the child's placement. If they could be trained in up-to-date American practices, New York ISS officials seemed to think, West German child welfare workers would no longer aid and abet people like Mabel Grammer.

This strategy to americanize German adoption practices proved less than successful for a number of reasons that Mende repeatedly tried to explain to her colleagues in New York. Although Mende professed to be convinced by the superiority of American methods, she represented herself as facing an entrenched German culture of child welfare.[59] The ISS, she reminded the New York branch, was merely a private agency in West Germany with no authority over public or religious youth offices or institutions. As such, the ISS could not dictate general principles or policy guidelines, but could only encourage cooperation. ISS personnel had to be realistic about their influence, she noted, since public youth offices (*Jugendämter*) looked to state and federal Ministries of the Interior for authoritative advice and expertise.

But apart from structural constraints, a number of practical considerations caused German child welfare officials to prefer to place the children with Americans—and especially American military families based in West Germany. The first was that they were willing to take children that most Germans would not consider adopting and eagerly contacted West German authorities in substantial numbers to inquire about available children. Mende depicted German youth officials as "pressured" by American couples to surrender German children (regardless of color) for adoption. Even into the turn of the 1960s, German ISS officials were reporting to New York that for youth offices in the vicinity of American military bases—towns like Birkenfeld and Kaiserslautern in Rheinland-Pfalz—80 to 100 percent of their adoption cases involved placements with American military families, even though increased numbers of German couples had become interested in adoption (albeit of white children). Of those babies adopted, 70 percent had already been promised prior to birth to American couples by the expectant mothers.[60]

Second, since most of the children subject to intercountry adoption were illegitimate, living in institutional or foster care, and therefore "supported by public means," German youth officials sought to place their "wards in an American family as soon as possible." In doing so, they were convinced they were acting "not only in the best interest of the child . . . but also in the best interest of the community in diminishing its expenditures." As a result, youth officials preferred not to work through official American agencies in making placements, since the process took too long. Instead they favored direct contact with American tourists or military families in Germany, or at minimum written communication with American citizens in the United States expressing interest in black German children. As Mende editorialized, "It is quite natural that for these hard-to-place children [German youth welfare officials] will not set up such high standards as you are accustomed to and for which we have such high admiration." After all, she continued, German public and private agencies have the "right to place a child with any family they deem suitable. They will of course prefer placement with

American families [over German foster parents since the former] take any child free of charge."[61]

As Mende's detailed explanations to her New York colleagues make clear, the impetus behind intercountry adoptions—proxy ones included—could not be attributed solely to the work of people like Grammer, or even to national differences in adoption culture and practices between the United States and West Germany. Rather, intercountry adoptions were also fueled by the practices and predilections of German youth workers, public and sectarian, who proved keen to offload the financial and social costs of "surplus" black German children onto a ready supply of black American parents.[62]

Given the circumstances in West Germany, Mabel Grammer was incensed by what she perceived as the ISS's myopic scrutiny of her work on behalf of "half-Negro" children and by the aspersions cast on the adoptive parents. Citing individual cases, she urged the ISS-New York to conduct home visits to judge the character and circumstances of the parents for themselves, rather than rely on spurious hearsay. She further reported to the New York office the insulting interview she had with a representative from the Munich office of the ISS, Fräulein Korner, who had visited her at her home in Mannheim in October 1953. Recently returned from an educational tour of the United States, Korner had informed Grammer that "leaders" in Atlanta, Washington, D.C., and Chicago—including educators and a group of female lawyers—had "told her that the colored German-American children [sic] would be much better off in Germany than in . . . prejudiced America" and that "they should be left in Germany."

> She told me of the jim-crow street cars and the places where colored people could not go . . . and she suggested that all colored people should leave the southern states. [She also told me] about the colored people being against the children because of their white mothers. . . . She pointed out that after this conversation the organization felt that the colored people would not make good parents for the children as they would discriminate against them. I am sorry that [the ISS] in New York did not point out to Miss Korner that there are thousands of colored people in America with mixture of blood. . . . I am a colored American and am very proud of the fact because despite the numerous sufferings of my people we have progressed rapidly and most of us certainly know how to treat other people. Why is it the people who are willing to improve the lot of these poor little children must be made to submit to so much ugly propaganda?[63]

Mabel Grammer was justified in her complaints. The American ISS *had* singled out black German children as an exceptional case when it came to intercountry placements, and gradually began to question the wisdom of their adoption to the United States. The reasons were several.[64] American ISS officials acknowledged publicly in 1954 that "there has indeed been a great deal of interest in these children among Negroes in America" and that the German children's "plight is indeed hard, [for] in an all-white population they carry on their faces proof of their illegitimacy . . . and a reminder of the Occupation." Nonetheless, they accentuated the great strides they believed had been taken among Germans to "help" the children, referencing the conferences sponsored by the Society for Christian-Jewish Cooperation/World Brotherhood as well as the pedagogical value of a range of other initiatives—such as the pamphlet *Maxi*, the popular movie *Toxi*, and even the interracial adoption of little Doni by Erich Lißner who, they added in tasteless prose, "spent much time traveling and speaking on the success of his venture."[65]

Unlike the NAACP, the American ISS avoided making pointed comparisons between American and West German race relations and declined to engage in explicit criticism of American racial practices or ideology. Their leaders were not, in terms of their temperaments or commitments, social critics or reformers. Rather, they suggested that West Germany might offer a friendlier environment for the children than one would assume and highlighted expectations of further improvement due to efforts on their behalf.

Beyond the cited activities of its racial liberals, West Germany's reputation for progressive practices in racial issues was further enhanced within the American ISS due to implicit comparisons with Korea and Japan. By the mid-1950s, ISS personnel in New York were handling increasing casework in intercountry adoptions from these countries and as a result documented the appalling physical, material, and social conditions of Asian children of American paternity there. Unlike in Germany, black Korean and Japanese orphans were subjected to such extreme prejudicial treatment that their lives were literally threatened, if they were fortunate enough not to have had them violently ended by acts of infanticide shortly after birth.[66]

As a result, the situation of biracial children in West Germany did not appear nearly as critical, and American ISS officials began to equivocate and wonder publicly whether American intervention was desirable. "Perhaps the best future for these half-Negro [German] children *is*, like in the case of Toxi, to be sent for by American fathers or some close relatives. Even so, we know it is no easy matter for such a child to adjust to an all-Negro community from an all-white one, unless he is so young as to be still unconcerned. For instance, little Otto, coming to an American Negro couple who adopted him by proxy at the age of four, was too aware ever to fit happily into his new home. His adoptive parents want now to return him to Germany as rapidly as possible. . . . To let him return to Germany with a sense of failure added to his obvious trials is intolerable."[67]

The concerns expressed by the American ISS president in this case were legitimate. The ideologies and social practices of race are nationally articulated to a large degree, and migration from one national context to another can result in personal and psychological trauma, particularly when a member of a targeted minority is entering a racially segregated society as a vulnerable child. ISS-New York officials were justified to worry about what it would "do to a half-Negro child to find himself for the first time in an all-Negro community."[68] But they were less justified in making the issue of racial adjustment the primary one. For in doing so they deflected attention both from the more numerous cases of biracial orphans who integrated more happily into their new American families (and the white ones who didn't), and from the misery, neglect, or social isolation of children in Germany that Mabel Grammer had so poignantly documented.

Protecting "Our" German Children: Between Emigration and Integration

Although the legal prescriptions regarding the status and treatment of black German children were unambiguous (since the West German Basic Law prohibited racial discrimination), over the course of the early 1950s, a tension developed between commitment to the *principle* versus the *practice* of integration. While West German officials congratulated themselves and their new democratic state for endorsing and enacting racially liberal policies—and not incidentally basked in the positive international attention provided by the African American press's coverage of the children's treatment in West Germany—they simultaneously continued to pursue strategies of emigration and segregation.

If one looks closely at the rationale for considering, and in some cases supporting, such action, a number of things become apparent. First, in addition to the political and economic considerations discussed above, West Germans advocating emigration and even segregation did so by invoking the psychological and emotional well-being of the children, who were considered too vulnerable, sensitive, or maladjusted to deal in healthy ways on a day-to-day basis with their difference from white classmates. Black German children described in state, school, and social worker reports as "healthy" or "well-adjusted" were those who exhibited neither self-consciousness regarding possible phenotypical differences between themselves and their playmates nor sensitivity on occasions in which their attention was drawn to such differences by callous or casual remark. If such behavior was observed (as it frequently was) the child typically was considered at risk for developing more severe emotional problems, which could lead to social alienation and socially pathological behavior, such as licentiousness or criminality, once s/he approached puberty and adulthood. In charting these problems, West German academics, social workers, and educators alike mentioned the "occasional" insensitivity of white adults, who persisted in viewing social relations and individual worth in racialist terms. Nonetheless, they concluded optimistically that postwar white German children were largely free of such racist response unless it was drilled into them by their narrow-minded elders. Liberal commentators, in particular, recognized that unexamined racism continued to be a significant social problem in Germany but suggested that racial understanding was gradually evolving via a younger generation of Germans who retained the "natural" color-blindness of youth provided they were not exposed to tainted old ideologies.[69]

This tendency to underplay the impact of larger social environment on the children's development and behavior meant that observers searched elsewhere for causal explanations. Unremarkably, given the accepted mythology of the children's origins, German educators and social workers returned to the maternal source and, in a series of local reports written for the federal Ministry of the Interior over the course of 1954 through 1955, indicated that the children at greatest risk of posing future danger to themselves and their communities were the product of broken homes and unregenerate, inattentive, employed, or in some cases overprotective mothers. As a result, even some liberal commentators counseled intervention for the sake of these children and the social order.[70]

Tellingly, intervention—in the form of facilitating the children's emigration via foreign adoption or segregation into privately administered homes for "Negermischlinge" on German soil—was packaged as providing more protective and nurturing environments for their wards. And consistently (as was the case in the pamphlet Maxi and in German press coverage of the issue) West German advocates highlighted the central role to be played by a surrogate mother who, in keeping with the diagnosis of the problem, would compensate for the failings of the original mother through an infusion of appropriate maternal love and attentiveness.[71]

Segregated privately run homes for "Negermischlingskinder"—although they remained a more controversial solution—were made palatable to West German officials with the appeal to the soothing balm of motherly nurture. The most prominent home to win a measure of official attention and support was the Albert-Schweitzer-Children's Home in North-Rhine Westphalia run by Irene Dilloo, a white German pastor's wife. In this instance, the home benefited from the respectability afforded by the

Christian maternalism of Frau Dilloo, who was widely represented in the press as a self-sacrificing German grandmother laboring diligently on behalf of outcast or troubled biracial children. This impression was further enhanced by the use of Albert Schweitzer's name, as well as the letter of support she solicited for the home from the highly esteemed native German doctor who was popularly associated with selfless race-based charitable work in Africa.[72]

Calls for nonintegrationist intervention cannot, however, be written off as a conservative reaction against postwar liberalizing impulses on the race issue. Advocates of separate homes for biracial children or their adoption abroad supported such measures as a means to protect the children from the psychological and emotional toll of living as a colored minority in a historically white land. They therefore, in good postwar liberal fashion, frequently if obliquely appealed to the legacy of past crimes and persistent racism that continued to plague German society.[73]

Some youth welfare officials sought out segregated homes for black German children because of their perceived rehabilitative function. Since the monthly costs of residence at the Albert-Schweitzer-Home were significantly higher than those of other children's homes, public officials needed to be persuaded that the extra expense to the public purse was merited. Evidence suggests that they tended to send only their most troublesome wards, typically black German boys approaching puberty, to receive the special ministrations of Frau Dilloo's segregated home.[74]

It is instructive, if heartbreaking, to learn that in 1955 one white German foster mother returned her nine-year-old black foster son to institutional care merely because she feared keeping him under the same roof as her white foster daughter as he got older. Frau Dr. Struve, who supervised this case for the city of Nuremberg, noted that school examinations of black schoolchildren—including presumably this one—had characterized many "as especially large or strong . . . a situation that is not an advantage but rather indicates the precocious sexual maturation and physical development of these Mischlingskinder. This has already been established by anthropologists, . . . can lead to disruptions in classrooms and homes, and can render Mischlingskinder, due to no fault of their own, morally threatening elements."[75] Frau Dilloo proved more than willing to take on the cases city youth officials found "difficult."

Drawing on the advice of Albert Schweitzer, Dilloo promised to instill in her wards exceptional knowledge of foreign languages so they might avail themselves, upon attaining majority, of opportunities to emigrate to the United States or Liberia, where contacts she cultivated promised employment for well-trained black German youth. These children, once they matured, could also serve German interests as "Ambassadors of

Frau Irene Dilloo, surrounded by her wards, with a
picture of Dr. Albert Schweitzer, the namesake of her children's
home, on the wall in the background. Courtesy of The
Newberry Library, Chicago.

Goodwill" since the Federal Republic "will need colored agents to boost
her trade among colored countries," she reportedly argued.[76]

Dilloo continued to pursue international contacts and in 1959 hosted
a visit of biracial children from a "Home for Toxis" (as the German press
put it) located in Dakar, West Africa. Dilloo's apparent intention was to
use the visit to advertise both her home and the international dimension
of the "problem of mixed-blood children." Unfortunately, local press coverage took a different editorial slant and highlighted a visiting teenager's
staged performances under the headline: "Nicole from Dakar dances to
the Beat of a Jungle Drum at Edersee," the site of the Albert-Schweitzer-

Heim. Although the article went on to praise the work done on behalf of *Mischlingskinder* in Dakar and in Dilloo's home, its packaging—via title and photo—unabashedly played to the presumptive prejudices of its white readers by associating blackness with imported African exoticism and primitivism.[77]

German policy toward the children was similarly ambivalent. Unswerving attention to the children's difference and even genuine concern for their welfare encouraged some Germans to abandon an exclusive policy of integration into German society. World Brotherhood leader Hermann Ebeling, who opened the 1952 West German conference on *"Mischlingskinder"* with an appeal for racial tolerance and integration, reportedly arranged the placement of four black German children at a Swiss school, the Ecole d'Humanité, two years later.[78] Thus emigration and segregationist measures received the support of less racially enlightened officials as well as some of their more progressive counterparts. And although the latter were not numerous, their voices were not insignificant and added a luster of respectability to the pursuance of such "solutions."[79]

However, neither segregation nor emigration could solve the social problem of postwar *Mischlingskinder* for a simple, if unanticipated, reason: only a small percentage (under 13 percent) of the children's birth mothers were willing to surrender their custodial rights and allow them to stand for adoption. Indeed, substantially fewer black than white occupation children were adopted to the United States. This was beholden in part to their smaller numbers. But it was also attributable to the fact, as German youth and state officials frequently complained, that white American families would not adopt them and American officials were not eager to have them sent to their country.[80]

With the suspension of the Statute of Occupation in 1955, a noticeable shift occurred in West German discussions regarding the children's fate, as the federal Interior, Family, and Foreign Ministries began issuing memos to German youth offices and social welfare organizations discouraging the adoption of *"Negermischlingskinder"* to the United States. One reason for this reversal had to do with negative coverage of such adoptions in the West German press, which picked up on ISS criticisms of proxy adoptions. Stories circulated about wily German lawyers pocketing quick cash after entering the proxy adoption business. Press reports alleged that state youth offices were "selling" German children to the highest bidder—usually to well-off American couples who ordered children via expensive long-distance arrangements rather than make the trip to select the son or daughter they were to nurture to adulthood. Grave concerns about the market mentality of Americans extending into the intimate sphere of the family were expressed by national leaders in German youth matters such as Heinrich Webler, director of the German Institute for Youth Guardianship. In May 1955, Webler published an article urging native youth officials to clamp down on transatlantic adoptions. While conceding in passing that some American adoptive parents acted out of a desire to help the children, he listed other "frequent" and much less admirable motives for adoptions, such as unwillingness to bear one's own children (a swipe at the putatively independent yet indolent modern American woman); desire for a tax break; and, more sinister yet, adoption with the intention of selling the child to a third party or even into indentured servitude. Webler, among others, argued that with the rapid improvement of the postwar German economy, the pressing material crisis that originally motivated foreign adoptions had disappeared. As a result, occupation children previously considered foreign became recharacterized as "our German children."[81]

According to Webler, a domestic solution would ensure the fiscal and physical health of the new West German state by helping to reverse the demographic trend of low birth rates and an increasingly aging population: "Our entire social welfare system is built upon the requirement that the young generation does not disappear." It is striking, then, that as the number of intercountry adoptions increased over the first half of the decade, suspicions regarding the reasons for—and national implications of—this upswing also flourished. Nonetheless, it is notable that the children's race was rarely mentioned in these accounts, which suggests that Webler was concerned primarily with the overseas adoption of white German children.[82]

Webler's anti-American screed and language of national self-defense was likely provoked as much by American media coverage as by American adoptive practice. Through the mid–1950s, glossy magazines like *Woman's Day* crudely advertised postwar Germany as yielding a "bumper crop" of children ripe for the picking. Boasting "We Found a Baby Bonanza in West Germany," a November 1954 feature noted the ease and frequency with which American couples were able to locate and lay claim to a German child. And what a child! The *Woman's Day* article described the experience of an American master sergeant and his wife seeking to adopt in Frankfurt am Main. Following the lead of a telephone call from the city's train station reporting that an abandoned infant was found "checked in, just like a bundle," the sergeant and his wife rush over to take a look. "Minutes later" they discover "a 14-day-old baby girl of pure German parentage—very blonde, like the sergeant's wife—and wrapped only in an incredibly dirty cotton blanket. They looked at the infant, then at each other. Agreement was silent and swift.

'That's for us,' exploded the sergeant. 'Why, she's beautiful.' . . .

Within half an hour the Americans had signed the adoption contract with the German mother."[83] The well-timed call, fast-paced action, and happy resolution could be straight out of Hollywood. Scripted as a family romance, the story's narrative logic and denouement hinges on a dramatic moment of racial recognition. Rather than connote national difference, "pure German parentage" signals similarity, desirability ("very blond, like the sergeant's wife") and racial kinship—all of which suggested that, while seemingly miraculous, this match was "meant to be."

West German officials begged to differ. The *Women's Day* article found its way into the files of the Bavarian Interior Ministry at a time when its federal counterpart was beginning to demand better state oversight and regulation of localities' loose intercountry adoption practices. Bavaria and Hesse were particular targets of federal Interior Ministry concern since these two states ("but especially Bavaria") generated the greatest number of international adoptions to the United States.[84]

Following the formal end of occupation in 1955, federal Interior Ministry officials convened a meeting of the highest ranking youth officials from the state Interior Ministries and private welfare organizations to address the unwelcome increase in adoptions of German children abroad. The July 1955 meeting resulted in an agreement to better regulate such adoptions and to abide by the procedural recommendations of the German ISS (especially the need for full reports on the character and circumstances of prospective parents before the child was delivered to them). For intercountry adoptions to the United States in particular, federal Interior Ministry officials asked state Interior Ministries to assume an active supervisory role and keep officials at the federal Interior Ministry, the German Foreign Office, and the German Consulate apprised of such cases.[85]

Participants at the meeting also agreed on the need to work with German couples to increase domestic adoptions. By the mid-1950s, following the loosening of restrictions on domestic adoption, larger numbers of prospective German parents from "all economic and professional levels and of diverse ages" were beginning to express interest in adopting. Nonetheless, social workers noted that for "many couples in elevated circumstances, we are lacking children of good heritage [*Herkunft*]" and bemoaned the "absence of nice, common, educable parents for simple [*einfache*] children."[86] Reportedly, couples of higher economic and social standing tended to request orphans and often refused children born out of wedlock. Moreover, like their white American counterparts, most prospective German parents expressed a strong "continuing preference" for infant or toddler "girls, blond and blue-eyed."[87] Federal and state interior ministers were aware of these preferences. At their July 1955 meeting they advocated finding ways to instill in German couples the "American" conviction, based upon "modern insights of psychology and pedagogy," that illegitimate children's intellectual, spiritual, and moral characteristics were not innate and immutable, but could be positively influenced by a healthy and caring family environment.[88] Still, one of the reasons that international adoptions seem to have touched a nerve in Bonn and elsewhere in the 1955 Federal Republic was that prospective German parents were competing with American couples to keep their most "desirable" progeny at home. Implicitly, then, these discussions—and the resulting policies—were keyed to the notion of "normative" white German children.

Mischlingskinder, on the other hand, were treated as a separate, if related, category that raised distinctive challenges.[89] When it came to black German children, German authorities articulated a different rationale for discouraging intercountry adoptions to the United States. To explain their policy shift, the federal ministries repeatedly referenced the case of "Otto," earlier spotlighted in American ISS reports critical of proxy adoptions. Charging that the child suffered severe emotional trauma after being placed with an African American family, ministry memos analyzed the placement problem as twofold: first, the child's shock at and inability to adjust to an all-black family and neighborhood in the United States; and second, the child's subjection to racial segregation and Jim Crow laws in democratic America. Since white German families were still not adopting biracial children in any significant numbers (apart from a handful of well-publicized exceptions like the Lißners and Fiegerts),[90] the preferred destination for the children placed for adoption became Denmark where, German commentators curiously insisted, racial prejudice was nonexistent.[91]

By the early 1960s, intercountry adoptions of black German children to Denmark outpaced those to the United States. The Central Adoption Office of the Protestant Inner Mission was a primary force behind these adoptions and cooperated with public youth offices to identify black children to be shipped to Danish parents. German youth officials attributed Danish interest in the children to the exceedingly small number of native children available for adoption in Denmark, where prospective parents could wait up to a decade for a Danish child.[92] Since 1955, handfuls of black German children had been sent to the Danish children's camp Stig Guldburg in Nysted for several weeks of recuperative vacation by public youth welfare officials.[93] Such visits were organized by a Danish woman, Frau Tytte-Botfeldt. On the basis of this experience, she began to publicize the plight of black German children throughout Denmark and advocate their adoption by Danish couples and families—an initiative that came to be called "the Guldberg Plan." Over the course of the early 1960s, the statistics of the Protestant Central Adoption Office show that adoptions of *Mischlingskinder* to the United States were all but ended, while some 160 of the children were legally transferred to Denmark for adoption. Danish newspapers reported the illegal transport of hundreds more, but this allegation was denied by authorities in West Germany.[94]

In August 1962, the director of the German Protestant Youth Welfare Association visited Denmark in order to gauge the success of the adoption placements and determine whether this program should be continued or terminated. His experiences of meeting the adoptive families and observing the children were summarized in a report to the Association membership:

> In the children's demeanor we perceived in general only joy. The children appeared healthy and well cared for . . . and felt at home. These were children who were growing up well protected in a good parental home. The economic circumstances of the adoptive parents were thoroughly very favorable (engineer, business owners, teachers, etc.).
>
> Everywhere we went we were met with Danish hospitality by the adoptive parents and were able to gather some insight into the relationship between the parents and children. Everywhere it was the same picture. The children snuggled up to the parents trustingly and, when upset, sought them out. Some of the children were a bit nervous about our visit, for they feared that they'd again be separated from their parents. . . . The children learned Danish surprisingly fast, even those who were older. Because relatively many Danes know some German, the children's acclimatization was made somewhat easier. In the Danish schools things went well. There is great understanding for these children, especially since many teachers themselves have taken in one or two Mischlingskinder.[95]

In contrast to the troubling reports on adoptive black German children issuing from the United States, this report painted a picture of easy integration because of the class background of the parents and their assured cultural competence in easing the children from a German to a Danish context. Unlike the United States, Denmark is portrayed in terms of cultural similarity: it was like Germany, only better. This assessment was based on the perception that prospective Danish parents were "more broad-minded about the children's origins" than their German counterparts: while *Mischlingskinder* presented something of a race problem in Denmark, it was "not of the same type as in the Federal Republic." Because Denmark was deemed more culturally compatible than the United States and more tolerant than the children's country of birth, the German Protestant Youth Welfare Association, in reviewing these findings, strongly advocated that Germans "not deny Mischlingskinder a *Heimat* with Danish parents."[96]

This assessment was shared by the leading expert on German *Misch-lingskinder* at the time, University of Hamburg psychologist Klaus Eyferth, who had recently completed a federally funded sociopsychological study comparing two hundred white and two hundred "colored" occupation children.[97] Published in 1960, the resulting book, *Farbige Kinder in Deutschland* (Colored children in Germany), became the authoritative source of information and policy recommendations on the children. On the topic of intercountry adoption, Eyferth and his coauthors noted that in their research they often confronted the mistaken "notion that where large groups of colored people exist among the population, there must be fewer impediments" for the children. This misconception, they argued, accounted for the frequency with which the children's mothers expressed a desire to "emigrate together with the child to North America or to entrust it to American adoptive parents." Invoking his experience in the United States, Eyferth enumerated several reasons for his "principled" rejection of America as a destination for children and their mothers. First and foremost, he argued, the general population's practices of "segregation and discrimination against the Negro is still so evident that, despite progressive laws and the efforts of numerous open-minded people, much time will need to pass before the Negro can achieve full equality. . . . Even in the Northern U.S. states, Negroes are still treated as second-class citizens by the majority of whites." What is more, Eyferth observed, such social practices led to the racialization of "even European women who marry a Negro." German women accompanying their black husbands to the United States were "treated as a 'Negro' by the [white] population" and were denied social contacts with whites. Moreover, he noted, since "Negroes too often strictly observe racial differences, they reject whites who try to enter their circles." As a result, Eyferth warned, white German women and their "colored children" faced a future of social isolation in the United States.

When it came to the adoption of black German children—even motherless "*Heimkinder*"—by black American families, Eyferth and his coauthors also expressed grave concerns. In large measure, their negative disposition was predictable since it reiterated criticisms articulated in earlier ISS and West German federal Interior Ministry memos. Nonetheless, Eyferth's rationale for rejecting adoptions to the United States, and in particular by African American families, did distinguish itself in one important way: by reinterpreting the character of black motherhood vis-à-vis the black German child. Instead of representing "the American Negro mother" as natural nurturer to the black German child as earlier German commentators had done, Eyferth echoed the criticisms of American racial liberals of the 1940s and 1950s by suggesting that her maternal effectiveness was undermined by an overbearing demeanor and marked lack of decorum and restraint. In the case of American social science, this negative image of black motherhood was used to explain the origins of black Americans' alleged social and psychological pathologies.[98] In the case of this German psychologist, it served a different function. Eyferth employed the extant negative image of black motherhood to delineate national-cultural difference and distinguish between a putatively more refined set of European gender practices and sensibilities and their baser (African) American counterpart: "For the [child's] acclimatization into the colored American family, the role of the mother has proved to be a burden since it is articulated differently than in Germany. The mother of the American Negro family is in general much more domineering and emotional in her behavior than is usual here among us. Since children in Germany very seldom get the opportunity to meet a colored woman, they have no conception of their new 'Mama.' Should they already be old enough to expect a certain comportment among women, they will become cowed and intimidated if introduced into this completely different situation."[99]

Through his explicit comparison of black American and white German motherhood, Eyferth retreated from the earlier German tendency to treat blackness as the exclusive indicator of identity and belonging. While blackness remained a crucial component of the children's identity for Eyferth, he conceived it not as a monolithic racial category, but one conditioned by national and cultural factors. In effect, Eyferth's analysis proposed a distinction between American and German Blacks on the basis of their social environments, upbringings, and practices. Given the choice between the United States and Germany as a destination for the children, Eyferth and his colleagues unambiguously chose the latter since in Germany, they reasoned, the child "will be recognized as something more than just a member of a group": "In spite of all of the prejudice here, we still hold that the possibilities of attaining a respected place in society in Germany are greater than the chances, in North America, of finding people who have not been influenced by customary racial segregation."[100]

· · ·

Like virtually all statements by German public and private welfare organizations of the period, Eyferth's study and the Protestant Youth Welfare report stressed the need for youth officials to proceed with "great care, deliberation, and responsibility" in matters concerning German *Mischlingskinder*. Language to that effect became formulaic in official discussions of the children—from the level of local youth offices to the federal Ministry of the Interior—and emphasized that decisions regarding the children's placement were not taken arbitrarily but were based upon careful evaluation of the children's present welfare and future prospects.

From the mid-1950s, the West German state—following the lead of organizations like the ISS and the Protestant Youth Welfare Association, as well as the expert counsel of academic specialists like Eyferth—cultivated its role as protector and sought for its wards a more suitable and humane destination. In the process, the children's identity was reimagined, and the earlier indelible mark of (presumed) black *American* ancestry faded in importance. In confronting the issue of international adoptions and relocation, West German officials now encouraged a solution that would allow the children to "retain" their essential identity as Europeans (if not always as Germans).[101]

By embracing this more critical stance toward U.S. adoptions, West German officials were likely influenced by high political considerations. Appeal to their experience with adoptions of black German children to the United States provided a useful comparative perspective on social progress in both Western democracies and permitted a positive public reassessment of the success of postwar German racial reeducation. While federal and state officials stopped short of engaging in explicit social criticism of their Cold War patron, their altered stance on transatlantic adoptions alerted both national publics—along with an international network of social and Christian welfare organizations—that the United States had been tested, and found wanting, on the very principles with which it had come armed to democratize Germany. At home in West Germany, academics and the press leveled their criticism more explicitly. As Herbert Hurka noted: "One shouldn't overlook the fact that even in the U.S.A. the professed ideal and the practiced reality are not always identical. The illusion that America is, among other things, also a paradise for colored people should not be nourished." Or, as a regional West German newspaper pithily and provocatively put it: "The USA prefers 'Blonds.'"[102]

By the mid-1950s, *Ebony* magazine, along with black newspapers in New York, Chicago, and Philadelphia were reporting the "frictionless" integration of German schools at a time when the national guard was needed to compel compliance in the American South. The African American press perhaps proved a bit too willing to take Germans at their word, showcasing Erich Lißner's celebration of his multihued family and, several years later, lauding the "smooth integration" of biracial youth into the German workplace. But even though such press reports sometimes lacked critical historical and sociological perspective, their authors can surely be excused for their overly positive assessments. After all, they measured the apparently rapid racial progress made by postwar Germans against American responses to integrationist initiatives at home, which were more often than not marked by violent reprisals of antiblack racists. Given the protracted civil battle over racial integration raging in the United States, it is not surprising that in 1960 *Ebony*, in a feature titled "Brown Babies Go to Work," would quote with approval Nuremberg youth office official Dr. Dorothea Struwe's speech on the topic to fellow social workers: "The incidents in Little Rock have caused much indignation in Germany. I hope that no one will ever have reason to tell us Germans to clean [our own house]. . . . It is essential that our colored children can expand and develop their talents and abilities so that they will be firmly rooted in our community and will not some day constitute a source of unrest. They can help us make good some of the guilt we have laden upon us in the past. We can do so by approaching these children with tolerance and free of prejudice and by giving them full possibilities for their development."[103] In just over a decade since Hitler's defeat, a chastened nation appeared to have surpassed its tutor in the lessons of democracy and was "credentialed" to that effect by the favorable reviews of African American organizations and the press. By the turn of the 1960s, West German officials could point to their treatment of *Mischlingskinder* and claim a moral victory in the area of race relations.

This self-congratulatory assessment was not merely the conceit of a handful of federal and state ministry officials. Rather, it was reinforced by a series of publications by West German academics, youth workers, educators, and the press from the midfifties onward which touted the overall success of West German efforts to integrate schools and—as the oldest began entering their teenage years—the national workforce.[104] By the close of the 1950s, official and public attention increasingly turned away from the question of where black German children most properly belonged to focus instead on documenting efforts to aid the absorption of resident black German children into the West German economy. For despite the avid efforts devoted to international adoptions of black German children throughout the 1950s, the majority of the children had not, after all, been surrendered by their mothers for shipment abroad but remained in their country of birth.

Chapter Six

LEGACIES: RACE AND THE POSTWAR NATION

> Our social environment is the mirror in which we perceive
> what we ourselves are.
>
> —Klaus Eyferth[1]

As Black Germans, we are surrounded by silence;
surrounded by a society that denies our existence and negates the fact of racism;
surrounded by white peers who shut their mouths in incomprehension
when we talk about humiliation and anger;
surrounded by a wall of silence when we start to ask about our roots.

> —Sheila Mysorekar[2]

IN 1959, representatives of federal and state employment ministries, worker welfare organizations, industry, unions, and the press gathered in Frankfurt am Main to discuss how to facilitate the "frictionless professional incorporation" of the first wave of fifteen hundred black German teenagers, scheduled to leave school in the spring of 1960, into apprenticeships and employment. On hand as resident expert was University of Hamburg psychologist Klaus Eyferth, author of the influential comparative study of two hundred white and two hundred "colored occupation children. Emphasizing that his research detected no significant differences in intelligence, interests, or inclinations of black and white German children, he nonetheless argued that antiblack prejudice was real and widespread among white Germans, who continued to respond negatively to black children's color, illegitimacy, and origins in military occupation. While he urged the need to encourage public tolerance as well as practical assistance for the teens as they entered the job force, Eyferth counseled officials and employers to avoid singling them out for special treatment. He forcefully rejected segregationist proposals that had been bandied about to collect all "colored youth" into a handful of special apprentice homes or into one large industrial firm.[3] Despite Eyferth's concerns, the conference concluded with an optimistic prognosis. Provided West German officials and employers proceeded with sensitivity and helped cultivate a "shared sense of public responsibility for our *Mischlingskinder*," the teenagers' colleagues at work "would very quickly forget their differently colored skin and come to recognize and appreciate the human beings beneath it."[4]

By the turn of the 1960s, as the oldest of postwar black German youth concluded their education, the issue of the children's integration into the Federal Republic increasingly became narrowed to a myopic focus on job placement. Thanks to a strong economy and low unemployment—some West German industries had begun, with state support, to import southern European and Turkish "guest workers" to address a growing labor shortage—municipal and state offices reported the ready cooperation of West German employers in providing training and jobs for biracial youth, and generally painted a rosy picture of welcoming coworkers and unbiased absorption into working life.[5]

In the state of Hesse, which kept good records on the numbers and experiences of black German youth beginning job training, apprenticeships, or full-time employment during the years 1960–61, the state youth office reported that the 150 "colored youth" leaving school in the spring of 1960 would easily be accommodated since some ten thousand jobs and apprenticeships were available statewide. Subsequent reports from cities and towns throughout Hesse confirmed that the vast majority of black German teens had little trouble locating positions, either on their own initiative or with the help of the local public employment office. Moreover, after placement, follow-up interviews with employers and training personnel established that most were well satisfied with the teens' performance.

In a handful of instances, employers made a point of specifically requesting *"Mischlingskinder"* to fill apprenticeships. Officials scrutinized such requests carefully, refusing, for example, to accommodate a chocolate manufacturer on the suspicion that the firm intended to exploit the teens for marketing purposes, given the persisting historical association between black skin and chocolate confections in German advertising. Officials also declined the offer of a large auto manufacturer to take on numerous black German apprentices, fearing that a concentration of black youth in the workplace would hinder easy on-the-job integration. Hessian state officials monitored the placement of black teens, on the lookout for problems that might arise. In one case, the white proprietor of an Esso gas station in Frankfurt am Main attracted media and official attention when he came to the defense of his black trainee, K., who was threatened with the loss of his position by the Esso corporation, which vetted both the academic and job performances of its trainees. K. was not a particularly good student at school, but his boss praised his work and judged him "very handy, industrious, respectable, and well-liked by colleagues and customers." K.'s possible dismissal by the Esso corporation "struck [the boss] as inhumane." The director of the Frankfurt Employment Office followed up on the case and, after speaking to the proprietor of the gas station, reported the "impression that [the man] feels confirmed in his humanity since ... he's received over a hundred telephone calls praising his benevolent behavior. . . . One is left with the perhaps not unfounded suspicion that he wants to keep the boy at the station at all costs because he serves as a attraction and draws customer recognition of his humane attitude, which is not bad for business."[6]

If state employment officials scrutinized the motives of the gas station owner skeptically behind closed doors, they never aired their analysis publicly. Moreover, the press covered such "heroic" gestures avidly, celebrating them as proof of how far everyday Germans had progressed in their attitudes toward race.[7]

What received less public attention was the teens' placement into overwhelmingly manual and sometimes menial jobs. In good measure, this was beholden to German officials' oft-stated conviction that "among *Mischlingskinder* practical abilities predominate over theoretical intelligence."[8] This official bias persisted from the children's early school days, despite evidence to the contrary, and together with their often depressed socioeconomic background conditioned their educational trajectory.[9] Black German children were disproportionately routed into rudimentary *Hauptschulen* and school-leaving by the age of fourteen, rather than into the *Realschulen* or *Gymnasien*, which extended their formal education up to another half decade and, in the case of the latter, prepared students for university study. When it came to job placement, the boys apprenticed or took work as gas station attendants (a common occupation), in laundries or dry cleaners, as cooks, sheet-metal workers, painters, lathe operators, mechanics helpers, or automobile, truck, or machine mechanics. Girls, on the other hand, tended to take jobs as domestic help (in private homes or institutions), in laundries, or less frequently as office help. Some became salesgirls (typically in small grocery stores or bakeries) or worked as hairdressers. Although a notable number of teenaged girls expressed interest in careers in sales or in hair salons, they were often discouraged from pursuing them. This was due in large measure to negative response from prospective employers who claimed to anticipate hostile customer reaction. One salon owner, for example, suggested that his clients did not want to be touched by black hands. In another case, a laundry owner initially hired a biracial girl only to fire her shortly thereafter because of the "strong peculiar odor of her dark skin"—a long-standing allegation of white racists intent on establishing Blacks' fundamental and pervasive difference, down to and in-

Orphaned Afro-German maids at work at the Bavarian villa of
German movie star Curd Jürgens, shown with his wife, Simone. The teens
lived with a foster-mother in a nearby village *Ebony* reported in 1960.
Courtesy of The Newberry Library, Chicago.

cluding the olfactory. Given the uncertain climate of reception, some
teens proved reticent to expose themselves to the possibility of rejection
or humiliation on the basis of race and appear to have abandoned their
aspirations untried.[10]

By the early 1960s, at the level of social representation if not social reality, West German press reports, official memos, and academic assessments projected the image of a stable and prosperous postwar nation
whose bureaucrats and employers operated in accordance with the principles of social justice and economic rationality.[11] As a result, the specter
of racist irrationality was declared banished from the reconstructed West
German state, but only because integration was defined and pursued in

exclusively economic, rather than broadly social, terms.[12] This approach, to paraphrase David Abraham, valued the children's labor over their aspirations and dreams: "Instead of hope, it offered them only a job."[13]

The (Economic) Miracle of the Vanishing *Mischlingskind*

After declaring the integration of *Mischlingskinder* an overwhelming success, official and media attention to the children—and the postwar problem of race—sharply subsided in the Federal Republic. The color-blind aspirations of postwar liberalism, fueled by an expanding economy, allowed West German officials to declare equality achieved and racial difference irrelevant. The early 1960s initiated a shift away from the domestic discussions of race and national belonging that characterized the 1950s. One significant step in this direction was the resistance encountered by the federal Ministry of the Interior when its officials in 1960 ordered West German *Länder* (states) to conduct another survey of the numbers of *Mischlingskinder* in their jurisdictions. The state cultural minister of Schleswig-Holstein refused outright, citing both pragmatic concerns (understaffing) and legal principle (the Basic Law's prohibition of singling out individuals on the basis of race). While it bears noting that these objections issued from a state with a minute black population, it is nonetheless significant that the rebuke effectively nullified the German Interior Ministry's practice, since the Nazi years, of keeping separate statistics on its black citizens.[14]

Indicative of the postwar retreat from a focus on race was an article on black German youth entitled "They Have the Same Prospects as Whites," which found its way into the files of the federal Ministry of Youth and Family as an authoritative comment on the issue. In it, Ruth Bahn-Flessburg interviewed a handful of biracial teenagers and attested to their easy integration into the West German economy. She also, however, visited the teens' families and provided the following assessment: "If I conclude my interviews with my visit to a mother who lives in two small rooms near the city limits with her *seven illegitimate children*—all from different fathers—, it is only to indicate that the difficulties the majority of colored occupation children have to battle are caused not by skin color but by their origins [*Herkunft*]; they have to cope with the same problems as white children who grow up in similar circumstances." At the end of her essay, Bahn-Flessburg posed the question: "Does the problem of colored occupation children exist in the Federal Republic?" and answered it with an unequivocal "No." "But what continues to exist in the closing

years of the twentieth century," she maintained, "is the problem of illegitimate children."[15]

Bahn-Flessburg's analysis was far from anomalous. Her arguments
were echoed in numerous memos and publications by West German
youth and social workers at the turn of the 1960s, as well a film docu-
mentary "How Toxi really lives" (*Wie Toxi wirklich lebt*, 1958). When, in
1960, a Munich newspaper featured an article titled "*Not* all children are
equal under the law" it was decrying the prejudicial treatment of illegitimate, rather than "colored," children.[16]

By the early 1960s, reports of successful integration increasingly down-
played the social significance of race in the Federal Republic and in effect
initiated a tendency to derace the nature of the postwar *Mischlingkind's*
difference. This response, moreover, became symptomatic of a shift in
West German public discourse during the early 1960s, which declared
racial integration accomplished and the postwar period of racial reexam-
ination and reeducation closed. In a reversal of the rhetorical strategy of
postwar racial liberalism of the 1950s that uncoupled the mother and
child to save the latter, early 1960s liberalism removed the biracial child
from center stage—in this case by shifting moral scrutiny back to the
behavior of their white German mothers. One consequence of this
new public understanding was that it reinforced the representational
link between unregenerate femininity and social disorder by nimbly
transforming a social dilemma of national-historical proportions into
a "timeless" problem rooted in aberrant white female sexuality and
socialization.

The second consequence was the disappearance of the postwar
Mischlingskind as an object of social policy. This absence had a profound
effect, for it was accompanied by a silencing of official and public
discussions regarding the role of race *within* German society and
national identity. What is more, it authorized a cultural atmosphere of
racial exclusivity in defining the nation. That is, while contemporary
Germans, since the 1960s, have recognized an increasing ethnic diversity within their borders as a demographic fact, they have interpreted
this as resulting from an influx in foreign laborers and asylum seekers,
attracted by Germany's strong economy and social welfare provisions.
However, *membership in the nation* in the form of citizenship was culturally imagined and, until 1999, to a large extent legally prescribed as
the more exclusive domain of homogeneous whiteness. This perceptual
racial narrowing of "nation" left little space—social or psychological—
for German citizens of color who, to borrow from W.E.B. DuBois,
daily felt the "doubleness" of their lives as Blacks and Germans in a
hostile, or at best, indifferent society that was their own. The silence
that overtook issues of race in West Germany muted discussions of the

relationship between blackness and German-ness for two decades, until its reemergence in the 1980s in the form of identity politics and discussions of German multiculturalism.[17]

"*Die Toxis Sind Erwachsen*": Black Skin and Black Sexuality in the West German Press

While social policy interest in black German children subsided by the early 1960s in West Germany, sporadic media attention continued. Under headlines announcing that "the Toxis are now grown up"—and accompanied by eye-catching photos of the attractive physical attributes of the females among them—a handful of articles in the national press over the course of the 1960s and 1970s provided occasional updates on the personal and professional experiences of the young adults.[18]

Although this press coverage overtly professed interest in how "the Germans with dark skin" were faring since they reach adulthood, and chronicled examples of racial prejudice and racist epithets they had weathered during their lives, the tenor of the articles was upbeat and optimistic. True, black Germans experienced adversity and were sometimes treated as "second-class Germans" by their white neighbors. Nonetheless, press reports suggested, such experiences strengthened the young adults' resilience and resolve. They covered the stories of black Germans who had not only survived, but prevailed.[19]

In large measure, this was due to a tendency in the popular press to focus on the biographies of performers, personalities, or sports figures—celebrities whose careers contrasted sharply with the mundane blue- and pink-collar work performed by most young black Germans—and package them as representative of the larger social group of grown *Mischlingskinder*. We have already seen this phenomenon in the case of the child star, Elfriede Fiegert, and certainly the West German press continued to run irregular sequels to her "story" into the 1970s. Popular weekly magazines also highlighted the achievements of black German males like "Jimmy" Georg Hartwig, who grew up in miserable circumstances in Offenbach and braved childhood taunts of "nigger pig" and "whore's son" to become a soccer star of the "1860 München" team. Or Georg Steinherr who had to learn to protect himself from bullies as a small child and put his resulting "aggressiveness" to good use as a professional boxer. Steinherr was quoted as saying, "I attribute my cleverness in the ring to that shot of Negro blood. There are also advantages to being a Mischling."

By the 1970s, the popular West German magazine *Quick* invoked the American phrase, "Black is beautiful," and reported on the various ways that biracial German women benefited from the current mode and marketability of their black skin. There was, for example, Nicky, "a poor orphan child, abandoned by her parents," now transformed into a long-legged knockout (featured in a full-page photo), who worked in a Munich boutique and turned the heads of men as she walked down the street. Or Rosi, cruelly ridiculed as a "Niggerkind" by classmates, who as a child tried to scrub her "dark skin clean." She was now a fashion model, earning a lucrative daily rate of six to eight hundred German marks, thanks to her "dark, exotic" looks. Sweet revenge, the article suggested.

In a reversal of racial liberals' admonishment to white Germans in the early 1950s not to fret about what would become of postwar *Mischlingskinder* after they reached puberty, West German media coverage of the mid-1960s through late 1970s reveled in exploring precisely this issue in explicitly sexual terms. Magazine articles betrayed a voyeuristic fascination with black female physicality and sexuality in particular, and overtly invested these with power to stimulate white male desire.[20] Even respectable newspapers like the *Frankfurter Allgemeine Zeitung* invoked the young women's "attraktive Andersartigkeit," or attractive racial difference, in sociological discussions of the teens' integration into the workforce.[21] Illustrated weeklies, on the other hand, ran photo essays that promised an intimate peek into the personal lives and interracial relationships of Black Germans.

One particularly egregious exposé appeared in the magazine *Neue illustrierte Revue* in early 1975 under the title *"Adam und Eva: Ein Mädchen wie Toxi fand sein Glück an der Elbe"* (Adam and Eve: How a girl like Toxi found happiness on the Elbe).[22] While ostensibly focused on the domestic happiness achieved by the cohabiting couple of Carole, a black German child-care worker, and her boyfriend, Dieter, a white German salesman, the feature and interviews on which it is based were organized around a salacious fascination with black sexuality, interracial sex, and the long-range intentions of the white male partner. When asked how the couple met, Dieter, "a tall, good-looking man who says he has never lacked opportunities with the female sex," described his first impression of Carola, whom he observed while at the movies one autumn day: "As I saw her in the partial darkness of the cinema I thought: 'What a pretty exotic bird . . .' I was not averse to the usual little adventure." Although Dieter quickly adds that he "soon learned that Carola is not the type for a fleeting romantic adventure," the magazine feature suggested the opposite. In fact, it emphasized both Carola's sexual appeal and the sexual nature of the relationship in text and photos. In a full-page nude photo of Carola and Dieter facing each other in profile, Carola stands fully extended and tilted slightly forward, with forearms leaning on the back of a wooden chair to better expose breasts and buttocks. As she looks down into the admiring eyes of a squatting Dieter, offset to the lower right-hand corner, Carola's nude, sexualized body is clearly the focus and dominates the frame. However the photo and text are as much about white male desire for black-skinned women—both overtly, through Dieter's story and experience, and more implicitly through such strategies of reader titillation.[23]

Particularly duplicitous, yet telling, was the interviewer's opportunistic attempt to draw Dieter out on the issue of marriage while Carola ran out to the bakery for sweets to accompany coffee. Dieter thinks for a moment, we are told, and then responds: "It may sound strange but we have never spoken about it. I really haven't ever thought about it either. Our life is so . . . so satisfying. No, that word isn't quite right. Well, I can only speak for myself, and I find that life at the moment feels fine, the way it should." When Carola returns—reportedly bearing *Mohrenköpfe* or "moor's heads," a chocolate confection—she is not asked the marriage question. She is, however, asked whether it bothers her to be caring for other people's kids on a daily basis, rather than her own. She responds, "I've gotten used to it, taking care of others' kids. After all, it's my job."[24]

Although the article self-consciously adopted a kind of swinging-seventies tone of enlightened openness on issues of race and sex, it was riddled with cultural biases—reaching back to the 1950s and before—that informed official and media approaches to black Germans. When preparing black German teens for school-leaving, for example, state officials and social workers emphasized that it was particularly important to give black German girls good job training since they would have meager marriage prospects.[25] *Adam und Eva* reinforced this assumption by depicting Carola as the lover of a white man, on the one hand, and the caretaker of her employer's white children, on the other. Interracial marriage and motherhood were ruled out for her. She was not consulted about her sentiments on the topic or her aspirations for the future, but was portrayed as a sweet, and thoroughly sexualized, modern mammy.[26]

In a side-bar column to the article, moreover, Carola is posed a couple of "candid" questions about black male sexuality and her experiences with her former husband, a medical student from Ghana. "Finally we can get it firsthand," wrote the interviewer, "how 'great' it really is to sleep with a *Neger*." To which Carola calmly replied:

> The widespread notion regarding the insatiable and incessant potency of the Negro is a legend, one that really seems to excite many people's imagination. The joke, at least in relation to our current discussion, is

that Blacks in Europe feel pressured to live up to their reputations as
lady-killers. . . .

Neue Revue: But Carola, you were married for two years to a black man. So
your husband wasn't a "wonder-wand" in bed?

Carola, in response, attempted to humanize her former husband and
subvert the interviewer's obvious intent of differentiating black male
sexuality from white. "Wonder-wand in bed—that's good. Haha. What I
really liked about him then was his manner, his character. It was really
just a matter of chance that he wasn't white. Since he was also the first
man with whom I had physical relations, I had no point of comparison
at the time. These days I know that good lovers and bad lovers come in
all skin colors."[27]

One could, of course, dismiss the images of black sexuality portrayed
in this article as the result of its author's individual obsession or a trashy
magazine's sensationalist marketing ploy. No doubt they were a bit of
both. But more significant is the fact that this portrayal (minus, perhaps,
the nude photos) was not outrageous for the time, but well within the
cultural mainstream. Although official reference to blackness gradually
disappeared from social policy following the turn of the 1960s, the tendency to stereotype and sexualize Blacks in German cultural and media
representations persisted.

One aspect of postwar German reconstruction that has gone unrecog-
nized are issues of continuity and rupture in social norms regarding sexual relations between white Germans and ethnic minorities. It is significant, in this connection, that 1945 represented neither a social nor moral
challenge to the prerogatives of white German men to engage in nonmat-
rimonial, nonreproductive sexual relations with women perceived as racial others. There was no social break in the cultural acceptability of *these*
types of relationships. One remarkable scene in a serialized novel from
1961, *Meine schwarze Schwester* (My black sister), which centered on the
troubled domestic life of a teenaged Afro-German girl, suggested continuities with sexual violence committed by German soldiers on racialized
women in conquered territories during World War II, when the girl's
white stepfather, who fought in the Wehrmacht on the Eastern front in
the war, nearly rapes her one day when they are alone together at home.
Stimulated by the sight of his stepdaughter's exposed "soft brown skin"
when he, in the heat of an argument, tugs at her bathrobe, he nonetheless
rationalizes his barbaric urge as revenge for his wife's rape by an African
American soldier, the girl's biological father.[28]

As the drama of this serialized novel and my earlier chapters make
clear, it was the sexual and romantic relationships between white women
and foreign black troops that represented a decisive break in German so-

cial norms and moral behavior from the point of view of most white Germans after 1945. White women's accessibility to men of color nullified Nazi social policy by challenging racialized gender ideology and effectively terminating state regulation of white women's reproductive sexuality. Interpreted as a threat to German honor, white masculinity, and national community both before and after 1945, interracial relations involving white German women encouraged continuities in the pejorative depiction of black male sexuality—if not always, after about the mid-1950s, in the depiction of black men sans sexuality. In press coverage of the 1960s and 1970s—unlike that of the late 1940s and 1950s—relationships between black German men and white German women go virtually unrepresented.[29]

The West German press sometimes raised, only to dismiss or dispel, the grave social biases experienced by black German youth and young adults. A couple of articles, for example, mentioned the ease with which some boyish black teenagers dated white girlfriends. Yet only one printed a teenager's fears that, although he had no trouble getting dates with white girls, they would prove unwilling to marry him when he got older. Such fears provide little insight into the social behavior and personal choices of individual white German women. Nonetheless, they were generated in response to normative social ideologies and practices, as well as cultural biases, regarding the perceived attraction and repulsion of black male sexuality. It bears remembering that it was mostly black German boys reaching puberty who were shipped to Frau Dilloo's Albert-Schweitzer-Home for segregated living, and later, to Denmark for adoption by white families there. German officials and social welfare workers, that is to say, were perceptibly nervous about both the "integrationist potential" of postpubescent black German males, as well as its ensuing social consequences.[30]

Black German girls also appear to have suffered from their cultural image as sex objects. Carola, in "*Adam und Eva*," mentioned that before she could reconcile herself to a relationship with Dieter, she first needed to surrender the "I-just-want-to seduce-you-complex" she had internalized at an earlier age vis-à-vis white men. Another young woman was reported by a social worker (in an article titled "Skin color is no problem"!) to have attempted suicide after a one-night stand with a white German partner. Additionally, an Afro-German acquaintance, in discussing her experiences as a teenager in the late 1950s and 1960s, has mentioned being repeatedly subjected to unwanted sexual innuendo and propositions by male acquaintances and strangers on the street—this after nuns who were raising her admonished that she, as a black girl, would need to choose between a future as a Christian missionary or a prostitute. To them, she was not only more sexualized than her white counterparts, she was presumed to be potentially morally abject as well.[31]

These examples are admittedly anecdotal.[32] However, they help to provide context for a poem, published by a Black German named Tumoi in the 1990s, titled "White Love":

> I am just a substitute
> sitting on a rock
> I am just a second song
> waiting for the dance
>
> The *experience to be told*
> back at home
> *The artifact to be bought*
> *from the depths of the dark*
>
> I am just an african fruit
> waiting to be tasted
>
> An image for the camera
> *Furniture for the sitting room*
> I am just a substitute
> painted in black![33]

Such feelings of debased objectification, profound alienation, and racial difference were not, however, featured in the media reports on Black Germans through the late 1970s in the Federal Republic. In 1977, for example, the popular magazine *Quick* highlighted, among others, the success story of Ramona. Dubbed "Germany's most famous Mischling," Ramona was the twenty-three-year-old lead singer of the pop group Silver Convention, with a hit single "Fly, Robin, Fly" that was played abroad and a fast-selling second album. Questioned about the impact of *her* racial difference on her life, Ramona indicates it has had no perceptible negative effect: "Neither my color nor my Negroid nose ever bothered me. My skin color was and is no problem for me. I would surely be just as happy if I were green." By the 1970s, such press coverage challenged the earlier liberal German assumption that "Mischlingskinder *suffered from their skin color.*" Nonetheless, that persistent notion, which held sway in the 1950s, did not disappear completely in the 1970s. Rather, it coexisted with an emerging focus on the substantial benefits bestowed by black skin and exotic otherness in a capitalist land attuned to cosmopolitan cultural trends. Black skin came to be represented in the media in a dual manner: as either an obvious physical and commercial advantage to be exploited or a psychological burden to be borne. Together they suggested there were "healthy" and "unhealthy" ways to be black in

West German society.[34] These were, of course, two sides of the same coin. Both emphasized individual disposition and choice over social analysis. And both derived from the tendency to minimize the existence and impact of racism in a dominant German society that remained convinced of, and committed to, its own intrinsic whiteness.

The Pursuit of Visibility and Voice: Black German Identity and Political Subjectivity

> In the spring of 1984, I spent three months at the Free University in Berlin teaching a course in Black American women poets and a poetry workshop in English for German students. One of my goals on this trip was to meet Black German women, for I had been told there were quite a few in Berlin.
>
> Who were they, these German women of the Diaspora? Beyond the details of our particular oppressions—although certainly not outside the reference of those details—where do our paths intersect as women of color? . . . [W]hat can we learn from our connected differences that will be useful to us both, Afro-German and Afro-American?
>
> Afro-German. The women say they've never heard that term used before. . . .
>
> "I've never thought of Afro-German as a positive concept before," she said, speaking out of the pain of having to live a difference that has no name; speaking out of the growing power self-scrutiny has forged from that difference.
>
> I am excited by these women, by their blossoming sense of identity as they say, "*Let us be ourselves now as we define us. We are not a figment of your imagination or an exotic answer to your desires. We are not some button on the pocket of your longings.*"[35]

Thus wrote poet Audre Lorde in the original preface to *Farbe Bekennen* (*Showing our Colors*) which appeared in 1986 in the Federal Republic. Considered an important foundational text for the establishment of Black German identity and community, *Farbe Bekennen* was one of the first publications to establish the historical presence of Blacks in Germany, as well as explore—through the perspective of autobiography, family histories, interviews, discussions, and poetry—both the social experiences of Afro-Germans, and the emotional and personal repercussions of being treated as alien in a country that is your own.[36]

As Lorde's observations indicate, the articulation of "Afro-German" (later "Black German") as a positive personal and social identity emerged through Black German women's intellectual contact with, and mentoring by, individual African American women who were poets, scholars, and, not coincidentally, feminists. Asserting self and voice, in this context, engaged the dual interlocking identities of race and gender: not only what it meant to be black in a predominantly white Germany, but what it meant to be a black woman in that context as well.

To make this point is not to claim that Afro-German identity is somehow derivative of Afro-American, as it was then called. Rather, it is to recognize *both* that feminism developed a language with international application and resonance *and* that the articulation of Black German identity occurred within the larger conceptual framework of an international Black Diaspora, based upon shared experiences of "oppression," as Lorde suggested, even if these experiences were inflected differently according to distinct national experiences of colonialism, slavery, state-sanctioned civil inequality, or more informal forms of social inequality. Thus, in the 1980s (as in the late 1940s and 1950s), reformulations of notions of race, identity, and nation in Germany were part of a larger transnational dialogue with African Americans and the American experience of race and gender. This can be seen in the critical concepts and terminology that Lorde introduced to her students in Berlin in the early 1980s, which assisted them in their social analysis and allowed them to reject their received identities as *"Mischlinge," "Besatzungskinder,"* or *"Negerin,"* in order to conceive of themselves in a positive way as Afro-Germans. One can say that Afro-German identity was galvanized through dialogue with African American intellectuals. While extremely influential, however, comparisons with the African American experience were only one point of reference for the development of Afro-German subjectivity. Black Germans have also looked to postcolonial experiences and social theorizing of other Black Europeans. And since they hail from diverse family backgrounds, some Black Germans have traveled to African countries in search of their fathers, self-knowledge, political engagement, or a sense of belonging.[37]

The publication of *Farbe Bekennen* has been recognized as a milestone since it helped stimulate the creation of a national movement committed to the empowerment and political solidarity of Black Germans. This has been accomplished, with some degree of success, through the creation of organizations such as Initiative Schwarze Deutsche (ISD) in 1985 and Afro-deutsche Frauen (ADeFra) in 1986; by founding Black German publications (such as *afro-look, Afrakete,* and *AfroCourier*); and by sponsoring a German Black History month (after the American model) and annual Bundestreffen, or nationwide conferences of Black Germans.[38]

Although these initiatives grew from the efforts of Afro-German citizens, they have expanded to encompass a diversity of ethnic minorities of color residing in Germany. From the early 1990s, in fact, the ISD's magazine *afro-look* adopted a bilingual approach, publishing in German and English in order to reach both immigrants who had not yet mastered the local language in Germany as well as people of color in the United States, Anglophone Africa, and the Caribbean.[39] By that time, as historian Tina Campt has described it, the Black German movement, "along with other ethnic groups throughout Europe," was "engaged in a process of reappropriation and rearticulation of the concept of blackness, redefining it as a political position ... of strength and self-definition.... [B]y reclaiming 'Schwarzsein' [the condition of being black] in public and political forums ... and within leftist and feminist political coalitions among individuals of Arabic, Turkish, Latin American, Afro-German, Jewish and other heritages, individuals of different ethnic backgrounds draw on the collective strengths and commonalities of their shared experiences of racism, oppression, and marginalization. At the same time they are reciprocally compelled to confront their own individual differences."[40] Thus defined, the term "Black German" has become a much more expansive politically inflected social category, a kind of antiracist front directed against the upsurge of ethnic prejudice and violence in contemporary Germany. Rather than refer, as the term "Afro-German" does, to a smaller population of Black German *citizens*, "Black German" encompasses a broader multihued, multiethnic population of *residents* committed to the cause of social equality and justice within Germany.

"Black German" is therefore an identification with certain elasticity. This elasticity, moreover, is dependent on specific national histories and conditions. The umbrella effect of "Black German" in Germany, employed in part as political strategy to unite people of color to fight an ostensibly resurgent racism in the Federal Republic, has not found a parallel in the United States. There, a "Black German Cultural Society" was founded in January 1998 in Chicago. Although it drew inspiration from the Black German movement in Germany, it does not have close connections with organizations in Germany. And although its members, like its German counterparts, are committed to human equality and the fight against racism, it defines its membership in a narrower way: as persons of color of German birth or descent. Like Afro-Germans in the 1980s, a significant focus appears to be the quest for self-definition as Black Germans, including recognition of their history and experiences. While Afro-Germans in Germany have struggled to revise the dominant myth of the lily-white nation, for Black Germans in the United States, the unitary narrative against which they define themselves tends to be subnational, rather than national. The cultivation of a Black German identity in the

United States derives from a desire for recognition of their unique histories in the Black Diaspora. Although they crossed the Atlantic, their ancestors were not necessarily part of the Middle Passage. They resist having their histories subsumed by more dominant African American origin narratives centered on slavery. Although they identify as black, they want to retain a sense of their German cultural heritage, and in some instances feel that they have been subject to prejudice by African Americans in the United States because of it. That said, one of their goals is to "build upon relationships with the African American community and other groups . . . to improve opportunities for all people of color." Since some of the Society's members are Black German women, adopted by African American couples or married to African American husbands, or both, with children who self-identify as African American, those relationships can be extremely close. Moreover, because of these personal histories, many are American citizens. As a result, the identification of "Black German" in the United States tends to be cultural and elective. As such, Black Germans cannot be readily counted. Currently, the membership of the Black German Cultural Society is small and geographically scattered, and their organization consists mostly in the virtual world of the Internet. But they have recently launched a new web site and are making plans for a conference, so the activities and possibilities of self-definition continue.[41]

The number of Black Germans in the Federal Republic is likewise difficult to establish. This is due, ironically, to the success of the color-blind liberalism introduced in the 1950s and the subsequent effacement of race as a category of census taking and social analysis, if not social experience. Estimates of the numbers of Black Germans range widely from a low of 30,000 (for Black German citizens) to a high of about 700,000 (as a combined total of all citizens and residents of color in Germany). What is clear is that they are a heterogeneous population, ranging from Afro-Germans whose families held German citizenship since the nineteenth century, to children of troops that occupied the Rhineland after 1918 or Germany after 1945, to children of so-called guest workers or international students entering either of the Cold War Germanys since the 1950s, to more recent immigrants or asylum seekers. What is more, they constitute a significant minority in contemporary Germany—yet one that has not received much recognition from German officials or the German public. They are, one could say, undetected by the radar screen of German social consciousness.

This is not to say that white Germans are unaware of minorities in their midst. In fact, for the past couple of decades, and especially since German unification in 1990, minorities living in Germany found themselves at the center of heated debates regarding immigration and citizenship law, as well as the impact of immigration on the German nation, culture, and economy. There has also been a good deal of attention devoted to displays of bias and violence toward ethnic minorities in German society, due in part to a marked increase in asylum seekers and immigration from Eastern Europe and the former Soviet Union since the end of the Cold War.

As a result, in the past few decades, German officials, social scientists, and the press have tended to interpret expressions of ethnic prejudice and violence in the Federal Republic as "xenophobia," or hatred toward *foreigners*, and have not investigated these behaviors as reflecting a more generalized German racism. While this focus is in part understandable, given the upsurge in immigration, it has had the consequence of constructing the problem of racist violence and its victims in a distortedly narrow way. The interpretative act of attributing the violence to "xenophobia" and identifying its victims as "foreigners" casts the problem as a short-term one: an uncomfortable period of adjustment issuing from the end of the Cold War, the demise of socialism and the East German state, and the ensuing civil, social, and economic crises that these circumstances have unleashed. It locates the *origins* of the problem as *external* to the German nation and German history, rather than treating the problem as connected to a longer and deeper German history of racism and racist violence.

This response goes a long way toward explaining the absence of public awareness of the existence and experiences of Afro-Germans.[42] When their presence does register, many white Germans assume that they too are immigrants: African asylum-seekers or even visiting African Americans. Their daily reception in public has been prefigured by a public policy focused on immigration. What is lacking is a social and historical consciousness. Blacks have had a long history of residence and citizenship within Germany.[43] For well over a century, they have been part of the German nation. However, their presence has not been sufficient to alter the conception of the German nation as fundamentally homogeneous and white.

Nonetheless, there have been moments in German history when their presence was publicly noted and perceived as intimately tied to the health and well-being of the white German citizen, family, and nation. That is the story I have tried to tell here: of an extended historical moment after 1945 when Afro-Germans attained a highly charged visibility in West German society, only to be rendered invisible once their value for the democratizing nation had dissipated. The challenge for contemporary white Germans—and for contemporary historians of white Germany—is to find a way to reconceptualize the nation and its narratives to recognize the existence and experiences of its minorities, not on the basis of "difference" but as Germans and equals.

If you do an internet search on "*Mischlinge*" these days, you will turn up scores of web pages devoted to dogs, the advantages of owning mixed breeds over pure breeds, and the occasional dog shelter advertising a lovable mutt for adoption. The notion of "mixed blood" has finally been transferred from human reproduction back to its origins in animal breeding in contemporary Germany. Now this is social progress. However, if you have a few more moments to spend at the computer and search the electronic database WorldCat, which catalogs published literature worldwide, you will find that "race"is something that Germany has very little of when compared to Britain, France, or the United States.[44] Some might argue that this is a predictable product of those latter countries' longer imperial or colonial histories. But when it comes to twentieth-century Germany, it has also been something of a historiographical blind spot.

•   •   •

The story I have told here has been a predominantly German one. It has suggested that postfascist sensibilities regarding race were formulated around a focus on "race mixing" and in ongoing, often intimate, interaction with American racial practices and ideologies. Surely, in the process, postwar Germans were reeducated in matters of race. But just as surely, this process of racial reeducation took a terrible toll on the family lives and social relationships of Afro-German children and their white mothers.

We know less about the children's fathers and the personal, professional, even psychological impact on them of their time in Germany. Most, following their military stint abroad, returned to the United States and, depending on their specific destination, to the official or informal practices of racial segregation and discrimination that governed their lives. Yet, times were a-changing, if slowly, in the postwar United States as well. It may well be that the impetus for the American civil rights movement cannot in the main be attributed to the specific eye-opening experiences of black American soldiers in occupied Germany. However these experiences certainly contributed to the gradual shift in social practices, perceptions, and policies governing interracial marriages, reproduction, and child rearing in the United States that began in earnest after 1945.[45]

Nonetheless white fears regarding the social consequences of "race mixing" did not dissipate quickly and may initially have intensified in

Courtesy of Lisa M. Hein Dixon.

response to a growing civil rights movement and an enlivened postwar liberalism intent on casting critical light on the shameful national problem of race.[46] The transformation of social policies and ideologies of race after 1945 was neither rapid nor one directional in either the United States or West Germany. For a good quarter century following the end of the war, the social acceptance of black-white marriage among whites in the both countries remained at a low level. The real-life result was that

black-white marriages remained rare; white women involved in such relationships were socially stigmatized and often economically disadvantaged; and black German children grew up deprived of at least one biological parent.

One such child was Lisa, who was four years old when this photo was
taken in 1949. She stands with her mother and baby sister: "A happy
family," she remarks, "torn apart because of racial issues." The photo
was one of the last to depict little Lisa's intact family. Shortly thereafter,
she was sent to live in a children's home by a mother who could no
longer care for her.

This book has primarily explored the public dimensions of racial reconstruction after 1945. But as Lisa's photo reminds us, the consequences
of prejudice are deeply and devastatingly personal—and often target the
most vulnerable. "I remember that day vividly," she recalls in retrospect
about the frozen moment in time just before her family dissolved. My
hope is that this book has provided some essential historical context to
the pressures that shaped her mother's decision and, ultimately, young
Lisa's life.

ABBREVIATIONS OF ARCHIVES CONSULTED

ADW—Archiv des Diakonisches Werkes der Evangelische Kirche Deutschlands, Berlin

BAB—Bundesarchiv, Berlin-Finckensteinallee

BAK—Bundesarchiv Koblenz

BayHStA—Bayerisches Hauptstaatsarchiv, Munich

DIF—Deutsches Institut für Filmkunde, Frankfurt am Main

HessHStA—Hessisches Hauptstaatsarchiv, Wiesbaden

HStAStg—Hauptstaatsarchiv Stuttgart

LAB—Landesarchiv Berlin

NAACP—Papers of the National Association for the Advancement of Colored People (on microfilm), Library of Congress, Washington, D.C.

NARA-CP—U.S. National Archives and Records Administration, College Park, Maryland

SA Nürnberg—Stadtarchiv Nürnberg

SdK—Stiftung deutsche Kinemathek/Filmmuseum, Berlin

StA Augsburg—Staatsarchiv Augsburg

StA Freiburg—Staatsarchiv Freiburg im Breisgau

SW—Social Welfare History Archives, University of Minnesota Libraries, Minneapolis

NOTES

INTRODUCTION
DEMOCRATIZING THE "RACIAL STATE": TOWARD
A TRANSNATIONAL HISTORY

1. Benedict Anderson, *Imagined Communities* (New York, 1994, first published 1983), 149; George Frederickson, *Racism: A Short History* (Princeton, 2002), 73. Frederickson was referring, of course, to those Germans and Americans who considered themselves white. The title's reference to the Third Reich as "racial state" comes from Michael Burleigh and Wolfgang Wippermann, *The Racial State: Germany, 1933–1945* (Cambridge and New York, 1991, reprinted 1993).

2. ADW, HGSt 1161, letter of Elisabeth Müller to Frl. Bäcker, 25 July 1952. On the history of black Germans prior to 1945, see the work of Tina Campt, Fatima El-Tayeb, Pascal Grosse, Katharina Oguntoye, Clarence Lusane, Lora Wildenthal, Paula Reed-Anderson, Susann Samples, Christian Koller, and Reiner Pommerin, as well as the memoir of Hans J. Massaquoi and the oral histories in May Opitz, Katharina Oguntoye, and Dagmar Schultz, eds. *Farbe bekennen. Afrodeutsche Frauen und den Spuren ihrer Geschichte* (Berlin, 1986).

3. ADW, HGSt 1161, letter of Frl. Bäcker to Schwester Elisabeth Müller, 19 July 1952.

4. NAACP, Reel 8: Group II, Box G11 "Brown Babies 1950–58," Walter White press release, 18 September 1952. Also Allan Gould, "Germany's Tragic War Babies," *Ebony* (December 1952): 74–78; and Erich Lißner, "We Adopted a Brown Baby," *Ebony* (May 1953): 38–45.

5. Although following the language of my sources, I explore black-white relations, it is important to remember that the multiethnic U.S. military forces were more diverse. West German officials and social workers ultimately did not attempt to distinguish between various ethnicities but collapsed them into the category of "colored," which came to be understood as a synonym for "Negro." A social history of the interactions between Europeans and Hispanic, Asian American, Native American, African American, and other minorities in the U.S. military during World War II and the Cold War remains to be written.

6. See for example Brenda Gayle Plummer, *Rising Wind: Black Americans and U.S. Foreign Affairs, 1935–1960* (Chapel Hill, 1996); and Carol Anderson, *Eyes Off the Prize: The United Nations and the African American Struggle for Human Rights, 1944–1955* (New York, 2003). Also Stuart Svonkin, *Jews against Prejudice: American Jews and the Fight for Civil Liberties* (New York, 1997); and Marc Dollinger, *Quest for Inclusion: Jews and Liberalism in Modern America* (Princeton, 2000). On the gendered dimensions of racial liberalism, see Ruth Feldstein, *Motherhood in Black and White: Race and Sex in American Liberalism, 1930–1965* (Ithaca, N.Y., 2000).

7. See for example Brenda Gayle Plummer, ed., *Window on Freedom: Race, Civil Rights, and Foreign Affairs, 1945–1988* (Chapel Hill, N.C., 2003).

8. Of course this meant turning a blind eye to the inconvenient fact of U.S. propaganda's own well-documented anti-Japanese racism. On this point see John Dower's *War without Mercy: Race and Power in the Pacific War* (New York, 1986).

9. United Nations General Assembly, "International Declaration of Human Rights" (New York, 1948). Also UNESCO, *The Race Concept*. (New York, 1952).

10. Mary Dudziak, *Cold War Civil Rights* (Princeton, 2000) examines this relationship. The quote is from a review of the book by John Summers, "Right Think, Wrong Reason," *Commonweal* (18 May 2001). Also Thomas Borstelmann, *The Cold War and the Color Line: American Race Relations in the Global Arena* (Cambridge, Mass., 2001).

11. An exception is the recent study by Maria Höhn, *GIs and Fräuleins* (Chapel Hill, 2002), which focuses in part on racial conflict in American occupation forces in Germany.

12. Other recent work that looks at social interactions between American military forces and occupied populations are: Petra Goedde, *GIs and Germans* (New Haven, Conn., 2003); Höhn, *GIs and Fräuleins*; Perry Biddiscombe, "Dangerous Liaisons: The Anti-fraternization Movement in the U.S. Occupation Zones of Germany and Austria, 1945–1948," *Journal of Social History* (Spring 2001); Yukiko Koshiro, *Trans-Pacific Racisms and the U.S. Occupation of Japan* (New York, 1999); Katharine H. S. Moon, *Sex among Allies: Military Prostitution in U.S.-Korea Relations* (New York, 1997).

13. Some exceptions are Opitz, Oguntoye, and Schultz, *Farbe bekennen*, and more recently, Uta G. Poiger, *Jazz, Rock, and Rebels: Cold War Politics and American Culture in a Divided Germany* (Berkeley and Los Angeles, 2000); Heide Fehrenbach, "Rehabilitating Fatherland: Race and German Remasculinization," *Signs: Journal of Women in Culture and Society*, 24, no. 1 (Autumn 1998): 107–27; Heide Fehrenbach, "Of German Mothers and 'Negermischlingskinder': Race, Sex, and the Postwar Nation," in *The Miracle Years: A Cultural History of West Germany, 1949–1968*, ed. Hanna Schissler, 164–86 (Princeton, 2001); Sara Friedrichsmeyer, Sara Lennox, Susanne Zantop, eds. *The Imperialist Imagination: German Colonialism and Its Legacy* (Ann Arbor, 1998); and Maria Höhn, "Heimat in Turmoil: African-Americans GIs in 1950s West Germany," in Schissler, *The Miracle Years*, 145–63.

14. Poiger, *Jazz, Rock, and Rebels*.

15. Barbara Fields, "Race and Ideology in American History," in *Region, Race and Reconstruction*, ed. J. M. Kousser and J. M. McPherson (New York, 1983), 154.

16. Matthew Frye Jacobsen, *Whiteness of a Different Color: European Immigrants and the Alchemy of Race* (Cambridge, Mass., 1998); Matthew Pratt Guterl, *The Color of Race in America, 1900–1940* (Cambridge, Mass., 2001).

17. For a discussion of this question in relation to cultural and gender identities, see Heide Fehrenbach, *Cinema in Democratizing Germany: Reconstructing National Identity after Hitler* (Chapel Hill, 1995), 6.

18. In an expanding literature on these points, see Robert G. Moeller, *Protecting Motherhood: Women and the Family in the Politics of Postwar West Germany* (Berkeley and Los Angeles, 1993); Atina Grossmann, "A Question of Silence: The Rape of German Women by Occupation Soldiers," *October* 72 (1995): 43–63; Eliz-

abeth Heineman, "The 'Hour of the Woman' ": Memories of Germany's 'Crisis Years' and West German National Identity," *American Historical Review* 101 (1996): 354–95; Elizabeth Heineman, *What Difference Does a Husband Make? Marital Status in Germany, 1933–1961* (Berkeley and Los Angeles, 1999); Fehrenbach, *Cinema*, chaps. 3–5; and Fehrenbach, "Rehabilitating Father*land*." Also Robert G. Moeller, " 'The Last Soldiers of the Great War' and Tales of Family Reunions in the Federal Republic of Germany," *Signs: The Journal of Women and Culture in Society* 24, no. 1 (1998): 129–46; Uta G. Poiger, "A New, 'Western' Hero? Reconstructing German Masculinity in the 1950s," *Signs: The Journal of Women and Culture in Society* 24, no. 1 (1998): 147–62; also Robert G. Moeller, *War Stories: The Search for a Usable Past in the Federal Republic of Germany* (Berkeley and Los Angeles, 2001), esp. 88–170; and Poiger, *Jazz, Rock, and Rebels.*

19. See, among others, Moeller, *War Stories*; Norbert Frei, *Adenauer's Germany and the Nazi Past: The Politics of Amnesty and Integration*, trans. Joel Golb (New York, 2002); Donald Bloxham, *Genocide on Trial: War Crimes Trials and the Formation of Holocaust History and Memory* (New York, 2001); Adalbert Rückerl, *The Investigation of Nazi Crimes, 1945–1978: A Documentation* (Heidelberg, 1979); Omer Bartov, Atina Grossmann, and Mary Nolan, eds., *Crimes of War* (New York, 2002); and Rebecca Elizabeth Wittmann, "The Wheels of Justice Turn Slowly: The Pretrial Investigations of the Frankfurt Auschwitz Trial, 1963–1965," *Central European History* 35, no. 3 (2002): 345–78.

20. Moreover, as historian Frank Stern has shown, after 1945 antisemitism transmogrified into a related philosemitism, which could be likened to antisemitism's photographic negative. That is to say, non-Jewish Germans, in public rhetoric and gesture, would attempt to prove and display their lack of antisemitic credentials by advertising and embracing admirable characteristics of Jews as a group (rather than denouncing Jews as a group for their negative stereotyped traits). Frank Stern, *The Whitewashing of the Yellow Badge: Antisemitism and Philosemitism in Postwar Germany* (New York, 1992); also Atina Grossmann, *Victims, Victors, and Survivors: Germans, Allies, and Jews in Occupied Germany, 1945–1949* (Princeton, forthcoming).

21. In *The Language of the Third Reich*, survivor Victor Klemperer recounts a conversation with a woman who had absorbed the lessons of the ubiquitous racist vocabulary circulating in Nazi Germany, such as *artfremd* (alien), *deutschblütig* (of German blood), *niederrassig* (of inferior race), *nordisch* (Nordic), and *Rassenschande* (racial defilement/racial shame). Klemperer, *The Language*, trans. Martin Brady (New Brunswick, N.J, 2000), 94 and 133 (quote in text).

22. A discussion of the role of antiblack racism in social policy during the Third Reich will be taken up in chapter 3. For recent literature on German colonialism and the French occupation of the Rhine, see the works of Fatima El Tayeb, Lora Wildenthal, Reiner Pommerin, and Koller cited in that chapter.

23. Historical studies of, and memoirs by, black Germans are listed in the bibliography of this book.

24. George Frederickson has emphasized the comparative dimension of racism in his *The Comparative Imagination: On the History of Racism, Nationalism, and Social Movements* (Berkeley and Los Angeles, 1997). Work has begun to be published on some of these issues by historians of Japan. See for example the excel-

lent book by Koshiro, *Trans-Pacific Racisms*. Interesting work has also begun on the postwar reformulation of notions of race and British identity. However, in that context the United States and the influence of American social science appears to play a subordinate role vis-à-vis decolonization and postimperial adjustments. Chris Waters, " 'Dark Strangers' in Our Midst: Discourses of Race and Nation in Britain, 1947–1963," *Journal of British Studies* 36, no. 2 (April 1997): 207–38; Kathleen Paul, *Whitewashing Britain: Race and Citizenship in the Postwar Era* (Ithaca, N.Y., 1997); Marcus Collins, "Pride and Prejudice: West Indian Men in Mid-Twentieth-Century Britain," *Journal of British Studies* 40, no. 3 (2001): 391–418.

25. Some of the historians who have begun to investigate these issues in the social and cultural realms are Atina Grossmann, Uta Poiger, Elizabeth Heinemann, and Maria Höhn.

26. Bamshad, Michael J., and Steve E. Olson, "Does Race Exist?" *Scientific American* 289, no. 6 (December 2003): 78–85.

27. Tina Campt has noted that " 'Black German' emphasizes the constructedness of blackness in German society and the fact that public perception of blackness in Germany is not restricted to the attribute of skin color." For astute observations on Black German identity and German multiculturalism, see Tina M. Campt, "Reading the Black German Experience: An Introduction"; Michelle M. Wright, "Other-from-Within from Without: Afro-German Subject Formation and the Challenge of Counter Discourse"; and Carmen Faymonville, "Black Germans and Transnational Identification," *Callaloo* 26, no. 2 (2003): 288–94, 296–305, and 364–82 respectively. For thoughtful critical commentary on the meanings and politics of multiculturalism, see Stuart Hall, "Conclusion: The Multicultural Question," *Un/Settled Multiculturalisms: Diasporas, Entanglements, "Transruptions,"* ed. Barnor Hesse (New York, 2000), 209–41. On the presence of African Americans and African American culture in twentieth-century Europe more generally, see Heike Raphael-Hernandez, ed., *Blackening Europe: The African American Presence* (New York, 2004).

Chapter One

Contact Zones: American Military Occupation and the Politics of Race

1. William Gardner Smith, *Last of the Conquerors* (New York, 1948), 67–68 and 141.

2. For a recent discussion of postwar German-American "intercultures" centered on tourism, see Rudy Koshar, " 'Germany Has Been a Melting Pot': American and German Intercultures, 1945–1955," in *The German-American Encounter: Conflict and Cooperation between Two Cultures, 1800–2000*, ed. Frank Trommler and Elliot Shore (New York, 2001). While Koshar's concept of interculture is not particularly relevant for these purposes, his focus on "intersocial transfer," "transsocial mixing," and "official and unofficial encounters" represents an approach similar to mine in this chapter.

3. See for example, "Long-Range Policy Statement for German Reeducation" in U.S. Department of State Publication 2783: *Occupation of Germany: Policy and*

Progress, 1945–1946. Also Stern, *Whitewashing*; Bloxham, *Genocide on Trial*; James Tent, *Mission on the Rhine* (Chicago, 1983); Dewey A. Browder, *Americans in Post–World War II Germany: Teachers, Tinkers, Neighbors, and Nuisances* (New York, 1998), 55–95; Habbo Knoch, *Die Tat als Bild. Fotografien des Holocaust in der deutschen Erinnerungskultur* (Hamburg, 2001); Fehrenbach, *Cinema*, chap 2. For discussions on the reeducation of German POWs in American camps, see Arthur L. Smith, *The War for the German Mind: Re-educating Hitler's Soldiers* (Providence, R.I., 1996) and especially Matthias Reiss, *"Die Schwarzen waren unsere Freunde." Deutsche Kriegsgefangene in der amerikanischen Gesellschaft, 1942–1946* (Paderborn, 2002). For an interesting discussion of how "race" was officially mobilized in issues of cultural consumption and control after 1945 in East and West Germany, see Poiger, *Jazz, Rock, and Rebels*.

4. For examples of Germans' irritation at official American ambitions to reeducate them, see Volker Berghahn, *America and the Intellectual Cold Wars in Europe* (Princeton, 2001), esp. chap. 3; and Fehrenbach, *Cinema*, chap. 2. For a discussion on how American films constructed Nazi psychology in contrast to "gendered democratic subjectivity" in the immediate postwar period, see Andrea Slane, *A Not So Foreign Affair: Fascism, Sexuality and the Cultural Rhetoric of American Democracy* (Durham, N.C., 2001), esp. chaps. 4 and 5, quotation from 113.

5. For recent studies of German responses to American racism, African American troops, and African American culture in the 1940s and 1950s, see: Poiger, *Jazz, Rock, and Rebels*; Johannes Kleinschmidt, "Besatzer und Deutsche: Schwarze GIs nach 1945," *Amerikastudien* 40, no. 4 (1995): 646–65; Höhn, *GIs and Fräuleins*; David Braden Posner, *Afro-America in West German Perspective, 1945–1966* (Ph.D. diss., Yale University, 1997); Reiss, *"Die Schwarzen waren unsere Freunde"*; John Willoughby, *Remaking the Conquering Heroes: The Social and Geopolitical Impact of the Post-war American Occupation of Germany* (New York, 2001); and Fehrenbach, "Rehabilitating Father*land*," 106–27. For a detailed study of transition to American occupation on the ground in Germany, see Klaus-Dietmar Henke, *Die amerikanische Besatzung Deutschlands* (Munich, 1995).

6. Religious worship was divided by confession and by race on most U.S. military bases. Harvard Sitkoff quoted one base's worship schedule as distinguishing between "Catholics, Jews, Protestants, and Negroes." Sitkoff, "Racial Militancy and Interracial Violence in the Second World War," *Journal of American History* 58, no. 3 (1971): 667.

7. For detailed discussions of the politics and chronology of the integration of the U.S. military, see Richard M. Dalfiume, *Desegregation of the U.S. Armed Forces: Fighting on Two Fronts, 1939–1953* (Columbia, Mo., 1969); Morris J. MacGregor, Jr., *Integration of the Armed Forces, 1940–1965* (Washington, D.C., 1981); Bernard C. Nalty, *Strength for the Fight: A History of Black Americans in the Military* (New York, 1986); Richard O. Hope, *Racial Strife in the U.S. Military: Toward the Elimination of Discrimination* (New York, 1979); Sherie Mershon and Steven Schlossmann, *Foxholes and Color Lines: Desegregating the U.S. Armed Forces* (Baltimore, 1998).

8. Nalty, *Strength*, 261.

9. Even then it was executed under considerable political duress and was initially planned to be implemented in such a way to ensure that each base intro-

duced only a minority of African Americans, equivalent to African Americans' proportion of the overall domestic U.S. population, which hovered around 10 percent. However, nervousness regarding potential Soviet expansion into Western Europe led American officials in 1951 to triple the number of U.S. military troops in Europe to 234,000, which effectively tripled the number of African American troops from 9,000 to 27,000. Due to the logistical problems caused by such vast increases of personnel, the European Command was unable to integrate its forces in a way that ensured a 90 percent white majority in all units as originally desired. As a result, the principle of maintaining an overwhelming white majority of troops at all locations was compromised due to practical consideration. Historical Division, Headquarters United States Army, Europe, *Integration of Negro and White Troops in the U.S. Army, Europe, 1952–1954* (1956), 32–33, 41–46; and Nalty, *Strength*, 260–62. For personal recollections by African American soldiers in Germany, see Maggi M. Morehouse, *Fighting in the Jim Crow Army: Black Men and Women Remember World War II* (Lanham, Md., 2000), 215–16.

10. Military desegregation was not successfully completed across the board by 1954; there were striking holdouts in the southern United States well into the 1950s. Even when racial segregation was effected, racial discrimination persisted. See MacGregor, *Integration*, 473–529; Nalty, *Strength*, 267–86. See the discussion in "Dependent Children and Integrated Schools" on military bases (especially in the United States), in MacGregor, *Integration*, 487–500; for a discussion of how interracial marriages affected the base assignments of black GIs in the U.S., see "When Negro Servicemen Bring Home White Brides," *U.S. News and World Report* (11 October 1957): 110–12. For reminiscences of African Americans involved in aspects of military desegregation, see Morehouse, *Fighting*, 218–27.

11. For example, Jacobsen, *Whiteness*; Peggy Pascoe, "Miscegenation Law, Court Cases, and Ideologies of 'Race' in 20th-Century America," in *Sex, Love, Race: Crossing Boundaries in North American History,* ed. Martha Hodes, 464–90 (New York, 1999); Desmond King, *Making Americans: Immigration, Race, and the Origins of the Diverse Democracy* (Cambridge, Mass., 2000); Guterl, *The Color of Race*; Dollinger, *Quest for Inclusion.*

12. See for example Dudziak, *Cold War Civil Rights*. The interwar and wartime efficacy of the NAACP is discussed in Dalfiume, *Desegregation*; Grace Elizabeth Hale, *Making Whiteness: The Culture of Segregation in the South, 1890–1940* (New York, 1999), 203–40; and Joyce Thomas, "The 'Double V' was for Victory: Black Soldiers, the Black Protest, and World War II" (Ph.D. dissertation, Ohio State University, 1993). For a broad historical interpretation of the evolution of the ideology of race and whiteness in the United States, see Jacobsen, *Whiteness.*

13. The first excerpt is quoted in Dalfiume, *Desegregation*, 109–10. The second, by James, is quoted in Morehouse, *Fighting*, 18.

14. Quoted in Dalfiume, *Desegregation*, 109–10. Schuyler's original (pre–Pearl Harbor) statement read, "our war is not against Hitler in Europe, but against the Hitlers in America."

15. Ibid., 113, and more generally 105–47.

16. Although the Surgeon General certified that there was no biological justification for the policy, the Army insisted throughout the war that it was "not advisable to collect and mix Caucasian and Negro blood indiscriminately for later administration to members of the armed forces." Dalfiume, *Desegregation*, 107; MacGregor, *Integration*, 36. Mershon and Schlossmann, *Foxholes and Color Lines*; Walter White, *A Rising Wind* (Garden City, N.Y., 1945). NARA-CP, RG 107, Entry 188, Boxes 204, 217, 221 document some of the abuses in the United States and abroad.

17. NARA-CP, RG 107, Entry 188, Boxes 204, 217, and 221. Harry W. Roberts, "The Impact of Military Service upon the Racial Attitudes of Negro Servicemen in World War II" *Social Problems* 1, no. 2 (October 1953): 67. Also Nat Brandt, *Harlem at War: The Black Experience in World War II* (Syracuse, N.Y., 1996); Harold W. Burrow, "An Exploration of the Attitudes of the Chicago Defender towards the Negroes' Role in World War II" (Master's Thesis in History, Northern Illinois University, 1966); Maureen Honey, *Bitter Fruit: African American Women in World War II* (Columbia, Mo., 1999); Michael Keith Honey, *Black Workers Remember: An Oral History of Segregation, Unionism, and the Freedom Struggle* (Berkeley and Los Angeles, 1999); Morehouse, *Fighting*; Mary Penick Motley, ed., *The Invisible Soldier: The Experience of the Black Soldier in World War II* (Detroit, 1975); Thomas, "The 'Double V' "; White, *A Rising Wind*.

18. For letters of complaint regarding misassignment by individual African American soldiers, see NARA-CP, RG 107, Entry 188, Box 217.

19. Claude Ramsey, interviewed in Motley, *Invisible Soldier*, 172.

20. For a detailed discussion of some of these issues, as well as retrospective recollections of former German POWs of their experience in the United States, see Reiss, *"Die Schwarzen waren unsere Freunde."*

21. Interview in Motley, *Invisible Soldier*, 162.

22. Interview in ibid., 266.

23. Brandt, *Harlem at War, 108*. Brandt also notes that African American soldiers were treated in segregated, black only medical facilities, while German and Italian POWs were treated at the same medical facilities as white U.S. soldiers.

24. A recent book by Matthias Reiss, which I encountered after this chapter was written, reinforces some of these points. See *"Die Schwarzen waren unsere Freunde,"* particularly 112–28, 133–41, 215–30, 282–305.

25. Walter White's wartime tour resulted in the book *A Rising Wind*. Reports on his trip are also filed in NARA-CP, RG 107: Entry 188, Box 221. On his wartime visit to Britain and the political concerns it raised there, see Thomas Hachey, "Walter White and the American Negro Soldier in World War II: A Diplomatic Dilemma for Britain," *Phylon* 39, no. 3 (September 1978): 241–49. In 1948 Walter White took a follow-up tour that included stops in France and Germany. In 1946 and 1948, a delegation from the Negro Newspaper Publishers Association news service and seven black newspaper editors, respectively, toured Europe and reported back to the Secretary of War. NAACP, reel 8: Group II, Series G, Veterans Affairs Files. II: G11, Folder 1, 1948, "Report of Walter White on his trip to Germany," n.d. Also MacGregor, *Integration*, 210; and Lem Graves, Jr., "Editors Blast Segregation in Armed Services," *Pittsburgh Courier*, 5 June 1948, 1 and 5.

26. Dalfiume, *Desegregation*, 82–104; Robert Franklin Jefferson, "Making the Men of the 93rd: African American Servicemen in the Years of the Great Depression and the Second World War, 1935–1947" (Ph.D. diss., University of Michigan, 1995), 295–98.

27. Dalfiume, *Desegregation*; MacGregor, *Integration*.

28. Dalfiume, *Desegregation*, 95.

29. While demoralization did lead to a lack of motivation in some cases, statistics show that once called up, very few African American men failed to report for military duty and only "a few hundred individuals among three million Negro registrants" were charged for draft evasion. Morehouse, *Fighting*, 18.

30. Thomas, "The 'Double V,' " 202–6. Sitkoff, "Racial Militancy."

31. The civilian aide to the secretary of war also kept a file of reports, "Trends of the Negro Press," assessing the war years through the period of German occupation. NARA-CP, RG 107, Entry 188, Box 223. See also Barbara Dianne Savage, *Broadcasting Freedom: Radio, War, and the Politics of Race, 1938–1948* (Chapel Hill, 1999); Brandt, *Harlem at War*; A. Russell Buchanan, *Black Americans in World War II* (Santa Barbara, 1977); Honey, *Black Workers Remember*; Honey, *Bitter Fruit*; Jefferson, "Making the Men"; Motley, *Invisible Soldier*; Thomas, "The 'Double V' "; Richard J. Stillman II, *Integration of the Negro in the U.S. Armed Forces* (New York, 1968); and Neil A. Wynn, *The Afro-American and the Second World War* (New York, 1975). For a discussion of *The Negro Soldier*, see Thomas Doherty, *Projections of War: Hollywood, American Culture, and World War II* (New York, 1999), 205–26; on attention to "Negro morale" in the war effort, see Savage, *Broadcasting Freedom*, 106–53.

32. MacGregor, *Integration*, 212, for the first quote by McNarney and the quote by Clay. McNarney's "failure" quote comes from "Army: A General on Negroes," *Newsweek*, 30 September 1946, 25.

33. The issue was raised in September 1944 by John McCloy, assistant secretary of War. He concluded that "Operations Division does not consider that the German population merits special consideration in this regards." Memo of the War Department General Staff dated 23 September 1944, quoted in Kleinschmidt, "Besatzer und Deutsche," 648.

34. Nalty, *Strength*, 224; MacGregor, *Integration*, 176–86. The issue of political prestige and effectiveness was also extended to POW camps in the United States, where African American soldiers were initially not permitted to guard German prisoners of war. See Reiss, *"Die Schwarzen waren unsere Freunde,"* 59–67.

35. In 1946–47, the proportion of African American troops in Europe ranged between 10.33 and 9.95 percent. This percentage only jumped substantially in the early 1970s, with the creation of the All Volunteer Forces. Between 1970 and 1972, the percentage of Blacks in the U.S. army (not just in Germany) jumped from 13.5 to 17 percent, and in all branches from 11 to 12.6 percent. Willoughby, *Remaking the Conquering Heroes*, 129; and Daniel J. Nelson, *A History of U.S. Military Forces in Germany* (Boulder, Colo., 1987), 119–20. Between 1955 and 1966 U.S. troop strength in Germany ranged from a low of 237,000 to a high of 280,000 in 1962, following the Berlin crisis. See Oliver J. Fredericksen, *The American Military Occupation of Germany* (Washington, D.C., 1953), 46, 50; and Nelson, *A History of U.S. Military Forces*, 45 and 81.

36. On the slower demobilization of black soldiers, see Morehouse, *Fighting*, 187–93. For an example of reports submitted on cases of indiscipline by black troops in Bavaria, see NARA-CP, RG260, OMGUS, Records of the Executive Office, Office of the Adjutant General, Gen. Correspondence, Box 43, File AG 250.1, Incidents-American.

37. For statistics see MacGregor, *Integration*, 208–15. Also Frank E. G. Weil, "The Negro in the Armed Forces," *Social Forces* 26, no. 1 (October 1947): 97–98. The NAACP questioned the basis of and practices behind these statistics, and pointed to instances of racism in the execution of military justice. For a more detailed discussion of policy toward African American troops in occupied Germany, see Willoughby, *Remaking*. For a fictional account of white U.S. officers' illicit strategies in occupied Germany to eject black soldiers from their command, see the novel by William Gardner Smith, *The Last of the Conquerors*, 198–211.

38. MacGregor, *Integration*, 212. Also Truman Gibson, "Meader's Report Seeks to Remove GIs" in *Pittsburgh Courier*, 14 December, 1. My thanks to Helen Bailitz for bringing this article to my attention.

39. Gibson, "Meader's Report," 1, 4.

40. Marcus H. Ray, "Report of Tour of European Installations, 16 November–17 December 1946," in *Blacks in the United States Armed Forces: Basic Documents*, ed. Morris J. MacGregor and Bernard C. Nalty (Wilmington, Del., 1977); and MacGregor, *Integration*, 210–11.

41. MacGregor, *Integration*, 152–86, 224–29. Also Fredericksen, *The American Military Occupation*, 173. For a discussion of the treatment of African American GIs in occupied Germany, see Willoughby, *Remaking*, chaps. 3 and 6.

42. Nalty, *Strength*, 228–29.

43. Lem Graves, Jr., "Editors Bash Segregation in Armed Forces," *Pittsburgh Courier*, 5 June 1948, 1, 5, summarizes the report of seven "Negro newspaper editors" after a four-week tour of Army installations in Europe.

44. The first quotation is from "An Outrageous Occupation Policy" in *Chicago Defender*, 8 June 1946. The Nidda complaints are from Report of the Negro Newspaper Publishers Association, dated 18 July 1946. NARA-CP, RG 407, File 291.2. My thanks to Helen Bailitz for bringing this to my attention.

45. In Auerbach, conditions were improved according to an Army incident report filed two months later. NARA-CP, RG 407. File 291.2, U.S. Army; AG Decimal File 1946–48. "291.2 Race to 292 Employment," "Complaint concerning Negro Personnel at Auerbach, Germany," quoted in an unpublished paper by Helen Bailitz, "Caught in the Crossfire," 16 and 18–19.

46. Quoted in "Trends of the Negro Press" for the period ending 3 July 1948 from an article by Ollie Stewart in the *Baltimore Afro-American*, 22 June 1948. NARA-CP, RG 107; Entry 188, Box 223. Such assessments were also to be found in the white American press. See for example Alice Blankfort, "They Live as Conquerors," *Survey* 86 (September 1950): 408–11, which relays one German's observation on black-white relations in the American military in Germany.

47. In 1947, 84 percent of Germans polled said that they would have chosen to live under the Americans; the vast majority felt that economic conditions were better in the American zone. By 1951, moreover, a national survey among West

Germans judged the United States. "by far the most solicitous toward Germany's well-being." Richard L. Merritt, *Democracy Imposed: U.S. Occupation Policy and the German Public, 1945–1949* (New Haven, 1995), 259–60. On the indelible impression made by U.S. troops, see, for example, Kleinschmidt, "Besatzer und Deutsche," 650–53. I heard the comment about white American teeth from a number of older German women, most memorably, however, from a German neighbor of mine in Munich, who married a British soldier in the 1950s, which gave her an intimate point of comparison.

48. For a summary of survey results of postwar German attitudes toward the four Allied powers, see Merritt, *Democracy Imposed*, 259–61. German POWs also remember being pleasantly astonished by the abundant food and quality accommodations during their stay in American POW camps, see Reiss, "*Die Schwarzen waren unsere Freunde,*" 143–49. Also Höhn, *GIs and Fräuleins*; Kaspar Maase, *Bravo Amerika. Erkungungen zur Jugendkultur der Bundesrepublik in den fünfziger Jahren* (Hamburg, 1992); Poiger, *Jazz, Rock, and Rebels*; Heide Fehrenbach and Uta G. Poiger, ed., *Transactions, Transgressions, Transformations: American Culture in Western Europe and Japan* (New York, 2000).

49. The quotation is from Heineman, *What Difference*, 77. See also Grossmann, "A Question of Silence"; Heineman, "The Hour of the Woman"; Moeller, *War Stories*, 51–87; and Norman Naimark, *The Russians in Germany: A History of the Soviet Zone of Occupation, 1945–1949* (Cambridge, Mass., 1995), especially 69–140.

50. Naimark, *The Russians*, 92–93; Heinemann, *What Difference*, 96.

51. Even before the ban on fraternization was lifted, American occupation troops sought out Germans for any number of reasons, including the pursuit of souvenirs, services, or sex; an interest to socialize to learn more about Germany and its culture, and for many German American soldiers, a desire to locate and visit relatives still residing in the old *Heimat*. See Fredericksen, *The American Military Occupation*, 129–39; Willoughby, *Remaking*, 112–15; Höhn, *GIs and Fräuleins*, 52–85; Goedde, "From Villains to Victims: Fraternization and the Feminization of Germany, 1945–1947," *Journal of Diplomatic History* 23, no. 1 (Winter 1999): 1–20.

52. Reliable estimates of the number of rapes perpetrated by Soviet and American soldiers are hard to come by. Atina Grossmann notes that rapes by members of the Red Army in Berlin alone have been cited as ranging from between a low of 20,000 to a high of 1 million, yet she suggests that the number of 110,000, cited by Barbara Johr, seems possible. At least 10,000 women were killed. As for rapes by American troops, historian Hans Woller has been cited as fixing the number around one thousand. Grossmann, "A Question of Silence" and Sieglinde Reif, "Das 'Recht des Siegers.' Vergewaltigungen in München 1945," in *Zwischen den Fronten. Münchner Frauen in Krieg und Frieden 1900–1950*, ed. Sybille Krafft, 360–71 (Munich, 1995), here 365. For a discussion of allegations of sexual assault by American soldiers in Berlin, see Jennifer V. Evans, "Protection from the Protector: Court-Martial Cases and the Lawlessness of Occupation in American-Controlled Berlin, 1945–1948" in *GIs and Germans: The Military Presence, 1945–2000*, ed. Detlev Junker and Phillip Gassert (Cambridge, forthcoming).

53. Naimark, *The Russians*, 94–95.

54. Fredericksen, *The American Military Occupation of Germany, 1945–1953*, 123–34; Willoughby, *Remaking*, 117–20; Annemarie Jakob, "Die amerikanische Garnison in Bamburg von 1945–1975, externe Situation, I. Teil" (Zulassungsarbeit, Politikwissenschaft, Gesamthochschule Bamberg, 1977), 26; Höhn, *GIs and Fräuleins*, 36–51.

55. Richard Joseph, with Waverly Root, "Why So Many GIs Like the Germans the Best," *Reader's Digest* (March 1946): 5–8. Also Daniel Glaser, "The Sentiments of American Soldiers Abroad toward Europeans," *American Journal of Sociology* 51, no. 5 (March 1946): 433–38; and Henry Elkin, "Aggressive and Erotic Tendencies in Army Life," *American Journal of Sociology* 51, no. 5 (March 1946): 408–13, here 409, 413. On the tendency of German American GIs to seek out their relatives in Germany, see Fredericksen, *The American Military Occupation*, 130.

56. For an assessment of Soviet-German relations, see Naimark, *The Russians*, 92–94. For a detailed discussion of the resentments caused, especially among German men, by heterosexual fraternization, see my discussion in chapter 2 and Biddiscombe, "Dangerous Liaisons." The concluding point about normalization derives in part from Willoughby, *Remaking*, 39.

57. The title of this section is drawn from two sources, Arthur Furr's 1947 book, *Democracy's Negroes*, which chronicles the accomplishments of black Americans in World War II, and a quote from a black GI in Germany in an article by Bill Smith, "Few GIs Eager to Return to the States," *Pittsburgh Courier* (22 February 1947): 1.

58. Motley, *The Invisible Soldier*, 154 and 170; also soldiers comments in Samuel A. Stouffer et al., *The American Soldier: Adjustment during Army Life*, vol. 1 (Princeton, 1949), 544 and 548. For discussions of experiences in Italy and England, see Morehouse, *Fighting*, 172–74; Sonya Rose, "Girls and GIs: Race, Sex, and Diplomacy in Second World War Britain," *International History Review* 19, no. 1 (February 1997): 146–60; David Reynolds, *Rich Relations: The American Occupation of Britain, 1942–1945* (New York, 1996); Graham Smith, *When Jim Crow met John Bull: Black Soldiers in World War II Britain* (New York, 1987); Stouffer et al., *The American Soldier*, 544–45.

59. From David Rodnick, *Postwar Germans: An Anthropologist's Account* (New Haven, Conn., 1948), 192, quoted in Kleinschmidt, Besatzer und Deutsche.

60. Quoted in Höhn, *GIs and Fräuleins*, 94. For other negative German impressions, see Merritt, *Democracy Imposed*, 258–59.

61. Late in the war, for example, the Nazi government spread rumors that black GIs were infected with venereal disease and leprosy, which they were spreading in Germany, and that "bordellos of German women were constructed" for the sexual pleasure of GIs, both white and black. Kleinschmidt, "Besatzer und Deutsche," 650–51. Also Niethammer, "Privat-Wirtschaft: Erinnerungsfragmente einer anderen Umerziehung," in ed. Lutz Niethammer, *Hinterher merkt man, daß es richtig war, daß es schiefgegangen ist* (Berlin and Bonn, 1983), 22–34.

62. The figure for relationships with white GIs was 28 percent. Merritt, *Democracy Imposed*, 258. Merritt emphasizes the continued racism among Germans in his analysis of OMGUS and HICOG surveys, which I will discuss in later chap-

ters. However, it seems to me that the evidence also indicates a significant minority of Germans did interact willingly with black troops.

63. NARA-CP, RG306, USIA Box 3, File 119: Confidential report, "The German Appraisal of the Allied Forces in West Germany with recommendations for improved Citizen-Soldier Relations," dated 28 January 1952.

64. While I am aware of no parallel poll taken in the United States regarding interracial social relations, polls were taken over the course of the 1940s to gauge American opinion regarding segregation of the U.S. military. In 1943, 90 percent of Americans polled favored military segregation; by June 1948, that number had dropped to 68 percent, with another 26 percent saying they favored integration of the military. In May 1949, a survey of white U.S. military personnel showed that 32 percent of respondents were "definitely opposed" to desegregation; 39 percent said they were "not definitely opposed"; 61 percent said they were "definitely opposed to complete integration," and 68 percent "expressed tolerance for partial desegregation," saying they would be willing to work together but not live or eat together. Mershon and Schlossman, *Foxholes and Colorlines*, 177–78.

65. The two quotations are from Kleinschmidt, "Besatzer und Deutsche," 652 and 653. See also Merritt, *Democracy Imposed*, 256–59, and Vernon W. Stone, "German Baby Crop Left by Negro GIs," *Survey* (November 1949): 579–83.

66. Posner, "Afro-America," 37, 35, and more generally 32–39.

67. NARA-CP, RG 260: OMGUS, Executive Office, Office of the Adjutant General, General Correspondence, Box 43, File: 250.1. The incident discussed occurred in mid-1946.

68. Black American soldiers who fought in the war were less likely to have a positive impression of Germans than the new recruits who replaced them over the course of 1945–46. Capt. John D. Long, Commander of the B Company, 761st Tank Battalion, for example, recalled:

> War is a strange thing. You are trained to do a job, even to the killing of men, but you do your job. It is an impersonal thing. . . . This is the way I looked at the Germans until the day we liberated our first concentration camp.
>
> Have you ever seen a stack of bones with skin stretched over it? . . . When we busted the gate the inmates just staggered out with no purpose or direction until they saw a dead horse recently struck by a shell. . . . They tottered over to that dead carcass and threw themselves on it, eating raw flesh. We cut ourselves back to one-third rations and left all of the food we could at the camp. . . . we later learned our food killed many of them. . . . From that incident on Jerry was no longer an impersonal foe. The Germans were monsters! I have never found any way to find an excuse for them. . . . We had just mopped them up before but we stomped the shit out of them after the camps.

Quoted in Motley, *Invisible Soldier*, 154–55, for more positive evaluations, 170; also Smith, *Last of the Conquerors*; "Racial: Mädchen and Negro," *Newsweek* (16 September 1946); 29–30; "Germany meets the Negro Soldier," *Ebony* (October 1946): 5–11; Stone, "German Baby Crop," 579–83.

69. The quotation is from Bill Smith, "Few GIs Eager to Return to the States," *Pittsburgh Courier* (22 February 1947): 1. Historian Lary May noted that West Germany was the preferred destination for African American soldiers he knew in the 1950s (conversation with author, May 1996). See also "Germany meets the Negro Soldier" in *Ebony* (October 1946): 6; David Brion Davis, "The Americanized Mannheim of 1945–1946," *Americanized Places: Encounters with History. A Celebration of Sheldon Meyer*, ed. William E. Leuchtenberg, 79–91 (New York, 2000); Morehouse, *Fighting*, chaps 5 and 6. For a fictional account of an African American soldier's experience in occupied Germany by a twenty-one-year-old African American novelist who served in the military there, see Smith, *Last of the Conquerors*. For discussions of the African American diaspora in postwar Europe, and especially Paris, see Tyler Stovall, "Harlem-sur-Seine: Building an African American Diasporic Community in Paris." *Stanford Electronic Humanities Review* 5, no. 2 (1997) (www.standord.edu/group/SHR/5–2/Stovall.html); and James Campbell, *Exiled in Paris: Richard Wright, James Baldwin, Samuel Beckett, and Others on the Left Bank* (Berkeley and Los Angeles, 2003).

70. "Germany meets the Negro Soldier," *Ebony* (October 1946): 5–10.

71. Smith, "Few GIs Eager to Return to States," 4.

72. Morehouse, *Fighting*, 201.

73. Leroy S. Hodges, Jr., *Portrait of an Expatriate: William Gardner Smith, Writer* (Westport, Conn., 1985), 17 and more generally 10–18.

74. Smith, *Last of the Conquerors*, 67–68.

75. Smith, "Few GIs Eager to Return to States," 1, 4. Also Weil, "The Negro in the Armed Forces," 98. Smith appears to have based his characters in the novel upon those he quoted in interviews for his reports to the *Pittsburgh Courier*. While there was no doubt creative license taken in the writing of his novel, Smith also shows a proclivity for drawing from autobiographical experience. On this point and the novel in general, see Hodges, *Portrait*, 10–18.

76. In Germany, these men were said to "live outside the big cities" or "congregate" in the Soviet zone of Berlin. The quotation comes from articles from the years 1952–53 in the Baltimore *Afro-American* and *Pittsburgh Courier* and appears in Plummer, *Rising Wind*, 208. The Soviet zone as a preferred destination over return to the United States was mentioned by William Gardner Smith in *Last of the Conquerors*, 107–8. I have been unable to find specific data on black American soldiers that may have taken up residence in the Soviet zone of Germany. However in 1946, the *Chicago Defender* featured a front-page article, "Soviet Fight on Racism Irks British, Americans," highlighting both the USSR's commitment to racial equality for "dark-skinned peoples all over the world" and the Soviets' international campaigns to expose and embarrass Britain, South Africa, and the United States for their racist policies. Beginning in the late 1950s, *Ebony* magazine published a couple of articles based upon the experiences of black American expatriates there and critical of the Soviet record on race. Homer Smith, "Russia is Not the Promised Land," *Ebony* (March 1958); William B. Davis, "How Negroes Live in Russia," *Ebony* (January 1960): 65–72. For a discussion of black American expatriates' experience in 1950s Paris and Western Europe more generally, see William Gardner Smith, *Return to Black America* (Englewood Cliffs,

N.J., 1970), particularly his chapter titled "In Search of Shangri-La" in the section "Black Men in Europe," 59–71.

77. Quoted in Morehouse, *Fighting*, 200–201, more generally for issues of transformative effect, see 202–27.

78. Smith, *Last of the Conquerors*, 238.

79. See also the discussions of Willoughby, *Remaking*, 30–34, 39–47, 60–64; and Höhn, *GIs and Fräuleins*, 85–108.

80. Fatima El-Tayeb, *Schwarze Deutsche. Der Diskurs um "Rasse" und nationale Identität, 1890–1933* (Frankfurt/Main, 2001); Lora Wildenthal, *German Women for Empire, 1884–1945* (Durham, N.C., and London, 2001); and Burleigh and Wippermann, *The Racial State*.

81. Martha Hodes, *White Women, Black Men: Illicit Sex in the Nineteenth Century South* (New Haven, 1999); Martha Hodes, ed., *Sex, Love, Race: Crossing Boundaries in North American History* (New York, 1999); Werner Sollors, ed., *Interracialism: Black-White Intermarriage in American History, Literature, and Law* (New York, 2000); Hale, *Making Whiteness*.

82. Smith, *Last of the Conquerors*, 44.

83. A disconcerting characteristic of this passage, at least to the historian, is the way that it resurrects Wannsee, the infamous site of the Nazi Regime's order to systematically murder European Jews, into a domestic sanctuary of interracial harmony. The instrumentalization of race and the relationship between antiblack racism and antisemitism will be discussed in following chapters. Smith, *Last of the Conquerors*, 238–39. Italics, misspellings, and ellipses are in the original text.

84. As William Gardner Smith later put it, most African American expatriates in Europe were seeking to "escape the 'race problem' in the U.S.—not just its existence, but above all, its seeming insolubility." *Return to Black America*, 62.

85. In Paris in the 1950s Smith became desk editor at the Agence France-Presse and continued to write for the *Pittsburgh Courier* in a regular column called "European Backdrop." He also began living with an East German woman there, the wife of an East German communist functionary, and made at least one trip to East Germany in the mid-1950s. Hodges, *Portrait*, 31–102, esp. 49–54, and Campbell, *Exiled in Paris*, 90–94.

86. The transcriptions of interviews of returning servicemen can be found in NARA-CP, RG 107, Civilian Aide to the Sec'y of War, Entry 189, Box 265, Technical Intelligence Reports. Description of fighting from interview of Lieutenant Colonel Purdue, 13 July 1945.

87. Quote is from White, *A Rising Wind*, 18.

88. NARA-CP, RG107, Entry 189, Box 265, interview with Howard M. Ducharme, dated 29 June 1945.

89. First sentence of the quotation is drawn from Dalfiume, *Desegregation*, 133. My thanks to Helen Bailitz for supplying the second half of the quotation from Owsley's letter, dated 16 September 1946, to the Secretary of War. NARA-CP, RG 107. Entry 188, File 291.2, Office of the Administrative Asst. to the Secretary of War.

90. E. T. Hall, Jr., "Race Prejudice and Negro-White Relations in the Army," *American Journal of Sociology* 52, no. 5 (March 1947): 401–9, here 403.

91. For a discussion of tensions between white and black American servicemen in 1950s West Germany, see Höhn, *GIs and Fräuleins*, 95–108.

92. Dudziak, *Cold War Civil Rights*.

93. "Friendship with 'Frauleins' Results in Racial Tensions," *Ebony* (Oct 1946): 7. The *New York Times* covered a fight between white and black GIs, due to white soldiers' resentment of interracial dating, in May 1951. David G. Mandelbaum, *Soldier Groups and Negro Soldiers* (Berkeley, Calif., 1952), 124. Also Motley, *The Invisible Soldier*, 191; Biddiscombe, "Dangerous Liaisons," 21.

94. Höhn, *GIs and Fräuleins*, 95–102.

95. Ibid., 102.

96. See ibid., 95–108. Also Jakob, "Die amerikanische Garnison in Bamberg von 1945–1975, externe Situation," 40–42.

97. See for example the interview in Motley, *The Invisible Soldier*, 191.

98. Willoughby, *Remaking*, 68–69.

99. Major L. Thomas, "Inside Germany," *Chicago Defender* (16 November 1946): 2.

100. This is evident in the descriptions of women fraternizing with black GIs in NARA-CP, RG260, Box 43, File AG 250.1, Incidents—American.

101. Stouffer et al., *The American Soldier*, 548; Rose, "GIs and Girls," 156–57.

102. Smith, *Last of the Conquerors*; the quotation is from 196, the episode is described in 191–97.

103. NARA-CP, RG260, Box 43, File AG 250.1.

104. On early American occupation policy regarding Jews, and on postwar German responses to Jews, see Stern, *Whitewashing*; Julius H. Schoeps, ed., *Leben im Land der Täter. Juden im Nachkriegsdeutschland* (Berlin, 2001); Leslie Morris and Jack Zipes, eds., *Unlikely History: The Changing German-Jewish Symbiosis, 1945–2000* (New York, 2002); and Juliane Wetzel, "An Uneasy Existence: Jewish Survivors in Germany after 1945" in H. Schissler, *The Miracle Years*.

CHAPTER TWO
FLACCID FATHERLAND: RAPE, SEX, AND THE REPRODUCTIVE
CONSEQUENCES OF DEFEAT

1. Quoted in Reif, "Das 'Recht des Siegers,' " 368. This English translation and all others are mine unless otherwise noted. Similar poems circulated as pamphlets in parts of Germany and Austria, and in one case was sent as in an anonymous letter, on old Wehrmacht stationery, to a German woman whose marriage to an American soldier was announced in the newspaper. Suzanne zur Nieden, "Erotic Fraternization. The Legend of German Women's Quick Surrender," in *Home/Front. The Military, War and Gender in Twentieth-Century Germany*, ed. Karen Hagamann and Stefanie Schüler-Springorum (New York, 2002), 297–310, here 302–3. Also Sonja Hosseinzadeh, *Nur Trümmerfrauen und Ami-Liebchen? Stuttgarterin in der Nachkriegszeit* (Tübingen, 1998), 100.

2. James P. O'Donnell, "Occupation: The GI Legacy in Germany," *Newsweek* (June 16, 1947): 48–50.

3. My initial citation of the word "Aryan" has quotation marks to remind readers that I am referring to a Nazi term; subsequently I drop the quotation marks, but am still invoking Nazi usage to which I do not subscribe.

4. Anette F. Timm, "Sex with a Purpose: Prostitution, Venereal Disease, and Militarized Masculinity in the Third Reich," *Journal of the History of Sexuality* 11, no. 1–2 (January/April 2002): 227.

5. This phrase is borrowed from Dagmar Herzog, "Hubris and Hyprocrisy, Incitement and Disavowal: Sexuality and German Fascism," *Journal of the History of Sexuality* 11, no. 1–2 (January/April 2002), 9.

6. Timm, "Sex with a Purpose," 246. For excellent recent scholarship on these issues, see the special double issue "Sexuality and German Fascism" edited by Dagmar Herzog in *Journal of the History of Sexuality* 11, no. 1–2 (January/April 2002). In particular, Herzog, "Hubris and Hypocrisy"; Timm, "Sex with a Purpose"; Patricia Szobar, "Telling Sexual Stories in the Nazi Courts of Law: Race Defilement in Germany, 1933–1945," 131–63; Birthe Kundrus, "Forbidden Company: Romantic Relationships between Germans and Foreigners, 1939–1945, 201–22." Also Gabriele Czarnowski, "Hereditary and Racial Welfare (Erb- und Rassenpflege): The Politics of Sexuality and Reproduction in Nazi Germany," *Social Politics* (Spring 1997): 114–35; Birgit Beck, "Rape: The Military Trials of Sexual Crimes Committed by Soldiers in the Wehrmacht, 1939–1944," in Hagamann S. Schüler-Springorum, *Home/Front*, 255–73; and Bartov, *Hitler's Army.*

7. While there has been some research on this topic, much more work needs to be done. See Moeller, Grossmann, Heinemann, Sander/Johr, also Anette Timm, "The Legacy of *Bevölkerungspolitik*" in *Canadian Journal of History* 33 (August 1998): 173–214. For an interesting discussion of how discourses on sex and National Socialism evolved in the two decades after the war, see Dagmar Herzog, "Desperately Seeking Normality: Sex and Marriage in the Wake of the War," in *Life after Death: Approaches to a Cultural and Social History of Europe during the 1940s and 1950s*, ed. Richard Bessel and Dirk Schumann, 161–92 (New York, 2003).

8. The term "racial state" is borrowed from Burleigh and Wippermann, *The Racial State.*

9. Robert G. Moeller, *Protecting Motherhood: Women and the Family in the Politics of Postwar West Germany* (Berkeley and Los Angeles, 1993). Elizabeth Heinemann has explored the relationship between collective memory of women's experiences and the articulation of national identity in "The Hour of the Woman," 354–95.

10. The census was from October 1946. Quotation and census information is from Moeller, *Protecting Motherhood*, 27. Numbers for the Soviet-occupied area of Berlin were 1,000 men to 1,446 women. Kirsten Poutrus, "Von den Massenvergewaltigungen zum Mutterschutzgesetz. Abtreibungspolitik und Abtreibungspraxis in Ostdeutschland, 1945–1950," in *Die Grenzen der Diktatur. Staat und Gesellschaft in der DDR*, ed. Richard Bessel und Ralph Jessen (Göttingen, 1996), 170–98, here 173.

11. Annemarie Tröger, "Between Rape and Prostitution: Survival Strategies and Chances of Emancipation for Berlin Women after World War II," trans. Joan Reutershan, in *Women in Culture and Politics: A Century of Change*, ed. Judith

Friedlander et al., 97–117 (Bloomington, Ind., 1986); and Barbara Willenbacher, "Zerrüttung und Bewährung der Nachkriegs-Familie," in *Von Stalingrad zur Währungsreform: Zur Sozialgeschichte des Umbruchs in Deutschland*, 3d ed., ed. M. Broszat, K.-D. Henke, and H. Woller, 595–618 (Munich, 1990). See also my discussion in *Cinema*, 92–117, and the interesting discussions by Svenja Goltermann, "Im Wahn der Gewalt. Massentod, Opferdiskurs und Psychiatrie, 1945–1956," in *Nachkrieg in Deutschland*, ed. Klaus Naumann (Hamburg 2001), 343–63; and Timm, "The Legacy of *Bevölkerungspolitik.*" On the issue of "remasculinization" of postwar Germany, a term drawn from Susan Jeffords's study of the United States, see the essays by Robert Moeller, Uta Poiger, Susan Jeffords, and Heide Fehrenbach in *Signs: Journal of Women in Culture and Society* 24, no. 1 (Autumn 1998): 101–69.

12. For a discussion of these issues, see Moeller, *Protecting Motherhood*; Heinemann, "The Hour of the Woman" and *What Difference*; also Fehrenbach, *Cinema*, chap. 3. For discussions of masculinity and German reconstruction after 1945, see Frank Biess, "Men of Reconstruction—The Reconstruction of Men. Returning POWs in East and West Germany, 1945–1955," in Hagamann and Schüler-Springorum *Home/Front*, 335–58. Frank Biess, "Survivors of Totalitarianism: Returning POWs and the Reconstruction of Masculine Citizenship in West Germany, 1945–1955," in *The Miracle Years*, ed. H. Schissler, 57–82 (Princeton, 2001). Robert Moeller, "The 'Remasculinization' of Germany in the 1950s: Introduction," *Signs* 24, no. 1 (1998): 101–6; Moeller, "The Last Soldiers of the Great War," 129–46; Fehrenbach, "Rehabilitating Father*land*,"107–28.

13. See Helke Sander and Barbara Johr's controversial book, *BeFreier und Befreite. Krieg, Vergewaltigungen, Kinder* (Munich, 1992). For estimates of the number of rapes by Allied troops in 1945, and debates regarding these estimates, see Sander and Johr, *Befreier und Befreite*; Grossmann, "A Question of Silence"; Naimark, *Russians*; Hosseinzadeh, *Nur Trümmerfrauen und Ami-Liebchen?* 37.

14. Quotation is from Tröger, "Between Rape and Prostitution," 102–4. Regina Mühlhauser, "Vergewältigung in Deutschland, 1945. Nationaler Opferdiskurs und individuelles Erinnern betroffener Frauen," in Naumann, *Nachkrieg in Deutschland*, 400–401; Reif, "Das 'Recht des Siegers,' " 360–71.

15. In another notable case, an ailing husband was rendered speechless and then angry when he learned of his wife's rape in an interview with a local police official who was investigating the wife's application for abortion because of the rape. StA Augsburg, Nr. 30 Gesundheitsamt Sonthofen, interview dated 5 October 1945. For interviews of women's experience, see Mühlhauser, "Vergewaltigung in Deutschland, 1945," 404–5; in general, see Helke Sander, "Remembering/Forgetting," 22–23; *October* 72 (1995): 15–25. Grossmann, "A Question of Silence"; Heineman, "The Hour of the Woman"; and Marlene Epp, "The Memory of Violence: Soviet and East European Mennonite Refugees and Rape in the Second World War." *Journal of Women's History* 9, no. 1 (1997): 58–87. Also the film *Befreie und Befreite. Krieg, Vergewaltigungen, Kinder* (Director Helke Sander, 1992).

16. Moeller, *Protecting Motherhood*, 102–3. Moeller's quotations of Adenauer are drawn from Gottfried Niedhardt and Normen Altmann, "Zwischen Beurteilung und Verurteilung: Die Sowjetunion im Urteil Konrad Adenauers," in *Adenauer und die Deutsche Frage*, ed. Josef Foschepoth, 102. For elaboration of these

points, see the important recent volume, Eduard Mühle, ed., *Germany and the European East in the Twentieth Century* (New York, 2003).

17. On Germans' perceptions of and politics toward Eastern Europe after 1945, see Eduard Mühle, "The European East on the Mental Map of German *Ostforschung*"; Michael Müller, "Poland and Germany from Interwar Period through to the Time of *Détente*"; and Axel Schildt, "Mending Fences: The Federal Republic of Germany and Eastern Europe," all in Mühle, *Germany and the European East*, 107–30, 91–106, and 153–80. On West Germans' responses to "migrants from the east" after the war, see Ulrich Herbert, *A History of Foreign Labor in Germany, 1880–1980: Seasonal Workers/Forced Laborers/Guest Workers*, trans. W. Templer (Ann Arbor, 1990), especially 198–202; also Karen Schönwälder, "Invited but Unwanted? Migrants from the East in Germany, 1890–1990," in *The German Lands and Eastern Europe: Essays on the History of their Social, Cultural and Political Relations*, ed. Roger Bartlett and Karen Schönwälder (New York, 1999), 198–216. For the Nazi period, see Gerhard Hirschfeld, "Nazi Germany and Eastern Europe," in Mühle, *Germany and the European East*, 67–90. For a longer historical view of German attitudes toward "the East," see Bartlett and Schönwälder, *The German Lands and Eastern Europe*.

18. The quotation is from Moeller, *War Stories*, 67, and in general 51–87. Also Heinemann, "The Hour of the Woman" and Grossmann, "A Question of Silence."

19. On historical debates on this point—the so-called Historikerstreit of the late 1980s—see Geoffrey Eley, "Nazism, Politics and Public Memory: Thoughts on the West German *Historikerstreit*, 1986–1987" in *Past and Present* 121 (November 1988): 171–208; Charles Maier, *The Unmasterable Past: History, Holocaust, and German National Identity* (Cambridge, Mass. 1988); Richard J. Evans, *In Hitler's Shadow: West German Historians and the Attempt to Escape from the Nazi Past* (New York, 1989). Also Moeller, *War Stories*, esp. chaps. 3 and 5; Bartov, *Hitler's Army.*

20. It bears noting that Germans in 1945 appear to have anticipated brutal retribution from not only the Soviet victors but also surviving victims of Nazi death camps and forced labor units. While some Jewish survivors admitted to entertaining fantasies of violence or sexual revenge against Germans in the aftermath of war, there is little evidence that they actualized those fantasies in any numbers. Soviet troops were another matter. Atina Grossmann, "Victims, Villains, and Survivors: Gendered Perceptions and Self-Perceptions of Jewish Displaced Persons in Occupied Postwar Germany," *Journal of the History of Sexuality* 11, no. 1/2 (2002): 310. Also Sander, "Remembering/Forgetting"; Grossmann, "A Question of Silence"; Heineman, "The 'Hour of the Woman' "; Moeller, "War Stories"; Mühlhauser "Vergewaltigung." See also the 1992 film by director Helke Sander, *Befreie und Befreite. Krieg, Vergewaltigungen, Kinder*, pt. 1.

21. Naimark, *The Russians in Germany*, esp. 134–40. On oral testimony taken by German expellees from the eastern territories of the expanded Reich, see Moeller, *War Stories*, esp. 65–72. For an interesting recent discussion of the rape of Hungarian and Austrian women by Soviet soldiers, as well as its treatment in postwar social policy and memory, see Andrea Petö, "Memory and the Narrative of Rape in Budapest and Vienna in 1945" in Bessel and Schumann, *Life after Death*, 129–48.

22. Quoted in Mühlhauser, "Vergewaltigung," 395.

23. See Robert Moeller's analysis of this project, along with other West German official, academic, and cinematic responses to the war, in his excellent study *War Stories*.

24. Quoted in Mühlhauser, "Vergewaltigung," 393.

25. Moeller, *War Stories*, 59, and in general, 51–74. Sonja Hosseinzadeh notes that in her interviews during the mid-1990s with women in Stuttgart who lived through the period of rapes, they exclusively recalled instances of rape by black or Russian soldiers, rather than by white soldiers.

26. Such stories were readily woven into national narratives of victimization precisely because they deepened and broadened emotional resonance with appeals to German chauvinism, social and sexual patriarchy, antimiscegenation, and anticommunism—a potent constellation of values that could play equally well to unreconstructed fascists or budding converts to capitalist democracy.

27. Rapes by the Soviet army in eastern Germany and especially in Berlin have dominated the historical research. The most important contributions shaping historical knowledge on this topic have been: Schmidt-Harzbach, "Eine Woche im April: Berlin 1945—Vergewaltigung als Massenschicksal" *Feministische Studien* 2 (1984): 51–65; Tröger, "Between Rape and Prostitution"; Helke Sander's film, *Befreie und Befreite* (1992); the special issue of *October* 72 (Spring 1995), "Berlin 1945: War and Rape: Liberators Take Liberties," especially the essays by Helke Sander, Gertrud Koch, and Atina Grossmann; Naimark, *Russians in Germany*, 69–140; Heineman, "The 'Hour of the Woman' "; and Moeller, *War Stories*, 51–87. Recent essays that depart from this exclusive focus on Berlin and the Soviet army are Reif, "Das 'Recht des Siegers,' " and Hosseinzadeh, *Nur Trümmerfrauen*, 31–48.

28. Quotes are taken from Christian Koller, "Enemy Images: Race and Gender Stereotypes in the Discussion on Colonial Troops," in Hagemann and Schüler-Springorum, *Home/Front*, 144. Also Christian Koller, *"Von Wilden aller Rassen niedergemetzelt." Die Diskussion um die Verwendung von Kolonialtruppen in Europa zwischen Rassismus, Kolonial- und Militärpolitik, 1914–1930* (Stuttgart, 2001), esp. 249–61; Sally Marks, "Black Watch on the Rhine: A Study in Propaganda, Prejudice, and Prurience," *European Studies Review* 13 (1983): 297–334; Keith L. Nelson, "The 'Black Horror on the Rhine': Race as a Factor in Post–World War I Diplomacy," *Journal of Modern History* 42, no. 4 (December 1970): 606–27; Robert C. Reinders, "Racialism on the Left: E. D. Morel and the 'Black Horror on the Rhine,' " *International Review of Social History* 13 (1968): 1–28; Reiner Pommerin, *"Sterilisierung der Rheinlandbastarde": Das Schicksal einer farbiger deutschen Minderheit, 1918–1937* (Düsseldorf: Droste, 1979); Paul Weindling, *Health, Race, and German Politics between National Unification and Nazism, 1870–1945* (New York, 1993); and Burleigh and Wippermann, *The Racial State*. See also the brief perceptive discussion by Tina Campt, Pascal Grosse, and Yara-Colette Lemke-Muniz de Faria, "Blacks, Germans, and the Politics of Imperial Imagination, 1920–1960" in Sara Friedrichsmeyer, Sara Lennox, and Susanne Zantop, *The Imperialist Imagination* (Ann Arbor, 1998); Opitz, Oguntoye, and Schultz, eds., *Showing our Colors*, 41–55.

29. *Heimat* histories focused on the local life of a town or province. Examples of press coverage include "Die Wahrheit über Freudenstadt," *Münchner Illustrierte* 18 (30 April 1955): 6–9; "Eine Stadt lebt in Angst. Donaueschingen fürchtet die Marokkaner," *Münchner Illustrierte* 43 (27 October 1956): 10–11; "Das Gespenst der Angst kommt aus Marokko," *Bunte Deutsche Illustrierte* 49 (5 December 1959): 9–11. For a discussion of the historical development and meanings of *Heimat* in modern German history, see Celia Applegate, *A Nation of Provincials: The German Idea of Heimat* (Berkeley and Los Angeles, 1990); Alon Confino, "The Nation as Local Metaphor" in *History and Memory* 5, no. 1 (1993): 42–86; and Alon Confino, *The Nation as Local Metaphor: Württemberg, Imperial Germany, and National Memory, 1871–1918* (Chapel Hill, 1997). On the role of *Heimatfilm* in the creation of postwar German identities, see Fehrenbach, *Cinema,* 148–68; and Johannes Moltke, "Trapped in America: The Americanization of the Trapp-Family, or 'Papas Kino' Revisited," *German Studies Review* (October 1996): 455–78.

30. On postwar discourses of German victimhood, see Moeller, *War Stories* and Heinemann, "The Hour of the Woman."

31. Hans Rommel, *Vor zehn Jahren. 16./17. April 1945. Wie es zur Zerstörung von Freudenstadt gekommen ist* (Freudenstadt, 1955).

32. Rudolf Albart, *Die letzten und die ersten Tage. Bamberger Kriegstagesbuch 1944/46* (Bamberg, 1953), 116–17, boldface in the original. This is also evident in archival sources. See, e.g., the statements of witnesses (as well as the women themselves) accompanying German women's application for abortion following alleged rape by an Allied soldier in StA Augsburg, Nr. 30: Gesundheitsamt Sonthofen.

33. See Atina Grossmann's brief discussion of Soviet rape of Jewish women in "Victims, Villains, and Survivors," 306–7; also Epp, "The Memory of Violence" for the distinction she makes between the experience of *Reichsdeutsche*, or German nationals, and *Volksdeutsche*, ethnic Germans. Also see Robert Moeller's discussion of Jews as an "absent presence" in early West German construction of *Zeitgeschichte* or contemporary history. Moeller, *War Stories*, 80–87. On the shift to ethnoracial definitions of citizenship in Nazi Germany, see Rogers Brubaker, *Citizenship and Nationhood in France and Germany* (Cambridge, Mass., 1992), 165–71.

34. In her essay on rapes in Munich, for example, Sieglinde Reif notes that German police reports for that city during the period of 1 May to 31 December 1945 recorded 152 rapes. In 100 of the 152 cases, the nationality of the attacker was given; 55 were Americans and 36 were German. Reif, "Das 'Recht des Siegers,' " 370 n. 11. Also Tröger, "Between Rape and Prostitution," 105, 111–12, and Sibylle Meyer and Eva Schulze, *Wie wir das alles geschafft haben. Alleinstehende Frauen berichten über ihr Leben nach 1945* (Munich, 1985), 51.

35. Moeller also makes this point in *War Stories*, noting that "[a]lthough detailed information on the ethnic composition of the Red Army awaits a comprehensive social-historical account of the war's last months, evidence suggests that 'Asiatic' troops were not overrepresented among those responsible for the Soviet army's worst acts against Germans." (66). Teresa Rakowska-Harmstone, " 'Brotherhood in Arms': The Ethnic Factor in the Soviet Armed Forces,"in *Eth-*

nic Armies: Polyethnic Armed Forces from the Time of the Habsburgs to the Age of the Superpowers, ed. N. F. Dreisziger (Waterloo, Ontario, 1990), 123–57.

36. For a discussion of the ethnic composition of French colonial troops, see Myron Echenberg, "Race, Ethnicity, and Social Class in the French Colonial Army: The Black African *Tirailleurs,* 1857–1958" in *Ethic Armies;* and also Myron Echenberg, *Colonial Conscripts: The* Tirailleurs Sénégalais *in French West Africa, 1857–1960* (Portsmouth, N.H., 1991).

37. Strikingly, in oral interviews with older women in and around Stuttgart some fifty years after the end of the war, all who discussed the issue (but not their own experience) of rape referred to soldiers of color. Not one woman mentioned the fact that white Allied troops too had been among the perpetrators. Hosseinzadeh, *Nur Trümmerfrauen,* 36–37.

38. For a discussion of these issues see Grossmann, *Reforming Sex: The German Movement for Birth Control and Abortion Reform, 1920–1950* (New York, 1995), 150–52, and in general chapter 6. Also Gisela Bock, "Antinatalism, Maternity, and Paternity" in *Nazism and German Society,* ed. David Crew (New York, 1993); Gabriele Czarnowski, "Frauen als 'Mütter der Rasse.' "

39. Grossmann, *Reforming Sex,* 193, also 153. Poutrus, "Von den Massenvergewaltigungen," 179–80, and Grossmann, "A Question of Silence," 56.

40. StA Augsburg, Nr. 30: Gesundheitsamt Sonthofen, Memo from the Bürgermeister des Marktes Sonthofen, regarding "Schwangerschaftsunterbrechung" dated 7 June 1945. Also StA Augsburg, Nr. 30: Gesundheitsamt Sonthofen, Memo of Reichsministerium des Innern, "Unterbrechung von Schwangerschaften" dated 14 March 1945.

41. Estimates range from between 350,000 to 1 million in a German population of 64.5 million. Poutrus, "Von den Massenvergewaltigungen," 193, 178–80.

42. Estimates suggest that some 360,000 out of 500,000 abortions in 1945 were done for reasons of racial eugenics. As historians Atina Grossmann and Kirsten Poutrus have pointed out, in the months following military defeat abortions *in practice* were permitted in the case of medical, eugenic, "moral" (*ethisch*— a carryover from the Nazi period, meaning impregnation by a non-Aryan man), and—given the miserable material and nutritional conditions of the early postwar period—even social reasons. Nonetheless, social indications do not appear to have been an acceptable legitimating reason for abortions in southern Germany. The willingness of some German officials to consider the social circumstances of women was a clear departure from Nazi practices, as Grossmann points out, and indicated that abortion policy after 1945 (especially in the Soviet zone and in Berlin) also hearkened back to more progressive "social necessity" discourse of the Weimar Republic. On this point, see *Reforming Sex,* 194–95. On the continued role of eugenic thinking among high-ranking health officials with regard to marriage counseling see Timm, "The Legacy of *Bevölkerungspolitik.*"

43. The "Gesetz über die Aufhebung des Gesetzes zur Verhütung erbkranken Nachwuches" took effect in November 1945. In the Soviet zone, German Länder adopted new legislation on abortion within the first three years of occupation. All five states in the Soviet zone permitted abortions for "medical and moral [ethische] indications." In addition, Thüringen, Mecklenberg, and Brandenburg allowed abortion in instances of "social need," and Mecklenburg permitted

abortion for eugenic reasons. BAB, Stiftung Archiv der Parteien- Massenorgani-sationen der DDR: DY30/IV 2/17/28 SED Zentralkomitee—Frauen [Abtrei-bung], "Merkblatt, 1.6.48: Die neue Gesetzgebung zur Schwangerschaftsverhü-tung in der sowjetischen Besatzungszone."

44. Grossman, *Reforming Sex*, chapter 8; Poutrus, "Von den Massenvergewalti-gungen."

45. StA Augsburg, Nr. 30 Gesundheitsamt Sonthofen, Memo from Bürger-meister des Marktes Sonthofens, dated 7 June 1945. StA Augsburg, Gesund-heitsamt, File 19: Neuburg, memo from Bayerisches Staatsministerium der Justiz dated 2 August 1945; memo dated 12 November 1945; also File 30: Gesund-heitsamt Sonthofen, memo dated 19.12.1946. Memos on "Unterbrechung der Schwangerschaft bei Notzuchtfällen"

46. StA Augsburg, Nr. 30, Gesundheitsamt Sonthofen; Nr. 19, Gesund-heitsamt Neuburg; and VA Lindau 1946: Einzelfälle.

47. StA Augsburg, Nr. 30: Gesundheitsamt Sonthofen, Memo from the Bür-germeister des Marktes Sonthofen, regarding "Schwangerschaftsunterbrech-ung" dated 7 June 1945. Also StA Augsburg, Nr. 30: Gesundheitsamt Sonthofen, Memo of Reichsministerium des Innern, "Unterbrechung von Schwangerschaf-ten" dated 14 March 1945.

48. StA Augsburg, Gesundheitsamt File Nr. 19: Neuburg, Memos from Bay-erisches Staatsministerium des Innern and den Regierungspräsidenten, dated 2 August 1945 and 12 November 1945 (the memo from 20 June 1945 was refer-enced in the August memo).

49. StA Augsburg, Gesundheitsamt File Nr. 19: Neuburg, Memos from Bay-erisches Staatsministerium des Innern and den Regierungspräsidenten, 12 November 1945.

50. StA Augsburg, Kreispräsidium Lindau, Nr. 161, transcription of memo from Staatssekretariat, Landesdirektion der Justiz, Tübingen, to Gerichte und Staatsanwaltschaften, 18 January 1946.

51. StA Augsburg, Nr. 30 Gesundheitsamt Sonthofen, applications for abortion.

52. Quoted in Hosseinzadeh, *Nur Trümmerfrauen*, 41.

53. StA Augsburg, Nr. 30 Gesundheitsamt Sonthofen and Nr. 19 Gesund-heitsamt Neuberg. One cannot discount the possibility of infanticide or inten-tional neglect by German women in the case of unwanted births. Following the end of the war, material provisions were poor and the infant mortality rate was high. However, none of the evidence I have consulted suggests that local offi-cials had either the inclination or the ability to investigate causes of death among infants born in the immediate postwar years.

54. For a discussion of abortion policy in East Germany, see Poutrus, "Von den Massenvergewaltigungen," who argues that access was available for women with medical, eugenic, or social indications through 1950, after which it was increasingly restricted. In *Reforming Sex*, Grossmann indicates that by that time, East German officials feared that legalization caused an "abortion addi-tion" among German women: "the more applications were granted, the more were submitted" (198). After 1950, and earlier in Western Germany, abortion began to be recriminalized. For a discussion of both Germanies after 1945, see

Grossmann, *Reforming Sex*, 189–212. For an analysis of East German policy after 1950, see Donna Harsch, "Society, the State, and Abortion in East Germany, 1950–1972," *American Historical Review* 102, no. 3 (1997): 53–84.

55. StA Augsburg, Gesundheitsamt File Nr. 19: Neuburg, Memos from Bayerisches Staatsministerium des Innern and den Regierungspräsidenten, dated 2 August 1945 and 12 November 1945 (the memo from 20 June 1945 was referenced in the August memo).

56. By 1950–51, Bavarian doctors were ordered to report all miscarriages so that officials could investigate whether the affected women were attempting to pass off an intentional abortion as an "act of God." StA Augsburg, Gesundheitsamt, File 19: Neuberg; and File 91: Nördlingen. For a discussion of abortion policy in East Germany see Harsch, "Society, the State, and Abortion," 53–84.

57. StA Augsburg, Nr. 30: Gesundheitsamt Sonthofen, applications for abortions, 1945–46; and Gesundheitsamt (GA), Nr. 19: Neuburg. By mid-1946, German and American officials were constructing images of criminality linking African American troops and their white German mistresses. NARA-CP, OMGUS, Executive Office, Office of the Adjutant General, General Correspondence, Box 43, File: Incidents-American. For a more general discussion of *"Amiliebchen"* and *"Negerliebchen"* see Heinemann, *What Difference* and "The Hour of the Woman"; also Höhn, *GIs and Fräuleins*.

58. "From that moment on, even the mere thought of saying something to another person about my misfortune was terrible," remarked the woman in question. StA Augsburg, Nr. 30 Gesundheitsamt Sonthofen, petition for abortion.

59. For example, StA Augsburg, VA Lindau, 1946, Einzelfälle. There is also evidence of North African men returning to Europe illegally to reunite with their German or Austrian girlfriends and children. Luise Frankenstein, *Soldatenkinder. Die uneheliche Kinder ausländischer Soldaten mit besonderer Berücksichtigung der Mischlinge* (Munich, 1954), 29.

60. There is no evidence that Allied soldiers of other nationalities were similarly targeted for castration or antifraternization action in general. Biddiscombe, "Dangerous Liaisons."

61. Kundrus, "Forbidden Company," 209–10.

62. Quoted in Biddiscombe, "Dangerous Liaisons," 11–12, also more generally 15–19. Translation his.

63. "Rundschreiben" des Stuttgarter Oberkirchenrats, 20 March 1946. Quoted in Clemens Vollnhals, "Die Evangelische Kirche zwischen Traditionswahrung und Neuorientierung," in Broszat et al., *Von Stalingrad zur Währungsreform*, 151–52. This concern outlived the occupation. See my discussion of the furor provoked in state and church offices by the 1951 film, *Die Sünderin*, which thematized the failure of masculine will. Fehrenbach, *Cinema*, 92–117.

64. These women were characterized in the press and by social workers and sociologists as asocials, mentally impaired, or as professional or informal prostitutes. This characterization persisted into the 1950s, although nearly one-third of German mothers of biracial children questioned in a survey at the beginning of the decade offered that their involvement with African American soldiers was motivated by love, and one-fifth of those questioned said they hoped to marry

their partner. These percentages are likely low since it required substantial courage on a woman's part to make such admissions, given the unambiguously critical public assessment of interracial fraternization in postwar Germany at the time. See Herbert Hurka, "Die Mischlingskinder in Deutschland, Teil I: Ein Situationsbericht auf Grund bisheriger Veröffentlichungen" in *Jugendwohl* 37, no. 6 (1956): 213–21.

65. "Weekly Intelligence Summary" no 29, 31 January 1946. NARA-CP, RG 59, State Dept., quoted in Biddiscombe, "Dangerous Liaisons," 21–22.

66. See for example reports on the debriefing of black and white American military service personnel returning from overseas on the performance of "Negro troops" abroad in NARA-CP, RG 107: Civilian Aide to Sec'y of War, Entry 189, Box 265 "Technical Intelligence Reports" from 1945. Also Box 223, for transcripts of reports by the African American press on the duties and treatment of black U.S. soldiers abroad.

67. Nevertheless, some U.S. officials in Germany were simultaneously acutely embarrassed by the hypocrisy of American occupation policy, which proclaimed and promoted democratic values and equality yet maintained a racially segregated military. Consequently (and in order to avoid inflaming African American opinion back home), they sometimes backed off from meting out harsh punishment for misdemeanors. NARA-CP, RG 260: OMGUS, Executive Office, Office of the Adjutant General, General Correspondence, Box 43, File: 250.1. The two incidents discussed occurred in the summer and fall of 1946.

68. Willoughby, *Remaking*, 64–72, provides a concise discussion of VD and crime rates among American troops in Germany.

69. In late 1947, the Public Welfare Branch of OMGUS undertook an internal study of illegitimate German births of American paternity; like the German surveys they preceded, statistics on white and "colored" soldiers were tallied separately. The survey of American paternity in Bavaria can be found in NARA-CP, RG 260: OMGUS, Bavaria, Civil Affairs Div., Public Welfare and DP Branch, General Records, Box 37, File: "Children of American Fathers." For a corrective to the official view of African American soldiers' behavior, see NARA-CP, RG 107: Civilian Aide to Sec'y of War, Entry 189, Box 223, for transcripts of reports by the African American press on the duties and treatment of black U.S. soldiers abroad; also the fictional account of interracial fraternization by an African American novelist who served in occupied Germany, Smith, *Last of the Conquerors*.

70. Some Germans justified their negative reaction to black troops by pointing out the racist treatment by white U.S. soldiers of their African American compatriots; similar justifications were given for antisemitic responses to Jewish-American soldiers. See Alfons Simon, *Maxi, unser Negerbub* (Bremen, 1952), 40; and in general Stern, *Whitewashing*.

71. Even though the workhouses were finally closed by American order in 1949, they were reopened in 1951 in parts of Bavaria. SA Nürnberg, C88/I Pflegeamt/Allgemeine Akten 1908–93: Nr. 6, Führung der Kriegschronik, Berichte, 1939–52; Nr. 7, Massnahmen gegen Prostitution.

72. In a memo analyzing "prostitution in Germany," which found its way into the files of East German officials in the governing Social Unity Party, Dr. Luise

Jürgensen argued that "one must mention the race problem, since the sex appeal of black men is an important factor that exacerbates the problem [of prostitution]." BAB, DQ1/4632 Ministerium für Gesundheitswesen, "Protokolle von Sitzung mit Bezirksvenerologen unter Teilnahme der SMAD" and "Die Lage der Prostitution in Deutschland."

73. Frankenstein, *Soldatenkinder*, 24, and 16–20; for descriptive assessments of individual women by German social workers, 16–20. Also ADW, Mischlingskinder und Adoption/Heime, "Ergebnis der Rundfrage des Central-Ausschusses für die Innere Mission—Mitteilung Nr. 25 von 22.4.52."

74. In their survey of 552 mothers of biracial children, German social workers found that only 3 percent were the result of rape. See for example the reports of social welfare workers regarding the mothers of black occupation children in Frankenstein, *Soldatenkinder*, 16–19, 23–24. During the occupation, informal prostitution was prevalent, as German women attempted to feed themselves and their families in years of extreme scarcity. Nonetheless, if we take "sex for material compensation" as the working definition of prostitution, virtually all German girlfriends of American troops—white and black—would be guilty of engaging in at least casual prostitution since there was an unstated expectation that beaus would provide for their romantic or sexual partners. This form of material beneficence was, after all, one of the important ways that American men distinguished themselves from their German—and other Allied—competitors. Nonetheless, the derogatory characterization of German women who associated with black troops persisted into the 1950s.

75. A U.S. opinion poll taken in June 1956 among 1,646 West Germans showed that nearly 50 percent judged the prestige of women who bore children of foreign troops to be either "low" or "very low." NARA-CP, RG 306, USIA, Research Reports on German Public Opinion, Boxes 9, Report C-1 "Assessment of Troop-Community Relations, 30–32.

76. The information in this paragraph is drawn from Herzog, "Desperately seeking Normality," 173. The surveys mentioned were taken by *Costanze* magazine and the Institute for Statistical Market and Opinion Research and by the *Wochenend* weekly in concert with the Institute for Demoscopy in Allenbach.

77. NARA-CP, RG260: OMGUS/Bavaria-CAD, PWDP, General Records, Box 25 and 37.

78. For an expanded discussion of this point, see Fehrenbach, "Rehabilitating Father*land.*" On the issue of the construction of German masculinity in the 1950s see also Moeller, "The 'Remasculinization' of Germany in the 1950s"; Moeller, "Fathers, Sons, and Foreign Relations"; Poiger, "A New 'Western' Hero?"; Poiger, "Krise der Männlichkeit. Remaskulinisierung in beiden deutschen Nachkriegsgesellschaften," in Naumann, *Nachkrieg in Deutschland*, 227–63. Also Biess, "Survivors of Totalitarianism"; and Fehrenbach, *Cinema*, chaps. 3, 5, and 6.

79. For a corrective to misconceptions, see Stone, "German Baby Crop Left by Negro GIs," *Survey* 85 (November 1949): 579–83, an American whose study in the late 1940s included 600 German mothers. Some 210 had completed a Volksschule education; 218 reported less than eight years of education, but 172 reported more. One hundred were unskilled workers, 90 semiskilled, 90 were professionals, and 60 were skilled workers, with 250 mothers unclassified be-

cause they "never had been required to earn for themselves." Also Frankenstein, *Soldatenkinder*, 23, whose statistics show that while 49.5 percent of the women were unskilled workers (such as domestic help), 30 percent were semiskilled workers (in factories, at dressmakers, in retail trades), and nearly 22 percent were classified as skilled in a trade or profession (such as nurse, teacher, translator, sculptor). Frankenstein's information was drawn from three German youth offices and included a consideration of 657 children and 602 mothers.

80. Stone, "German Baby Crop," 582. In another study from the early 1950s, one-third of German mothers of biracial children questioned declared that their involvement with African American soldiers was motivated by love, and one-fifth of those questioned said they hoped to marry their partner. Frankenstein, *Soldatenkinder*.

81. This holds true for nearly all of the leading anthropological, social, and psychological studies on *"Mischlingskinder,"* which followed the unbroken pattern of considering the social, moral, and mental backgrounds of the children's mothers. See Frankenstein, *Soldatenkinder*; Hermann Ebeling, "Zum Problem der deutschen Mischlingskinder," *Bild und Erziehung* 7, no. 10 (1954): 612–30; Rudolf Sieg, "Mischlingskinder in Westdeutschland: Eine anthropologische Studie an farbigen Kindern," *Beiträge zur Anthropologie* 4 (1955): 9–79; Gustav von Mann, "Zum Problem der farbigen Mischlingskinder in Deutschland," *Jugendwohl* 36, no. 1 (January 1955): 50–53; Hans Pfaffenberger, "Zur Situation der Mischlingskinder," *Unsere Jugend* 8, no. 2 (1956): 64–71; Hurka, "Die Mischlingskinder in Deutschland," 257–75. The only studies that depart on this issue are those of American Vernon Stone, and Walter Kirchner, "Eine anthropologische Studie an Mulattenkindern in Berlin unter Berücksichtigung der sozialen Verhältnisse" (doctoral dissertation, Freie Universität Berlin, 1952).

82. StA Augsburg, VA Lindau, 1948. Also Siegfried Boschan, *Die Vormundschaft* (Cologne, 1956); Deutsches Institut für Vormundschaftswesen, *Neues Unehelichenrecht in Sicht. Vorträge der Arbeitstagung in Coburg am 25., 26. und 27. Mai 1961* (Heidelberg, 1961); Franziska Has, *Das Verhältnis der unehelichen Eltern zu ihrem Kinde. Eine soziologischer Beitrag zur Reform des Unehelichenrechts* (Berlin, 1962); and Barbara Schadendorf, *Uneheliche Kinder. Untersuchungen zu ihrer Entwicklung und Situation in der Grundschule* (Munich, 1964). For a historical survey of legal guardianship of children in Germany since the nineteenth century, see Edward Ross Dickinson, *The Politics of German Child Welfare from the Empire to the Federal Republic* (Cambridge, Mass., 1996); for the post-1945 period, Elizabeth Heineman, "Complete Families, Half Families, No Families at All: Female-Headed Households and the Reconstruction of the Family in the Early Federal Republic," *Central European History* 29, no. 1 (1996): 19–60. For a survey of twentieth-century German social policy toward "illegitimacy," see Sybille Buske, "Die Debatte über 'Unehelichkeit,' " in *Wandlungsprozesse in Westdeutschland. Belastung, Integration, Liberalisierung, 1945–1980*, ed. Ulrich Herbert, 315–47 (Göttingen, 2002); for a more detailed discussion, see Sybille Buske, *Fräulein Mutter und ihr Bastard* (Göttingen, 2004).

83. A memo from 14 January 1947 between the Youth Office of Bremen and that of Stuttgart insists that German youth officials should work with American authorities to "do away with the difficulties" involved in permitting marriages

between black soldiers and German women since "the number of Negerkinder will surely increase over the course of the occupation." HStA Stuttgart [hereafter HSAStg] , EA2/007 Akten des Innenministeriums Württemberg-Baden and Baden-Württemberg, Nr. 1177, Vol. 1.

84. Marriage between American soldiers and German women was officially permitted by January 1947, but nevertheless continued to be officially discouraged and subject to the rigorous review and approval of one's superior officer and military chaplain. Marriage applications were further subject to the "six months and three" rule, which allowed a GI only a narrow temporal window of opportunity to petition to marry his German girlfriend. He had to have no more than six months and no fewer than three remaining in his tour-of-duty; after petitioning he had to wait three months for approval, and then another five months (unofficially dubbed the "cooling off period," by which time he would have returned home) before he would be permitted to import his fiancée for the nuptials. OMGUS, Circular 181.

85. O'Donnell, "The GI Legacy in Germany," 49.

86. Stone, "German Baby Crop," 583; Frankenstein, *Soldatenkinder*, 25, 29–30.

87. For a discussion of the social treatment and legal debates over "illegitimacy" in twentieth-century Germany, see Buske, "Die Debatte über 'Unehelichkeit.' "

88. Nonetheless, in 1946 doctors in the southwestern state of Baden were secretly ordered by the Interior minister there to report all births of children "of apparently Moroccan, Indochinese or other colored paternity." StA Freiburg, C15/1: Südbadisches Ministerium des Innerns, #257, Rassenbiologie: Allgemeine Regelung der Erbgesundheitspflege 1933–46, "Auszug aus dem Protokoll über die Amtsarzttagung am 16. Mai 1946."

89. HStAStg, EA2/007: Akten des Innenministeriums Baden-Württemberg, memo dated 14.1.47, also "Vorbemerkung" from 7 February 47.

90. "Wer zahlt die Alimente?" in *Revue* (n.d.), clipping in BayHStA, Minn 81083. Deutscher Bundestag, 23. Ausschuss, Protokoll Nr. 149: "Kurzprotokoll der 149. Sitzung des Ausschusses für Rechtswesen u. Verfassungsrecht am 21. Jan 1952." Articles also appeared in the American press, such as "400,000 Babies Left Behind," *U.S. News and World Report* (23 September 1955) and "The Sins of the Fathers," *Redbook* (April 1956): 22–25, 82–86.

91. Buske, "Die Debatte über 'Unehelichkeit.' " For a general discussion of the reestablishment of patriarchy in West Germany, see Moeller, *Protecting the Family*; and Heinemann, *What Difference*.

92. Deutscher Bundestag, 1. Wahlperiode 1949: Drucksache Nr. 2191, "Antrag der Fraktion der SPD, betr. Uneheliche Kinder der Besatzungsangehörigen. Also supporting memos of the Bundesministerium des Innerns, B153/342, especially memo from the Statistisches Bundesamt to the Bundesministerium des Innern regarding results of a telephone survey of occupation children and paternity, dated 30 October 1951.

93. In Britain, paternity suits either had to be filed in the home country while the alleged father still resided in Germany or the father had to declare paternity voluntarily. In France, the Napoleonic Civil Code did not permit paternity suits by illegitimate children except if conception occurred as a result of rape, seduc-

tion, or kidnapping. Soviet law, on the other hand, prohibited illegitimate children from establishing paternity regardless of the circumstances of their conception, and child support could be claimed only by legitimate children. What is more, with the end of Allied occupation and the start of the supervisory phase of the Allied High Commission (HICOG), HICOG law explicitly prohibited Germans from lodging paternity suits against any of its military or civilian personnel. BAK, B153/342 "Aufzeichnung zur Frage der Unterhaltsansprüche unehelicher deutscher Kinder gegen ihren ausländischer Erzeuger, soweit dieser nicht unter das Gesetz Nr. 13 der Alliierten Hohen Kommission fällt," Spring 1951. StHStA, EA2/007 Aken des Innenministeriums, Nr. 1179.

94. For example, of the 14,786 occupation children born in 1950–51, well over half lived in what had been the American zone. BAK B153/342, Memo from the Statistisches Bundesamt to the Bundesministerium des Innern, dated 30 October 1951.

95. Karl Ey, "Wer zahlt für die Besatzungskinder?" *NWZ-Göppinger Kreisnachrichten* (18 April 1952): 7, clipping in HStStg, EA2/007, Nr. 1177.

96. NARA-CP, RG 306, USIA, Research Reports on German Public Opinion, Box 9, C-1: Assessment of Troop-Community Relations, 15 August 1956, 32.

97. The Deutscher Verein für öffentliche und private Fürsorge worked in conjunction with the International Association for Youth Assistance in Genf (IAYA), which in 1951 appeared before the Social Commission of the United Nations to facilitate or compel child support payments by the fathers of "soldiers' children" conceived (and abandoned) abroad. Although the IAYA claimed to be laboring on behalf of all "soldiers' children" regardless of nationality or paternity, the report it returned focused predominantly on occupation children in postwar Germany and devoted particular attention (and the largest number of pages) to German "*Mischlingskinder*." Frankenstein, *Soldatenkinder*, 8–9. For a nuanced discussion of the emergence and growth of "human rights" as a legal term and "political agenda" see Kenneth Cmiel, "The Recent History of Human Rights," *American Historical Review* 109, no. 1 (February 2004): 117–35. Atina Grossmann is exploring the application of the notion of human rights to the situation of Jewish Displaced Persons in postwar Germany in her forthcoming study, *Victims, Victors, and Survivors.*

98. BAK B153/342, Kurzprotokoll der 149. Sitzung des Ausschusses für Rechtswesen und Verfassungsrecht, 21 January 1952, 4–5; and Deutscher Verein für offentliche und private Fürsorge, Frankfurt/Main, report, "Uneheliche Kinder von Besatzungsangehörigen," 15 January 1952. Also Frankenstein, *Soldatenkinder.*

99. An informal survey of "*farbige Besatzungskinder*" was ordered by the West German federal Interior Ministry in late 1950 for the former French and American occupation zones of Baden, Bayern, Hesse, Rheinland-Pfalz, Württemberg-Baden, and Württemberg-Hohenzollern. In 1954, the West German federal Ministry for Family and Youth Issues (Bundesministerium für Familien- und Jugendfragen) undertook a nationwide survey of all *Besatzungskinder*; statistics on children of color were kept separate. BAK, Bundesministerium für Familien- und Jugendfragen, B153/342; and BAK, Bundesministerium für Jugend und Familien, B189/6858. Also BayHStA, MInn 81089, "Uneheliche Kinder von Be-

satzungsangehörigen—Berichte der Jugendämter"; and BayHStA, MInn 81083, 81085, 81086, 81088, 81090, 81094.

100. BAK, B153–327 "Jugendgefährdung in Gegenden großer Truppenansammlungen,insb. durch Prostitution"; BAK, B189/6858 Besatzungs- u. Flüchtlingskinder, ff; B189/6859 "Unterhaltsansprüche unehelicher Kinder gegen Angehörige der NATO-Truppen"; B189/6861, "Durchsetzung von Rechtsansprüchen unehelicher Kinder gegenüber Mitgliedern der ausländischen Stationierungsstreitkräfte auf der Grundlage des NATO-Truppen Statuts und der Zusatzvereinbarungen"; B189/6863 "Versorgung von Kindern, die durch Vergewaltigung durch Angehörige der Besatzungsmachte gezeugt worden." Also BayHStA, Minn 81083, 81084.

101. "Auf Unterhaltszahlung verklagt," *Stuttgarter Nachrichten*, 23 August 1955, clipping in HStStg, EA2/008, Akten des Innenministeriums, Nr. 1176.

102. BayHStA, Minn 81087, Memo from the Bayerischen Ministerium der Justiz to the Bundesminister der Justiz, 23 April 1956. Memoranda from the German and U.S. delegations to the Status of the Forces conferences, as well as correspondence for individual cases, can be found in BayHStA, MInn 81088 and MInn 81085.

CHAPTER THREE
"MISCHLINGSKINDER" AND THE
POSTWAR TAXONOMY OF RACE

1. LAB, Rep. 12, Senatsverwaltung für Gesundheitswesen, Letter from Herman Muckermann to Dr. Meyer, Landesgesundheitsamt Berlin, dated 24 July 1951. World Brotherhood, Gesellschaft für Christlich-Jüdische Zusammenarbeit, *Protokoll der Arbeitstagungen über das Schicksal der farbigen Mischlingskinder in Deutschland*, 3–4.

2. Ebeling, "Zum Problem der deutschen Mischlingskinder," 2.

3. In 1946, for example, the Jewish birthrate in Bavaria was 29 per 1,000 and the German birthrate was 7.35 per 1,000; by 1948 the Jewish birthrate jumped to 35.8 per 1,000. Atina Grossmann, "Trauma, Memory, and Motherhood: Germans and Jewish Displaced Personal in Post-Nazi Germany, 1945–1949." *Archiv für Sozialgeschichte* 38 (1998): 215–39; and "Victims, Villians, and Survivors: Gendered Perceptions and Self-Perceptions of Jewish Displaced Persons in Occupied Postwar Germany." *Journal of the History of Sexuality* ll, no. 1–2 (2002): 291–318. The majority of Jewish DPs were located in the American zone. Fredericksen, *The American Occupation of Germany*, 73–80; Dietrich, Susanne, and Julia Schulze Wessel, *Zwischen Selbstorganisation und Stigmatisierung. Die Lebenswirklichkeit jüdisher Displaced Persons und die neue Gestalt des Antisemitismus in der deutschen Nachkriegsgesellschaft*, Veroffentlichungen des Archives der Stadt Stuttgart, vol. 75. Stuttgart: Klett-Cotta, 1998; and Zeev Mankowitz, *Life between Memory and Hope: The Survivors of the Holocaust in Occupied Germany* (New York, 2002), Grossmann, *Victims, Victors, and Survivors*.

4. For an interesting study on the postwar treatment of Sinti and Roma, see Gilad Margalit, *Germany and Its Gypsies: A Post-Auschwitz Ordeal* (Madison, Wisc., 2002).

5. BayHStA, MInn 81083, "Entwurf" vom Bayerischen Landesjugendamt an die Stadt-Kreisjugendämter, dated 22 November 1950. The federal Ministry of the Interior petitioned state Ministries of the Interior in the former French and American zones of occupation for a head count of "Negro mixed-blood children" in November 1950. By mid-1951, a survey of all occupation children was initiated by the Deutscher Verein für öffentliche und private Fürsorge, which requested separate tabulation of white and black children. This survey was undertaken with the assistance of the state Ministries of the Interior as well as state and local youth offices, and commanded the interest of the federal Ministry of the Interior and the Foreign Office. BAK, B153: Bundesministerium für Familien- und Jugendfragen, #342: Fürsorge für uneheliche Kinder von Besatzungsangehörigen, insb. für Mischlingskinder. Also BayHStA, MInn 81089; and HStAStg EA2/007, Nr. 1177.

6. A rare contemporary criticism of this racial ideology, see Gustav Blume, *Rasse oder Menschheit?* (Dresden, 1948).

7. For an analysis focusing on the images and investigations of Blacks in German racialism and racism of the period see El-Tayeb, *Schwarze Deutsche.*

8. Brubaker, *Citizenship and Nationhood in France and Germany.* For discussion of pre-1933 racial science and notions of race, see P. Weingart, J. Kroll, and K. Bayertz, *Rasse, Blut und Gene. Geschichte der Eugenik und Rassenhygiene in Deutschland* (Frankfurt/Main, 1992) and El-Tayeb, *Schwarze Deutsche.* For an instructive discussion of racial studies during World War I, see Andrew D. Evans, "Anthropology at War: Race Studies of POWs during World War I" in *Worldly Provincialism: German Anthropology in the Age of Empire,* ed. H. Glenn Penny and Matti Bunzl (Ann Arbor, Mich., 2003), 198–229. See also Gerhard Hirschfeld, "Nazi Germany and Eastern Europe," 67–90, and Müller, "Poland and Germany," 91–106, which emphasize the longer history of anti-Slav stereotypes among Germans, as well as the recent work by Elizabeth Harvey, *Women in the Nazi East: Agents and Witnesses of Germanization* (New Haven, 2003).

9. For an interesting historical discussion, see Norman Naimark, *Fires of Hatred: Ethnic Cleansing in Twentieth-Century Europe* (Cambridge, Mass., 2001).

10. Certainly racist depictions of Soviet communism persisted into the 1950s; in this case, the racist stereotype of the "Slavic subhumans" was used to make a political point. However, by the 1950s the social behavior of Soviet troops was no longer a threat to West Germans. As a result, the reproductive consequences of defeat by the Red Army dissipated, as did its perceived threat to West German racial integrity. Less is known about East German responses in the 1950s to both the continued presence of Soviet soldiers and to the influx of migrant labor from Poland and other Eastern European countries. On this point, see the brief comments of Schönwälder, "Invited but Unwanted?" 208–9.

11. See Statistisches Bundesamt/Wiesbaden, "Statistische Berichte: Die unehelichen Kinder von Besatzungsangehörigen im Bundesgebiet und Berlin (West)" Arb.-Nr. VI/29/6, 10 October 1956.

12. Ibid, 4; BAK, B153/342: "Uneheliche Kinder von Besatzungsangehörigen, 5 (#323).

13. Not all illegitimate children of Soviet paternity were unwanted. Instances are recorded in which such children were accepted by women's German hus-

bands and raised within the family. In one case in 1947, a child was removed temporarily from the mother's household in order to avoid "surprising" her husband, who was scheduled to return from a POW camp. "After only 14 days the husband declared that he was willing to raise the Russenkind as their third child." ADW-BP: Provinzial-Ausschusses für Innere Mission in der Provinz Brandenburg, BP 1937: Jugendfürsorge, 1946–48 and BP 2226: Mütterhilfe zu Para. 218, 1947–48. On policy toward *"Russenkinder,"* see W. Karin Hall, "Humanity or Hegemony: Orphans, Abandoned Children, and the Sovietization of the Youth Welfare System in Mecklenburg, Germany 1945–1952 (doctoral dissertation, Stanford University, 1998), 146–61.

14. However, popular use of the term *"Russenkinder"* did persist after 1946. Hall, "Humanity," quotation from 147.

15. BAK, B153/342, "Ergebnis der Rundfrage betreffend Negermischlinge"; Statistisches Bundesamt/Wiesbaden, "Statistische Berichte: Die unehelichen Kinder von Besatzungsangehörigen im Bundesgebiet und Berlin (West)."

16. BAK, B189: Akten des Bundesministeriums für Jugend und Familie, 6858, 6859, 6861; BAK, B153: Bundesministerium für Familien- und Jugendfragen, File 1335, I–II; HStAStg, EA2/007, Akten des Innenministeriums Baden-Württemberg, Nr. 1177: "Jugendwohlfahrt: Statistik und Unterhalt der unehelich geborenen Kinder . . . , 1951–55"; HStAStg, EA2/008, Akten des Innenministeriums, Nr. 1176, "Jugendwohlfahrt: Unterhalt für uneheliche Kinder—Unterhaltsverpflichtung von Mitgliedern ausländischen Streitkräfte (1955–70)"; BayHStA, MInn 81087, "Verfolgung von Unterhaltsansprüchen gegen Angehörige von ausländischen Streitkräften—Pariser Verträge, 1955–57.

17. Walter Kirchner, "Eine anthropologische Studie an Mulattenkinder in Berlin unter Berücksichtigung der soziale Verhältnisse (doctoral dissertation, Free University Berlin, 1952), 10, 49; Rudolf Sieg, "Mischlingskinder in Westdeutschland. Eine Anthropologische Studie an farbigen Kinder," *Beitrage zur Anthropologie* 4 (1955), 10–11. Sieg received permission from the Central-Ausschuss für die Innere Mission and from the Caritas Verband to conduct his examination of *Mischlingskinder* in their orphanages (Kinderheime) located in the regions of Bremen/Bremerhaven, Heidelberg/Mannheim, Kaiserlautern, Mainz/Wiesbaden, Nuremberg, and Stuttgart (16). For a recent analysis of these studies compatible with mine, see Tina Campt and Pascal Grosse, " 'Mischlingskinder' in Nachkriegsdeutschland: Zum Verhältnis von Psychologie, Anthropologie und Gesellschaftpolitik nach 1945" *Psychologie und Geschichte* 6, no. 1–2 (1994): 48–78.

18. Kirchner, "Eine anthropologische Studie;" Sieg, "Mischlingskinder."

19. This is not to argue that German anthropology successfully reformed itself after 1945. For critical discussions of continuities in that discipline after the war, see Heidrun Kaupen-Haas and Christian Saller, eds., *Wissenschaftlicher Rassismus. Analysen einer Kontinuität in den Human- und Naturwissenschaften* (Frankfurt/Main, 1999).

20. El-Tayeb, *Schwarze Deutsche*; Lora Wildenthal, *German Women for Empire, 1884–1945* (Berkeley and Los Angeles, 2001), 79–171; Tina Campt, "Converging Spectres of an Other Within: Race and Gender in Prewar Afro-German History," *Callaloo* 26, no. 2 (2003): 322–41.

21. Weingart et al., *Rasse, Blut, und Gene*, 100–103; El-Tayeb, *Schwarze Deutsche*, 83–92, quote from 91.

22. El-Tayeb, *Schwarze Deutsche*, 141. Emphasis added.

23. Koller, "Enemy Images"; Koller, *'Von Wilden aller Rassen'*; Marks, "Black Watch on the Rhine"; Nelson, "The 'Black Horror on the Rhine' "; Reinders, "Racialism on the Left"; Pommerin, *"Sterilisierung"*; Weindling, *Health, Race, and German Politic*; Burleigh and Wippermann, *The Racial State*. Also Campt, Grosse, and Lemke-Muniz de Faria, "Blacks, Germans, and the Politics of Imperial Imagination"; Campt, "Converging Spectres"; and El-Tayeb, *Schwarze Deutsche*.

24. Pommerin, *Sterilisierung*, 23–40, 91. For an English synopsis, see Pommerin, "The Fate of Mixed Blood Children in Germany," *German Studies Review* 5 (1982): 315–23.

25. Abel's original report was destroyed, but the results of his study were published in 1937 in the *Zeitschrift für Morphologie and Anthropologie*. Pommerin, *Sterilisierung*, 46–48.

26. StA Freiburg, C15/1 Südbadisches Ministerium des Innerns, #257: Rassenbiologie: Allgemeine Regelung der Erbgesundheitspflege 1933–46, Memo from Reichsminister des Innern, 9 April 1934, and responses.

27. Ibid. *"Affenliebe"* appears in dictionaries and is defined as "blinde Liebe [blind love]" or "doting affection." *Der Sprach-Brockhaus*, 6th ed. (Wiesbaden, 1952), 16, and *Cassell's German-English, English-German Dictionary* (New York, 1982), 22.

28. StA Freiburg, C15/1 Südbadisches Ministerium des Innerns, #257: Rassenbiologie: Allgemeine Regelung der Erbgesundheitspflege, 933–46, Memo from Reichsminister des Innern, 9 April 1934, and responses.

29. Ibid. In her recent book, Claudia Koonz notes the lack of consensus among German scientists and medical doctors during the 1930s regarding eugenics and racial value, see *The Nazi Conscience* (Cambridge, Mass., 2003).

30. Pommerin, *Sterilisierung*, 56.

31. Ibid., 52–87.

32. Ibid.; also Pommerin, "Fate," 322. For the autobiography of a Black German of Liberian paternity, not affected by the sterilization action, see Hans Massaquoi, *Destined to Witness: Growing up Black in Nazi Germany* (New York, 1999).

33. For a recent overview of research on the KWI during the Third Reich, see Carola Sachse and Benoit Massin, *Biowissenschaftliche Forschung an Kaiser-Wilhelm-Instituten und die Verbrechen des NS-Regimes. Informationen über den Gegenwärtigen Wissenstand* (Berlin, 2000).

34. Jeremy Noakes, "The Development of Nazi Policy towards the German-Jewish 'Mischlinge,' 1933–1945," *Leo Baeck Institute Yearbook* 34 (1989): 291–354; Beate Meyer, *"Jüdische Mischlinge," Rassenpolitik und Verfolgungserfahrung, 1933–1945* (Hamburg, 1999); James F. Tent, *In the Shadow of the Holocaust: Nazi Persecution of Jewish-Christian Germans* (Lawrence, Kans., 2003). There are also numerous autobiographies, such as Ilse Koehn, *Mischling, Second Degree: My Childhood in Nazi Germany* (New York, 1977). Robert Gellately has emphasized that antisemitism and exclusionary policies towards Jews increased gradually over the course of the 1930s. See his *Backing Hitler: Consent and Coercion in Nazi Germany* (New

York, 2002); also the excellent social history by Marion Kaplan, *Between Dignity and Despair: Jewish Life in Nazi Germany* (New York, 1998).

35. On its postwar reincarnation and it loose affiliation with the Max-Planck-Institut, see Hans-Peter Kröner, *Von der Rassenhygiene zur Humangenetik. Das Kaiser-Wilhelm-Institut für Anthropologie, menschliche Erblehre und Eugenik nach dem Kriege* (Stuttgart, 1998), 195–208.

36. Between 1933 and 1945, an estimated 300,000 to 400,000 people had been forcibly sterilized. Weingart et al., *Rasse, Blut und Gene*, 215, 234, 245, 295, 385–86, 536, 562, quotation from 386.

37. Kröner, *Von der Rassenhygiene*, 24–25.

38. See for example Benno Müller-Hill, *Murderous Science: Elimination by Scientific Selection of Jews, Gypsies, and Others in Germany, 1933–1945*, trans. G. F. Fraser (Plainview, N.Y., 1998), 154. Also the interesting discussion on the cultivation of "respectable racism" in Koonz, *Nazi Conscience*.

39. In total, 4,776 "children of colored paternity" were recorded in the 1955 census. Of these, the most resided in Bavaria (1,681), Baden-Württemberg (1,346), Hesse (881), and Rheinland-Pfalz (488). The balance were scattered among Nordrhein-Westfalen (151), Bremen (95), (West) Berlin, (72), Lower Saxony (51), Hamburg (10) and Schleswig-Holstein (1). Statistisches Bundesamt, "Statistische Berichte: Die uneheliche Kinder von Besatzungsangehörigen im Bundesgebiet und Berlin (West)," 10 October 1956, 9.

40. Kirchner, "Eine anthropologische Studie," 2–3.

41. Ibid., 12, 35; also Sieg, "Mischlingskinder," 27.

42. Kirchner thought it significant in this connection to cite Yerkes's 1921 study of the American Army claiming that light-skinned soldiers performed better on intelligence tests 7, 17, 42; Sieg, "Mischlingskinder," 22, 24–25.

43. Kirchner, "Eine anthropologische Studie," 40–49; Sieg, "Mischlingskinder," 25–62. It bears noting that these same attributes were mentioned in school reports on the children in 1954–55, which were ordered by the federal Ministry of the Interior. See discussion later in this chapter.

44. Kirchner, "Eine anthropologische Studie," 13–14.

45. Sieg, "Mischlingskinder," 24–25.

46. Kirchner, "Eine anthropologische Studie," 61, 35; Sieg, "Mischlingskinder," 65, emphasis added.

47. Kirchner, "Eine anthropologische Studie," 62.

48. Stern, *Whitewashing*, 310–11 and more generally 310–34. Also Frank Stern, "Deutsch-jüdisches Neubeginnen nach 1945? Ein Rückblick auf die Gründungen der Gesellschaften für Christlich-Jüdische Zusammenarbeit," *Journal für Geschichte* 6 (1989): 18–27.

49. Everett R.Clinchy's "confidential report" of his 1947 trip, in diary form, is deposited at University of Minnesota's Social Welfare History Archives. SW, NCCJ, Box 9, File 35: "Clinchy's Journal of European Trip." Josef Foschepoth, *Im Schatten der Vergangenheit. Die Anfänge der Gesellschaft für Christlich-Jüdische Zusammenarbeit* (Göttingen: Vandenhoeck & Ruprecht, 1993), 155–203. The web site of the contemporary Koordinierungsrat der Gesellschaft für Christlich-Jüdische Zusammenarbeit can be found at www.deutscher-koordinierungsrat.de.

50. For discussions of these developments in the United States, see Svonkin, *Jews against Prejudice*.

51. Simon, *Maxi*.

52. This liberal discourse of race, moreover, was rooted both in American *and* German traditions of liberalism. For the German historical context, I use the broader definition of liberalism forwarded by Konrad Jarausch and Larry Jones in their edited volume *In Search of Liberal Germany* (New York, 1990): "[A]lthough liberalism functioned as an organized political movement . . . it also represented a set of cultural attitudes, social practices, and economic principles. . . . Liberalism, therefore, refers not merely to programs, institutions, and modes of political operation in the public realm, but also to patterns of social, economic, and cultural interaction that define the larger context in which the struggle for liberal Germany has taken place" (13). However, my approach to the study of West German liberalism is compatible with Ruth Feldstein's recent book on the racial and gender dimensions of American liberalism. In it, she notes that while liberalism "was never singular . . . certain assumptions consistently recurred," such as "the assumption that progress was possible; the conviction that social and political problems could be remedied through rational intervention; and the expectation that the federal government could play a role in remedying these problems in ways that helped a collective body politic while simultaneously strengthening the individual citizens in it." These were also characteristic of postwar German liberalism. My understanding of "liberal discourse" is also similar to Feldstein's. As she puts it, "To speak of liberal discourse is to refer to a process: one through which different texts from various social, cultural, and political arenas are produced, circulated, and sometimes contested intertwined assumptions about gender, race, and liberalism. . . . [D]iscourse . . . refers to a system of ideas and practices, including individual behavior and institutional policies, which help to produce reality." *Motherhood in Black and White: Race and Sex in American Liberalism, 1930–1965* (Ithaca, N.Y., 2000), 10.

53. World Brotherhood, *Protokoll*, 3.

54. Ibid., 3–4.

55. See for example Hans Pfaffenberger, "Farbige Kinder im Heim—ein Prüfstein," *Unsere Jugend* 5, no. 12 (1953): 534; Kirchner, "Eine anthropologische Studie"; Herbert Hurka, "Die Mischlingskinder in Deutschland, Teil I: Ein Situationsbericht auf Grund bisheriger Veröffentlichungen," *Jugendwohl* 37, no. 6 (1956): 213–21; Gustav von Mann, "Zum Problem der farbigen Mischlingskinder in Deutschland," *Jugendwohl* 36, no. 1 (1955); 50–53; and Hans Pfaffenberger, "Hilfe für unsere Mischlingskinder—aber wie?" *Neues Beginnen* 8 (1955): 113–15.

56. World Brotherhood, *Protokoll*, 5.

57. *Der Sprach-Brockhaus*, 6 ed. (Wiesbaden, 1952), 187.

58. I am not addressing popular attitudes in this argument. For a discussion of some of these issues at the grass-roots level see for example, Stern, *Whitewashing*; Julius H. Schoeps, ed., *Leben im Land der Täter: Juden im Nachkriegsdeutschland* (Berlin, 2001); Julia Schulze Wessel, *Zur Reformulierung des Antisemitismus in der deutschen Nachkriegsgesellschaft: Eine Analyse deutscher Polizeiakten aus der Zeit von 1945 bis 1948*; Wolfgang Benz, *Feindbild und Vorurteil* (Munich, 1996); and Höhn, *GIs and Fräuleins*. For postwar German perceptions of Eastern Europeans, see

Mühle, *Germany and the Euopean East* and Bartlett and Schönwälder, ed., *The German Lands and Eastern Europe.*

59. On shifts in U.S. understandings of race, see Jacobsen, *Whiteness*; Guterl, *Color of Race.*

60. Simon, *Maxi*, 10.

61. These characterizations appeared in media coverage of the children as well as anthropological, sociological, and school reports on the children . See for example Kirchner, "Eine anthropologische Studie," and Sieg, "Mischlingskinder," as well as teachers and youth worker reports on the children in BayHStA, Minn 81084; HStAStg, EA2/007 Akten des Innenministeriums, Nr. 1177: "Jugendsozialhilfe"; StA Freiburg, Bestand F110/1, #176; and Archiv des Diakonischen Werkes der EKD, Berlin (ADW), HGSt 1161.

62. In her opening comments of the 1952 Wiesbaden conference, Claire Guthmann declared that souls of *Mischlings Kinder* "were not blacker than those of white children." A similar comment was made at the conference by Erich Lißner. World Brotherhood, *Protokoll*, 3, 7.

63. Simon, *Maxi*, 14.

64. Ibid., 5 and 29.

65. For a discussion of this phenomenon in the United States, see Svonkin, *Jews against Prejudice*; Daryl Michael Scott, *Contempt and Pity: Social Policy and the Image of the Damaged Black Psyche, 1880–1996* (Chapel Hill, N.C., 1997); and Feldstein, *Motherhood.*

66. Simon, *Maxi*, 18.

67. Ibid., 7. See also the discussion in Posner, *Afro-America in West German Perspective.*

68. Simon, *Maxi*, 7. For a more detailed discussion of *Maxi*, see Fehrenbach, "Of German Mothers and 'Negermischlingskinder.' "

69. See chapter 5. Also Lißner, "We Adopted a Brown Baby"; and "Weisser Vater, schwarzer Sohn" *Revue* (15 September 1951).

70. For further discussion see Fehrenbach, "Rehabilitating Father*land.*"

71. Simon, *Maxi*, 7.

72. World Brotherhood, *Protokoll*, 6–7; Lißner, "We Adopted a Brown Baby."

73. World Brotherhood, *Protokoll*, 18–20.

74. StA Freiburg, F110/1, Nr. 176: Oberschulamt Freiburg; BayHStA, MK 62245, Memo from Ständige Konferenz der Kultusminister, Bonn, 27 February 1956.

75. Herbert, *A History of Foreign Labor in Germany*, 195.

76. This in spite of the fact that the social and especially economic integration of ethnic German "expellees" was a significant issue in the late 1940s and early 1950s in West Germany. Although some 12 million ethnic Germans entered the American, British, and Soviet zones of occupation after the war, with most settling in the American zone, "this influx . . . has never been regarded as immigration." This had to do in part with historical definitions of German-ness and German citizenship, which emphasized ethnicity and jus sanguinis. However, it is also notable that all black German occupation children after 1945 were minors, which was not the case for ethnic Germans, who became very active political lobbyists and founded their own political party, Block der Heimatvertriebe-

nen und Entrechteten. Wolfgang Seifert, "Social and Economic Integration of Foreigners in Germany," 83, and Rainer Münz and Rainer Ohliger, "Long Distance Citizens," 155–201, both in *Paths to Inclusion*, ed. Peter Schuck and Rainer Münz, vol. 5 in Migration and Refugees Series, ed. Myron Weiner (New York: Berghahn Books, 1998). Also Schönwälder, "Invited but Unwanted?"; and Stefan Senders, "Laws of Belonging: Legal Dimensions of National Inclusion in Germany," *New German Critique* 67. Special issue on "Legacies of Antifascism (Winter 1996): 147–76.

77. StA Freiburg, F110/1, Nr. 176: Oberschulamt Freiburg; BayHStA, MK 62245, Memo from Ständige Konferenz der Kultusminister, Bonn, 27 February 1956, summarizing report results from the states. Also HessHStA, 504, Nr. 906, reports from school districts to Hessisches Ministerium für Erziehung und Volksbildung, 1955–56.

78. The children's film, *Zehn kleine Negerlein*, was released in 1954 and directed by Rolf von Sydow. Actors in the film included Josefine Bachert, "Jamie," Harry Mambo, and Thomas Ngambi, among others. I have not been able to locate or view a copy of the film.

79. BayHStA, MK 62245, Senator für Jugend und Sport, Berlin, "Bericht über uneheliche deutsche farbige Mischlingskinder in West-Berlin" (copy of a copy), 8 November 1955. A representative from the Inner Mission in Stuttgart reported that a three-and-a-half-year-old girl living in one of their children's homes declared, "I can't stand my mother because she made me black." This poignant example illustrates that feelings of social isolation and alienation extended into the intimate sphere of family. For a discussion of the tensions in mother-child relationships as articulated by adult Afro-Germans, see Francine Jobatey, "*Afro-Look:* Die Geschichte einer Zeitschrift von Schwarzen Deutschen." (doctoral dissertation, University of Massachusetts, 1998), chapters 3–4. The Stuttgart quote comes from ADW, HGst1161, letter from Verband der Inneren Mission in Württemberg, 11 November 1955.

80. Black German's subjectivity and social experience has begun to be documented in memoir writing. For the postwar cohort of Black Germans discussed in this book, see Opitz, Oguntoye, and Schultz, *Showing Our Colors*; Ika Hügel-Marshall, *Invisible Woman: Growing Up Black in Germany*, trans. E. Gaffney (New York, 2001); Helga Emde, "I Too Am German: An Afro-German Perspective," in *Who Is German? Historical and Modern Perspectives on Africans in Germany*, ed. Leroy T. Hopkins, Jr. (Washington, D.C., 1999), 33–42; also discussions of autobiographical essays in the magazine *afro-look* in Jobatey, "*Afro-Look.*" For contemporary discussions of Black German identity, see Campt, "Reading the Black German Experience"; Wright, "Others-from-Within from Without"; Faymonville, "Black Germans and Transnational Identification"; and Karen K. Goertz, "Showing Her Colors: An Afro-German Writes the Blues in Black and White," *Callaloo* 26, no. 2 (2003): 306–19. Also Erin Crawley, "Rethinking German-ness: Two Afro-German Women Journey 'Home,' " in *Other Germanies*, ed. K. Jankowsky and C. Love (Albany, N.Y., 1997), 75–95.

81. The strategy of mother-blaming could take a devastating toll on personal relations within the family. Klaus Eyferth, a Hamburg University psychologist who published an authoritative study titled "Colored Children in Germany"

wrote of one three-year-old girl who hated her mother "because she blames her for her 'condition.' " This tendency to blame the mother did not begin to wane until the early 1960s, when Eyferth quite consciously attempted to address the bias against mothers by proposing that it was perhaps only the children's mothers who could successfully look beyond the children's racial difference to see the multifaceted human being. Klaus Eyferth, "Die Situation und die Entwicklungsaussichten der Neger-Mischlingskinder in der Bundesrepublik," *Soziale Arbeit* 7, no. 11 (1958): 469–78, quote from 476. Also Klaus Eyferth, Ursula Brandt, and Wolfgang Hawel, *Farbige Kinder in Deutschland* (Munich, 1960), 33–37.

82. Such workhouses persisted in at least Bavaria and Hesse after 1945. Unlike the pre-1945 period, when male inmates predominated, in the postwar period, workhouse populations were up to 80 percent female. Wolfgang Ayass, *Das Arbeitshaus Breitenau: Bettler, Landstreicher, Prostituierte, Zuhälter und Fürsorgeempfänger in der Korrektions- und Landarmenanstalt Breitenau, 1874–1949* (Kassel, 1992), 328–45.

83. Bock, "Antinatalism, Maternity, and Paternity in National Socialist Racism," 233–55, here 251. On West Germany, see Moeller, *Protecting Motherhood*; for a comparison of East and West Germany, see Heineman, *What Difference*.

84. Feldstein, *Motherhood*, 1.

85. Ibid., 3.

86. Feldstein's analysis of the American experience proves instructive: "Mother-blaming cannot be explained as simply a conservative backlash, or only as an expression of reactionary misogyny. One might easily (and at times correctly) reason that those who blame mothers for all of society's ills want to keep women in the home, bring feminism to a grinding halt, and preserve the status quo. But it is perhaps even more important to consider how and why progressive thinkers have used mother blaming, for . . . many thinkers who favored increased social justice, an expansive liberal welfare state, and greater racial equality relied on mother-blaming in central ways. . . . [M]other-blaming was relevant to changes in both race *and* gender relations." Feldstein, *Motherhood*, 2–3.

CHAPTER FOUR
RECONSTRUCTION IN BLACK AND WHITE: THE *TOXI* FILMS

1. The first quotation comes from World Brotherhood, *Protokoll*, 3. The second is from the 1952 West German film *Toxi*. The original German version is: Ich möcht' so gern nach Hause geh'n / Die Heimat möcht' ich wiederseh'n / Ich find' allein nicht einen Schritt / Wer hat mich lieb und nimmt mich mit?

2. SdK, Nachlass R. A. Stemmle, newspaper clippings "So fanden wir Toxi!" (1952) and "TOXI—Alle Menschen sind nett zu mir" (1963).

3. *Toxi*. FONO-Film, 1952. Director: R. A. Stemmle. Screenplay: Maria Osten-Sacken and R. A. Stemmle (based on an idea by Peter Francke and Maria Osten-Sacken). The film has never been released commercially on video or, as far as I can tell, been shown on German television. A copy is available for viewing at the Bundesarchiv Filmarchiv in Berlin.

4. See clippings file on microfiche for *Toxi* at DIF. Also SdK, clippings in Nach-lass R. A. Stemmle. Quote from "Toxi auf Raten," *Sie* (31 August 1952).

5. SdK, "Aktuelle Film Nachrichten," 3, no. 1 (1 August 1952): 7.

6. On the representation of Jews in postwar German cinema, see Frank Stern, "Film in the 1950s: Passing Images of Guilt and Responsibility" in *The Miracle Years*, ed. H. Schissler (Princeton, 2000), 266–80; Robert R. Schandley, *Rubble Films: German Cinema in the Shadow of the Third Reich* (Philadelphia, 2001), 77–115; and Omer Bartov, *The "Jew" in Cinema: From "The Golem" to "Don't Touch My Holocaust"* (Bloomington, Ind., 2005).

7. This shot occurs in *Toxi* at 0:37:28–0:38.00.

8. I do not intend to minimize the suffering of marginalized and institutional-ized children, but rather to make the point that the film, in formulating the prob-lem it seeks to solve, shifts the focus from racism (a white-generated problem) to the children themselves. The sociological data on biracial children in postwar Germany show that just over 10 percent of the children were uncared for by their mothers or mothers' relatives. Nonetheless, commentators continually as-sumed that black German children were in the main raised in institutions and not by their families. This assumption, of course, affected both the way the "problem" of the children and its solution were understood.

9. Günter Herbst, "Fünfjähriges Negerkind spielt sein Schicksal" *Bonner Rundschau*, (20 May 1952).

10. Ellen Geier, "Farbige 'Toxi' soll Adoptionsziffer steigen," *Abendpost* 18 August 1952.

11. BAK, B149: Bundesministerium für Arbeit und Sozialordnung, #8679. Also BayHStA, Papers of the Bavarian Innenministerium, MInn 81084 "Fürsorge für Kinder ausländischer Väter 1954–60," letter from Dr. Rothe of the Bundes-ministerium des Innerns, 9 September 1955. For a discussion of the mutating West German policies on international adoptions of occupation children, see chapter 5.

12. Biracial children were "raced" as black rather than white. The pull of blood was never perceived to work in the direction of their white mothers.

13. My friend did not see the film as a child, nor, I suspect, did most Afro-German children at the time.

14. Fears that this would be the "fate" of black German children underlay much of the liberal discourse on race in West Germany. See especially the influ-ential publications of the Hamburg psychologist Klaus Eyferth: "Die Situation und die Entwicklungsaussichten der Neger-Mischlingskinder in der Bundesre-publik," 469–78; and Eyferth, Brandt, and Hawel, *Farbige Kinder in Deutschland*.

15. Shortly after Theodor's conversion in the film, we see a scene that takes place in the kitchen on Christmas eve involving the family's cook and the police investigator in which the latter discloses that he has learned the identity of the person who left Toxi on the doorstep. When asked by the cook why he had not made a more general announcement of the fact, he responds that he wanted the child "to enjoy a peaceful Christmas first." This signals his compassion, but more importantly indicates that Toxi's status in the white bourgeois home was necessarily temporary and quickly nearing an end.

16. *Der dunkle Stern*. WEGA-Film GmbH, 1955. Director: Hermann Kugelstadt. Screenplay: Maria Osten-Sacken and Hermann Kugelstadt (based upon an idea of Peter Francke and Georg Hurdalek).

17. My discussion of this film will necessarily be schematic since it is based upon descriptions culled from film bills, publicity, press reports, and a more detailed novelized account of the film. Despite multiple attempts with German film archives and the German film company holding its rights, I have been unable to locate or gain access to either a film or video copy of *Der dunkle Stern*. Unlike many films from the 1950s, it has not been screened on German television, perhaps for obvious reasons given the film's narrative. See Lia Avè, "*Der dunkle Stern*: Ein Roman." *Hermes Film-Roman Magazin*, 17 (Munich: Hermes Film- und Bühnen-Verlag, n.d.).

18. This is a quotation from the publicity material of WEGE Film for *Der dunkle Stern*, located in the SdK Schriftgutarchiv.

19. Avè, "*Der dunkle Stern*," 5.

20. One new postwar reality, connected with national belonging, was the need to integrate millions of ethnic German refugees from eastern Europe. See the discussion below.

21. For a longer discussion of the ideology of the postwar *Heimatfilm*, see Fehrenbach, *Cinema*, esp. 148–68. For a discussion of postwar films that respond more overtly to the war and its aftermath, see Moeller, *War Stories*, 123–70. The history of the modern concept of *Heimat* is explored in Applegate, *Nation of Provincials*, and Confino, *Nation as Local Metaphor*.

22. Avè, "*Der dunkle Stern*," 8.

23. The Reich Inheritance Law (*Reichserbhofgesetz*) of November 1933 restricted farmers to "those of German or similar blood," and explicitly prohibited those with "Jewish or colored (*farbiges*) blood" from inheriting landed property.

24. At the end of *Der dunkle Stern*, Moni joins the community of circus performers and ponders her fate: "Would she really become a trapeze artist in the world-renowned act of the Bellanis? Really a famous, if also dark, star in the circus heaven as was predicted? She wished it from the bottom of her heart because she must—no, she wanted to—find a new *Heimat* in this colorful world." Avè, "*Der dunkle Stern*," 55.

25. It is notable that although ethnic Germans hailed from Hungary, Romania, and Yugoslavia, they are consistently depicted in the West German films of the 1950s as blond haired and blue eyed—a stereotyped representation of "Germanness" that cast ethnicity in biogenetic rather than cultural terms. My thanks to Bob Moeller for this observation.

26. On the film and *Heimatfilme* more generally, see Fehrenbach, *Cinema*, 148–68; also Moeller, *War Stories*, 123–70.

27. Nonetheless, a number of *Heimatfilme* from the 1950s used black characters as a visual reference or a plot device to enable the romance of white protagonists. In the first postwar *Heimatfilm*, *Schwarzwaldmädel* (1950/1), a shot of a large black man in orientalist garb with naked chest opens the scene at a masked ball at which the white German lovers first meet. Toward the end of the decade, the opening scene of *Heimat, deine Lieder* (Dir: Paul May, 1959) introduces heroine Eva to her love interest when Paul narrowly avoids hitting Eva's charge, a black

German child, with his car. Her use to the plot expended, the child disappears among the other orphans in the SOS-Children's Village Eva runs. The popular film *Liane-Das Mädchen aus dem Urwald* (Dir: Eduard von Borsody, 1957) opened with ethnographic-style clip of unspecified native African women dancing bare-breasted to an African-inspired beat. Setting up a contrast between black African and white German femininity, the film's plot revolves around the "rescue" of a scantily dressed blond-haired, blue-eyed, orphaned German teenage girl from life in the African jungle and her assimilation into the household of a rich uncle in Hamburg.

28. It is interesting in this connection that neither Celia Applegate nor Alon Confino discusses the relationship of German Jews to *Heimat* in their studies. For examples of postwar *Heimat* histories that build their mythology on descriptions of racial violence (especially black-on-white rape and murder) see, Albart, *Die letzten und die ersten Tage* and Hans Rommel, *Vor zehn Jahren*; for a brief analysis of this mythology see Fehrenbach, "Rehabilitating Father*land*," 110–12. For a critical discussion that deals explicitly with the issue of race and *Heimat* after 1945 in terms of social experience, see Maria Höhn, *GIs and Fräuleins*, 85–125.

29. Avè, "*Der dunkle Stern*," 50 and 55.

30. The instances of this are too numerous to list, but a couple of the more popular article titles are "Toxi spielt ihr eigenes Schicksal" or, in the case of *Der dunkle Stern*, "Toxi landet im Zirkus," "*Der dunkle Stern*—ein neuer Film mit Toxi!" In the credits for *Das Haus in Montevideo*, Elfie Fiegert is listed as Toxi Fiegert.

31. The following are merely the press clippings I have come across that dubbed the children "Toxis" in the title or the body of the article: Liselotte Deinert, "Weil Toxis Haut braun ist wird sie nicht Friseuse: Farbige Besatzungskinder müssen die gleichen Berufschancen haben," *Welt der Freizeit*, no. 36 (4 September 1959); "Nicole aus Dakar tanzt zum Klang einer Urwaldtrommel am Edersee: Mischlingskinder aus Französisch-Westafrika verleben Ferien im Albert-Schweitzer-Heim," *Kassler Stadtausgabe*, no. 193 (22 August 1959); Hermann Schreiber, "Wenn 'Toxi,' das Negerkind, erwachsen sind," *Stuttgarter Zeitung* (26 September 1959); "Keine Sorge um Mischlingskinder," *General-Anzeiger* (Bonn) (8 April 1961), clippings of which are found in ADW, HGSt 3949. Also "Die 'Toxis' sind erwachsen—und haben Heiratssorgen," *Welt am Sonntag*, 26 March 1967, article clipping was found in BAK, B189/6858: Bundesministerium für Jugend und Familie, "Untersuchung des Situation der Neger-Mischlingskinder in der Bundesrepublik."

32. It is perhaps telling that some educators and social workers warned against singling out "*Mischlingkinder*" for too much positive attention—whether on the playground or in the media—since this allegedly resulted in a "star situation" that spoiled the child and (mis)led her into thinking she was something special. The reference to a "Starsituation" comes from Waldemar Lichtenberger, "Mischlingskinder in unseren Schulklassen," *Jugend Literatur* 3 (1963): 97–110, quote from 102.

33. "TOXI. Alle Menschen sind nett zu mir," R. A. Stemmle Nachlass, SDK, Berlin.

34. In addition to the films discussed in this chapter, Elfriede Fiegert also appeared in bit parts in the feature films *Zwei Bayern im Harem* (1957, director: Joe Stöckel) and *Unsere tollen Tanten* (1961, director: Rolf Olsen), as well as the television documentaries *Wiedersehen macht Freude* and *Color Me German* (NBC-TV with ZDF). See "Toxi auf Raten," "Wiedersehen macht Freude," "Toxi—Alle Menschen sind nett zu mir," "Filmkind Toxi geht nach Afrika," "Das ist Toxi heute," "Keine lauten Töne," "So wird's nie wieder sein," from SDK-Berlin, Nachlass R. A. Stemmle. Also "Die 'Toxis' sind erwachsen—und haben Heiratssorgen."

CHAPTER FIVE

WHOSE CHILDREN, THEIRS OR OURS? INTERCOUNTY ADOPTIONS
AND DEBATES ABOUT BELONGING

1. SW 109, Box 10, file 19. Letter from Mabel Grammer to International Social Service (ISS), German Branch, 3 June 1953; Lißner, "We Adopted a Brown Baby," 38, 45.

2. "Mammies für die Negerlein," *Stern* 3, no. 35 (27 August 1950): 29. Also "German War Babies: Red Tape Balks Adoption of Orphans by Teacher," *Ebony* (January 1951): 35–38.

3. By March 1951, the following bodies were authorized by the West German federal government to conclude adoptions for German children: state and local public youth offices throughout West Germany, as well as thirty offices or associations affiliated with the Protestant Inner Mission; sixty offices or associations affiliated with the Catholic Deutscher Caritasverband; and twenty-four branches of the Arbeiterwohlfahrt (Workers' Welfare Association). ADW, CAW 843, Bundesrat Sekretariat, BR-Drucks. Nr. 15/52.

4. SW109, 30, #1(b); also SW109, 3, #3. "Four thousand Orphans," March 1954, 7.

5. In the late 1940s, coverage in the black American press adopted a critical stance toward black GI's presumed love-'em-and-leave-'em behavior. See Douglas Hall, "What's Become of Them? Berlin's 'Wild Oats' Babies," *Afro-American* (25 October 1947): 1; "How Many 'Wild Oats' Babies in Germany?," *Afro-American* 8 May 1948: 11. For a fuller discussion of how the children's fathers were treated by the African American press, see Yara-Colette Lemke Muniz de Faria, *Zwischen Fürsorge und Ausgrenzung. Afrodeutsche "Besatzungskinder" im Nachkriegsdeutschland* (Berlin, 2002), 103–5.

6. NAACP, Reel 8: Group II, Box G11, "Brown Babies 1950–58": Letter from Thomasina Norford to Walter White, 7 July 1950. A 1948 newspaper article alleged that "brown babies [in Germany were] turned into side-show attractions . . . with neighbors paying 20 cents to see them" and that some were killed. See "Brown Babies Turned into Side Show Attractions," *Pittsburgh Courier* (17 July 1948): 3. Also correspondence between Pearl Buck and Walter White, 1951–53, in NAACP, Reel 8: Group II, Box G11, "Brown Babies 1950–58". Pearl Buck and her daughter Henriette were featured in "Should White Parents Adopt Brown Babies?" *Ebony* (June 1958): 26–30.

7. Articles appeared in such publications as *Survey, Newsweek, Time, Redbook, Woman's Day, Chicago Tribune,* and *U.S. News and World Report,* as well as *Ebony, Afro-American, Pittsburgh Courier,* and *Chicago Defender.* In addition, the writer Kurt Vonnegut published a story on a black occupation child, deceptively titled "D.P." in his collection *Welcome to the Monkey House* (1953; reprint, New York, 1988). My thanks to Anna Holian for bringing this story to my attention.

8. Lemke Muniz de Faria mentions these initiatives in *Zwischen Fürsorge,* 102–3. *The Pittsburgh Courier* ran the following articles: " 'Brown Babies' Need Help, Nunn Writes" (29 May 1948): 1, 4; P. L. Prattis, "Germany's 'Brown Babies' Must Be Helped! Will You?" (30 April 1949): 1, 5; "U.S. Santa Visits 'Brown Babies' " (24 December 1949): 7; "Adopt Brown Babies" (24 January 1953): 1.

9. SdK, Archivgut, *Aktuelle Film-Nachrichten* 3, no. 1 (1 August 1952): 7.

10. It appears that the special "Mischlingskinder Adoptionsaktion" and the follow-up reports did not occur. ADW, HGSt 1161, transcription of memo from the Sozialminister des Landes Nordrhein-Westfalen to all of its state youth offices, 7 June 1952. Also BayHStA, MInn 81096, letter to Stadtjugendamt Marktredwitz from Küchler, Editor of the *Revue,* 22 February 1952, and draft memo and letter from Drs. Laubenthal and Lutz, Oberregierungsrat, 16 July 1954. *Revue*'s "Adoptionsaktion" was similar to, and may have been copied from, that of the Baltimore *Afro-American.* On the initiatives of the *Afro-American* see the discussion on Mabel Grammer below as well as Lemke Muniz de Faria, *Zwischen Fürsorge,* 108–9.

11. "Mammies für die Negerlein," 29; "German War Babies," 36–37.

12. See for example, Dudziak, *Cold War Civil Rights;* Borstelmann, *The Cold War and the Color Line.*

13. German biases against raising a "blutfremdes Kind"—literally a child of alien blood—applied to white children as well as black, as is clear in from educational pamphlet on adoptions, published in West Germany in 1951, that attempted to dispel such concerns. Margarete zur Nieden, *Fremdes Kind wird eigenes Kind* (Stuttgart; per 1951). In the 1920s, German adoptions were estimated to have numbered about 4,000 per year; with the advent of the Third Reich and the strengthening of eugenic and racial controls, numbers of adoptions plummeted. From 1950 through 1955, adoptions in West Germany rose from 4,279 to 8,205. However, these numbers included international adoptions, which grew in number from 709 in 1952 to 2,568 in 1955 and represented a jump from 12 to 31 percent of all adoptions concluded in West Germany. Helmut Glässing, *Voraussetzungen der Adoption: Eine rechtspolitische und rechtsvergleichende Studie* (Frankfurt/Main; 1957), 25–26, 37.

14. The translated quote is from Edmund C. Jann, "The Law of Adoption in Germany," Typescript, Library of Congress, Law Library, Foreign Law Section (Washington, D.C., 1955), 4, and refers to sec. 1754 of the German Civil Code (emphasis added). Nazi amendments to adoption law included: "Gesetz über Vermittlung der Annahme an Kindesstatt vom 19.4.1939," the text of which appeared in *Reichsgesetzblatt I,* p. 795; commentary on the law can be found in *Deutsche Justiz* (1939): 701. Also "The Law to Change and Supplement the Regulations on Family Relations and to Regulate the Legal Status of Stateless Persons" of 14 April 1938 (*Reichsgesetzblatt* I, p. 380); and "The Marriage Law of 6 July 1938" (*Reichsgesetzblatt* I, p. 807). These laws were preceded in the fall of

1935 by the "Law for the Protection of German Blood," which prohibited sexual relations or marriage between "Aryan" Germans and "Jews, Negroes, or Gypsies [Sinti and Roma] or their bastards." For an English overview of German legislation on adoption through the early postwar period, see Jann, "Law."

15. ADW, CAW 843, Bundesrat Sekretariat, BR-Drucks. Nr. 15/52. Also Nieden, *Fremdes Kind*, 18; and Glässing, *Voraussetzungen*, 44–56.

16. ADW, CAW 843, "Gutachliche Äusserung zur Frage der Adoptionsvermittlugn," 11 March 1948.

17. According to the letter, the "main considerations" behind the law were "the elimination of unreliable, poorly instructed and inexperienced agencies" and the "strengthening of public and State influences on the agencies in order to direct their activities." ADW, CAW 843, Letter of Religious Affairs Branch (U.S.) to Pastor Münchmeyer, Centrral Ausschuss für die Innere Mission der Deutschen Evangelischen Kirche, 1 June 1948.

18. The American military government law was: MG Law No. 59, Article 81, "Re-establishment of Adoption," which was issued on 10 November 1947 and permitted applications to vacate the cancellation of adoptions that took place between 30 January 1933 (Hitler's accession to the German chancellorship) and 8 May 1945. Jann, "Law," 20–21. Jann presents a good legal overview of adoption during the occupation, including all American MG law. He also comments briefly on law in the British, French, and Soviet zones.

19. By the mid-1950s, some white American couples were beginning to adopt "Amerasian" children from Korea and Japan. It took until the early 1960s, however, until serious discussion began about the appropriateness of white couples adopting black children in the United States. SW 109, Boxes 10–11.

20. ADW, CAW 843, "Gutachliche Äusserung zur Frage der Adoptionsvermittlugn," 11 March 1948. Only married couples could adopt.

21. In August 1950, a temporary modification of the adoption law was passed by the Bundestag ("Gesetz zur Erleichterung der Annahme an Kindes Staat") to allow German families with children to adopt. This law was renewed in 1952 to extend to 1955. ADW, CAW 843, Deutscher Bundestag, 1. Wahlperiode 1949, Drucksache Nr. 3931. See also the popular German magazine, *Revue* (Munich), for its "Adoptionsaktion" in 1951.

22. In 1948 Bavaria, for example, the justification for the amendment of the state adoption law invoked the "great losses of many families due to the war and the availability of a huge number of orphans," arguing: "It is also especially important to think such cases in which people, married with children, desire to adopt children of relatives, friends, or neighbors, above all from the eastern regions [of the former German empire (Ostgebieten)] whose parents were killed in the war or its aftermath. Often it is the illegitimate child of a fallen son one wants to adopt." BayHStA, Staatskanzlei (StK) 130324. "Rechtsausschuss, Antrag aus der Ausschusssitzung vom 5. November 1948."

23. SW 109, 30, #1(a).

24. NARA-CP, OMGUS, OMG-Hesse, CAD, Public Welfare Branch, Box 1069: "Correspondence: Child and Youth Welfare," Memo of Conference with Regierungsrat Crueger, 17 July 1947.

25. For example, ADW, HGSt 1161, transcription of memo from Sozialminister des Landes Nordrhein-Westfalen, 11 June 1952.

26. The program was ended in June 1952. USCOM, *Memorandum Concerning Official Basis of the Program of the United States Committee for the Care of European Children, Inc.*, 1953.

27. BAK, B153/342, "Vermerk" to Dr. Rothe, 26 February 1951; letter of McVey to Kitz, 13 March 1951.

28. Ministry officials continued to consult Heibl for his advice and "expertise" over the course of the following year as they pursued possibilities for the children's emigration. BAK, B153/342, Correspondence and "Vermerke" of Rothe and Weider to and regarding Heibl, 28 October 1950, 30 June 1951, 24 July 1952.

29. Emphasis added. BAK, B153/342, "Vermerk" to Dr. Rothe, 25 May 1951. The German Interior Ministry officials present were Drs. Kitz (Ministerialdirekor) and Scheffler (Ministerialrat).

30. Ibid.

31. In attendance were nineteen men and women, black and white, representing the NAACP, Urban League, Phelps Stokes Fund, Child Welfare League of America, European-Jewish Children's Aid, National Catholic Welfare Conference, Catholic Committee for Refugees, Church World Service, National Lutheran Council, Methodist Committee on Overseas Relief, and U.S. Committee for the Care of European Children.

32. NAACP, Reel 8: Group II, Box G11, "Brown Babies 1950–58." Minutes of the "Meeting of the Committee to Consider Possibilities and Resources for the Immigration of a Group of German Orphans of Negro Blood," 29 January 1951, p. 2.

33. Ibid, 5, 7.

34. Ibid, 5–8.

35. Ibid. Also Eugenie Hochfeld and Margaret A. Valk, *Experience in Intercountry Adoptions*, (New York, 1957), 12.

36. BAK, 153/342 correspondence dated 12 January and 24 January 1952, 340–41.

37. Letters from Marget Pfeiffer (Göttingen), 10 November 1950; Maria Schenk (Darmstadt), 19 September 1951; Irene Dilloo, founder of the "Albert Schweizer Kinderheim," 14 October 1952; and from Frau Maya Angowski, head of the "Hilfsorganization 'Das Besatzungskind' e.v. in Munich from 18 May 1954, who later founded the first German Branch of the NAACP there. NAACP papers, Reel 8: Group II, Box G11, "Brown Babies, 1950–58."

38. Letter of Roy Wilkins to Maria Schenck, 13 September 1951; exchange of letters between Walter White and J. Oscar Lee, July–October 1952.

39. Walter White press release, NAACP, Reel 8: Group II, Box G11 "Brown Babies 1950–58."

40. "Meeting of the Committee to consider . . . the Immigration of . . . German orphans of Negro Blood," 29 Jan 1951. NAACP papers, Reel 8: Group II, Box G11, "Brown Babies, 1950–58."

41. Allan Gould, "Germany's Tragic War Babies," *Ebony* (Dec 1952): 78.

42. Ibid.

43. Walter White press release, 18 September 1952. NAACP, Reel 8: Group II, Box G11 "Brown Babies 1950–58."

44. Walter White press release, 18 September 1952. NAACP, Reel 8: Group II, Box G11 "Brown Babies 1950–58." Similar points were made in Allan Gould, "Germany's Tragic War Babies," *Ebony* (Dec 1952): 74–78.

45. NAACP Reel 8, Group II, Box G11., Brown Babies. "German Waifs Find a Friend," *Chicago Daily New*, 15 May 1953.

46. SW109, Box 10, #19, letter from Susan T. Pettiss, dated 13 March 1962.

47. Ibid; also SW109, Box 10, #19; SW109, Box 11, #21, 29. Press articles include "How You Can Help," *Afro-American* (27 November 1948): 3; "*Afro* Arranges Adoption of First Brown Babies," *Afro-American* (24 January 1953): 1; "Is This the End of the Brown Baby Plan?" *Afro-American* (7 August 1954): 1, 6; "Letter from Germany: Brown Babies Ask for Your Help," *Afro-American* (1 February 1958): 3; "German Brown Babies Ask Aid from Americans," *Afro-American* (15 March 1958): 5; also P. L. Prattis, "Germany's 'Brown Babies' Must Be Helped! Will You?" *Pittsburgh Courier* (30 April 1949): 1, 7; "How to Adopt a German War Baby," *Jet* (23 October 1952): 16–21. For a discussion of the role played by the *Afro-American* in Grammer's adoption initiative, see Lemke Muniz de Faria, *Zwischen Fürsorge*, 106–10.

48. For example, BayHStA, MInn 81096, memo from Landratsamt Roding (Bezirksfürsorgeverband), 7 November 1953.

49. SW109, Box 10, #19.

50. Correspondence from Mabel A. Grammer dated 3 June 1953 and 18 March 1954. The children's names have been changed by the author. SW109, Box 10, #19.

51. SW109, Box 23, #23; Box 3, #3;

52. SW109, Box 3, #3, "Four Thousand Orphans," 7; also SW109, Box 10, #19.

53. SW109, Box 10, #19, letter of M.Grammer to ISS-NYC, 18 March 1954.

54. SW109, Box 3, #3, "Four thousand orphans," 3. Also Laurin Hyde and Virginia P. Hyde, "A Study of Proxy Adoptions," June 1958.

55. SW109, Box 10, #38. S. T. Petiss, "Proxy Adoptions," n.d., 1.

56. SW109, Box 3, #3, "Four thousand orphans," 7. Also Hyde and Hyde, "Study of Proxy Adoptions."

57. The American Branch of the ISS was founded in 1924, the German Branch in 1928. After 1933, with the National Socialist Party's assumption of power, the German branch was compelled to sever its relationship with the ISS council when it could no longer "comply with the essential ISS principle—service without political, racial, or religious discrimination." The branch was refounded after the war in 1952. By the early 1950s, the ISS had offices in the Australia, Austria, Belgium, Brazil, France, Great Britain, Greece, Italy, Japan, the Netherlands, North Africa, Switzerland, Uruguay, Venezuela, West Germany, and the United States. Short institutional histories can be found in Ruth Larned, "International Social Service: A History, 1924–1955" (New York, typescript, 1956); Eugenie Hochfeld and Margaret A. Valk, "Experience in Inter-country Adoptions" (New York, typescript, 1957); Ruth Larned, *The Story of the International Social Service* (New York, 1960). The ISS-New York's rich archival record is deposited at the University of Minnesota's Social Work History Archives and merits its own full-length historical study.

58. Hochfeld and Valk, "Experience."

59. For history on the subject, see Edward Ross Dickinson, *The Politics of German Child Welfare from the Empire to the Federal Republic* (Cambridge, Mass., 1996). Also SW109, Box 30, #5: "Relationship of ISS German Branch with German Social Services."

60. SW109, Box 30, 1(c). Memos from 16 June and 3 August, 1961. SW109, Box 30, 1 (a). Interview with Alice L. Shugars, 23 April 1954; letter from Mende to ISS-New York, 8 August 1955, and further correspondence of Mende from 1955 to 1956. Also SW109, Box 30, #5, reports on ISS German Branch, 1955–62.

61. SW109, Box 30, 1(a). Letter from Mende to ISS New York, 8 August 1955, and further correspondence of Mende from 1955–56.

62. The Protestant Inner Mission in Germany, for example, was publicly criticized by American ISS representatives for concluding 258 proxy adoptions for German children to America by 1955. SW109, Box 30, 1(a).

63. SW109, Box 10, #19. Letter of Grammer to ISS-New York, 18 March 1954.

64. In official publications, American ISS officials devoted separate discussions to "half-Negro" German children. In statistics on intercountry adoptions to the U.S. conducted under ISS-auspices, separate figures were kept on "Caucasian," "Negro," "Eurasian," and "Oriental" children from abroad. SW109, Box 3, #3 and Box 11, #9.

65. SW109, Box 3, #3. Burns, "Four Thousand Orphans."

66. SW109, Boxes 10–11.

67. Burns, "Four Thousand Orphans," 7.

68. Ibid, 10.

69. See for example school reports on black German children in BayHStA, MInn 81084 and Staatsarchiv Freiburg, Bestand F110/1, Nr. 176. Also Wilhelmine Hollweg, "Ohne Ansehen der Rasse . . . ," *DPWV-Nachrichten* 5, no. 6 (June 1955), 2–3, filed in BAK, B153/342; "Zur Frage der Aufnahme farbiger Kinder in Heimen," *Unsere Jugend* 5, no. 8 (August 1953): 376–77; Hans Pfaffenberger, "Farbige Kinder im Heim—ein Prüfstein," *Unsere Jugend* 5, no. 12 (December 1953): 533–36; "Farbige Kinder im Heim," *Unsere Jugend* 5, #12 (December 1953): 571–72; and the anthropological studies by Kirchner and Sieg.

70. Responses to a request issued by the federal Ministry of the Interior to state youth offices, the Centralauschuss für die Innere Mission der Deutschen Evangelischen Kirche, the Deutscher Caritasverband, and the Arbeiterwohlfahrt for inquiries regarding the special characteristics and problems of *"Mischlingskinder."* BayHStA, Minn 81084; HStAStg, EA2/007 Akten des Innenministeriums, no. 1177: "Jugendsozialhilfe"; and StA Freiburg, Bestand F110/1, #176. See also the earlier reports submitted in 1952 to the Centralausschuss für die Innere Mission der Deutschen Evangelischen Kirche, ADW, HGSt 1161.

71. BAK, B153/342.

72. On Dilloo and the Albert-Schweitzer-Kinder Heim, which operated between 1955 and 1959, see BAK, 153/342 and ADW, HGSt 1161 and HGSt 1193. Also the numerous press reports including Hollweg, "Ohne Ansehen der Rasse"; u.h.l., "Eine Frau mit warmer Herz," *Freie Presse* (13 March 1956); anon., "Lebensglück auch für sie," *Hor zu* (24–30 May 1953), among others. Dilloo was also the subject of sympathetic articles in *Ebony* magazine, including "Children Nobody Wants: German Pair Open 'Brown Baby' Home," *Ebony* (May 1959): 59–

62. For a critical appraisal of Dilloo and her work, see the comments of D. Otto Ohl (Geschäftsführender Direkor des Landesverbandes Innere Mission Rheinland) in ADW, HGSt 1161 and 1193; for a detailed historical analysis, based in part upon Dilloo's correspondence, see Lemke Muniz de Faria, *Zwischen Fürsorge*, 120–56.

73. This description also applies to Irene Dilloo. For a discussion of her motives and emotional investment in the Albert-Schweitzer-Home, see Lemke Muniz de Faria, *Zwischen Fürsorge*, 122–25, 144–45.

74. SA Nürnberg, C25/I, F Reg: Gesamtbestand Sozialamt, Nr. 489: Kinderfürsorge, nun: Minderj.-Hilfe, 1954–55.

75. SA Nürnberg, C25/I, F Reg, Gesamtbestand Sozialamt, Nr. 489, Kinderfürsorge, letter 28. March 1955.

76. The reference to Liberia is in Hollweg, "Ohne Ansehen der Rasse," 3. Dilloo's plans to train children for emigration appear in BAK, B153/342 and ADW, HGSt 1161 and 1193. Her statement about the children as West German economic agents appeared in "Operation Brown Babies," *Our World* (May 1954): 31.

77. "Nicole aus Dakar tanzt zum Klang einer Urwaldtrommel am Edersee: Mischlingskinder aus Französisch-Westafrika verleben Ferien im Albert-Schweitzer-Heim," *Kasseler Stadtausgabe* Nr. 193 (22 August 1959), clipping in ADW, HGSt 3949.

78. Ebeling's initiative was reported in "Operation Brown Babies," *Our World* (May 1954): 24–31.

79. Officials at the Protestant Inner Mission were skeptical of Dilloo's enterprise. Ultimately the home was closed in 1959 at the initiative of the Hessian State Youth Office in Wiesbaden which had been critical of both its professional management and, following the earlier recommendations of the SCJC/World Brotherhood, the segregationist model of socialization and education. For details, see Lemke Muniz de Faria, *Zwischen Fürsorge*, 148–56.

80. ADW, HGSt 1161; also HStAStg, EA2/007, Nr. 1177. The smaller number of petitions by prospective African American adoptive parents reflected and reproduced a racial difference in the culture and management of out-of-wedlock births and adoptions during this period in the United States. Rickie Solinger, *Wake Up, Little Susie: Single Pregnancy and Race before "Roe vs. Wade"* (New York, 1992).

81. Heinrich Webler, "Adoptions-Markt" in *Zentralblatt für Jugendrecht und Jugendwohl* 42, no. 5 (May 1955): 123–24. Also BAK, B153: Bundesministerium für Familien- und Jugendfragen, File 1335, I–II: "Material über Probleme des Internationalen Adoptionsrechts"; HStAStg, Akten des Innenministeriums, EA2/007: Vermittlung der Annahme an Kindesstatt, Band II, 1955–66, especially the copy of the memo from the Internationaler Sozialdienst to the Bundesministerium für Familien- und Jugendfragen dated 27 January 1958; and Franz Klein, "Kinderhandel als strafbare Handlung" *Jugendwohl*, Heft 3 (1956): 95.

82. Webler, "Adoptions-Markt."

83. Charles Lanius, "We found a Baby Bonanza in West Germany," *Woman's Day* (November 1954): 42 ff., filed in BayHStA, MInn 81096.

84. ADW, HGST 1161, "Kurzbericht über die Sitzung . . . dem 12. Juli 1955 im Bundesministerium des Innern."

85. Ibid. Private welfare organizations were represented by the Central Association of Private Welfare Services (Zentrale der Verbände der freien Wohlfahrtspflege). Also BayHStA, MInn 81906, memo of Bundesministerium des Innern, 6 September 1955. On the apparent increase in the German ISS's influence at the federal level, MInn 81096, memos from the Bundesminister des Innern, 27 May 1955; report of Generalkonsulat der BRD, New York, 29 October 1954; draft letter of Bayerisches Landesjugendamt to the Generalkonsulat der BRD, 14 May 1954.

86. ADW, CAW 845, "Bericht über die Adoptionsvermittlung für das Jahr 1955."

87. Prospective German parents were particularly interested in two-to-three year old girls. ADW, CAW 845, "Bericht über die Adoptionsvermittlung für das Jahr 1955." This preference for girls continued into the mid-1960s according to statistics kept by the Central Adoption Office of the Diakonisches Werk der EKD. ADW, HGst 3949, reports from 1960–63.

88. BayHStA, MInn 81906, memo of Bundesministerium des Innern, 6 September 1955. This educational pitch had been made earlier in a promotional pamphlet on adoption in 1951. However, it now received official support. See Nieden, *Fremdes Kind*.

89. In memos, minutes, and reports, separate sections were typically devoted to the discussion of *"Mischlingskinder."*

90. According to the Protestant Central Adoption Office, German adoptions of black German children remained flat (no more than three a year), even though applications for white children from prospective German adoptive or foster parents during these years ranged between five hundred and one thousand per annum. ADW, HGSt 3949, Auszug aus dem Bericht über die Tätigkeit der Adoptionszentrale für den Verwendungsnachweise, Zuschuss 1961 and 1963.

91. The unstated basis for this claim may have been Danish success in protecting the lives of Danish Jews under German occupation in the Second World War by smuggling them to other Scandinavian countries. BAK, B153: Bundesministerium für Familien- und Jugendfragen, File 1335, I-II: "Material über Probleme des Internationalen Adoptionsrechts." HStAStg, Akten des Innenministeriums, EA2/007: Vermittlung der Annahme an Kindesstatt, Band II, 1955–66, especially Internationaler Sozialdienst memo to the Bundesministerium für Familien- und Jugendfragen, 27 January 1958. Heinrich Webler, "Adoptions-Markt," 123–24; Franz Klein, "Zur gegenwärtige Situation der Auslandsadoption," *Unsere Jugend* 9 (1955), 401–8; Franz Klein, "Kinderhandel als strafbare Handlung," in *Jugendwohl*, 3 (1956), S. 95.

92. On this point, see Ruth Bahn-Flessburg, "Die Hautfarbe ist kein Problem," *Frankfurter Allgemeine Zeitung*, Nr. 238: 68.

93. SA Nürnberg, C25/I, F Reg: Gesamtbestand Sozialamt, Nr. 489 Kinderfürgsorge, "Beschluss des Wohlfahrtsausschusses vom 15.6.1955.

94. ADW, HGst 3949. A few articles, all positive, on the adoption of black German children to Denmark also appeared in the African American press: "Danish Lady Shows Love for German Brown Baby," *Chicago Defender* (3–9 February 1962): 11; "Germany's Brown Babies Visit Denmark," *Pittsburgh Courier*, sec. 2 (3 February 1962): 16–17; and "What Is Danish Attitude? What Future for Brown Babies in Germany?" *Pittsburgh Courier*, sec. 2 (24 February 1962): 4.

95. ADW, HGSt 3949, Evgl. Jugendfürsorgeverein Rheinland e.V., 13 May 1963.

96. Ibid.

97. The study was funded by funded the West German federal Ministry of the Interior and the German Research Council (Deutsche Forschungsgemeinschaft); interestingly, Eyferth earlier inquired in the United States about Ford Foundation funding, but it is not clear whether he submitted a formal application. Eyferth, Brandt, and Hawel, *Farbige Kinder in Deutschland.*

98. See the interesting recent studies, Feldstein, *Motherhood*, and Scott, *Contempt and Pity.*

99. Eyferth grudgingly noted that children under the age of two could perhaps be considered for adoption to the United States. Eyferth, *Farbige Kinder,* 90–91.

100. As for black German *Heimkinder* who could not find placement in Germany, Eyferth judged that certain European destinations—and "especially the Scandinavian ones"—offered a superior solution since children could be placed into a supportive family environment and national culture "in which, due to tradition and upbringing, prejudices are much rarer than here in Germany." Eyferth, *Farbige Kinder,* 91–92.

101. This reclassification of the children as "European" also appears in a serialized novel about a black German girl, see Ursula Schaake, "Meine schwarze Schwester. Der Roman eines Besatzungskindes," *Revue* no. 42 (Weihnachten, 1960)—no. 15 (9 April 1961).

102. The first quote is from Hurka, *Die Mischlingskinder in Deutschland, Teil II,* S. 275; the second is from an article on U.S. immigration and the McCarran bill to "ensure the purity of the race." "Die USA bevorzugen 'Blonde' ", *Rheinische Post,* 24 July 1952, press clipping in BAK, B106 Bundesministerium des Innern, File 20620. Also Eyferth, *Farbige Kinder,* 90–93.

103. "Brown Babies Go to Work: German Launches Smooth Integration of 1,500 Negro Youths in Its Work Force," *Ebony* (November 1960): 97–108.

104. Ebeling, "Das Problem der deutschen Mischlingskinder"; Erna Maraun, "Zehn kleine Negerlein," *Der Rundbrief. Fachliches Mitteilungsblatt des Hauptjugendamtes Berlin* 3, no. 1 (1953), 2–6; Erhard Schneckenburger, "Das Mischlingskind in der Schule," *Neues Beginnen,* no. 1 (1957), 24; and BayHStA, MK 62245, report by the Ständige Konferenz der Kulturminister on the integration of "*Mischlingskinder*" into West German schools, 27 February 1956.

CHAPTER SIX
LEGACIES: RACE AND THE POSTWAR NATION

1. Klaus Eyferth, "Die Situation und die Entwicklungsaussichten der Negermischlingskinder," *Soziale Arbeit* 7, no. 11 (1958): 469–78, here 473.

2. From "Pass the Word and Break the Silence," *Moving beyond Boundaries,* ed. C. Boyce Davies and M. Ogundipe-Leslie (New York, 1995), 82, quoted in Carmen Faymonville, "Black Germans and Transnational Identification," *Callaloo* 26, no. 2 (2003): 373–74.

3. BAK, B149, Bundesministerium für Arbeit und Sozialordnung, 8679: Berufsberatungs und Vermittlung von Ausbildungsstellen für unehelicher farbiger Besatzungskinder deutscher Staatsangehörigkeit, report in *Unsere Jugend*, October 1959. Also Eyferth, "Die Situation und die Entwicklungsaussichten der Neger-Mischlingskinder," 469–78; Eyferth, Brandt, Hawel, *Farbige Kinder.*

4. HessHStA 940/77, Report on conference, "Verantwortung für unsere Mischlingskinder," sponsored by the Arbeiterwohlfahrt in Frankfurt am Main, 20 August 1959.

5. For an overview of the history of foreign workers in Germany, see Herbert, *A History of Foreign Labor in Germany.* Foreign workers constituted 0.8 percent of total employed (166,000 out of 26.4 million) in the Federal Republic in 1959; by 1967, their numbers had risen to almost 5 percent, or 1,023,000 out of 26.6 million employed. Herbert, *History of Foreign Labor in Germany,* 291. See also the forthcoming book by Rita Chin, *The Guest Worker Question: Debating Diversity in the Federal Republic of Germany, 1955–1990.*

6. HessHStA 940/77. Memo from Director, Arbeitsamt Frankfurt a.M. to Präsidenten des Landesarbeitsamt Hessen, 30 June 1960.

7. West German press reports tended to follow the upbeat prognosis articulated at the 1959 conference in Frankfurt/Main. Every once in awhile, however, they would document individual instances of prejudice toward biracial youth, but these were presented as anomalies in the larger narrative of racial progress in West Germany. See for example Liselotte Deinert, "Weil Toxis Haut braun ist wird sie nicht Friseuse," *Welt der Freizeit* (4 September 1959), clipping in ADW, HGSt 3949.

8. This quote is from HessHStA 940/77, draft letter dated 14 July 1960; however this bias was widely expressed in reports from youth and employment office officials throughout Hesse.

9. See for example the school reports on black German children from the early to mid-1950s. BayHStA, Minn 81084; HStAStg, EA2/007 Akten des Innenministeriums, Nr. 1177: "Jugendsozialhilfe"; and StA Freiburg, Bestand F110/1, #176.

10. This discussion is based upon the reports in HessHStA 940/77. For a small sample of interviews of Afro-Germans' experience as teens and young adults, see "Die Deutschen mit der dunklen Haut," *Quick* 46 (3–9 November 1977): 82–89. Also Ruth Bahn-Flessburg, "Sie haben die gleichen Chancen wie die Weissen: Auf der Suche nach den farbigen Besatzungskindern," *Unsere Jugend* 20 (1968): 295–303; and Ruth Bahn-Flessburg, "Die Hautfarbe ist kein Problem: Farbige 'Besatzungskinder'—Vierzehn Lebensläufe," *Frankfurter Allgemeine Zeitung* (1968). This last article was filed in ADW, HGSt 3949. Strikingly, details of Bahn-Flessburg's interviews subvert her rosy depiction of race relations in West Germany.

11. These attributes (tolerance, rational argument and practice, humanistic values, and protection of the individual) were the historical hallmarks of German liberalism and were enshrined in West Germany's Basic Law. Dieter Langewiesche, *Liberalism in Germany* (Princeton, 2000) and Konrad H. Jarausch and Larry Eugene Jones, ed., *In Search of Liberal Germany* (New York, 1990).

12. Eyferth remained the exception to this trend, and while he was called upon and quoted for his expertise, the reception of his work was decidedly se-

lective. For assessments of integration into apprenticeships and the workforce, see in particular the material from BAK, B149: Bundesministerium für Arbeit und Sozialordnung, #8679; BayHStA, MInn 81126, press clippings on "Mischlingskinder," 1960–61; BayHStA, MK62245, "Volksschulwesen Negerkinder"; HessHStA, Abt. 940/77; Elly Waltz, "Mischlinge werden jetzt Lehrlinge," *Münchner Merkur* 164 (9–10 July 1960); and "Farbige Lehrlinge—wieder sehr gefragt," *Münchner Merkur* 63 (15 March 1961). For a more critical assessment, see Klaus Eyferth, "Gedanken über die zukünftige Berufseingliederung der Mischlingskinder in Westdeutschland," in *Neues Beginnen* 5 (May 1959), 65–68.

13. David Abraham, "American Jobs but Not the American Dream: Lessons from Europe about Guest Worker Programs," *New York Times*, Op-Ed Section (9 January 2004): A21. Abraham was commenting critically on U. S. President G. W. Bush's immigration reform proposal announced on 7 January 2004. His essay concludes by asserting that the proposal "values immigrants' talents over their dreams. Instead of hope, it offers them simply a job."

14. BayHStA, MInn 81094, correspondence regarding the 1960 survey of occupation children and *"Mischlingskinder,"* 1960–61. However, as we have seen the state of Hesse continued through 1961 to collect separate information on the integration of black German youth into the workforce.

15. Bahn-Flessburg, "Sie haben," 295–303, emphasis in the original. This article was filed in BAK 189/6859.

16. "Vor dem Gesetz sind *nicht* alle Kinder gleich," *Abendzeitung* 19–20 March 1960, in BayHStA, MInn 81126. Also Bahn-Flessburg, "Sie haben"; and ADW, HGst 3949, Bahn-Flessburg, "Die Hautfarbe." My thanks to Maria Höhn for providing me a verbal description of her viewing of the film *Wie Toxi wirklich lebt*. For a discussion of the debates regarding the legal status of illegitimacy in 1960s West Germany, see Buske, *Fräulein Mutter*.

17. For example, Karen Thimm and DuRell Echols, *Schwarze in Deutschland* (Munich, 1973); Katharina Oguntoya, "Die Schwarze deutsche Bewegung und die Frauenbewegung in Deutschland," *Afrekete: Zeitung von afro-deutschen und Schwarzen Frauen* 4 (1989): 3–5, 33–37; Opitz, Oguntoye, and Schultz, *Showing our Colors*; Tina Campt, "Afro-German Identity and the Politics of Positionality," *New German Critique* 58 (Winter 1993): 109–26; and May Ayim, "Die afro-deutsche Minderheit," in *Ethnische Minderheiten in der Bundesrepublik Deutschland*, ed. Cornelia Schmalz-Jacobsen and Georg Hansen (Munich, 1995).

18. The articles I have found in the course of my research and that I will be drawing on for this discussion are: "Lehrlinge mit dunkler Haut," *Frankfurter Allgemeine Zeitung* 185 (12 August 1961); Gerhard Nebel, "Nicky," *Frankfurter Allgemeine Zeitung* 181 (8 August 1961); "Wiedersehen macht Freude," *Quick* (28 April 1963): 38; "Toxi: Alle Menschen sind nett zu mir," ca. 1964, no periodical title given, photo-essay filed in SDK, Berlin, Nachlass R. A. Stemmle; "Die 'Toxis' since erwachsen—und haben Heiratssorgen," *Welt am Sonntag* (26 March 1967), 6; Bahn-Flessburg, "Sie haben"; Bahn-Flessburg, "Die Hautfarbe"; "Adam und Eva: Ein Mädchen wie Toxi fand sein Glück an der Elbe," *Neue illustrierte Revue* 7 (10 February 1975), 47–50; "Die Deutschen mit der dunkler Haut," *Quick* 46 (3–9 November 1977): 82–89.

19. This was particularly the case for coverage in the 1970s.

20. A couple of serialized novels featuring black German teenaged girls were also published in the early 1960s. See Ursula Schaake, "Meine schwarze Schwester," *Revue* no. 42 (Weihnachten, 1960) through no. 15 (9 April 1961); Stefan Doerner, "Mach mich weiss, Mutti!" *Quick* 16, no. 17 (28 April 1963) through no. 27 (7 July 1963).

21. "Lehrlinge mit dunkler Haut," *Frankfurter Allgemeine Zeitung* (12 August 1961), clipping in ADW, HGSt 3949.

22. "Adam und Eva," 47–50.

23. For more recent musings of a white German male academic, see Andreas Mielke, " 'Black Cherries are Sweeter': A Note on African-German Erotic Relations," *Who Is German? Historical and Modern Perspectives on Africans in Germany*, ed. Leroy T. Hopkins, Jr., Harry and Helen Gray Humanities Program Series, vol. 5 (Washington, D.C., 1999), 55–75.

24. "Adam und Eva," 50.

25. Ika Hügel-Marshall also makes this point in her memoir, *Invisible Woman: Growing Up Black in Germany* (New York, 1999). In school, nuns wanted to train her to be a child-care worker since they did not expect her to marry.

26. The West German press pursued the issue of whether and whom black Germans were marrying, and in 1967 the popular *Welt am Sonntag*, reported turning up only two marriages of "*Mischlingsmädchen*": one married a "white American" and the other a "German student [sic!]." "Die 'Toxis' sind erwachsen." An article in the following year in the *Frankfurter Allgemeine Zeitung* cited two further marriages: between a black German man and a white German woman (much was made of her poor family circumstances), and between a black German woman and a white German toolmaker. Bahn-Flessburg, "Die Hautfarbe."

27. "Adam und Eva," 50. William Gardner Smith also reflected on white European fascination with black male sexuality in *Return to America*, 67.

28. In part, it is Heinz's reflection on this behavior and his love for his wife that convinces him to accept the girl, Gisela, into the family. Ursula Schaake, "Meine schwarze Schwester," Revue no. 42 (Weihnachten 1960)–no. 15 (9 April 1961). This scene occurs in the second installment of the novel, 22.

29. In the two occasions they do appear, much is made of the grim moral background and lower-class milieu of the white bride. See Bahn-Flessburg, "Sie haben." Of course the 1970s produced two famous films depicting sexual relationships between white German women and foreign men of color, both by director Rainer Werner Fassbinder: *Ali, Fear Eats the Soul* (1974), which focuses on a romance between a white German cleaning woman and an Arab auto mechanic from North Africa; and *The Marriage of Maria Braun* (1978), the allegorical tale of West German reconstruction told through the social and economic mobility of a seductive white German woman whose early postwar affair with a black GI results in his murder when her white German husband returns from the war. *Maria Braun*'s iconic stature was brought home to me repeatedly, when presenting my research at conferences, by scholars in the audience who would inevitably reference the film in way that suggested it provided the basis for their historical knowledge of the postwar phenomenon of interracial relationships between white German women and black GIs. What is more interesting about

the film, however, is the way Fassbinder reproduced, uncritically, socially conservative representations of white women's behavior that dominated the West
German public discourse in the late 1940s and the 1950s.

30. SA Nürnberg, C25/I, F Reg, Nr. 489; also ADW, HGst 1161.

31. "Adam und Eva," 47–48; also Bahn-Flessburg, "Die Hautfarbe."

32. See the contribution of Helga Emde, "An 'Occupation Baby' in Postwar
Germany" in Opitz, Oguntoye, and Schultz, *Showing our Colors*, 101–11. For can-
did discussions of being black and female in the West Germany of the 1970s
and 1980s, see Thimm and Echols, *Schwarze in Deutschland*; and Laura Baum,
Katharina Oguntoye, and May Opitz, "Three Afro-German Women in Conversa-
tion with Dagmar Schultz," 145–64; and contributions of Ellen Wiedenroth,
Corinna N., Angelika Eisenbrandt, Abena Adomako, Opitz, and Oguntoye in
Opitz, Oguntoye, and Schultz, *Showing our Colors*, 145–217.

33. Jobatey, "*Afro-Look*," quoted on 147.

34. This characterization also informed white Germans' assessments of black
Germans' self-identity. As one commentator in the prominent West German
newpaper, *Frankfurter Allgemeine Zeitung*, put it in 1961 when discussing a "long-
legged, graceful" young acquaintance named Nicky, an Afro-German of black
American paternity:

> The flip side of her suffering is her racial consciousness. While in Bonn, she
> waved to every colored person who crossed our path, even the Indonesians
> and Moroccans. She took her place in the "Afro-Asiatic front." She opted
> for the Party of one-quarter Negro Blood and forgot the three-quarters Eu-
> ropean blood. . . . She wants to be a doctor, something she will not achieve
> intellectually, and then go to Africa—not to America. She appears to have
> heard that racial equality will be achieved there before long. She would like
> to wash off her race, but now because her race has proved indelible, she
> makes the best of it and is sickly proud of it. She acts like her race is a fateful
> injustice and therefore seeks solidarity with all who have been similarly
> treated unjustly—with all non-Europeans.

This quote begs an analysis of how African and Asian decolonization movements affected German notions of race and blackness, something that is beyond
the scope of this book. Nebel, "Nicky."

35. Audre Lorde, "Foreward to the English Language Edition," Opitz, Oguntoye, and Schultz, *Showing Our Colors*, vii–viii. Italics added.

36. *Farbe Bekennen* appeared in English translation as *Showing Our Colors:
Afro-German Women Speak Out* (Amherst, 1992). The following discussion is
based upon *Showing Our Colors*; and Tina Campt, "Afro-German Cultural
Identity and the Politics of Postionality: Contests and Contexts in the Forma-
tion of a German Ethnic Identity," *New German Critique* 58 (Winter 1993): 109–
26. Also Special Issue on the Black German Experience, *Callaloo* 26, no. 2 (2003);
Erin Crawley, "Rethinking Germanness: Two Afro-German Women Journal
Home," 75–95 in *Other Germanies*, ed. K. Jankowsky and C. Love (Albany,
N.Y., 1997); Hopkins, *Who Is German?* See also the book edited by Patricia
Mazon and Reinhild Steingröver, *Not So Plain as Black and White: Afro-*

German History and Culture from 1890 to 2000 (University of Rochester Press, 2005).

37. Paul Gilroy and Stuart Hall have been influential voices on Blacks and blackness in a European context. For a biographical portrait of one Black German woman who decides to see her extended family, see the 1995 ZDF production, *Ich wollte immer blond sein auf der Haut.*

38. For a brief description, see Leroy Hopkins, Jr., "Race, Nationality and Culture," in Jankowsky and Love, *Who Is German,* 1–32; also Jobatey, *"Afro-Look,"* introduction. Web sites can be found at: http://www.isdonline.de/; http://www.woman.de/katalog/politik/adefra.html; and http://www.secession.com/afrolink/.

39. Jobatey, *"Afro-Look,"* 20.

40. Campt, "Afro-German Cultural Identity," 116, 123. Actually, *Farbe Bekennen's* publication postdated two other volumes that are not given as much critical attention. These are Thimm and Echols, *Schwarze in Deutschland* and Gisela Fremgen, *. . . und wenn du dazu noch Schwarz bist. Berichte schwarzer Frauen in der Bundesrepublik* (Bremen, 1984).

41. The web site of the Black German Cultural Society can be found at http://www.blackgermans.us.

42. Although public awareness is low, over the past few years academic attention to the study of the history and experiences of Black Germans and Europeans has increased. Conferences on the topic have been held at the University of Buffalo (1999); at the University of Leipzig (2000, sponsored by the German Historical Institute in Washington, D.C.); at the Universität zu Köln (2004; www.kopfwelten.org); and at the Haus der Kulturen der Welt in Berlin (2004; www.hkw.de). In addition, funding has been awarded by the Volkswagen Stiftung and Humbolt University in Berlin for a project on the "forgotten history of Black Europe." The University of Massachusetts, Amherst, which is involved with the project, plans to act as a clearinghouse for international scholarship on Black Europe. Personal communication with Sara Lennox.

43. For recent research that explores the presence of Blacks in eighteenth-century Germany, see Vera Lind, "Privileged Dependency on the Edge of the Atlantic World: Africans and Germans in the Eighteenth Century," in *Interpreting Colonialism,* ed. Byron Wells and Philip Stewart. Oxford, in press; and Vera Lind, "Africans in Early Modern German Society: Identity—Difference—Aesthetics—Anthropology," *Bulletin of the German Historical Institute* no. 28 (Spring 2001), 74–82.

44. A search of WorldCat on 8 March 2004 turned up the following for each country: when searched in conjunction with the phrase "race relations," the United States turned up 17,960 titles, Great Britain 1,237, France 255, West Germany 36, East Germany 19, and Germany (general) 481, virtually all of which concerned the Third Reich. There were fewer entries across the board for the broader designation "race," but the United States easily topped Germany (again mostly Nazi Germany), 287 to 162.

45. At the start of World War II, thirty-one of forty-eight American states prohibited marriage between Blacks and whites. By 1967, when the U.S. Supreme Court finally declared such laws unconstitutional, sixteen states still had such

laws on the books. In 1940, black-white marriages were rare; by 1960, the first date for which census data on interracial marriages exists, there were 51,000 black-white marriages recorded in the United States; by 2000 that number had increased to 363,000. For a detailed discussion of these issues in the United States after 1945, see the recent book by Renee C. Romano, *Race Mixing: Black-White Marriage in Postwar America* (Cambridge, Mass., 2003), 1–81; data from 2–3.

46. For the U.S., see Romano, *Race Mixing*, 44–81.

SELECT BIBLIOGRAPHY

Anderson, Carol. *Eyes off the Prize: The United Nations and the African American Struggle for Human Rights, 1944–1955*. New York: Cambridge University Press, 2003.

Arndt, Susan, ed. *AfrikaBilder. Studien zu Rassismus in Deutschland*. Münster: Unrast, 2001.

Ayim, May. "Die afro-deutsche Minderheit." In *Ethnische Minderheiten in der Bundesrepublik Deutschland*, edited by Cornelia Schmalz-Jacobsen and George Hansen, 39–52. Munich: Beck, 1995.

———. "The Year 1990: Homeland and Unity from an Afro-German Perspective." In *Fringe Voices: An Anthology of Minority Writing in the Federal Republic of Germany*, edited by Antje Harnisch, Anne Marie Stokes, and Friedemann Weidauer, 105–19. New York: Berg, 1998.

Back, Les, and Anoop Nayak. *Invisible Europeans? Black People in the "New Europe."* Birmingham, U.K: All Faiths for One Race, 1993.

Bartov, Omer. *Germany's War and the Holocaust: Disputed Histories*. Ithaca, N.Y.: Cornell University Press, 2003.

———. *The Holocaust: Origins, Implementation, Aftermath*. New York: Routledge, 2000.

Behrends, Jan C., Thomas Lindenberger, and Patrice G. Poutrus, eds. *Fremde und Fremd-Sein in der DDR. Zu historischen Ursachen der Fremdenfeindlichkeit in Ostdeutschland*. Berlin: Metropol, 2003.

Benz, Wolfgang. *Feindbild und Vorurteil. Beiträge über Ausgrenzung und Verfolgung*. Munich: Deutscher Taschenbuch Verlag, 1996.

Biddiscombe, Perry. "Dangerous Liaisons: The Anti-fraternization Movement in the U.S. Occupation Zones of Germany and Austria, 1945–1948." *Journal of Social History* 34 (2001).

Blackshire-Belay, Carol Aisha, ed. *The African-German Experience: Critical Essays*. Westport, Conn.: Praeger, 1996.

Bock, Gisela, and Charles Johnson. *Rassenpolitik und Geschlechterpolitik in Nationalsozialismus*. Göttingen: Vandenhoeck & Ruprecht, 1993.

Borstelmann, Thomas. *The Cold War and the Color Line: American Race Relations in the Global Arena*. Cambridge: Harvard University Press, 2001.

Brandt, Nat. *Harlem at War: The Black Experience in World War II*. Syracuse, N.Y.: Syracuse University Press, 1996.

Brubaker, Rogers. *Citizenship and Nationhood in France and Germany*. Cambridge: Harvard University Press, 1992.

Burleigh, Michael, and Wolfgang Wippermann. *The Racial State: Germany, 1933–1945*. New York: Cambridge University Press, 1993.

Campt, Tina. *Other Germans: Black Germans and the Politics of Race, Gender, and Memory in the Third Reich*. Ann Arbor: University of Michigan Press, 2004.

Campt, Tina, and Pascal Grosse. "'Mischlingskinder' in Nachkriegsdeutschland. Zum Verhältnis von Psychologie, Anthropologie, und Gesellschaftkritik nach 1945." *Psychologie und Geschichte* 6, no. 1/2 (1994): 48–78.

Campt, Tina, Pascal Grosse, and Yara-Colette Lemke-Muniz de Faria. "Blacks, Germans, and the Politics of the Imperial Imagination, 1920–1960." In *The Imperialist Imagination: German Colonialism and its Legacy*, edited by Sara Friedrichsmeyer, Sara Lennox, and Susanne Zantop, 205–29. Ann Arbor: University of Michigan Press, 1998.

Campt, Tina, and Michelle Maria Wright, eds. Special Issue, on "Reading the Black German Experience." *Callaloo* 26, no. 2 (Spring 2003).

Crawley, Erin. "Rethinking Germanness: Two Afro-German Women Journey 'Home.'" In *Other Germanies: Questioning Identity in Women's Literature and Art*, edited by K. Jankowsky and C. Love. Albany: State University of New York, 1997.

Czarnowski, Gabriele. "Frauen als Mütter der 'Rasse.' Abtreibungsverfolgung und Zwangssterilisation im Nationalsozialismus." In *Unter anderen Umstaenden. Zur Geschichte der Abtreibung*, edited by Gisela Staupe and Lisa Vieth. Dresden: Deutsches Hygiene Museum, 1993.

Dietrich, Susanne, and Julia Schulze Wessel. *Zwischen Selbstorganisation und Stigmatisierung. Die Lebenswirklichkeit jüdischer Displaced Persons und die neue Gestalt des Antisemitismus in der deutschen Nachkriegesellschaft*. Veröffentlichungen des Archivs der Stadt Stuttgart, vol. 75. Stuttgart: Klett-Cotta, 1998.

Dudziak, Mary L. *Cold War Civil Rights: Race and the Image of American Democracy.* Princeton: Princeton University Press, 2000.

El-Tayeb, Fatima. *Schwarze Deutsche. Der Diskurs um 'Rasse' und nationale Identität*. Frankfurt/Main: Campus Verlag, 2001.

Epp, Marlene. "The Memory of Violence: Soviet and East European Mennonite Refugees and Rape in the Second World War." *Journal of Women's History* 9, no. 1 (1997): 58–87.

Eyferth, Klaus, Ursula Brandt, and Wolfgang Hawel. *Farbige Kinder in Deutschland. Die Situation der Mischlingskinder und die Aufgabe ihrer Eingliederung*. Munich: Juventa, 1960.

Fehrenbach, Heide. *Cinema in Democratizing Germany: Reconstructing National Identity after Hitler*. Chapel Hill: University of North Carolina Press, 1995.

———. "Rehabilitating Father*land*: Race and German Remasculinization." *Signs: Journal of Women in Culture and Society* 24, no. 1 (1998): 107–27.

Fehrenbach, Heide and Uta G. Poiger, eds. *Transactions, Transgressions, Transformations: American Culture in Western Europe and Japan*. New York: Berghahn Books, 2000.

Feldstein, Ruth. *Motherhood in Black and White: Race and Sex in American Liberalism, 1930–1965*. Ithaca, N.Y.: Cornell University Press, 2000.

Finzsch, Norbert, and Dietmar Schirmer, ed. *Identity and Intolerance: Nationalism, Racism, and Xenophobia in Germany and the United States*. New York: Cambridge University Press, 1998.

Foschepoth, Josef. *Im Schatten der Vergangenheit. Die Anfänge der Gesellschaft für Christlich-Jüdische Zusammenarbeit*. Göttingen: Vandenhoeck & Ruprecht, 1993.

Frankenstein, Luise. *Soldatenkinder. Die unehelichen Kinder ausländischer Soldaten mit besonderer Berücksichtigung der Mischlinge*. Munich: W. Steinebach, 1954.

Frederickson, George M. *Racism: A Short History*. Princeton: Princeton University Press, 2002.

Frei, Norbert. *Adenauer's Germany and the Nazi Past*. Translated by Joel Golb. New York: Columbia University Press, 2002.

———. *Vergangenheitspolitik. Die Anfänge der Bundesrepublik und die NS-Vergangenheit*. Munich: C. H. Beck, 1996.

Fremgen, Gisela. *. . . und wenn du dazu noch Schwarz bist. Berichte schwarzer Frauen in der Bundesrepublik*. Bremen: Edition CON, 1984.

Friedrichsmeyer, Sara, Sara Lennox, and Susanne Zantop, eds. *The Imperialist Imagination: German Colonialism and Its Legacy*. Ann Arbor: University of Michigan Press, 1998.

Gellately, Robert. *Backing Hitler: Consent and Coercion in Nazi Germany*. New York: Oxford University Press, 2002.

Gilman, Sander. *On Blackness without Blacks: Essays on the Image of the Black in Germany*. Boston: Hall, 1982.

Goedde, Petra. *GIs and Germans: Culture, Gender, and Foreign Relations, 1945–1949*. New Haven: Yale University Press, 2003.

Gregor, Neil, Nils Roemer, and Mark Roseman, eds. *German History from the Margins*. Bloomington: Indiana University Press, in press.

Grosse, Pascal. *Kolonialismus, Eugenik, und bürgerliche Gesellschaft in Deutschland, 1850–1918*. Frankfurt/Main: Campus, 2000.

Grossmann, Atina. "A Question of Silence: The Rape of German Women by Occupation Soldiers." *October* 72 (1995): 43–63.

———. *Reforming Sex: The German Movement for Birth Control and Abortion Reform, 1920–1950*. New York: Oxford University Press, 1995.

———. "Trauma, Memory, and Motherhood: Germans and Jewish Displaced Persons in Post-Nazi Germany, 1945–1949." *Archiv für Sozialgeschichte* 38 (1998): 215–39.

———. "Victims, Villians, and Survivors: Gendered Perceptions and Self-Perceptions of Jewish Displaced Persons in Occupied Postwar Germany." *Journal of the History of Sexuality* 11, no. 1/2 (2002): 291–318.

Hagemann, Karen, and Stefanie Schüler-Springorum, ed. *Home/Front: The Military, War, and Gender in Twentieth-Century Germany*. New York: Berg, 2002.

Harsch, Donna. "Society, the State, and Abortion in East Germany, 1950–1972." *American Historical Review* 102, no. 3 (1997): 53–84.

Heineman, Elizabeth D. *What Difference Does a Husband Make? Women and Marital Status in Nazi and Postwar Germany*. Berkeley and Los Angeles: University of California Press, 1999.

Herbert, Ulrich, ed. *National-Socialist Extermination Policies: Contemporary German Perspectives and Controversies*. New York: Berghahn Books, 2000.

Herzog, Dagmar, ed. Special Issue: "Sexuality and German Fascism." *Journal of the History of Sexuality* 11, nos. 1–2 (January/April 2002).

Hine, Darlene Clark, and Jacqueline McLeod. *Crossing Boundaries: Comparative History of Black People in Diaspora*. Bloomington: University of Indiana Press, 1999.

Hodges, Carolyn. "The Private/Plural Selves of Afro-German Women and the Search for a Public Voice." *Journal of Black Studies* 23, no. 2 (1992): 219–34.

Höhn, Maria. *GIs and Fräuleins: German-American Encounter in 1950s West Germany.* Chapel Hill: University of North Carolina Press, 2002.

Hopkins, Leroy T., Jr., ed. *Who Is German? Historical and Modern Perspectives on Africans in Germany.* Harry and Helen Gray Humanities Program Series, vol. 5. Washington, D.C.: American Institute for Contemporary German Studies, 1999.

Hügel-Marshall, Ika. *Daheim unterwegs. Ein deutsches Leben.* Berlin: Orlanda Verlag, 1998. Published in English as *Invisible Woman: Growing up Black in Germany.* Translated by Elizabeth Gaffney. New York: Continuum, 2001.

Hurka, Herbert. "Die Mischlingskinder in Deutschland. Ein Situationbericht auf Grund bisheriger Veröffentlichungen." *Jugendwohl* 6 (1956): 257–75.

Jacobsen, Matthew Frye. *Whiteness of a Different Color: European Immigrants and the Alchemy of Race.* Cambridge: Harvard University Press, 1998.

Jobatey, Francine. "*Afro-Look:* Die Geschichte einer Zeitschrift von Schwarzen Deutschen." Doctoral dissertation, University of Massachusetts, 2000.

Jones, Larry Eugene, ed. *Crossing Boundaries: The Exclusion and Inclusion of Minorities in Germany and the United States.* New York: Berghahn Books, 2001.

Kaupen-Haas, Heidrun, and Christian Saller, ed. *Wissenschaftlicher Rassismus. Analysen einer Kontinuität in den Human- und Naturwissenschaften.* Frankfurt/ Main: Campus Verlag, 1999.

Kesting, Robert W. "Forgotten Victims: Blacks in the Holocaust." *Journal of Negro History* 77, no. 1 (1992): 30–36.

Kestling, Robert W. (*sic,* aka Robert W. Kesting). "Blacks under the Swastika: A Research Note." *Journal of Negro History* 83, no. 1 (1998): 84–99.

Kirchner, Walter. "Der Schulerfolg von Negermischlingen in Deutschland." *Studien aus dem Institut für Natur- und Geisteswissenschaftliche Anthropologie Berlin-Dahlem,* 5, no. 31 (März): 366–72.

———. "Eine anthropologische Studie an Mulattenkindern in Berlin unter Berücksichtigung der sozialen Verhältnisse." Phil. Diss., Freie Universität, 1952.

———. "Untersuchungen somatischer und psychischer Entwicklung bei Europäer-Neger-Mischlingen im Kleinkindalter unter Berücksichtigung der sozialen Verhältnisse." *Studien aus dem Institut für Natur- und Geisteswissenschaftliche Anthropologie, no. 1.* (1952): 29–36.

Kleinschmidt, Johannes. "Besatzer und Deutsche. Schwarze GIs nach 1945." *Amerika Studien* 40, no. 4 (1995): 646–65.

Koller, Christian. "Enemy Images: Race and Gender Stereotypes in the Discussion on Colonial Troops; A Franco-German Comparison." In *Home/Front,* edited by Karen Hagemann and Stephanie Schüler-Springorum, 139–57. New York: Berg, 2002.

———. "*Von Wilden aller Rassen niedergemetzelt.*" *Die Diskussion um die Verwendung von Kolonialtruppen in Europa zwischen Rassismus, Kolonial- und Militaerpolitik 1914–1930.* Beiträge zur Kolonial- und Uebergeschichte, ed. Rudolf von Albertini and Eberhard Schmitt. Stuttgart: Franz Steiner Verlag, 2001.

Königseder, Angelica, and Juliane Wetzel. *Lebensmut im Wartesaal. Die jüdischen DPs in Nachkriegsdeutschland.* Frankfurt/Main: Fischer Taschenbuch, 1994.

Koonz, Claudia. *The Nazi Conscience.* Cambridge: Harvard University Press, 2003.

Koshiro, Yukiko. *Trans-Pacific Racisms and the U.S. Occupation of Japan*. New York: Columbia University Press, 1999.

Kraft, Marion, Rukhsana Shamim Ashraf-Khan, eds. *Schwarze Frauen der Welt. Europa und Migration*. Berlin: Orlanda Frauenverlag, 1994.

Krüger-Potratz, Marianne. *Anderssein gab es nicht. Ausländer und Minderheiten in der DDR*. New York: Waxmann, 1991.

Lemke Muniz de Faria, Yara-Colette. *Zwischen Fürsorge und Ausgrenzung. Afrodeutsche "Besatzungskinder" im Nachkriegsdeutschland*. Berlin: Metropol Verlag, 2002.

Lester, Rosemarie K. "Blacks in Germany and German Blacks: A Little-Known Aspect of Black History." In *Blacks and German Culture*, edited by Reinhold Grimm and Jost Hermand, 113–34. Madison: University of Wisconsin Press, 1986.

———. *Trivialneger. Das Bild des Schwarzen im westdeutschen Illustriertenroman*. Stuttgart, 1982.

Lind, Vera. "Africans in Early Modern German Society: Identity—Difference—Aesthetics—Anthropology," *Bulletin of the German Historical Institute*, no. 28 (Spring 2001): 74–82.

———. "Privileged Dependency on the Edge of the Atlantic World: Africans and Germans in the Eighteenth Century." In *Interpreting Colonialism*, edited by Byron Wells and Philip Stewart. Studies on Voltaire and the Eighteenth Century. Oxford: Oxford University Press, in press.

Lorbeer, Marie, and Beate Wild, ed. *Menschen Fresser, Neger Küsse. Das Bild vom Fremden im deutschen Alltag*. Berlin: Elefanten, 1991.

Lusane, Clarence. *Hitler's Black Victims*. New York: Routledge, 2003.

MacGregor, Morris J., Jr. *Integration of the Armed Forces, 1940–1965*, Defense Studies Series. Washington, D.C.: Center of Military History, 1981.

MacGregor, Morris J., and Bernard C. Nalty, eds. *Blacks in the United States Armed Forces: Basic Documents*. Wilmington, Del.: Scholarly Resources, 1977.

MacMaster, Neil. *Racism in Europe, 1870–2000*. New York: Palgrave, 2000.

Maiwald, Stefan, and Gerd Mischler. *Sexualität unter dem Hakenkreuz. Manipulation und Vernichtung der Intimsphäre im NS-Staat*. Hamburg: Europa Verlag, 1999.

Mankowitz, Zeev. *Life between Memory and Hope: The Survivors of the Holocaust in Occupied Germany*. New York: Cambridge University Press, 2002.

Martin, Philip L. *Germany: Reluctant Land of Immigration*. German Issues, no. 21. Washington, D.C.: American Institute for Contemporary German Studies, 1998.

Massaquoi, Hans. *Destined to Witness: Growing Up Black in Nazi Germany*. New York: William Morrow, 1999.

Mazon, Patricia, and Reinhild Steingröver. *Not So Plain as Black and White: Afro-German History and Culture from 1890 to 2000*. Rochester, NY: University of Rochester Press, 2005.

McGuire, Phillip. *Taps for a Jim Crow Army: Letters from Black Soldiers in World War II*. Santa Barbara, ABC-Clio, 1983.

Merritt, Richard L. *Democracy Imposed: U.S. Occupation Policy and the German Public, 1945–1949*. New Haven: Yale University Press, 1995.

Mershon, Sherie, and Steven Schlossman. *Foxholes and Color Lines: Desegregating the U.S. Armed Forces*. Baltimore: Johns Hopkins University Press, 1998.

Meyer, Beate. *"Jüdische Mischlinge." Rassenpolitik und Verfolgungserfahrung, 1933–1945*. Hamburg: Dölling und Galitz Verlag, 1999.

Moeller, Robert G. "'The Last Soldiers of the Great War' and Tales of Family Reunions in the Federal Republic of Germany." *Signs: Journal of Women in Culture and Society* 24, no. 1 (1998): 129–46.

———. *Protecting Motherhood: Women and the Family in the Politics of Postwar West Germany*. Berkeley and Los Angeles: University of California Press, 1993.

———. "The 'Remasculinization' of Germany in the 1950s: Introduction." *Signs: Journal of Women in Culture and Society* 24, no. 1 (1998): 101–6.

———. *War Stories: The Search for a Usable Past in the Federal Republic of Germany*. Berkeley and Los Angeles: University of California Press, 2001.

———., ed. *West Germany under Construction: Politics, Society, and Culture in the Adenauer Era*. Edited by Geoff Eley, Social History, Popular Culture, and Politics in Germany. Ann Arbor: University of Michigan Press, 1997.

Morehouse, Maggi M. *Fighting in the Jim Crow Army: Black Men and Women Remember World War II*. Lanham, Md.: Rowman and Littlefield, 2000.

Motley, Mary Penick, ed. *The Invisible Soldier: The Experience of the Black Soldier in World War II*. Detroit: Wayne State University Press, 1975.

Müller, Martina, Paulette Reed-Anderson, and Martin Issa. *Afrikaner in Berlin*. Berlin: Der Ausländerbeauftragte des Senats, 1993.

Naimark, Norman. *Fires of Hatred: Ethnic Cleansing in Twentieth-Century Europe*. Cambridge.: Harvard University Press, 2001.

———. *The Russians in Germany: A History of the Soviet Zone of Occupation, 1945–1949*. Cambridge: Harvard University Press, 1995.

Naumann, Klaus. *Nachkrieg in Deutschland*. Hamburg: Hamburger Edition, 2001.

Nelson, Daniel J. *A History of U.S. Military Forces in Germany*. Boulder, Colo.: Westview Press, 1987.

Niethammer, Lutz, Ulrich Herbert, Dirk van Laak, and Ulrich Borsdorf. *Deutschland danach. Postfaschistische Gesellschaft und nationales Gedächtnis*. Bonn: J.H.W. Dietz Nachfolger, 1999.

Noakes, Jeremy. "The Development of Nazi Policy towards the German-Jewish 'Mischlinge,' 1933–1945." *Leo Baeck Institute Year Book* 34 (1989): 291–354.

Oguntoye, Katharina. *Eine Afro-Deutsche Geschichte. Zur Lebenssituation von Afrikanern und Afro-Deutschen in Deutschland von 1884 bis 1950*. Berlin: Hoho Verlag, 1997.

Opitz, May, Katharina Oguntoye, and Dagmar Schultz, eds.. *Showing Our Colors: Afro-German Women Speak Out*. Translated by Anne V. Adams. Amherst: University of Massachusetts Press, 1986, 1992. Originally published in German as *Farbe bekennen. Afro-deutsche Frauen auf den Spuren ihrer Geschichte*. Berlin: Orlanda Frauenverlag, 1986.

Panayi, Panikos. *Ethnic Minorities in Nineteenth and Twentieth Century Germany*. New York: Longman, 2000.

Peck, Jeffrey. "Turks and Jews: Comparing Minorities in Germany after the Holocaust," In *German Cultures, Foreign Cultures: The Politics of Belonging*, edited by Jeffrey Peck. AICGS Report no. 8. Washington, D.C., 1997.

Plummer, Brenda Gayle. "Brown Babies: Race, Gender, and Policy after World War II." In *Window on Freedom: Race, Civil Rights, and Foreign Affairs, 1945–1988*, edited by B. G. Plummer, 67–91. Chapel Hill: University of North Carolina Press, 2003.

———. *Rising Wind: Black Americans and U.S. Foreign Affairs, 1935–1960*. Chapel Hill: University of North Carolina Press, 1996.

———, ed. *Window on Freedom: Race, Civil Rights, and Foreign Affairs, 1945–1988*. Chapel Hill: University of North Carolina Press, 2003.

Poiger, Uta G. *Jazz, Rock, and Rebels: Cold War Politics and American Culture in Divided Germany*. Berkeley and Los Angeles: University of California Press, 2000.

———. "A New, 'Western' Hero? Reconstructing German Masculinity in the 1950s." *Signs: Journal of Women in Culture and Society* 24, no. 1 (1998): 147–62.

Pommerin, Reiner. *"Sterilisierung der Rheinlandbastarde." Das Schicksal einer farbigen deutschen Minderheit, 1918–1937*. Dusseldorf: Droste Verlag, 1979.

Posner, David Braden. *Afro-America in West German Perspective, 1945–1966*. Doctoral dissertation, Yale University, 1997.

Raphael-Hernandez, Heike, ed. *Blackening Europe: The African American Presence*. New York: Routledge, 2004.

Rappaport, Lynn. *Jews in Germany after the Holocaust: Memory, Identity, and Jewish-German Relations*. New York: Cambridge University Press, 1997.

Reed-Anderson, Paulette. *Eine Geschichte von mehr als 100 Jahren. Die Anfänge der Afrikanischen Diaspora in Berlin*. Berlin: Ausländerbeauftragte des Senats, 1994.

Reif, Sieglinde. "Das 'Recht des Siegers.' Vergewaltigungen in München 1945." In *Zwischen den Fronten. Münchner Frauen in Krieg und Frieden, 1900–1950*, edited by Sybille Krafft, 360–71. Munich: Buchendorfer Verlag, 1995.

Reinemann, John Otto. "The Mulatto Children in Germany." *Mental Hygiene* 37, no. 3 (1953): 365–76.

Reiß, Matthias. *"Die Schwarzen waren unsere Freunde." Deutsche Kriegsgefangene in der amerikanischen Gesellschaft, 1942–1946*. Krieg der Geschichte Series, edited by Kroener Wegner Forster, vol. 11. Paderborn: Schoningh, 2002.

Riedel, Almut. *Algerische Arbeitsmigranten in der DDR. " . . . hatten ooch Chancen, ehrlich!"* Oplanden: Leske und Budrich, 1994.

Romano, Renee C. *Race Mixing: Black-White Marriage in Postwar America*. Cambridge: Harvard University Press, 2003.

Romberg, Otto R., and Susanne Urban-Fahr, ed. *Jews in Germany after 1945: Citizens or "Fellow" Citizens?* Frankfurt/Main: Edition Tribuene, 2000.

Samples, Susann. "African Germans in the Third Reich." In *Other Germanies: Questioning Identity in Women's Literature and Art*, edited by Karen Jankowsky and Carla Love. Albany: State University of New York Press, 1997.

Sander, Helke. "Remembering/Forgetting." *October* 72 (1995): 15–25.

Sander, Helke, and Barbara Johr, eds. *Befreier und Befreite. Kriege, Vergewaltigung, Kinder*. Die Frau in der Gesellschaft, edited by Ingeborg Mues. Frankfurt/Main: Fischer Taschenbuch, 1995.

Schissler, Hanna, ed. *The Miracle Years: A Cultural History of West Germany, 1949–1968*. Princeton: Princeton University Press, 2001.

Schmalz-Jacobsen, Cornelia, and Georg Hansen. *Ethnische Minderheiten in der Bundesrepublik Deutschland. Ein Lexikon.* Munich: C. H. Beck, 1995.

Schmidt-Harzbach, Ingrid. "Eine Woche im April: Berlin 1945—Vergewaltigung als Massenschicksal." *Feministische Studien* 2 (1984): 51–65.

Schoeps, Julius H., ed. *Leben im Land der Täter. Juden im Nachkriegsdeutschland (1945–1952).* Berlin: Jüdische Verlagsanstalt Berlin, 2001.

Schuch, Peter H., and Rainer Münz, eds. *Paths to Inclusion: The Integration of Migrants in the United States and Germany.* New York: Berghahn Books, 1998.

Scott, Daryl Michael. *Contempt and Pity: Social Policy and the Image of the Damaged Black Psyche, 1880–1996.* Chapel Hill: University of North Carolina Press, 1997.

Shukert, Elfrieda, and Barbara Scibetta. *War Brides of World War II.* Novato, Calif.: Presidio, 1988.

Sieg, Katrin. *Ethnic Drag: Performing Race, Nation, Sexuality in Postwar Germany.* Ann Arbor: University of Michigan Press, 2002.

Sieg, Rudolf. *Mischlingskinder in Westdeutschland. Festschrift für Frederic Falkenburger.* Baden-Baden: Verlag für Kunst und Wissenschaft, 1955.

Simon, Alfons. *Maxi, unser Negerbub.* Bremen: Gesellschaft für christlich-jüdische Zusammenarbeit, 1952.

Smith, William Gardner. *Return to Black America.* Englewood Cliffs, N.J.: Prentice Hall, 1970.

Stern, Frank. "Deutsch-Jüdisches Neubeginnen nach 1945? Ein Rüchblick auf die Gründungen der Gesellschaften für Christlich-Jüdische Zusammenarbeit." *Journal Geschichte* 6 (1989): 18ff.

Stern, Frank. *The Whitewashing of the Yellow Badge: Antisemitism and Philosemitism in Postwar Germany.* New York: Pergamon Press, 1992.

Stone, Vernon W. "German Baby Crop Left by Negro GIs." *Survey* (November 1949): 579–83.

Stillman, Richard J. *Integration of the Negro in the U.S. Armed Forces.* Special Studies in U.S. Economic and Social Development. New York: Praeger, 1968.

Svonkin, Stuart. *Jews against Prejudice: American Jews and the Fight for Civil Liberties.* Columbia Studies in Contemporary American History, edited by William E. Leuchtenberg and Alan Brinkley. New York: Columbia University Press, 1997.

Szobar, Patricia. "Telling Sexual Stories in the Nazi Courts of Law: Race Defilement in Germany, 1933–1945." *Journal of the History of Sexuality* 11, no. 1/2 (2002): 131–63.

Thimm, Karen, and DuRell Echols. *Schwarze in Deutschland.* Munich: Protokolle, 1973.

Timm, Annette, F. "Sex with a Purpose: Prostitution, Venereal Disease, and Militarized Masculinity in the Third Reich." *Journal of the History of Sexuality* 11, no. 1/2 (2002): 223–55.

Tröger, Annemarie. "Between Rape and Prostitution: Survival Strategies and Chances of Emancipation for Berlin Women after World War II." In *Women in Culture and Politics: A Century of Change,* edited by Judith Friedlander et al., 97–117. Bloomington: Indiana University Press, 1986.

UNESCO. *The Race Concept: Results of an Inquiry.* Paris: Unesco, 1952.

Weindling, Paul. *Health, Race and German Politics between National Unification and Nazism, 1870–1945.* Cambridge History of Medicine, edited by Charles Webster and Charles Rosenberg, New York: Cambridge University Press, 1993.

Weingart, Peter, Jürgen Kroll, and Kurt Bayertz. *Rasse, Blut, und Gene: Geschichte der Eugenik und Rassenhygiene in Deutschland.* Frankfurt/Main: Surkamp-Taschenbuch Verlag, 1992.

White, Walter. *A Rising Wind.* Garden City, N.Y.: Doubleday, 1945.

Wildenthal, Lora. *German Women for Empire, 1884–1945.* Durham, N.C.: Duke University Press, 2001.

———. "Race, Gender, and Citizenship in the German Colonial Empire." In *Tensions of Empire: Colonial Cultures in a Bourgeois World*, edited by Frederick Cooper and Ann Stoler. Berkeley and Los Angeles: University of California Press, 1997.

Willoughby, John. *Remaking the Conquering Heroes: The Social and Geopolitical Impact of the Post-war American Occupation of Germany.* New York: Palgrave, 2001.

World Brotherhood, Gesellschaft für christlich-jüdische Zusammenarbeit. *Protokoll der Arbeitstagung über Das Schicksal der farbigen Mischlingskinder in Deutschland.* Wiesbaden, 1952.

Zantop, Susanne. *Colonial Fantasies: Conquest, Family, and Nation in Precolonial Germany, 1770–1870.* Durham, N.C.: Duke University Press, 1997.

FICTION

Ave, Lia. "Der dunkle Stern." *Hermes Film-Roman Magazin*, 1955.

Demski, Eva. *Afra. Roman in fünf Bildern.* Frankfurt/Main: Frankfurter Verlagsanstalt, 1992.

Doerner, Stefan. "Mach mich weiss, Mutti!" *Quick* (April–July 1963).

Habe, Hans. *Walk in Darkness.* Translated by Richard Hanser. New York: Putnam, 1948.

Hildenbrandt, Fred. "Nacht ohne Gnade." *Quick* (July–September 1951).

McGovern, James. "Ballade der besiegten Frauen." *Quick* (1957).

———. "Fraeulein." *Quick* (July–October 1957).

Mohr, Michael. "Freudenstadt." *Die neue Illustrierte* nos. 11–25 (1960).

Schaake, Ursula. "Mein schwarze Schwester." *Revue* (December 1960–April 1961).

Smith, William Gardner. *Last of the Conquerors.* 1st ed. New York: Farrar, Straus and Co., 1948.

Vonnegut, Kurt. "D.P." In *Welcome to the Monkey House.* New York: Dell, 1953. Reprint, 1988.

INDEX

Abel, Wolfgang, 81, 84, 85, 87, 88, 102
abortion, 12, 56–62, 105, 211n. 42–43, 213n. 56
Abraham, David, 173
Adenauer, Konrad, 51
adoption; of Black German children 2, 12, 132–137, 145–56, 160; by African Americans, 133–37, 147–56, 165–66, 237n. 80; and Christian churches in Germany, 137, 139; to Denmark, 163–67, 239n. 100; within Germany, 137–39, 160–63; and German official preference for international placements, 136–37, 140–42, 152–54, 163–66; interracial, in the United States, 133, 233n.19; legal status under military occupation, 138–39, 233n. 17–18; and military adoption boards, 149–50; Nazi-era law regarding, 137–38; numbers, in Germany, 232n. 13; and post–1945 German reforms, 137–40, 231n. 3, 233n. 21–22; by proxy, 151–54, 155, 160–61; to the United States, 140–56, 160–68; of white German children, 139–40, 160–63; by white German parents, 162–63, 238n. 90. *See also* International Social Service.
Advisory Committee on Negro Troop Policies, 23
Afrakete, 182
African American press, 2, 3, 13, 20, 21, 23, 24–26, 28, 133–34, 146–48, 156, 167–68
African American troops, 12, 13; and allegations of indiscipline, 24–26, 63–65, 214n. 67; and experiences in postwar Germany, 17, 18, 25–28, 32–45, 202n. 68; as fathers, 117–20, 123–24, 133, 146, 186; and fraternization with German women, 35–45, 61–73; and interactions with Germans in general, 32–39; German responses toward, 28–30, 32–45, 201n. 61; and military policies of discrimination, 21–23, 25, 28, 146; numbers in postwar U.S. army, 25, 195–96n. 9, 198n. 35; U.S. policies toward in World War II, 19–25;

violence toward by white Americans, 21, 35, 37, 39–45. *See also* marriage; paternity; sexuality; violence
African Americans 3, 12–13, 19–25, 181–82; and history, 184
Afro American, The, 24, 28, 132, 133, 147, 148, 203n. 76
AfroCourier, 182
Afro-Deutsche Frauen (ADeFra), 182
Afro-Germans, *see* Black Germans
afro-look, 182, 183
Albert-Schweitzer-Children's Home, 157–60, 179, 237n. 79. *See also* Dilloo.
Algeria, 53, 55, 62, 65
Ali, Fear Eats the Soul, 242n. 29
Allied Control Council, 57
Allied troops, 9, 10; and rape, 55, 60; and sexual relations with German women, 47–56. *See also* African American troops; Soviet troops
American occupation troops in Germany, 191n. 5; and assessments of Germans, 31; German responses toward, 28–45, 199–200n. 47; and indiscipline among, 26, 41–45; and interactions with Germans, 4, 13, 17–45; racial practices among, 4, 18; and sexual relations with German women, 37–42, 44–45, 62–69; and venereal disease among, 26. *See also* fraternization; marriage; paternity; sexuality; violence
Americanization, 96
Anderson, Benedict, 1
anthropological studies of race, 80–96
anti-Americanism, 33, 41, 43
antiblack stereotype, 32, 34, 40–41, 84, 88, 90, 97, 103, 170, 171, 201n. 61; in film, 115–15, 121, 124–31, 229–30n. 27; in the German press, 175–80, 243n. 34; in rape narratives, 53–56, 59–61. *See also* racism; sexuality
anticommunism, 50–51, 209n. 26. *See also* Soviet troops; Soviet Union; Soviet zone;